This book traces the history of the Social Democratic movement in Germany from its beginnings during the revolutionary period of the 1840s to the present day. It shows how the German Social Democrats have always endeavoured to combine a commitment to the emancipation of the working classes with political freedom and reform in order to achieve a synthesis between socialism and democracy. Drawing on the latest research, the authors examine the major ideas and achievements of the party's leading representatives as well as the attitudes and lives of the grass-roots members, placing them against the wider political, economic and social background. This lucid, sympathetic but not uncritical account is accompanied and enhanced by the inclusion of selected key documents. Like its German original, this book will without doubt be accepted as a standard work on the evolution of the German Social Democratic Party.

**Susanne Miller** and **Heinrich Potthoff** have been members of a number of West German associations for historical research and have published widely in the field of German labour history.

# A History of German Social Democracy
## From 1848 to the Present

# Susanne Miller
# Heinrich Potthoff

# A History of
# German Social Democracy
## From 1848 to the Present

*Translated from the German by*
*J. A. Underwood*

## BERG
*Leamington Spa / Hamburg / New York*
*Distributed exclusively in the US by*
**St. Martin's Press  New York**

**Berg Publishers Limited**
24 Binswood Avenue, Leamington Spa, CV32 5SQ, UK
Schenefelder Landstr. 14K, 2000 Hamburg 55, West Germany
175 Fifth Avenue, New York 10010, New York, USA

English translation © Berg Publishers 1986
Originally published as *Kleine Geschichte der SPD.*
*Darstellung und Dokumentation 1848–1983*
Translated from the German by permission of the publishers,
Verlag Neue Gesellschaft GMBH, Bonn
© 1983 Verlag Neue Gesellschaft GMBH

**British Library Cataloguing in Publication Data**

Miller, Susanne
 A history of German Social Democracy from 1848 to the present
 1. Sozialdemokratische Partei Deutschlands
 — History
 I. Title    II. Potthoff, Heinrich
 III. Kleine Geschichte der SPD. *English*
 324.243′072        JN3946.583

 ISBN 0–907582–63–X

Library of Congress Cataloging-in-Publication Data

Kleine Geschichte der SPD. English.
 A history of German social democracy from 1848 to the
present.

   Translation of: Kleine Geschichte der SPD.
   Bibliography: p.
   Includes index.
   1. Socialism--Germany--History.  2. Sozialdemokratische
Partei Deutschlands--History.  I. Miller, Susanne,
1915-    . II. Potthoff, Heinrich. III. Title.
HX273.K5313 1986        335'.00943        86-21582
ISBN 0-90758-263-X

Printed in Great Britain by Billings of Worcester

# Contents

## Documents

## Statistical Information

# Abbreviations

| | |
|---|---|
| ADAV | *Allgemeiner Deutscher Arbeiterverein*, General German Workers' Association |
| ADGB | *Allgemeiner Deutscher Gewerkschaftsbund*, General German Trades Union Congress |
| AfA | *Arbeitsgemeinschaft freier Angestelltenverbände*, Alliance of Free Employees' Associations |
| CDU | *Christlich-Demokratische Union*, Christian Democratic Union; and |
| CSU | *Christlich-Soziale Union*, Christian Social Union; known collectively (CDU/CSU) as the Union parties |
| DAF | *Deutsche Arbeitsfront*, German Labour Front |
| DBB | *Deutscher Beamtenbund*, German Civil Service Association |
| DDP | *Deutsche Demokratische Partei*, German Democratic Party |
| DGB | *Deutscher Gewerkschaftsbund*, (Christian) German Trades Union Congress |
| DNVP | *Deutschnationale Volkspartei*, German National People's Party |
| DVP | *Deutsche Volkspartei*, German People's Party |
| FDP | *Freie Demokratische Partei*, Free Democratic Party |
| IWA | International Workingmen's Association (First International) |
| KAPD | *Kommunistische Arbeiterpartei Deutschlands*, Communist Labour Party of Germany |
| KPD | *Kommunistische Partei Deutschlands*, Communist Party of Germany |
| MSPD | *Mehrheitssozialdemokratische Partei Deutschlands*, Majority Social Democratic Party of Germany |
| NPD | *Nationaldemokratische Partei Deutschlands*, National Democratic Party of Germany |
| NSDAP (NS) | *Nationalsozialistische Deutsche Arbeiterpartei*, National Socialist German Labour Party |
| SA | *Sturmabteilung*, Storm Troopers |
| SAJ | *Sozialistische Arbeiterjugend*, Socialist Labour Youth |
| SAPD | *Sozialistische Arbeiterpartei Deutschlands*, Socialist Labour Party of Germany |
| SDS | *Sozialistischer Deutscher Studentenbund*, Socialist German Students' Association |
| SED | *Sozialistische Einheitspartei Deutschlands*, Socialist Unity Party of Germany (the East German Communist Party) |
| SHB | *Sozialdemokratischer Hochschulbund*, Social Democratic Univer- |

# Abbreviations

|          |                                                                                                                              |
|----------|------------------------------------------------------------------------------------------------------------------------------|
|          | sities Association                                                                                                            |
| Sopade   | [*Sozialdemokratische Partei Deutschlands*] the name adopted by the party in exile, based first in Prague and subsequently in Paris and London |
| SPD      | *Sozialdemokratische Partei Deutschlands*, Social Democratic Party of Germany                                                 |
| SS       | *Schutzstaffel*                                                                                                               |
| USPD     | *Unabhängige Sozialdemokratische Partei Deutschlands*, Independent Social Democratic Party of Germany                          |

*Part One*

HEINRICH POTTHOFF

# Social Democracy from its Beginnings until 1945

# Introduction

The name *Sozialdemokratische Partei Deutschlands* has been in official use since 1890. Through all the storms, crises, and new beginnings, it has remained unchanged to this day. The importance of the expression 'Social Democratic' is perhaps best shown by the fact that the 'Independent Social Democratic Party' that broke away from the mother party in 1917 retained it in its name. But it had already formed part of the name of the party founded by August Bebel and Wilhelm Liebknecht in Eisenach in 1869, the Social Democratic Workers' Party. The still widespread view that the 'Eisenachers' represented the Marxist element in the labour movement whereas the specifically Social Democratic element had its roots in Lassalle is one for which the nomenclature of the parties at least provides no support. Apart from its commitment to 'the struggle for the emancipation of the working classes' and the replacement of the capitalist mode of production 'by co-operative labour', the Eisenach programme was dominated by demands for freedom and democracy. Here its stance was unequivocal: 'Political freedom is the essential prerequisite for the economic emancipation of the working classes. The social question is therefore inseparable from the political, the solution of the former being dependent on the latter and possible only in a democratic state.'[1]

More than one hundred years ago, then, an official party programme brought out the central point that was to remain the hallmark of Social Democracy: the close connection between free democracy and Socialism. The Socialist International — and likewise Kurt Schumacher — embodied this conception of itself in its Frankfurt Declaration of 3 July 1951 in concise and impressive terms: 'There is no Socialism without freedom. Socialism can be brought into being only by democracy; democracy can be brought to completion only by Socialism.'[2]

This synthesis between Socialism and democracy had governed the conduct of the Social Democratic labour movement ever since its beginnings. Although with the adoption of Marxist analyses and

1. See Document 1, p. 236.
2. Quoted in, for example, Dieter Dowe and Kurt Klotzbach (eds), *Programmatische Dokumente der deutschen Sozialdemokratie* (Berlin/Bonn, 1973), p. 289.

3

dogmas such catchwords as 'the class struggle', 'revolution', and 'seizing political power' came to dominate the movement's theoretical statements, this was not seen as conflicting in any way with the goal to which it aspired, namely a freely democratic Socialism.

Faced with Lenin's form of the dictatorship of the proletariat and Socialism in Russia, the overwhelming majority of German Social Democrats, up to and including Rosa Luxemburg, were in no doubt about where they stood: the Russian way was not their way. Acceptance of democratic majority decisions, the constitutional state and the right to strike, freedom of the individual and of expression, and respect for human rights and human dignity were regarded by Social Democrats as indispensable prerequisites for a just social order. These were things that they had taken for granted and that had governed their conduct from the very beginning. Now, however, to draw a line of demarcation against Lenin's Communist movement, specific emphasis was laid on freedom and on the democratic aspects of Socialism. The experiences of Hitler's Fascism and Stalin's reign of terror further underlined the importance of a commitment to democracy and freedom. Social Democracy and democratic Socialism became overlapping and indeed largely interchangeable terms. Attempts have been made from time to time, both inside and outside the party, to draw a distinction between them, but in the light of historical development these look somewhat contrived.

Such interpretations have undoubtedly been encouraged by the fact that the so-called Godesberg Programme, the basic programme adopted by the SPD at Bad Godesberg in November 1959, failed to give any really precise definition of the term 'Socialism'. It cites 'freedom, justice, and solidarity' as being 'the fundamental values of Socialism'. Explicitly renouncing 'ultimate truths', the party here proclaims its acceptance of a principle of social dynamics and the conditionality of knowledge, of an ongoing struggle and call to action: 'Socialism is a constant task - to fight for freedom and justice, to preserve them and to live up to them.'[3]

The problems connected with the use of the words 'Socialism' and 'Socialist' are emerging with fresh clarity today. They are as old, of course, as the term 'Socialism' itself, which increasingly entered the political vocabulary of Europe from about 1800. After Marx and Engels, a reading gained currency among the adherents of Marxist theory according to which 'Socialism' referred to the society without exploitation and oppression that would emerge after the socialisation of the means of production. Alongside this reading, however, other

3. See Document 13, p. 274.

interpretations persisted, for example religious — and specifically Christian — Socialism, co-operative Socialism, guild Socialism, and state Socialism.

In addition the term 'Socialism' and to an even greater extent its adjective 'Socialist' were frequently used to characterise the great movement for the emancipation of labour in so far as this presented itself as an independent political and social force. The evidence of this is still there today in the names of European sister parties of the SPD. From this point of view 'Socialist' implies primarily a line of demarcation against employees' organisations in the Christian and Liberal camps. The name 'Socialist' movement thus covers the whole spectrum of the great social and liberation movement of the 'Fourth Estate' with, as its goal, a new social order based on freedom and justice. The struggle over the best way to achieve this turned not least upon the political and social order and the economic structure with which 'Socialists' found themselves confronted. Given that in the ranks of German Social Democracy too, from its beginnings until the present day, the words 'Socialism' and 'Socialist' have seldom been used in a uniform, unambiguous manner, it is impossible to start out from rigid definitions. Instead the terms must as far as possible be used in the way in which they were understood at the time by the persons and groups concerned.

A book such as this ought not to and indeed must not confine itself to theoretical considerations. The history of the Social Democratic movement in Germany must be seen against the background of political, economic, and social developments. It also needs to take some account of the counter-forces with which that movement found itself confronted. This we have attempted to do, so far as space and the present state of research allow. Many gaps have had to be left, of course, just as in our description of the actual evolution of the party it proved impossible to avoid stressing certain aspects — necessarily at the expense of others. Our concern throughout has been to show more than just the major ideas and achievements of the party's leading representatives. This study endeavours not least to trace the situation and get inside the mind of the ordinary, grass-roots Social Democrat and to describe the living conditions of the workers, the salaried employees, and the civil servants who felt drawn to Social Democracy. For obvious reasons this could only be done in fairly bold brushstrokes here. A comprehensive, multi-volume general history of democratic Socialism and its organisations in Germany has only now been embarked upon in the Federal Republic,[4] though we have had a

4. The title is *Geschichte der Arbeiter und der Arbeiterbewegung in Deutschland seit*

series of extensive specialist studies of individual areas. Our *History of the SPD*, by drawing together the research that has been done in this field, seeks to provide an insight into the movement that has done more than any other in Germany to fight for a just and free political and social order.

*dem Ende des 18. Jahrhunderts* ('History of the workers and of the labour movement in Germany since the end of the eighteenth century') and the general editor is Gerhard A. Ritter. Two volumes has so far appeared; they are by Heinrich August Winkler and cover the periods 1918–24 and 1924–30. In East Germany an eight-volume *Geschichte der deutschen Arbeiterbewegung* was published by the Berlin Institute for Marxism–Leninism under the auspices of the Central Committee of the SED in 1966.

# 1
# The Beginnings in the Revolution of 1848–1849

## 1. Political and Social Conditions in the Mid-Nineteenth Century

On a red flag preserved in the SPD archives the slogans 'Liberty, equality, and fraternity' and 'Strength through unity' appear above and below a wreath of oak leaves framing two hands clasped in a handshake. The wreath is tied with a ribbon bearing the date '23 May 1863' and the name 'Ferdinand Lassalle'.[1]

It is the old flag of the General German Workers' Association, the traditional standard of the SPD. The date, 23 May 1863, when Lassalle's *Allgemeiner Deutscher Arbeiterverein* was founded in Leipzig as an independent workers' party, is regarded as the birthday of German Social Democracy. There has been a Socialist labour movement in Germany continuously, without a break, from that day to this. An autonomous political organisation, its democratic and social demands supported by an independent body of theory, has been a consistent feature of the long uphill climb since that date, a climb marked by many crises and reverses. Yet for all the acknowledged importance of great individuals in determining the course of history, a movement such as Social Democracy is not created from nothing by a single act of will. It was only in particularly favourable political and social circumstances that that forceful will was able to find expression in reality.

The handshake depicted on the flag of the General German Workers' Association is a reminder of the fact that workers' associations had entered the political arena fifteen years earlier. The symbol went back to the 'Brotherhood of Workers' founded by the printer Stephan Born in August 1848 — the first time working men had come together in a permanent organisation under the banner of solidarity.

Only a few months before that, in February 1848, the *Communist*

---

1. The slogans in German are 'Freiheit, Gleichheit, Brüderlichkeit!' and 'Einigkeit macht stark!'

7

*Manifesto* had appeared. When its authors, Karl Marx and Friedrich Engels, spoke of proletarians 'who, having no means of production of their own, are reduced to selling their labour power in order to live',[2] they were thinking primarily of the industrial labour force. In central Europe at that time this constituted only a small section of the population. Unlike in Britain, which was more advanced, in Germany the process of industrialisation was still in its infancy. Nevertheless, the remark in the *Communist Manifesto* about the proletarians having 'nothing to lose but their chains' did in a modified sense apply to a whole stratum of society.

It was not industrialisation that, as is widely believed even today, created the poverty of a large, hard-working, yet starving unpropertied class; that 'Fourth Estate' — the 'proletariat', as it was called in the language of the day — already existed in other forms. The introduction of freedom of trade and the emancipation of the peasantry in the wake of the Enlightenment and the French Revolution, in conjunction with other factors not altogether explained as yet, led to a sharp increase in marriages among journeymen and younger sons of peasant families. Better nutrition (potato-growing), increased agricultural production (crop-rotation), an improved sytem of food distribution, an absence of plagues and other catastrophes, and the beginnings of hygiene (with the use of soap) are regarded as important causes of the population explosion that ensued. One effect was the phenomenon that economists call 'pauperism' — a large, mainly rural lower class only just capable of keeping itself alive. Social statisticians have calculated that in the first half of the nineteenth century nearly 50 per cent of the population belonged to this 'proletariat'. Remunerative work was virtually unavailable. The situation of the weavers and spinners of Silesia, Saxony, and Westphalia was particularly bleak, the profits from their cottage industry lying far below the minimum necessary for existence. In his play *The Weavers* (*Die Weber*, 1892), Gerhart Hauptmann portrayed graphically how their rebellions against hunger and exploitation had been ruthlessly suppressed by the army in the 1840s.

Factory labour, on the other hand, meant at least work and something to eat. For all its hardships it was an anchor of hope to which people clung. The chance of a job in industry was open to very few in Germany before 1850. The firm of Krupp, for example, launched in 1811 with seven workers, still employed a mere eighty in 1849. It was only after that time that numbers began to increase sharply, so that by

---

2. The *Manifesto* was published 'in the English, French, German, Italian, Flemish, and Danish languages'. The quotations in this chapter are taken from Karl Marx and Friedrich Engels, *The Communist Manifesto* (transl. Samuel Moore; Penguin Books, 1967).

1857 the company already had 1,000 on the payroll. Inefficient production methods and a surplus of labour characterised the early days of industrialisation in Germany as elsewhere. The unimaginable poverty of large sections of the population and the rapidly increasing prosperity of a small class of capitalists opened a widening gulf between the propertied and the unpropertied. Thirteen-, fourteen-, and in the 1840s up to seventeen-hour working days under the harshest conditions, falling wages that families sought to bolster with the even lower-paid labour of women and children, appalling living conditions, and the absence of any provision against accident, illness, and old age were typical of this period.

The dissolution of the old feudal social order and the advance of early liberalism were aspects of a fundamental process of change that gradually came to affect almost every sphere of political and social life. The guiding ethos of this *Manchesterliberalismus*, as it was called in Germany, could be summed up in the slogan: 'Make way for efficiency!' — the struggle for existence viewed as positive selection. The vehicle of this movement was first and foremost the bourgeoisie, which as the 'Third Estate' in the French Revolution of 1789 had made its bid for power unmistakably clear. In the German states, liberalism was frustrated in the political sphere by the old conservative ruling groups, but in the economic sphere it carried all before it. Here even the state professed liberalism — that is to say, it placed its faith in the self-regulatory forces and inherent dynamics of the economy. It was obvious where this early capitalism would lead. The strong, namely the owners of land, capital, and means of production, dictated to the weak, namely those who owned nothing. Only in extreme cases did the state bureaucracy, in which a certain pre-liberal welfare mentality survived, intervene when destitution reached acute levels.

An important move was made in Prussia in 1828 by one General Horn. He warned against exploiting children for night work on the grounds that 'the poor state of health thus induced' would lead to shortfalls in recruiting. Despite this concern about the future of the armed forces and despite warnings from other quarters as well, a further eleven years elapsed before measures were enacted prohibiting the regular employment of children under nine in factories and mines. These were very inadequately implemented and brought little improvement. Nevertheless, with its child-protection statute of 1839 Prussia was a step ahead of the other German states. Bavaria and Baden followed in 1840, Saxony in 1861, and Württemberg a year later. Such measures, however, were a mere drop in the ocean. Above all they took no account whatever of the main problem, namely the social question.

## 2. Theories for Solving the Social Question

From Britain, the homeland of industry and capitalism, this development had spread to the continent of western Europe — initially to France and Belgium. These three countries, the harbingers of the new form of production, also produced the earliest critiques of the consequences of industrialisation. Such critiques went further than simple denunciations of social conditions to discuss theories and design models that aimed at a radical solution of the problems arising out of the change from an agrarian feudal system to a bourgeois industrial economy and society.

The British manufacturer Robert Owen sought to implement his ideas for overcoming social injustice in the context of his own factory, initially, and later in America through the medium of a practical Communism based on the principle of total communion of goods. The American experiment was a failure, but Owen's theory and practice of co-operatives and of social reform stimulated subsequent developments. Owen became the father of the trade-union and co-operative movement in Britain. In France Saint-Simon, who saw the economy as the mainspring of social development, and Fourier, for whom the solution of all social problems lay in a just distribution of goods, produced the two principal models of Socialist and Communist social systems, and these rapidly began to influence social criticism in Germany. A more durable influence was that of Pierre-Joseph Proudhon, with his critique of capitalist private property as 'theft'. For him the path to a new social order led by way of the existing bourgeois state.

The ideas of the French Socialists were disseminated in Germany partly through the medium of a book by the conservative thinker and sociologist Lorenz von Stein calling for social reforms. A similar role was played by the poet Georg Büchner, who with his battle-cry 'Peace to cottages! War on palaces!' helped to propagate early Socialist thinking. A more influential figure than these was the tailor Wilhelm Weitling (1808–71), who steadfastly preached the violent overthrow of society. He found support for his ideas particularly among itinerant German craftsmen working abroad. With his call for communion of goods, the abolition of money and national frontiers, and the brotherhood of all men, Weitling aspired to a logically consistent equality Communism that he also saw as the proper message of Christianity.

Not until Karl Marx and Friedrich Engels, however, were solutions put forward that remained influential beyond the immediate present. The ideas of these two exponents of the social problem shaped and indeed transformed the world of the nineteenth and twentieth centuries.

## Marx and Engels

Karl Marx was born in Trier on 5 May 1818, the son of a Jewish lawyer. On completing his studies he went to work for a short while as a journalist on the liberal–democratic Cologne newspaper, the *Rheinische Zeitung*. After only six months he moved to Paris. Expelled from there in 1845, he settled in Brussels, where he joined Friedrich Engels (b. 28 November 1820), the son of a manufacturer from Barmen — now part of Wuppertal — whom he had met the year before and who was to remain a lifelong friend. In Paris and Brussels the two were in close touch with the so-called 'League of the Just'. In November 1847 a splinter group of this association, calling itself the 'League of Communists', commissioned Marx to draw up a comprehensive theoretical and practical party programme.

The programme was written for a small, radical, secret organisation, yet as the *Communist Manifesto* it has made history to an extent equalled by no other piece of writing in the modern age. The ideas in the *Manifesto* were based on what Marx had been thinking and publishing since the early 1840s. Milestones of that activity had been *A Critique of Hegel's Constitutional Law* (1843), *A Contribution to the Critique of Hegel's Philosophy of Law* (1843–4), *The Holy Family* (1844), and two works not published until much later: *A Contribution to the Critique of National Economy* (published in 1931) and, in collaboration with Engels, *German Ideology* (1845–6; published 1932).[3] In addition Engels' thorough study of *The Condition of the Working Class in England* (1845) had done much to clarify their point of view. The same author's *Principles of Communism*, published in 1847, had likewise done much of the groundwork for Marx. The *Manifesto of the Communist Party* — to give it its proper title — was published in February 1848. On the eve of the revolution it announced threateningly: 'A spectre is haunting Europe — the spectre of Communism.'

'The history of all hitherto existing society is the history of class struggles.' Distilled in this sentence from the *Manifesto* is the essence of what Engels was later to call the 'materialist interpretation of history'. What was meant, realistically, was that 'during its rule of scarce one hundred years' the bourgeoisie had brought about the greatest historical advance ever seen and let loose hitherto undreamt-of productive forces. The driving force of capitalism was breaking down the old barriers and traditions to expose the core of man's dependence

---

3. Respectively *Kritik des Hegelschen Staatsrechts, Zur Kritik der Hegelschen Rechtsphilosophie, Die Heilige Familie, Zur Kritik der Nationalökonomie,* and *Die deutsche Ideologie.*

on man: control of the means of production, i.e. property. 'Society as a whole is more and more splitting up into two great hostile camps, into two great classes directly facing each other — Bourgeoisie and Proletariat.' But 'the bourgeoisie is unfit any longer to be the ruling class in society . . . because it is incompetent to assure an existence to its slave within his slavery . . . '. Instead the capitalist mode of production creates a rapidly growing proletariat that its concentration in factories and the work of trade unions weld together into an ever stronger unity. But the mode of production, as Marx succinctly remarked in the foreword to his *Contribution to the Critique of Political Economy* (1859), dictates 'the social, political, and intellectual life process generally. It is not men's awareness that determines their being but on the contrary their social being that determines their awareness.'[4] The triumphal progress of the bourgeoisie and the capitalist mode of production is paralleled by the growth of the proletariat and its formation into a solid revolutionary class that is conscious of its power. The *Manifesto* continues: 'The development of Modern Industry, therefore, cuts from under its feet the very foundation on which the bourgeoisie produces and appropriates products. What the bourgeoisie, therefore, produces, above all, is its own gravediggers. Its fall and the victory of the proletariat are equally inevitable.'

Alongside such passages, in which Marx described the apparently ineluctable course of history, the *Manifesto* contained his calls for revolutionary action: 'The immediate aim of the Communists is the same as that of all the other proletarian parties: formation of the proletariat into a class, overthrow of the bourgeois supremacy, conquest of political power by the proletariat.' The Communists 'openly declare that their ends can be attained only by the forcible overthrow of all existing social conditions. Let the ruling classes tremble at a Communistic revolution. The proletarians have nothing to lose but their chains. They have a world to win. Working men of all countries, unite!'

Both this call to action and violent revolution and the theory of the 'inevitable' victory of the proletariat, as substantiated by Marx in his great theoretical work, *Capital*, have constantly occupied the minds of politicians and academics, revolutionaries and evolutionaries alike. For some, the change from the early capitalist system of exploitation to Social Democracy is proof that a different way from the one described by Marx was and is possible. Others subscribe to the theory that, now as always, the only way to Socialism is *via* the overthrow of the

4. Karl Marx (ed. Karl Kautsky), *Zur Kritik der politischen Ökonomie*, third edition (Stuttgart, 1909; '1859), p. lv.

bourgeois social order. In particular the obvious contradiction between a necessary development governed by laws of nature and pressure in the direction of political action, between dependence on economic and social laws and a freedom to act, has provoked repeated arguments as to what constitutes the true core of Marxist thought. Marx and Engels never came up with a clear, unambiguous answer to this problem. But the unity of theory and practice that characterised their thinking suggests as the most probable answer that, while they saw Socialism as a necessary consequence of social evolution, it also required 'the power of the human will as motivated by revolutionary awareness'.[5]

The ultimate goal of this transformation of society was for Marx the abolition of 'man's alienation from man', which in the capitalist system reduced the proletarian to a commodity and had led to the total loss of his humanity. The only freedom that private ownership of the means of production granted the worker seemed to him to be the bitter, twofold freedom: 'Free of means of production and free to sell his labour.' In contrast to this, Communism as a positive 'abolition of private property' ought to create the conditions under which man would become not merely free *of* something but free *for* something — able, in other words, to realise and fulfil himself. As the *Communist Manifesto* proclaimed its vision of society: 'In place of the old bourgeois society, with its classes and class antagonisms, we shall have an association, in which the free development of each is the condition for the free development of all.'[6]

### 3. 1848 and the First Workers' Organisations

With their words and ideas Marx and Engels eventually achieved what Marx, turning his back on traditional philosophy, had declared to be the true task of that science, namely to change the world.

As far as 1848 was concerned, however, the claim of the *Communist Manifesto* that 'Communism is already acknowledged by all European Powers to be itself a Power' was mere wishful thinking. As Engels later admitted, Marx and he entertained illusionary hopes at this stage. In Germany their manifesto initially reached only the tiny band of supporters of the League of Communists.

5. See Helga Grebing, *Geschichte der deutschen Arbeiterbewegung, Ein Überblick*, third edition (dtv, 1972), p. 32 (English trans.: *History of the German Labour Movement. A Survey*, Leamington Spa, 1985).
6. *Manifesto of the Communist Party*. See also Erich Fromm, *Das Menschenbild bei Marx*, (Frankfurt a.M.,³1969), p. 44.

Unlike in Britain, there was in Germany no trade-union movement before 1848, nor was there a political labour movement. The reason for this, apart from the much later onset of industrialisation as compared with the countries of western Europe, was the policy of repression conducted by the governments of the 'age of reaction'. Whereas in Britain trade unions were legalised as early as 1824–5, with the repeal of the Combination Act, in Germany they remained outlawed, together with all political associations of whatever kind, until the revolution of 1848. Tough press censorship played a part in keeping expressions of aspirations to freedom to a minimum. There were a few social self-help organisations in the shape of craftsmen's provident and burial funds, but political activity had of necessity to be confined to associations of itinerant journeymen working abroad.[7] 'New Germany', 'Young Germany', the 'League of Outlaws', and the 'League of the Just' were the principal associations in which journeymen got together to discuss political affairs.[8] They were based initially in France and Switzerland for the most part, though after 1840 the main centre was London. The League of the Just eventually gave birth, with the active assistance of Marx and Engels, to the League of Communists, which was founded in London in 1847. It lasted a little over three months.

In February 1848 revolution broke out in France, and it quickly spread to Germany. In contrast to France, however, where the revolution had a strong social content, in Germany it was primarily a movement in favour of national unity, democratic freedoms, parliaments, and constitutional government. For most people, therefore, the object was already achieved with the election, by universal suffrage, of the Constituent National Assembly that met in St. Paul's Church, Frankfurt, on 18 May 1848. But the Assembly was also the focus of wider expectations of a reform of political and social life in Germany. While Marx and Engels sought in the columns of the newspaper they now edited in Cologne, the *Neue Rheinische Zeitung*, to show democracy the way towards the conquest of political power and the completion of the revolution, largely unnoticed by them at first the German labour movement began to take shape.

Journeymen and workers had manned the front lines at the barricades when in March 1848 the revolutionary movement in Germany

7. For the early organisational mergers mentioned in this section, see particularly Ernst Schraepler, *Handwerkerbünde und Arbeitervereine 1830–1853* (Berlin/New York, 1972). For developments up until the First World War, see also Hedwig Wachenheim, *Die deutsche Arbeiterbewegung 1844–1914* (Cologne/Opladen, 1967).

8. Respectively 'Neues Deutschland', 'Junges Deutschland', the 'Bund der Geächteten', and the 'Bund der Gerechten'.

brought absolutism to its knees. The self-awareness thus aroused, together with the newly acquired freedoms, paved the way for the foundation of a wide variety of organisations. As well as the beginnings of trade-union-like combinations, in which printers and tobacco-workers gave the lead, it was mainly workers' educational associations, founded by middle-class democrats, that now made an appearance. They grew out of a social-welfare mentality that saw the liberal educational ideal summed up in the slogan 'Freedom through education' as representing the way out of poverty.

An organisation of a quite different kind was the 'Brotherhood of Workers' started by a printer named Stephan Born.[9] Founded at a conference of delegates from thirty-two workers' associations from all over Germany, which met in Berlin from 23 August to 3 September 1848, the *Allgemeine Deutsche Arbeiterverbrüderung* was an independent political organisation that soon commanded a total of 230 local and regional associations. Most members of the Brotherhood of Workers were journeymen and skilled workers. There was a clear gulf between them and unskilled manual workers, day labourers, and the so-called *Lumpenproletariat*. But precisely because these skilled men called themselves 'workers' and began to see themselves as belonging to the 'working class', a social self-awareness took root and grew here that enormously accelerated the subsequent rise of the labour movement.

The Brotherhood's election slogan, 'One for all, all for one' — later taken over by the Socialist trade unions — shows how much importance Born and his followers attached to the concept of solidarity. For them this lay at the root of the emancipation of the working class and its chance of becoming, through its own organisations, an autonomous political and moral force capable of pushing through social reforms in the context of a democratic state. In a circular dated 18 September 1848 the central committee of the Brotherhood outlined its policy once again: 'We workers must help ourselves — that is the principle that the Berlin conference took as its starting-point. On this basis — of the need for self-help — it drew up the resolutions that it now places before the court of public opinion. The workers of Germany must strive to constitute a moral force in the state, to become a powerful body that weathers every storm, that thrusts forward and ever forward and with its impetus defeats and sweeps aside all that stands in the way of a freer and better shaping of circumstances, that accepts into itself everyone who feels for the plight of the oppressed and is himself

9. See also Frolinde Balser, *Sozial-Demokratie 1848/49–1863. Die erste deutsche Arbeiterorganisation 'Allgemeine Arbeiterverbrüderung' nach der Revolution* (Stuttgart, 1962).

chained by the might of capital and obliged to hire out his physical or intellectual powers to one of the fortunate ones of this earth — everyone who works or wants to work.' There followed the call: 'Workers of Germany, we appeal to you once again: Be united, and you will be strong. Fear no obstacles; you will overcome them all, but only with the strength born of unity.'[10]

Their hopes were focused on St Paul's Church in Frankfurt, where sat the first popularly elected parliament for all Germany. They expected that parliament to agree to their concrete objectives: freedom of combination and a certificate of employment, health services and provident funds, consumer and production co-operatives, legislation for the protection of labour, and co-determination with regard to working-hours and wages. However, attempts by individual deputies to secure a legally guaranteed minimum wage, develop a body of social legislation, and introduce a right of co-determination for workers in the production process were consistently rebuffed by the majority.

That majority — a liberal one — wished to create a German national state and at the same time guarantee the people the middle-class freedoms. It owed this chance of doing so to a revolution that it regarded with very mixed feelings. On the one hand it opposed the only temporarily unseated monarchical conservatives in the state and society; on the other hand it found itself in confrontation with the democratic, republican, and social-revolutionary forces that wanted to push on to further conquests.

The deputies assembled in St Paul's Church disappointed not only the expectations of the workers' associations but also those of the middle-class radical democrats. Angry crowds demonstrated outside, while the parliament was protected by the soldiers of the Prussian king. The forces of reaction saw their opportunity to win back one lost position after another. The Austrian Monarchy began the process, followed by the King of Prussia. Parliaments were dispersed and the resistance of determined democrats suppressed by force of arms. One by one the workers' associations were banned and all political combinations made impossible.

The failure of the revolution of 1848–9 had a profound effect on the labour movement in Germany and its relations with the bourgeoisie. Broad sections of liberal opinion succumbed to de-politicisation, resignation, or accommodation with the ruling class. Marx and other champions of the 'Fourth Estate' gradually came round to the view

10. Quoted in Max Quarck, *Die erste deutsche Arbeiterbewegung. Geschichte der Arbeiterverbrüderung 1848/49. Ein Beitrag zur Theorie und Praxis des Marxismus* (Leipzig, 1924), pp. 369, 371. Reprinted in Horst Schlechte (ed.), *Die Allgemeine Deutsche Arbeiterverbrüderung 1848–1850* (Weimar, 1979), pp. 338ff.

that the bourgeoisie had failed in the 1848 revolution and capitulated before the forces of monarchical authoritarianism. The Social Democratic labour movement as it evolved over the next sixty years saw itself as the heir to that failed revolution. It took on the twofold task of achieving democracy and fighting for the emancipation of labour. In October 1848 the Democratic Congress, at which Stephan Born, Wilhelm Weitling, and disciples of Karl Marx were represented, had professed the principle that 'the solution of the social question is possible only in the democratic-Socialist republic'.[11] That principle became one of the political guide-lines of German Social Democracy.

11. Quoted in Ernst Schraepler, *op. cit.* (see above, note 7), p. 318.

# 2

# The Emergence of the Social Democratic Labour Movement

### 1. Ferdinand Lassalle and the General German Workers' Association

'After a fifteen-year slumber Lassalle — to his undying credit — roused the labour movement in Germany to wakefulness once again.'[1] With these words no less a person than Karl Marx paid tribute to the achievement of Ferdinand Lassalle. The political reaction of the years following the abortive revolution of 1848 had succeeded in stifling aspirations for freedom, democracy, and political equality but not in destroying them. The Italian unification movement, together with a brief relaxation of Prussian policy characterised by a turning-away from its one-sidedly agrarian, conservative orientation, launched a wave of politicisation that not only gave a powerful boost to the desire for national unity but also encouraged aspirations for emancipation among those strata of society that were excluded from political responsibility. In this situation the liberal middle class in Germany once again put itself forward as an eloquent advocate of parliamentarism, democratic rights, freedom, and national unity. In Prussia a struggle developed between parliament and king, a struggle that finally went against the liberal democrats in 1862 when an adversary of superior strength and energy took the field in the person of Bismarck.

The Prussian constitutional conflict was a pivotal experience for Ferdinand Lassalle. Where Marx and Engels had stated in the *Communist Manifesto* that Communists 'labour everywhere for the union and agreement of the democratic parties of all countries',[2] Lassalle became convinced that the liberals and with them the bourgeoisie as a whole were not prepared to put up a determined fight for democracy. In a bitter mood he wrote to the Düsseldorf businessman Gustav

---

1. Karl Marx in a letter to J. B. von Schweitzer, 13 October 1868; in *Die Neue Zeit*, XV, Vol. 1, No. 1, p. 8.
2. *Op. Cit.* (see ch. 1, note 1), p. 7.

Lewy: 'Believe me, I have looked very closely at the Progressive Party [the party of the liberals] here and their first law is: "Anything but revolution from below; we'd rather have despotism from above."'[3]

In his eyes the middle class had betrayed the ideals of 1848. The Fourth Estate alone still carried the flag of democracy. 'Its cause therefore truly is the cause of all humanity, its freedom the freedom of humanity itself, its rule the rule of all.'[4] In addition to ideological considerations there were thoroughly practical reasons for Lassalle's fierce hostility towards the liberal middle class. The workers he wished to win over were at this time organised — if at all — in so-called 'workers' associations' and 'workers' educational associations', which had been founded by middle-class democrats. When in the late 1850s and early 1860s the cry for freedom and unity rang out once again, the latter sought allies among the workers. Although the social factor played a part in such foundations, there could be no question of working-class interests being represented on equal terms. Saxony, where industrialisation was already comparatively far advanced, constituted a centre of these workers' associations. A particularly favourable circumstance here was that, as a result of the removal of the ban on coalitions in 1861, Saxon associations were subject to fewer restrictions than obtained in the other German states. An increasingly active minority in the Leipzig educational association aspired under the leadership of a shoemaker named Vahlteich and a cigar-worker named Fritzsche to become independent of their middle-class patrons and advocated that the association set itself political objectives. A 'Central Committee for the Convocation of a General German Workers' Congress', set up by this group, turned in February 1863 to the publicist Ferdinand Lassalle with the request that he draft a programme for them.

*Ferdinand Lassalle* (1825–64) had made a name for himself as Countess Sophie Hatzfeld's lawyer for many years. In addition to his preoccupation with philosophical works, concerning which he also corresponded with Marx and Engels, he increasingly addressed himself to the social problems of the workers. From the spring of 1862 onwards all his speeches and writings were devoted to the cause of labour. In lectures on 'The special connection between the present period of history and the concept of the working class' (the so-called 'Arbeiterprogramm' already quoted) and 'Science and the workers' —

3. Quoted in Willy Eichler, *Hundert Jahre Sozialdemokratie* (Bielefeld, 1963), p. 15.
4. Quotation from the 'Arbeiterprogramm', in Ferdinand Lassalle (ed. Eduard Bernstein), *Gesammelte Reden und Schriften*, Vol. 2 (Berlin, 1919), pp. 186f. On the programmatical ideas of Lassalle and the Social Democratic Party up until the time of the revisionism debate, see above all Susanne Miller, *Das Problem der Freiheit im Sozialismus. Freiheit, Staat und Revolution in der Programmatik der Sozialdemokratie von Lassale bis zum Revisionismusstreit*, (Berlin/Bonn, 1977).

both subsequently published in pamphlet form — he expounded his ideas on the subject.[5] On a trip to London he tried to establish a closer working relationship with Marx and Engels.

In his 'Open Reply' of 1 March 1863, a classic document of the Socialist labour movement, Lassalle set out for the benefit of the Leipzig committee his views on how to improve the political and social situation of the workers. His call for the foundation of a labour party independent of middle-class influence found an echo. In Leipzig on 23 May 1863 delegates from eleven localities set up the *Allgemeiner Deutscher Arbeiterverein* (ADAV; the 'General German Workers' Association') and elected Lassalle its president. In spite of Lassalle's tireless agitation, membership numbers remained relatively low at first (ca. 4,600 by the end of 1864); nevertheless the rousing influence of the Association fired working-class self-respect in a way that found its finest expression in Georg Herwegh's *Bundeslied*:

> *Mann der Arbeit, aufgewacht!*
> *Und erkenne Deine Macht!*
> *Alle Räder stehen still,*
> *wenn Dein starker Arm es will.*
>
> *Brecht das Doppeljoch entzwei!*
> *Brecht die Not der Sklaverei!*
> *Brecht die Sklaverei der Not!*
> *Brot ist Freiheit, Freiheit Brot!*[6]

Lassalle presided over the ADAV for a mere fifteen months before his death on 31 August 1864, following a duel fought over a woman. Yet that short space of time sufficed — particularly given the romantic circumstances of his death — to make him the idol of many working men. In their *Workers' Marseillaise*, written by Jakob Audorf, they sang with proud self-assurance:

> *Nicht zählen wir den Feind,*
> *Nicht die Gefahren alle!*
> *Der Bahn, der kühnen, folgen wir,*
> *Die uns geführt Lassalle!*[7]

5. 'Über den besonderen Zusammenhang der gegenwärtigen Geschichtsperiode mit der Idee des Arbeiterstandes' ('Arbeiterprogramm') and 'Die Wissenschaft und die Arbeiter'; see Ferdinand Lassalle, *Gesammelte Reden und Schriften*, Vol. 2, pp. 165ff., 242ff.

6. 'Wake up, man of labour, / and know your power. / Every wheel will halt / at the bidding of your mighty arm. / Smash the double yoke asunder. / Smash the poverty of slavery. / Smash the slavery of poverty. / Bread is freedom, freedom bread.'

The path that Lassalle had pointed them down was that of conducting themselves as an independent, firmly established workers' party in which the programmatic catchwords of universal equal suffrage, producer associations, exploitation, and the class struggle came to occupy a permanent place. With the theory of the 'iron law' of wages, according to which 'the average wage never rises above the necessary subsistence that a people normally requires in order to eke out a living and to procreate', Lassalle managed to oust his arch-rival, Schulze-Delitzsch, in the battle for the workers' hearts.

Hermann Schulze-Delitzsch, true to the tenets of early liberalism, rejected state aid as an inadmissible intervention and advocated self-help measures in the form of consumer co-operatives, health and disability insurance schemes, savings banks, and provident funds. Lassalle, however, argued that under the economic conditions of capitalism these were incapable of effecting any lasting improvement in the workers' situation. Only if the workers set up their own production co-operatives, so ending the 'divorce between pay and profits' and reaping the full reward of their labour, was a solution possible to what appeared to be a hopeless dilemma. Since the workers were not strong enough to do this on their own, the state must intervene with loans to promote and develop such facilities. The liberal non-interventionist state was to become, under pressure from the party of the working class, a welfare state fulfilling its true mission of 'facilitating and procuring the great cultural advances of humanity'.[8]

This estimate of the role of the state in the emancipation of the Fourth Estate also constituted the principal difference between Lassalle and Marx. Where the latter saw the state primarily as an instrument of oppression in the hands of the ruling class, Lassalle saw it as the positive organisational aspect of society. 'The purpose of the state,' he wrote in the 'Arbeiterprogramm', 'is not simply to protect individual freedom and property. . . ; the purpose of the state is precisely to put individuals in a position, as a result of this association, to achieve ends and attain a level of existence that they could never achieve as individuals, to enable them to acquire a sum total of education, power, and freedom that they would all, as individuals, find utterly beyond their reach.'[9]

Despite their antithetical views of the state, the different conceptions

---

7. 'Let us not count the enemy, / nor number every danger. / Let us tread the path, the fearless path, / that Lassalle bid us follow.'

8. The quotations here are from the 'Open Reply' of 1 March 1863; see Dowe and Klotzbach (eds), *Programmatische Dokumente* (1973), pp. 123ff.

9. Ferdinand Lassalle, *Gesammelte Reden und Schriften*, Vol. 2, pp. 197f.; he expressed himself in similar terms in 'Die Wissenschaft und die Arbeiter', *ibid.*, p. 267.

cannot be reduced — as people often seek to reduce them — to the simple duality: 'the Social Democratic reformism of Lassalle with its positive acceptance of the national state and the international, revolutionary Socialism of Marx and Engels'.[10] In their analysis of the capitalist system, in their assessment of the role of the working class and the labour movement, and even in terms of their ultimate objectives there was a broad measure of agreement. It was not for nothing that Marx described Lassalle's 'Arbeiterprogramm' as plagiarising his own ideas.[11] What he and Engels attacked as 'association with public funds' was for Lassalle simply a practical instrument and a first step towards changing the structure of the economy. For Lassalle, too, no solution of the social question was possible without the abolition of 'ownership of land and capital'.[12] It was just that in terms of day-to-day political agitation the revolutionary aspirations of the General German Workers' Association, for all its Communist objectives, came down to demanding universal suffrage and production co-operatives. The dualism so typical of nineteenth-century Social Democracy — between radical ideology and reformist practice — was thus already inherent in Lassalle's organisation.

## 2. The First International

Marx and Engels were sharply critical of Lassalle's one-sided battle-plan as directed against the liberal bourgeoisie. The tactics outlined in the *Communist Manifesto* stated that the working class must first fight against reaction in alliance with the democratic forces of the middle class. Only when certain specific economic and political conditions obtained did they see the time as being ripe for independent action on the part of the proletariat. Within a few years of Lassalle's death they were urging Wilhelm Liebknecht and his fellow-campaigner August Bebel to break with 'petty-bourgeois democracy' and establish an independent labour organisation.

Following the failure of the 1848 revolution Marx — together with his friend and patron Engels — settled in England in June 1849. There

10. The example quoted is Helga Grebing, *Geschichte der deutschen Arbeiterbewegung, op. cit.*, p. 57.
11. Letter to Engels, 28 January 1863; in Karl Marx and Friedrich Engels, *Gesamtausgabe* (published on behalf of the Marx–Engels Institute, Frankfurt/Berlin/Moscow, 1927–35), Part 3, Vol. 3, pp. 125f.
12. Letter from Lassalle to Karl Rodbertus, 28 April 1863; in Ferdinand Lassalle (ed. Gustav Mayer), *Nachgelassene Briefe und Schriften*, Vol. 6 (Stuttgart/Berlin, 1925), p. 329. For the context, see Susanne Miller, *Das Problem der Freiheit im Sozialismus, op. cit.* (see above, note 4), particularly pp. 35ff.

he was to remain until his death in 1883. Apart from intervening in the Cologne Communist trials and contributing series of articles to newspapers, he devoted most of those years to intense academic study. He wrote his famous analysis of Napoleon III's seizure of power, *The 18th Brumaire of Louis Bonaparte* (1852), and in the *Outlines of the Critique of Political Economy* (published posthumously in 1938) he produced the first draft of his major work, *Capital*.[13] The central ideas of *Capital*, the first volume of which appeared in 1867, were already clearly elaborated in the *Outlines*: the theory of the commodity character of human labour-power in the capitalist system and the theory of surplus-value. By 'surplus-value' Marx meant the difference between the value of the goods manufactured by the production worker and the wages he received for his labour.

Alongside his academic and journalistic work, Marx distinguished himself in these years primarily in the 'International Workingmen's Association' (the First International), a body founded on 28 September 1864 with himself at first a silent listener.[14] The initiative came from a group of British and French workers' representatives who had made contact at the International Exhibition in London in 1862. In the opinion of the British contingent, only international solidarity and an internationally integrated labour movement would help to relieve the pressure on wages resulting from cheaper foreign competition and the oppression of the proletariat. In September 1864 a great crowd of workers' representatives from Britain, France, Italy, and Germany met in London to establish an umbrella organisation for the labour organisations of all countries. Neither organisational differences (parties or trade unions) nor discrepancies of theoretical orientation were to be any obstacle to joining the IWA.

A broad spectrum of Socialist tendencies from French Proudhonists to British trade unionists was represented on the new body. National-revolutionary democrats such as the Italian Guiseppe Mazzini belonged to it, and there was even an anarchist wing. The affiliation of the Russian anarchist Mikhail Bakunin in 1868 led to fierce internal battles that eventually brought about a split in 1872. In 1876 the International, which had meanwhile transferred its headquarters to New York, was dissolved. Although it never assumed the character of a mass movement but rather represented a forum for the exchange of theoretical ideas, the IWA created a stir out of all proportion to its practical importance. Wherever strikes or disturbances occurred, the

13. The German titles of these works are *Der achtzehnte Brumaire des Louis Bonaparte*, *Grundrisse der Kritik der politischen Ökonomie*, and *Das Kapital*.
14. For a good general survey, see Karl-Ludwig Günsche and Klaus Lantermann, *Kleine Geschichte der Internationale* (Bonn, 1977), pp. 25ff.

ruling powers saw the hand of the International. They created the spectre of a gigantic revolutionary organisation that was secretly developing into a 'second power in the state, a second government'.[15]

In an 'Inaugural Address' written by Marx the International called for an end to class rule and for the establishment of co-operatives and independent political labour parties. At the Geneva conference of the International (1866) the Marxist majority declared its belief in an independent role for trade unions in the workers' fight for a new social order. At the same time the demand for the introduction of a statutory eight-hour day was incorporated in the programme against the resistance of a powerful minority. The IWA's appeal to the international revolutionary solidarity of the working class found an echo in Germany too, although at an organisational level it enjoyed only limited success there, attracting a total of only 385 members. So although Marx did not provide the decisive impulse towards the formation of a proletarian party in Germany, his vision of supra-national solidarity offered German workers, just as they were beginning to emancipate themselves, an alternative to the social and political isolation into which they had fallen after detaching themselves from the middle class in the 1860s. It was an alternative they seized on eagerly. A new German labour party, the 'Eisenachers', promptly became affiliated to the International Workingmen's Association.

### 3. The 'Eisenachers'

The failure of the Progressive Party in the Prussian constitutional conflict and the successes of Bismarck's strategy of armed conflict in the solution of the national question mercilessly exposed the weakness of bourgeois liberalism vis-à-vis the authoritarian state. Its proven inability — in Prussia — to implement democracy, its ambivalent attitude towards the national question, and its failure to deal with the social problems of the 'Fourth Estate' threw the politically awakening workers back on their own resources. Instead of the coalition that suggested itself between middle-class radical democrats and workers fighting for democracy and social justice, there emerged an alliance of interests between the old agrarian aristocracy and the new industrial leaders of the bourgeoisie.

The formation of independent Socialist-oriented parties that began with the General German Workers' Association was the logical 'an-

---

15. According to a Viennese public prosecutor quoted in Julius Braunthal, *Geschichte der Internationale*, Vol. 1, second edition (Berlin/Bonn, 1974), pp. 121f.

swer of the German labour movement to its exclusion from access to political equality of status and economic redistribution in the national state'.[16] An attempt by committed democrats to create a counterpart to Lassalle's ADAV in 1863 by drawing together local educational associations in the Union of German Workers' Associations was only briefly successful. With their one-sided emphasis on education and training they contributed greatly to what subsequently became a very widespread belief in Social Democratic circles — that knowledge is power. Yet increasingly the initiative was passing to those who strove for a more effective assertion of the political and social interests of the working class. The development of the young August Bebel was a model example of this.

*August Bebel* (1840–1913) had after years of wandering settled in Leipzig as a wood-turner and become active in the local industrial educational association. At first Bebel opposed any politicisation of the association and even rejected universal suffrage on the grounds that the workers were not yet ready for it. It was his clashes with the disciples of Lassalle, whom he had initially accused of unfurling the flag of Communism with all its terrors, that first set him on the road to Socialism and eventually, under the influence of Liebknecht, to the theories of Marx.[17]

*Wilhelm Liebknecht* (1826–1900) had fought in the 1848 revolution and after its collapse had emigrated to London, where he soon became a close friend of Karl Marx. As a convinced adherent of the latter's teachings, though he interpreted them in accordance with his own political ideas, he returned to Germany in 1862. In Leipzig he made the acquaintance of Bebel and with him founded the radical–democratic Saxon People's Party (*Sächsische Volkspartei*) in 1866. In the following year the two men both won seats in the Diet (*Reichstag*) of the North German Confederation.

Also in 1867 Bebel succeeded the liberal Dr Max Hirsch as chairman of the Union of German Workers' Associations. He immediately began a vigorous campaign for the politicisation of the associations. Bebel replaced the liberal conception that had prevailed hitherto with the kinds of viewpoint represented by the International. The Nuremberg conference of 1868 saw a break between the liberal democrats and the advocates of a Socialist orientation. A majority led by Bebel accepted the principle that the emancipation 'of the working classes' must be fought for by those same classes and voted for 'union with the

16. See Wolfgang Schieder, 'Das Scheitern des bürgerlichen Radikalismus und die sozialistische Parteibildung in Deutschland', in Hans Mommsen (ed.), *Sozialdemokratie zwischen Klassenbewegung und Volkspartei* (Frankfurt a. M., 1974), p. 21.
17. See Bebel's autobiography, *Aus meinem Leben*, Vol. 1 (Stuttgart, 1910), pp. 50ff.

endeavours of the International Workingmen's Association'.[18] At the same time members were encouraged to band themselves together in trade co-operatives (i.e. trade unions) that would more effectively represent their interests in the economic sphere. The split between the middle-class democrats and the future Social Democrats in the workers' associations was paralleled within the Saxon People's Party and similarly constituted political parties in other German states. The decisive initiatives came from Wilhelm Liebknecht and August Bebel, the second of whom was to become the dominant figure in the Social Democratic movement in the decades to come and the man who shaped the party more than any other.

The Social Democratic Workers' Party was founded in Eisenach, an ancient Thuringian city now in East Germany, on 7–9 August 1869. In addition to the ADAV, Germany now had a second party of labour. It drew its support chiefly from workers' associations in central and southern Germany, former adherents of the Saxon People's Party, and discontented members of the ADAV. In their programme the 'Eisenachers', as they were called, demanded the abolition of class rule and 'the establishment of a free republic'.[19] Other items in their programme included statutory maximum working-hours, the restriction of female and the prohibition of child labour, universal compulsory education, an independent judiciary, the replacement of all indirect taxes by a single income and inheritance tax, plebiscites, and universal, equal, direct suffrage. Consistently with this, the Eisenachers stood as candidates for election to the *Reichstag*, so declaring their faith in parliament as a sphere of activity. Their tenth demand was regarded as specifically Socialist: 'State backing for the co-operative movement and government loans for free producer co-operatives under democratic guarantees.'

The new party saw political freedom as 'the essential prerequisite for the economic emancipation of the working classes'. It further maintained: 'The social question is therefore inseparable from the political, the solution of the former being dependent on the latter and possible only in a democratic state.' Although the Eisenachers explicitly described themselves as a 'branch of the International Workingmen's Association', such concepts as Socialism and Communism were beyond the comprehension of many of its members. As Kautsky noted in retrospect, even men in leading positions had only the most superficial acquaintance with the teachings of Marx and Engels up until the end of

18. Reprinted in, for example, Hermann Weber, *Das Prinzip Links. Eine Dokumentation. Beiträge zur Diskussion des demokratischen Sozialismus in Deutschland 1847–1973* (Hanover, 1973), p. 29.
19. For this and the following quotation, see Document 1, p. 236.

the 1870s. The prime motivation of workers around this time stemmed from their everyday predicament, from the injustice and oppression that were their daily lot and that they sought by working together in solidarity to combat and to overcome.

The existence of two labour parties was therefore occasioned not so much by differences of theoretical approach as by current problems. On the national question, which dominated public discussion in the 1860s, the Eisenachers favoured a federalist, 'Greater German' course in the tradition of radical democracy. They rejected unification from above through the great-power machinations of Prussia because an imposed unity would be without freedom. On the other hand Lassalle and his followers placed their faith in Prussia. Whereas Lassalle sought the support of Bismarck in the struggle against his arch-enemy, the liberal bourgeoisie, Bebel and his friends had a deep aversion to the 'blood and iron' policies of the Prussian Junker. The authoritarian organisational structure that Lassalle gave the ADAV — that of a kind of plebiscitary dictatorship, which his successor, J. B. von Schweitzer, continued to operate in the same spirit — was bitterly opposed by the Eisenachers. Their party was structured democratically, from the base upwards. Its chief centres of support were in Saxony. Its membership numbered about 10,000 in 1870 and about 9,000 in 1875, while that of the ADAV stood at over 21,000 in 1870 and about 15,000 five years later.

## 4. Agreement at Gotha

The occasionally violent disagreements between the two competing parties began slowly to subside around 1873. On the one hand the resignation of the long-serving, controversial president of the ADAV, von Schweitzer, had removed a major personal obstacle, and on the other hand the foundation of the Reich and the consolidation of the Bismarckian state rendered old antagonisms obsolete. The Eisenachers were obliged to bury their hopes of a democratically united Greater Germany (including the German-speaking parts of the Austrian empire). But the hopes that the Lesser German, Prussian-oriented Lassalleans had placed in social concessions on the part of the state likewise turned out to have been illusory. The policy of governmental repression that set in after 1871 and that was implemented principally by Public Prosecutor Tessendorf affected both parties, the ADAV and the Eisenachers, in the same way, favouring a process of mutual understanding and reconciliation. Finally the economic crisis that began in 1873 compelled the two parties to direct their urgent attention to the immediate problems of the working class: strikes, housing shortages, and trade-union questions. In fact it was the rank and file that pushed them into merging.

At the so-called 'unification conference' held at Gotha on 23–27 May 1875 their aspirations were crowned with success. The programme adopted at Gotha by the new Socialist Workers' Party of Germany (*Sozialistische Arbeiterpartei Deutschlands*) fell foul of some scathing criticism by Marx in his 'Comments on the Programme of the German Workers' Party'.[20] Even today it is often maintained that the lack of a Marxist foundation was occasioned by concessions to the Lassalleans. In pouring scorn on Lassalle's nonsensical 'iron law' of wages, Marx was undoubtedly right. Undoubtedly, too, the statement he took to task about 'all other classes' constituting 'a single reactionary mass' vis-à-vis the working class was scientifically absurd and politically inept, for it impeded possible alliances with other party groupings. Yet what the statement expressed was the deep-rooted indignation of a minority that was largely ostracised by bourgeois society and harassed and denigrated by the state. It was precisely this ostracism and isolation that strengthened the idea of solidarity and enhanced the workers' awareness of themselves as a class.

In essence the Gotha programme was not at all what it is popularly made out to have been, namely a compromise between moderate Lassalleans with their acceptance of the state and Marxist Eisenachers. The argument with which Liebknecht later justified his suppression of the 'Comments' that had reached him from Marx bore little relation to the truth. The Lassalleans, who were in many respects more radical in their demands, would undoubtedly have accepted a more Marxist programme. Tölcke, for example, speaking for the ADAV, said that in the interests of unification he was prepared to adopt any programme, be it only a 'scrap of white paper with a clenched fist on it'.[21] In reality Liebknecht — whom Marx and Engels had long regarded as their 'only reliable contact' in Germany, despite frequent angry outburst at 'Willie's stupidity'[22] — had a largely free hand in drawing up the programme. Consequently his draft, apart from one or two elements of Lassallean thinking, was primarily a reflection of his own ideas. These

---

20. 'Randglossen zum Parteiprogramm der deutschen Arbeiterpartei', in Karl Marx, *Kritik des Gothaer Programms* (Berlin, 1946). For the programme itself, see Document 2, p. 238.
21. *Volksstaat*, No. 58, 23 May 1875. See also Georg Eckert, 'Die Konsolidierung der sozialdemokratischen Arbeiterbewegung zwischen Reichsgründung und Sozialistengesetz', in Hans Mommsen (ed.), *Sozialdemokratie zwischen Klassenbewegung und Volkspartei, op. cit.* (see above, note 16), pp. 47ff.
22. Letter from Engels to Marx, 7 August 1865; in Karl Marx and Friedrich Engels, *Gesamtausgabe*, Part 3, Vol. 3, p. 284.

deviated considerably from the theories of his friends Marx and Engels, but they met with the unanimous approval of the conference, Bebel withholding his own misgivings.

In these early years of the labour movement there could be no question of a solid, firmly established body of theory. Instead its programmatic rallies were organised with an urgent view to providing the labour movement with an effective weapon in its struggle and one that would appeal to its supporters and arouse their enthusiasm. In the years immediately preceding the Gotha conference any interest in abstract theorising had been overlaid by the very concrete problems arising out of the aggravation of social and political conflicts. Statutory limitation of working-hours, increased wages, labour-protection regulations, the banning of child labour, unlimited right of combination, and freedom to form associations and hold meetings — these were tangible concerns that preoccupied and motivated working people. Associated with them were the demand for universal, equal suffrage and political democracy, the call to battle against the domination of the 'single reactionary mass', and the profession of faith in international worker solidarity.

From this point on there was no returning to bourgeois social-reform movements.[23] Schultze-Delitzsch's concept of purely self-help co-operatives had been suffering a steady loss of support. An attempt by Württemberg democrats to revive the liberal approach to the social question soon ran aground. In the Roman Catholic camp such men as Bishop Ketteler of Mainz and Father Kolping recognised the potential explosiveness of social grievances and called for measures to get rid of the worst excesses of early capitalism. But Ketteler, like his Protestant colleague Wichern, saw social problems primarily in pastoral terms, while Kolping's efforts were coloured by the notion of welfare and directed not so much at workers as at craft-tradesmen. A more influential body in later years was an association of concerned academics calling themselves the 'Society for Social Affairs'.[24] In speeches and publications they sought to increase middle-class awareness of the dire predicament of the 'Fourth Estate', and they played a crucial role in stimulating the subsequent social policy of the government. But whereas in Britain, for example, links were forged between Social Democracy on the one hand and Christian Socialist politicians and middle-class social reformers on the other, in the German Reich this did not occur. Two events widened and deepened the gap between

23. On the questions discussed in this paragraph, see Carl Jantke, *Der Vierte Stand. Die gestaltenden Kräfte der deutschen Arbeiterbewegung im XIX. Jahrhundert* (Freiburg, 1955).
24. The *Verein für Sozialpolitik* was founded in 1872.

them until it seemed virtually unbridgeable: the Paris Commune and Bismarck's anti-Socialist legislation.

# 3
# From the Founding of the Reich to the Repeal of the *Sozialistengesetz*

## 1. The Paris Commune

The war-loans question that was to split the German Social Democratic movement in the First World War had already provided a bone of contention during the Franco-German war of 1870–1. On that occasion too the crucial problem was the same, namely whether the war was being fought for defensive purposes or not. In the *Reichstag* of the Prussian-dominated North German Confederation, Schweitzer of the ADAV and the Eisenacher F. W. Fritzsche voted in favour of the first bill while Bebel and Liebknecht abstained — a decision in which they were at odds with the majority opinion in the party, which was that Socialists, too, had, as Germans, to stand up for Germany. But when, following the abdication of Napoleon III, the 'enemy' became the French Third Republic, the Eisenachers and soon the Lassalleans, too, turned against continuation of the war and the proposed annexation of Alsace-Lorraine. As the waves of nationalist feeling beat higher and higher, a mere handful of people voiced a dissenting opinion and expressed solidarity not with annexation but with the revolt of the Paris Commune on 18 March 1871. Eisenachers and Lassalleans alike hailed the Parisian revolution as the dawn of a new age and protested in impassioned terms at the massacres of the last week of May, when with the tacit support of Bismarck French government troops drowned this experimental new kind of democracy and social order in a sea of blood. From the tribune of the *Reichstag* Bebel testified to his deep respect for the quashed Commune and thundered at his fellow-deputies that this was a mere outpost engagement and that 'before many decades have gone by the battle-cry of the Parisian proletariat — "War on palaces, peace to cottages, death to poverty and idleness!" — will be the battle-cry of the entire European proletariat'.[1]

1. See *Stenographische Berichte über die Verhandlungen im Deutschen Reichstag, I.*

Bismarck claimed subsequently, during the debate on the *Soziali-stengesetz*, that this speech had opened his eyes to the subversive nature of Social Democracy and the threat that it posed to the state. The claim skilfully stirred up the fear of revolution that had gripped the aristocracy and the bourgeoisie even more fiercely after the Commune uprising. This expression by the German Social Democrats of solidarity with the Parisian 'Communards', together with the 'Address' issued by the International, in which Marx, its author, extolled the constitution of the Commune as 'the discovery, at last, of the political form of the rule of the proletariat',[2] provided the arguments for condemning the German labour movement outright as a 'party of moral degeneration, political indiscipline, and social discontent',[3] dedicated to upheaval and violence. Undoubtedly the aggressive and often revolutionary language of Social Democracy helped to foster such fears, but the roots went deeper than that. Invoking the 'red peril' served the ruling classes — concerned to preserve their privileges — as a snare with which to bind the economically restless and thrusting middle class to the autocratic military state as the guarantor of law and order.

Objectively there was very little occasion for revolution phobia. Although with the 'myth' of the Commune German Social Democracy acquired a revolutionary tradition at the level of its theoretical statements of belief, in practice the very experiences of the Commune led the movement to interpret the 'revolutionary' overthrow of the social order as a process of non-violent change. It came to place greater reliance than ever on what many Social Democrats felt the Paris Commune had lacked, namely on building up a powerful, disciplined organisation. General elections held under universal, equal suffrage supplied a sure gauge of the strength of the movement. The two parties — the Eisenachers and the ADAV — increased their share of the vote from 3.2 per cent in 1871 to over 6.8 per cent in 1874, and in 1877, two years after Gotha, the united party received 9.1 per cent of votes cast. Neither government repression nor the creation of counter-organisations on the employers' side (e.g. the Central Association of Industrialists in 1875) had succeeded in stopping the movement. It was well on the way to becoming a factor in German internal affairs when the *Sozialistengesetz* diverted this development into a new channel.

---

*Legislaturperiode*, p. 921.
2. Hans Joachim Lieber (ed.), *Karl Marx. Politische Schriften* (Stuttgart, 1960), p. 953.
3. Thus Heinrich Treitschke, for example, in 'Der Sozialismus und seine Gönner', in *Preussische Jahrbücher*, Vol. 34 (1874), pp. 67ff., 248ff.

## 2. The *Sozialistengesetz*

Two attempts on the life of the emperor — with which the Social Democrats had nothing to do: they decisively rejected terrorist measures — supplied Bismarck with a welcome pretext for introducing his so-called 'Socialists Law'. As he saw it, the time had come to take action to stem any further growth of 'the dangerous band of brigands dwelling alongside us in our cities'. A general election held after the second assassination attempt gave him the compliant parliament he needed, although in spite of an unprecedented campaign against Social Democracy the party still attracted 437,000 votes in the principal ballot, compared with 493,000 in 1877. In October 1878 the *Reichstag* passed the 'Law against the dangerous activities of Social Democracy'[4] by a majority of 221 to 149 votes. The Social Democrats, the Roman Catholic Centre Party, and the left-wing liberal Progressive Party voted against the measure, while the conservative parties and the majority of the National Liberals, who had rejected such an exceptive law at first, voted in favour.

The *Sozialistengesetz* was initially valid for three years. It was renewed three times before being repealed at last on 30 September 1890. As Bebel aptly summed up the situation in a letter to his Bavarian colleague, Georg von Vollmar, the Social Democrats were now fair game: 'Justice and the law no longer exist for us.'[5]

The *Sozialistengesetz* prohibited all organisations 'that seek by means of Social Democratic, Socialistic, or Communistic activities to overthrow the existing political and social order' and all associations 'in which Social Democratic, Socialistic, or Communistic activities aimed at overthrowing the existing political and social order find expression in a manner endangering the peace and in particular the harmony of the classes of the population'.[4] All assemblies and publications 'in which Social Democratic . . .activities find expression' were likewise prohibited. In addition to the threat of imprisonment and fines, police forces were empowered to expel from their localities 'persons suspected of endangering public security'. The provisions of the law were worded in such a way as to give the authorities great latitude of interpretation. Not only party organisations but also trade unions associated with Social Democracy became subject to dissolution. By November 1878 a total of 153 associations and 175 newspapers and magazines had already been banned and 67 Social Democrats expelled from Berlin alone. Altogether between 800 and 900 'suspic-

4. *Reichs-Gesetzblatt* (1878), No. 34, p. 351.
5. Letter of 12 December 1878; quoted in August Bebel, *Aus meinem Leben*, Vol. 3, pp. 28f.

ious persons' with nearly 1,500 dependants were driven from their homes in the twelve years of the *Sozialistengesetz*. In the two years 1878–9 alone the courts imposed 600 years of prison sentences for offences under this repressive measure and 'offences against the sovereign', and by 1888 they had imposed a further 881 years. The only legal activity left open to Social Democracy was participation in elections to the *Reichstag* and the individual *Landtage* or state diets. Here it emerged that no restrictions and inducements could halt the movement for any length of time.

Following the eventual repeal of the *Sozialistengesetz* in 1890, August Bebel proudly took stock at the party conference in Halle: 'Our performance at general elections was as follows: in 1871, 102,000 votes; in 1874, 352,000 votes; in 1877 — two years after the unification conference of what until 1875 was a split party — 493,000 votes. That was the highest vote recorded before the Anti-Socialists Law. A year later the *Reichstag* was dissolved following the two attacks on the Emperor, a monstrous smear campaign was staged against our party, which was infamously accused of having been responsible for the attacks, and under pressure from the campaign our vote dropped in the summer of 1878 from 493,000 to 437,000; we received 56,000 fewer votes than eighteen months previously. Then came the Law with its blows, but despite everything, in the 1881 general election, held under quite unprecedented conditions, we polled 312,000 votes. This result was to be rated all the higher for the fact that under the emergency conditions and pressures of the time a great many constituencies were not even able to get leaflets and voting papers because no hostile printer was prepared to print them for us and our own printing presses had almost all been destroyed, and even where leaflets were available they could be distributed only with the greatest difficulty and danger. Then came the 1884 election. This time the picture was very different. The party had meanwhile made a substantial recovery; the Wyden [1880] and Copenhagen [1883] conferences were behind it and had significantly lifted the party's self-confidence. Successful attempts were even made here and there to start new papers, maintain printing presses, etc., and as a result we managed on this occasion to attract 550,000 votes, 238,000 more than in 1881. In 1887, however, we increased that to 763,000 and in the last general election earlier this year [20 February 1890], as you will all still remember, to 1,427,000 votes. We had become the largest party in Germany'.[6]

And this despite the fact that Bismarck, as well as wielding the big

6. See *Protokoll über die Verhandlungen des Parteitages der Sozialdemokratischen Partei Deutschlands, abgehalten zu Halle a. S. vom 12. bis 18. Oktober 1890* (Berlin, 1890), pp. 32ff.

stick, had offered the hand of charity. Even the Prussian Junker at the head of the new German Empire was aware that a movement such as Social Democracy had not grown out of nothing but had its roots in social and economic grievances. These he took as the starting-point for the social policy that was made the subject of an imperial pronouncement of 17 November 1881. A Health Insurance Law was passed by the *Reichstag* in 1883. This was followed in 1884 by a measure covering accident insurance and in 1889 by one covering disability and old-age insurance. It was the earliest legislation of its kind — its pioneering role is repeatedly extolled to this day — and it was based on the idea of government welfare, providing a kind of 'further development of the form underlying state poor relief', as Bismarck put it. The deeper motivation behind his social-policy initiatives can be inferred from his words to the *Reichstag*: 'If there were no Social Democracy and if there were not a great many people who are afraid of it, neither should we have the moderate advances that we have made in social reform up to now.'[7] Tactical political motives 'and possibly also the expression of a practical Christianity'[8] governed his conduct here. He introduced state benefits in the hope that they would pull the ground from under the feet of Social Democracy, which he hated, win the workers over to the existing conservative monarchical social order, and place them in the bureaucratic, authoritarian leading-strings of a strengthened state.

### 3. The Political Consequences of Repression

But the mass of the working population refused to be decoyed by this two-pronged strategy of the carrot and the stick. They wanted equal status and democratic autonomy for the provident funds that the labour movement had to some extent already built up for itself; they did not want alms condescendingly handed down from above. They knew from daily experience how that same state continued to persecute the Social Democratic labour movement. Many felt as August Bebel did: 'The fact that we were banished like vagabonds and criminals and forcibly separated from our women and children without trial I experienced as a mortal insult for which I would have sought retribution had I had the power. No trial, no condemnation ever aroused in me such feelings of hatred and bitterness as those expulsions

7. Speech in the *Reichstag*, 26 November 1884; see *Stenographische Berichte über die Verhandlungen des Reichstags, VI. Legislaturperiode, I. Session 1884–1888*, Vol. 1 (Berlin, 1885), p. 25.
8. Helga Grebing, *Geschichte der Arbeiterbewegung*, p. 75.

that were renewed year after year until at last the overthrow of what had become an untenable law put an end to that cruel game with human lives.'[9]

The goad of mistrust and embitterment drove deep into the hearts of Social Democratic working men, outlawed and denounced as enemies of the state. Nevertheless the anarchist putsch tactics advocated by a small group led by Johann Most and Wilhelm Hasselmann was decisively rejected by the party and punished with expulsion. And when the word 'legal' was deleted from the Gotha Programme at the 1880 party conference at Wyden in Switzerland, the intention was simply to give expression to the party's determination to continue its work in the condition of illegality forced upon it by the Law.

The deeper consequences of the *Sozialistengesetz* lay in a different plane. Indignation against the present state gave rise to a hostility, marked by mistrust and aversion, to the state as such. Who could blame the Social Democrats for seeing the state increasingly as no more than an instrument of repression in the hands of the ruling classes? Out of this radicalised awareness on the part of people who were outlawed by bourgeois society and persecuted by authority grew the need for a theoretical foundation that answered their embitterment, condemned the whole system, and offered a rosier future. They found that support and that alleviation of their lot in the ideas of Marx and Engels, in the propagation and popularisation of which Eduard Bernstein and Karl Kautsky played key roles. What made people turn to Marx was not a sophisticated understanding of his theories but a specific interpretation and accentuation that spoke to their level of awareness. Marx offered them a system that taught, on a scientific basis, the certainty of the inevitable decline of the bourgeois class society and predicted the absolutely necessary victory of the Socialist labour movement — and did so in aggressively revolutionary language that exactly matched their own emotions.

For all the party's outward radicality and talk of the proletarian revolution, its secretary for many years, Ignaz Auer, hit the nail on the head when he said: 'A party of revolution is something that German Social Democracy has never been and has no intention of becoming and no desire to become today, the [Socialists] Law notwithstanding. The power of German Social Democracy has always lain and continues to lie in the fact that it really is the representative of the politically aware working man. . . If we wish to be a mere sect, we can allow ourselves the luxury of a revolutionary party on principle; but if we wish to remain the party of the German working man, we must place

9. August Bebel, *Aus meinem Leben*, Vol. 3, p. 183.

in the forefront of our endeavours our desire to bring about, by way of peaceful — I do not say legal — propaganda in the political and economic spheres, reforms and radical changes that will benefit the working population and at the same time bring us a step nearer to the Socialist state.'[10]

In fact the *Sozialistengesetz* itself, which banned the party but allowed participation in elections and countenanced the work of its deputies in the *Reichstag*, favoured the development of a reformist practice. The parliamentary group, which of necessity took over the leadership of the party, rapidly acquired an importance of its own. The *Reichstag* offered a stage the advantages of which the Social Democrats learned to appreciate: here they could operate publicly and put forward their programme and their concrete demands. And after the initial setbacks the party's swiftly and, it seemed, ineluctably swelling share of the vote appeared to demonstrate that, given universal equal suffrage, the ballot box was the proper and most promising way of winning power and radically changing the system. One of those who endorsed this ballot-box optimism was Friedrich Engels with his 1895 foreword to Karl Marx's *The Class Struggles in France*. The successful application of universal suffrage by German Social Democracy 'brought an entirely new mode of combat by the proletariat into operation'. The 'mass' of the SPD was 'constantly on the increase. Its growth is as spontaneous, as steady, as unstoppable, and at the same time as calm as a process of nature.'[11]

The *Sozialistengesetz* thus had a twofold, self-contradictory effect: in terms of awareness it produced a radicalisation of theory; in terms of method it steered the party towards the practical work of achieving reform through parliament.

10. Quoted in Eduard Bernstein, *Ignaz Auer. Eine Gedenkschrift* (Berlin, 1907), pp. 37f.

11. Karl Marx, *Die Klassenkämpfe in Frankreich 1848 bis 1850*, new edition introduced by Friedrich Engels, 1895; Engels' introduction reprinted in Hartmut Mehringer and Gottfried Mergner (eds), *Friedrich Engels. Studienausgabe 4* (rororo no. 296), pp. 195ff.

# 4
# Between Radical Theory and Reformist Practice
## Social Democracy as a Mass Party from Erfurt to the First World War

At its Erfurt conference in 1891 German Social Democracy not only assumed a new name, calling itself the 'Social Democratic Party of Germany'; it also gave itself a fresh programme. Eight years after Marx's death on 14 March 1883, Engels declared triumphantly in 1891: 'We have the satisfaction that Marx's criticism [of the Gotha Programme] has taken effect completely.'[1] With the 'Erfurt Programme', Marxism became the official theoretical foundation of German Social Democracy. With very little discussion the party conference gave its unanimous approval to the draft presented by the party's leading theoreticians, Kautsky and Bernstein. These two — dubbed half in mockery and half in admiration the 'latter-day Early Fathers' of the party — were concerned to recast 'the intellectual weapons furnished by the Marx-Engels arsenal'[2] in a form suitable for everyday use. The result was something of a two-edged sword.

The Erfurt Programme falls into two quite distinct parts: a theoretical part and a practical political part. This bi-polarity is one of the features of the programme that has encouraged criticism of it as 'inconsistent'.

The first section, dealing with principles, was based almost verbatim in places on chapter 24 (paragraph 7) of Marx's *Capital*. It did not represent a programme in the proper sense but instead offered a brief analysis of the 'economic development of bourgeois society' and the consequences that necessarily ensued. The 'gap between propertied and unpropertied', it said, was growing ever wider, the 'army of

---

1. *Briefe und Auszüge aus Briefen von Joh. Phil. Becker, Jos. Dietzgen, Friedrich Engels, Karl Marx u.a. an F. A. Sorge und andere* (Stuttgart, 1906), p. 370.
2. Susanne Miller, 'Zur Rezeption des Marxismus in der deutschen Sozialdemokratie', in Heiner Flohr, Klaus Lompe, Lothar F. Neumann (eds), *Freiheitlicher Sozialismus* (Bonn, 1973), p. 24.

surplus workers' ever greater, poverty, enslavement, and exploitation ever more acute, and 'the class struggle between bourgeoisie and proletariat. . . ever more vehement'. 'Only the transformation of the capitalist private ownership of the means of production — land, mines, raw materials, tools, machinery, transport — into social ownership and the conversion of commodity production into Socialist production, pursued by society for society's benefit, is capable of bringing it about that big business and the constantly increasing yield capacity of social labour cease to be a source of poverty and oppression for the hitherto exploited classes and become a source of supreme welfare and all-round, harmonious improvement. This social transformation means the emancipation not only of the proletariat but of the whole human race as suffering under present circumstances.' Yet this was to be achieved by the working class alone — in 'economic struggles', by wresting political rights, and by seizing political power as a basis for 'the switch of the means of production to common ownership'.[3]

If it appears from the first part of the programme that only the socialisation of the means of production was capable of permanently improving the position of the workers, the second part makes practical demands in the direction of the democratisation of state and society and the social betterment of the working class. In addition to universal, equal suffrage under a proportional representation system for all parliaments, the election of public authorities, and self-government at every level, the programme called for such things as equality for women, secular education, free justice and medical attention, a change in fiscal and economic policy, the introduction of labour exchanges, the safeguarding of freedom of opinion and association and the right of combination, the 'assumption of all labour-insurance by the state' with democratic worker-involvement, and above all that 'the standard working day. . . be fixed at a maximum of eight hours'. The markedly plebiscitary elements in the Gotha and Eisenach programmes were toned down at Erfurt. Rather than 'jurisdiction by the people', the call now was for 'jurisdiction by judges elected by the people'. Direct legislation was qualified to indirect, and decisions regarding war and peace were no longer to be taken by the people, as had been demanded at Gotha, but by their representatives in parliament.

There is a conspicuous absence of any statement of principle regarding the organisation of the state. Engels had drawn the attention of the authors of the draft to the fact that, if they wished to 'grow into Socialism', they must recognise that the SPD would be able to come to power only 'under the form of a democratic republic'.[4] There was

3. See Document 3, p. 240.

indeed something missing here. To call for a democratic republic was hardly possible in the current legal climate in Germany, and as an immediate demand it was in any case illusory. Yet Marx and Engels themselves could not entirely escape blame in this respect. They had never clearly defined the relationship between inexorable historical development and practical action, between the revolutionary objective and the work of reform, pointing only to the resolution of the antithesis in the dialectical unity of theory and practice. With the Erfurt Programme and the interpretations of Kautsky, Social Democracy took over from the theories of Marx and Engels the belief in a social development unfolding according to the strict rules of a natural law and resulting in the abolition of class rule and the consequent superfluity of the state. Friedrich Engels expressed it vividly: 'The state will wither away and be placed in the museum of antiquities beside the spinning-wheel and the bronze axe.'[5]

Socialism would then have reached its goal. But precisely how that goal was to be achieved, how the seizure of political power by the proletariat was to be brought about, and what changes of socio-political structure and what institutional transition stages would be necessary in the process — these were things that, so far as the Erfurt Programme was concerned, had to be read between the lines. This very lack of precision led people to stress different aspects. Some invoked the programme in support, primarily, of the struggle to achieve democratic freedoms and social reforms; others sought on the basis of the principles cited to go for an intensification of class conflicts and for social revolution. Despite such divergent tendencies, the actions of the Social Democratic Party were governed throughout by what it had enshrined in the Erfurt Programme as its fundamental commitment: to fighting 'for the abolition of class rule and classes themselves and for equal rights and equal obligations for all without distinction of sex and birth' and against not only the exploitation of workers but 'every kind of exploitation and oppression, be it directed against a class, a party, a sex, or a race'.[6]

## 1. Economic and Social Change

At the general election of 20 February 1890, German Social Democ-

---

4. Said by Engels in his critique of the Erfurt Programme, an extract from which is reprinted in Hermann Weber (ed.), *Das Prinzip Links*, p. 65.

5. Friedrich Engels, *Herrn Eugen Dührings Umwälzung der Wissenschaft* ('Anti-Dühring'), third edition (Stuttgart, 1894), p. 311.

6. See Document 3, p. 240.

racy had won 19.7 per cent of the vote, thus becoming the most voted-for party in the country. The 1,427,000 voters who used their ballot papers to express their loyalty to the proscribed representatives of the 'Fourth Estate' marked the final breakthrough to a mass movement. Apart from a brief setback in 1907, the SPD continued to expand steadily until the First World War. After reaching 23.3 per cent in 1893 (1,786,000 votes), 27.2 per cent in 1898 (2,107,000 votes), 31.7 per cent in 1903 (3,010,000 votes), and 28.9 per cent in 1907 (3,258,000 votes), in 1912 its share of the poll climbed to 34.8 per cent or four and a quarter million votes.[7] Hundreds of thousands of men and women carried cards to proclaim their membership of the SPD, although doing so often brought them difficulties and disadvantages at their place of work. The 'first-past-the-post' system prevented the party's vote from finding expression in an appropriate number of seats in the *Reichstag*. The constituency boundaries drawn in the early years of the Reich had not been altered to take account of subsequent population shifts and now favoured the thinly populated rural areas against the conurbations. Not until 1912 did the SPD become the largest party in the *Reichstag*, with 110 seats. Despite this unparalleled upswing, Social Democracy remained essentially a party of the industrial working class. It failed either to achieve any significant successes among farm workers, most of whom voted Conservative under the influence of their employers, teachers, and ministers, or to penetrate the ranks of the Roman Catholic working population, among whom the Centre Party continued to predominate.

The trade-union movement experienced similarly rapid growth.[8] The printers and cigar-workers had already organised themselves during the 1848 revolution, and in the 1860s they were once again the first to become active. The founding of the Society of Cigar-Workers (*Zigarrenarbeiterverein*) in 1865 and the Printers' Association (*Buchdruckerverband*) in 1866, coupled with initiatives stemming from the Socialist parties, led to the creation of further associations of workers. Their attempt to erect a central superstructure in 1878 was frustrated by the *Sozialistengesetz*, to which the trade unions sympathising with Social Democracy also fell victim and under which they were able to continue only in a camouflaged form.

Not until the *Sozialistengesetz* was thrown out in 1890 did real trade-union work become possible once again. Differences of opinion regarding the right forms of organisation proved largely surmountable. In that same year the 'General Commission of German Trade Unions'

7. See Tables 1, 2, pp. 293, 294.
8. For an account of the history of the German trade-union movement, see Dieter Schuster, *Die deutsche Gewerkschaftsbewegung*, (Düsseldorf, [4]1973).

was set up, providing united if fairly loose leadership, and by 1891 it was able to boast over 277,000 trade-unionist members. Following a period of stagnation in the shadow of an economic crisis, a sharp upswing began in 1895. The 500,000 mark was passed in 1899. The year 1904 saw the first million members, 1910 the second million, and by the outbreak of the First World War there were some two and a half million German trade-unionists in the ranks of the General Commission. In addition to the self-styled 'Free Trade Unions', which were closely associated with Social Democracy, there were the Christian trade unions and the *Gewerkvereine*, which sympathised with the Liberals. Both these groups enjoyed only minority support and reached their pre-war maximum in 1913 with 340,000 and 105,000 members respectively.

The growth of the Social Democratic labour movement took place against the background as well as on the basis of an explosive economic expansion. In this the railways, with their demand for steel and their improvement of communications and transport, acted as the driving force behind the industrialisation process. The rail network expanded from 549 kilometres in 1840 to 6,044 kilometres in 1850 and 19,575 kilometres in 1870; by the end of the century the figure stood at 51,678 kilometres.[9] To take another example: from the year of the foundation of the Reich, when the industrial revolution first got into top gear, as it were, pig-iron production rose from 1.6 million tons to reach 14.8 million by 1910. New technical processes (the Bessemer converter, 1855–60, the dynamo in 1866, advances in chemistry) laid the foundations for the emergence of new branches of industry. Mushrooming joint-stock companies, trusts, and monopolies, the first big combines, for example in the electrical industry, big banks such as the Deutsche Bank and the Dresdner Bank, and a noticeable increase in reciprocal involvement between banks and combines were typical manifestations of this period. Germany was finally transformed from an agricultural to an industrial country. The slice of the gross national product contributed by agriculture dropped from 47 per cent in 1850 to 23 per cent in 1913, while in the same period industry's share increased many times over, reaching nearly 60 per cent by the outbreak of the First World War. Population growth (40 million in 1871, 67 million in 1914) together with mass migration from predominantly rural areas led to a concentration of population in the conurbations. Industrial centres on the Rhine, in the Ruhr, in Saxony, and in Berlin moulded the face of the new Germany — an economic great power. The number of industrial workers doubled between 1887 and 1914. Whereas in 1871

9. See Fritz Voigt, *Verkehr*, Vol. 2 (Berlin, 1965), pp. 505, 529, 537.

sixty-five per cent of the population had been living in villages and small towns, in 1910 only 40 per cent remained. Over the same period the proportion of the population living in cities of over 100,000 inhabitants rose from 5 to 20 per cent. Urbanisation and the flight from the country were accompanied by a dissolution of the traditional ties and a turning towards a new sense of community characterised by homogeneous working and living environments. Although labour productivity rose rapidly as a result of technical improvements and increased division of labour, this failed to lead to the mass unemployment predicted by the Erfurt Programme and earlier by Marx himself. On the contrary, unemployment sank to a relatively low level, which was what provided the conditions necessary for a potentially successful working-class struggle. Among unionised employees the unemployment rate oscillated between about 1 and 3 per cent.[10] At the same time, from the 1870s onwards there was a progressive reduction of the working day to twelve, then to eleven, and in some well unionised branches even to ten hours.

Wages exhibited a rising trend. What was important was that not only was there an increase in nominal wages but that real wages went up too, if not always continuously. Particularly in the years following 1881 there was a steep rise that perhaps better deserved to be called a 'genuine, material social reform'[11] than did Bismarck's system of social insurance. Whereas in 1850 a working-class family in Prussia had had to spend 58 per cent of its income simply on the food it needed, by 1913 the proportion was down to 33 per cent.

Even so, its income was only just sufficient for a moderately sized family to live on without serious food shortages but not to purchase adequate clothing as well and lead a life fit for human beings. In most working-class households it therefore remained literally vital that the wife should work as well. Housing conditions were deplorable. Most people existed after a fashion in gloomy back rooms or grey tenement blocks that had been thrown up in a hurry. As late as 1895 Berlin still had 25,000 dwellings consisting of a single room. More than 80,000 so-called *Schlafburschen* or night lodgers had no more than a sleeping-place that they rented in someone else's dwelling — and that they often had to share with others into the bargain, sleeping turn and turn about.

Economic hardships remained rife, despite many improvements, but it was not only material worries that oppressed working people: the roots of discontent ran deeper. The ostentatious wealth of the affluent,

10. See Gerhard Bry, *Wages in Germany 1871–1945. A Study by the National Bureau of Economic Research, New York* (Princeton, 1960), pp. 325ff.

11. Hans Rosenberg, *Grosse Depression und Bismarckzeit* (Berlin, 1967), p. 217.

the persistence of political and social discrimination, and above all the paucity of rights and prevalence of dependence in the labour process continually provoked legitimate feelings of bitterness against 'them up there', as the German worker put it. These were directed as much against foremen — contemptuously regarded as 'slave-drivers' — as against capitalists, employers, and entrepreneurs who, with notable exceptions such as Ernst Abbe and Robert Bosch, for the most part adopted a rigidly authoritarian 'I'm the boss' attitude. Their standpoint was expressed by the industrialist Emil Kirdorf when on the occasion of the 1899 miners' strike he declared high-handedly: 'Neither emperors nor kings have any say in our mills. There we alone decide.'[12]

On his own, the individual working man was a powerless object in the face of this kind of claim to power. Only through solidarity, through sticking together with his fellows, was there any chance of his effectively safeguarding his interests. It was this experiencing every day the same situation as his workmates that made him aware of how he belonged to one great class, the exploited and oppressed working class. In the eyes of that class, Social Democracy was the party that represented its interests and was fighting for a better future. In its organisations and in the trade unions working people found a community of like-minded folk among whom that feeling of powerlessness was a thing of the past. Social Democracy offered a shelter that was at the same time a home; it gave working people the conviction that their position and that of their class comrades was not hopeless but that exploitation and oppression would come to an end, one day in the not-too-distant future. Inspired by this belief in the imminent victory of Social Democracy and the promised Socialist society of the future, its adherents felt themselves to be proud, self-assured pioneers of a new era. These feelings were given typical expression by a young metalworker when he said: 'I never despair, because anyone as steeped in Socialism as I am believes in emancipation as if it were a new Gospel.'[13]

## 2. Practical Politics and Theoretical Conflicts

With the overthrow of the *Sozialistengesetz* and the fall of Bismarck

---

12. Dieter Schuster, *Die deutsche Gewerkschaftsbewegung*, p. 24. For the attitudes of two better-known industrialists, Alfred Krupp and Carl Ferdinand von Stumm-Halberg, see Ernst Schraepler, *Quellen zur Geschichte der sozialen Frage in Deutschland*, Vol. 2 (Göttingen, 1957), pp. 87ff.
13. Adolf Levenstein, *Die Arbeiterfrage* (Munich, 1912), p. 314.

indicating a change of direction in domestic affairs, Social Democracy found itself facing an altered situation. Discrimination still continued. Using official interventions, trials for *lèse majesté*, and the instrument of the law on associations, the state went on creating difficulties for the SPD and the trade unions. Moreover, from time to time attempts were made to employ new and more powerful weapons against Social Democracy. The best-known instances are the so-called 'Subversion Bill' of 1894–5 and the 'Prison Bill' of 1898–9. Both measures, however, failed to get through the *Reichstag*. Yet in spite of all these attempts at repression, from 1890 Social Democracy was at last able, in contrast to the previous twelve years, to operate as a party within a context of legality. This lifted the question of future political tactics into a fresh dimension.[14]

The opposition movement of the so-called 'Young Ones' (*Die Jungen*) with their polemicising against the 'leaders' and their revolutionary and in part anti-parliamentary, syndicalist-style slogans remained peripheral and was short-lived. It was no use their appealing to Engels: he accused them of being incapable of 'seeing the simplest things and when judging an economic or political situation making an unbiassed assessment either of the relative importance of the factors on hand or of the strength of the forces at issue'.[15]

Quite different principles than those of the 'Young Ones' movement underlay the rise of reformism, which corresponded to a 'real need', as Kautsky aptly analysed it: 'We are too big to go on being a mere protest party.'[16] In the same spirit Georg von Vollmar, long a member of the party's radical wing, called in 1891 in his celebrated 'Eldorado Speeches' (named after the premises where the party met in Munich) for a resolute policy of reform on the basis of the existing political and social order. Rather than frighten off other progressive forces operating outside its ranks with its intransigent stance and revolutionary speeches, Social Democracy ought to work together with them, the better to push through a determined policy of social and democratic reform. Using the slogan 'An open hand for goodwill, a fist for ill!',[17] Vollmar sought in the existing political context to accelerate the

14. See also Gerhard A. Ritter, *Die Arbeiterbewegung im Wilhelminischen Reich. Die Sozialdemokratische Partei und die Freien Gewerkschaften 1890–1900* (Berlin-Dahlem, 1959; second edition, 1963), and Hans-Josef Steinberg, *Sozialismus und deutsche Sozialdemokratie. Zur Ideologie der Partei vor dem Ersten Weltkrieg*, fifth edition (Berlin/Bonn, 1979).

15. Marx/Engels, *Werke*, Vol. 22, p. 84.

16. Karl Kautsky in a letter to Eduard Bernstein, 8 December 1896; quoted in Hans-Josef Steinberg, 'Die deutsche Sozialdemokratie nach dem Fall des Sozialistengesetzes', in Hans Mommsen (ed.), *Sozialdemokratie*, p. 54.

17. Georg von Vollmar, *Über die nächsten Aufgaben der deutschen Sozialdemokratie* (Munich, 1891), p. 7.

proletariat's struggle for emancipation by concentrating forces on the practical task of reform. August Bebel, on the other hand, warned the party around this time against the danger of dissipating its energies in detailed work and losing sight of its higher objective. He saw the final struggle as imminent. In criticising Vollmar's initiative he told delegates at the Erfurt party conference: 'I am convinced that the realisation of our goals is so close that few here in this hall will not live to see the day.'[18] Although Vollmar's suggestions were officially rejected at first, they met with an increasing response. In giving priority to *Realpolitik*, they largely coincided with the course pursued by the 'Free Trade Unions', who strove for improvements 'on the ground of present-day society'[19] and like the reformists were reluctant to be forced into a rigid theoretical mould.

The impassioned debate sparked off by Vollmar's sally must not be allowed to obscure the fact that in the day-to-day political affairs of the party a broad measure of agreement was the rule. The fight for democratic freedoms and social change, which Marx and Engels themselves expressly fought, was clearly prescribed in the second part of the Erfurt Programme and governed the actions even of those who preached implacable class warfare and the coming social revolution. Paul Kampffmeyer characterised this attitude in 1899 in the words: 'It is a curious thing that the present schism between radicals and possibilists runs right through the middle of the Erfurt Programme as it runs — you almost feel you can touch it — through the minds of our most gifted theoreticians and party leaders. On the one hand they heap anathema after anathema upon bourgeois society; on the other they labour with burning zeal to patch up and improve it.'[20]

The foundations of that labour were party organisations, state and national parliaments, trade unions, co-operatives, and collaboration in the institutions of social insurance and labour law. The party's organisational structure was elastically adapted to the limitations imposed by the law, making it possible for women too to play a part in most states; it was not until 1908 that the law allowed them open membership throughout the Reich. Following the 1900 repeal of the prohibition of combinations, the party had changed its organisational structure under the statute of 1905 from the hitherto prevalent system of informal organisers (*Vertrauensleute*) to associations with fixed membership

18. From the minutes of the conference. See *Protokoll über die Verhandlungen des Parteitages der Sozialdemokratischen Partei Deutschlands, abgehalten zu Erfurt vom 14. bis 20. Oktober 1891* (Berlin, 1891), p. 172.
19. From the proclamation of the General Commission in 1891; quoted in Dieter Schuster, *Die deutsche Gewerkschaftsbewegung*, p. 27.
20. Paul Kampffmeyer, 'Schrittweise Sozialisierung oder gewaltsame Sprengung der kapitalistischen Wirtschaftsordnung', in *Sozialistische Monatshefte*, 1899, No. 10, p. 466.

dues. These rose in a pyramid from local and constituency units through district, provincial, and state associations to the national organisation at Reich level, with the executive committee. The party's rise is documented in its swelling membership figures: 384,327 in 1905–6, 1,085,905 in 1913–14.[21] The growth of a party bureaucracy through the appointment of salaried functionaries was an almost inevitable concomitant of a mass party from which people expected advice and help in all situations. With its free advisory service provided by labour secretariats, most of them run by the trade unions, Social Democracy helped large numbers of people to understand and obtain their rights, particularly in the field of social insurance. In addition it was intensely active in education, organising hundreds of courses and individual lectures, its own libraries, theatrical performances and the setting-up of the *Freie Volksbühne* or 'Free People's Theatre', itinerant teachers, and the establishment of a central Workers' College of Education and the famous party college. In this way the SPD and the trade unions not only provided the arms and equipment for the political and trade-union struggle but in the process constituted a cultural movement in the broadest sense of the term.

Much more in the public eye, however, was the party's work in the parliamentary arena. Fundamental differences regarding the political and social order and the largely *en bloc* antagonism of the middle-class parties placed narrow limits on the effectiveness of Social Democracy in the *Reichstag*. Only in isolated instances was the party able to find allies in the bourgeois camp. In its campaign for more extensive parliamentary rights and a greater degree of democracy the SPD had most chance of finding support among the left-wing liberal groups, while in the realm of social policy it had already made contact with the Centre Party and its 'Christian Workers' wing. But on such crucial points as the demand for a statutory eight-hour day, for example, or the abolition of the discriminatory Prussian three-class electoral system, Social Democracy was virtually impotent in the face of a united bourgeois front.

The only way in which the SPD could occasionally, in borderline cases, exert a direct influence on the legislative process was by adopting compromise tactics. In 1894 the parliamentary party's first vote for a government bill went to a measure proposing to lower cereal import tariffs, which held out the hope of lower food prices. In 1913 its votes carried through new tax laws — made necessary by increased military expenditure — that at last affected the propertied classes as well. This

21. See Dieter Fricke, *Zur Organisation und Tätigkeit der deutschen Arbeiterbewegung (1890–1914). Dokumente und Materialien* (Leipzig, 1962), pp. 64ff.

rather made nonsense — in an important respect — of the 'Not a man and not a penny for this system' principle that found its most obvious expression in the party's rejection of the budget.

In the *Landtage* this had begun even earlier, starting in 1891 in Hesse and Baden. In 1894 the SPD parliamentary party in the Bavarian *Landtag* went against national party policy and voted for the budget. In Prussia, with its three-class electoral system graduated according to tax yield, it was not until 1908 that Socialist deputies were able to enter the Lower House, so that the north Germans were given conspicuous confirmation of their view of the state as a tool of repression in the hands of the ruling classes. In the south-German states of Baden, Hesse, Württemberg, and Bavaria, however, the prevailing climate was more liberal. Through electoral pacts with bourgeois parties and by voting for the budget and government bills, the SPD here achieved certain socio-political and democratic concessions, notably the replacement of classified electoral systems by universal, equal suffrage.

Social Democracy placed particular emphasis on work at local level, this starting a tradition of involvement in local politics that was revived and taken further after 1945. The unemployment-benefit schemes set up in certain localities and the introduction of local certificates of employment were due not least to the tireless efforts of Social Democrats. In 1913 the SPD numbered nearly 13,000 local and municipal councillors.[22] Here and in its work on administrative and representative bodies to do with industrial insurance, local certificates of employment, and industrial and commercial courts (in 1910 an estimated 100,000 Social Democrats sat on such bodies) lies one of the root causes of Social Democracy's having gradually become part of the political fabric of the German Empire.

Another arose out of the work of the trade unions. With their welfare institutions — on which they spent a total of 389.9 million marks in the period 1891–1914, including 143.5 million for strike pay, 89.9 million for unemployment relief, and 91 million for sickness benefit[23] — they offered their members a system of social insurance that also exercised a powerful attraction on the hitherto non-unionised. It was the strike fund that first made it possible to survive labour struggles for longer periods. And from the turn of the century the idea of the industrial agreement — advocates of which were pilloried at first as being 'daft on harmony' and 'traitors to the class struggle' — found increasing acceptance. Carl Legien, the chairman of

22. Detailed statistics are given in Gerhard A. Ritter, *Die Arbeiterbewegung im Wilhelminischen Reich*, pp. 233f.
23. See Paul Umbreit, *25 Jahre deutsche Gewerkschaftsbewegung 1890 bis 1915* (Berlin, 1915), particularly the table on p. 175.

the General Commission of the Free Trade Unions, saw it not merely as an effective instrument for improving wages and working conditions but also as providing 'recognition of the worker's right of co-determination with respect to the conditions of labour'.[24] Like Legien, most trade-union officials were reformist in their approach. Their activities, after all, were directed towards securing practical improvements. They did not think much of speeches about revolutionary theories or of abstract theories in general, anxious to avoid if possible anything that might threaten the solidarity of their organisation and jeopardise what they had already achieved in the field of social policy.

### 3. The Revisionism Controversy and the General Strike Debate

Even today the charge of 'revisionism' is one of the most serious known to Communist theory. Anyone harbouring doubts about the validity of the 'true teaching' was and still is swiftly denounced as a 'revisionist'. The term goes back a long way and is associated with a man who around the turn of the century sparked off violent discussions among German Social Democrats with the ideas he put forward. That man was Eduard Bernstein. The reformism of Vollmar and others aimed at changing the party's political strategy and its conception of its goal but did not directly question the substance of Marxist theory. It was in the debate sparked off by Vollmar, however, that voices were heard for the first time expressing doubts as to the universal validity of that theory. In terms of their practical consequences those clashes were the early symptoms of the revisionism controversy to come.

Eduard Bernstein gave the revisionist stance its theoretical justification. In a series of articles in *Die Neue Zeit* headed 'Problems of Socialism' (1896–7) and in a book on 'The Requirements of Socialism and the Tasks of Social Democracy' (1899)[25] he gave notice of reasonable doubts as to whether the way in which society was actually developing really conformed to the trend towards a two-class pattern prognosticated by the *Communist Manifesto* and the Erfurt Programme. The middle classes were not disappearing; they were merely changing their character. Nor had the predictions of steadily worsening crises associated with the catastrophe theory or the thesis of the increasing pauperisation of the working class turned out to be true as

24. Carl Legien, 'Tarifgemeinschaften und gemeinsame Verbände von Arbeitern und Unternehmern', in *Sozialistische Monatshefte*, 1902, No. 1, p. 29.
25. Respectively 'Probleme des Sozialismus' and *Die Voraussetzungen des Sozialismus und die Aufgaben der Sozialdemokratie*.

originally formulated. Instead, contrary tendencies were becoming apparent that suggested a process of transformation and a certain bridling of unbridled capitalism. He saw the reasons for this development primarily in the determined struggle being waged by organised labour for a democratic say in matters concerning it and for some betterment of its social position. A policy of reform was thus for him a means not just of stabilising but also of changing the system.

As Bernstein saw it, Social Democracy ought not to let its policy be dictated by the prospect of the 'impending great social catastrophe', the necessary collapse of capitalism and its inevitable replacement by Socialism. On the contrary, it must re-examine its radical revolutionary dogmas and specifically admit, it terms of its theoretical objective, to being 'what in reality it is today: a democratic–Socialist party of reform'.[26] It was in this sense that he wished people to construe his often misunderstood statement that 'the movement is everything to me while what people *commonly* call the goal of Socialism is nothing'.[27]

Bernstein's ideas, which were based chiefly on his study of industrial development in Britain but also on German statistics, provoked an impassioned discussion that went on for years. The condemnations of revisionism issued by the party conference — the last occasion was in 1903 — and the party's profession of Marxism as taught to it by Kautsky and passionately championed by Bebel were not the end of the matter. Although tactical questions of day-to-day politics were also involved, Vollmar could rightly say at the party conference that he knew of no occasion on which solid blocs of 'radical' Marxists and revisionists had opposed each other in the *Reichstag*. In essence the controversy did not turn on the problem of whether or not to pursue a policy of reform. The pivotal point was in fact the notion of an unstoppable evolution towards Socialism by way of the necessary transitional stage of a social revolution. Bernstein, who advocated an ethically grounded Socialism that 'has ideals to realise but no doctrines', dismissed this expectation as 'Utopianism'. For him the concept of revolution was tied up with such elements as direct action and the use of force. In the party, however, the word 'revolution' had virtually ceased to be used in this sense — the sense corresponding to normal usage. Kautsky's phrase about Social Democracy being 'a revolutionary but not a revolution-making party' suggests how complex the term had become.[28] What emerged as its crucial characteristic

---

26. Eduard Bernstein, *Die Voraussetzungen des Sozialismus und die Aufgaben der Sozialdemokratie* (Stuttgart, 1904; first edition, 1899), p. 165.
27. Letter to the 1898 party conference; see Document 4, p. 243.
28. Karl Kautsky, 'Zur Frage der Revolution', in *Die Neue Zeit*, 1893, No. 14; reprinted in Georg Fülberth (ed.), *Karl Kautsky, Der Weg zur Macht* (second edition,

was the seizure of political power by the working class and the radical restructuring of the economy. The struggle for social reform thus keyed in smoothly with the revolutionary objective.

The Marxists, who represented the dominant element in the party, saw the economic crises that had succeeded one another since the 1873 crash as heralding the collapse of capitalism. This helped to account for the belief — proclaimed by August Bebel and adopted by a broad section of the membership — that the end of capitalism would come with a final, severe economic crisis culminating in the breakdown of the traditional social order. 'In the end,' Bebel opined in 1884, 'a good jolt will bring the whole lot crashing down like a house of cards';[29] the age of Socialism would have dawned. In his book *Women and Socialism* (1883), the most widely-read book to come out of the Social Democratic movement, he painted an impressive picture of that age: a society enjoying perfect freedom and justice together with all the blessings of communal institutions, a society in which men could freely develop their creative potential in peace and harmony.

From the very beginning Social Democracy had seen itself as the standard-bearer of a new age. In this the theory of revolution performed a double function: firstly as offering a radical challenge to the existing exploitative class society, secondly as holding out the hope of a Socialist society in the future. From the teachings of Marx and Engels it drew fresh sources of strength and enthusiasm: the 'scientifically' supported certainty of being on the side of history and the conviction that the great vision of Socialism would become a reality as a matter of absolute necessity. It was against this twofold assurance that the doubts of the revisionists were directed, which is why Bebel accused them of robbing the Socialist labour movement of its faith and its inspiration.


This conviction of the imminent collapse of the bourgeois, capitalist social order and the inexorable victory of Socialism, which at the time of the adoption of the Erfurt Programme had drawn strength from an economic depression, soon received a powerful damper. The economic upswing that began in 1896 showed capitalism to possess powers of survival and adaptability that took the SPD by surprise. The turn of the century was a time of rising entrepreneurial profits and saw the beginnings of a stagnation in real wages, a halt in the government's

---

1910; reprinted Frankfurt a.M., 1972), pp. 15ff.
29. August Bebel in a letter to Hermann Schlüter, 24 February 1884; quoted in Hans-Josef Steinberg, 'Die deutsche Sozialdemokratie nach dem Fall des Sozialistengesetzes', in Hans Mommsen (ed.), *Sozialdemokratie*, p. 57.

social policy, and renewed attempts at political oppression in the shape of the 'Subversion' and 'Prison' bills. Even the party's massive success at the polls in 1912, when the Social Democrats had concluded a second-ballot pact with the left-wing liberal Progressive Party, brought it little advantage. Indeed, the principal effect was to mobilise its enemies. In the so-called 'Cartel of the Productive Classes' (*Kartell der schaffenden Stände*), pressure groups from industry, agriculture, and small business welded themselves into a powerful fighting force to campaign against Social Democracy.

The party's inability — which emerged more and more clearly around the turn of the century — to convert its growing electoral strength into corresponding political influence mobilised the forces within the party who were on the lookout for new ways forward. The discussion that now flared up about a political general strike was partly a reflex reaction to the worsening internal contradictions of the Reich and the impasse in which Social Democracy found itself. Engels, Bebel, and the Second International — formed in Paris in July 1889 — all rejected the general strike at first as being an unsuitable weapon. Not even on the occasion of the first May Day demonstration called for by the new body in 1890 did a mass withdrawal of labour come close to being a reality. Subsequently, however, the Belgian suffrage strikes, the 'Subversion Bill', the Russian revolution of 1905, and the justly feared plans of reactionary forces to seize power and abolish the one man/one vote system in elections for the *Reichstag* sparked off vigorous new discussions in the party press and at party conferences. The outcome was a resolution passed at the 1906 conference in Mannheim recognising the general strike as an appropriate means of defence in the event of an attack on the *Reichstag* suffrage and the right of combination. This implied not only a renunciation of any offensive use but also grave reservations with regard to defensive deployment of the general-strike weapon.

The wording of the resolution took account of the trade unions, who at their earlier conference in Cologne had firmly rejected any commitment to the general strike. They had secured the so-called 'Mannheim Agreement' whereby actions of this kind, affecting both organisations, must be decided on jointly. With this agreement they had also secured their long-fought-for guarantee of independence from the party, which was henceforth obliged to discuss all important political decisions with the unions' General Commission. In addition to the plan championed primarily by the trade unions — to avoid all unnecessary risks and consistently improve the strength and solidarity of their organisation — a second, quite different strategy began to take shape during the general-strike debate. Under the leadership of Rosa

Luxemburg, Franz Mehring, and Wilhelm Liebknecht's son Karl a 'left' emerged that saw the revolutionary components of Marxism as providing the answer to worsening class conflicts and the pointer to new horizons. Impressed by the Russian revolution of 1905–6, they came to regard the political general strike as the decisive weapon for mobilising the masses. A spontaneous uprising by the working class — to prevent a war, for example — would develop into revolutionary struggles and finally usher in the Socialist revolution. However, these left-wing radicals likewise failed to develop a consistent strategy for the seizure of political power. They sought to arouse the masses' revolutionary will to fight, only to discover that the working class had very little time for so risky a course of action.

At one point their plan chimed with the ideas of the leading man on the reformist wing of the party, Ludwig Frank, and even with certain of Bernstein's views. Frank, whom August Bebel regarded as his 'crown prince' for a time and who urged an activation of party policy from the right, wished to use the general-strike weapon to force through a reform of the Prussian electoral system. It was all part of his strategy of a 'total mobilisation of the party's forces in the service of the democratisation of Germany', the strategy by means of which he sought to steer Social Democracy in the direction of becoming a systematic democratic–Socialist party of reform.

Of these two tendencies urging action, neither gained acceptance — neither the left, which wished to take revolutionary theory really seriously in practice, nor the right, which wished to make democratic–Socialist reformism the sole guide of the party's actions and statements.[30] The slogans of the radical left largely failed to find an echo among the wider membership. Involvement in the practical, 'here-and-now' work of the trade unions with their relief funds, coupled with the proven, long-term effectiveness of the government's social-insurance scheme, ultimately led to a partial integration of the working class in the existing state. A further contributory factor was that Social Democracy had managed, with much laborious effort, to build up its own very varied organisational world of *Volkshäuser* (literally 'houses of the people'; political, social, and cultural centres for the use of the movement), publications, educational institutions, and self-help services — of all of which it was justly proud. There was a growing belief among a not inconsiderable section of the working population that the existing social order could be reformed and that they had rather more to lose than their chains. If in spite of these

30. For the background here, see Detlef Lehnert, *Reform und Revolution in der Strategiediskussion der klassischen Sozialdemokratie* (Bonn, 1977).

tendencies revisionism as a theory failed to win general acceptance, the chief reason was simply that it was incapable of providing an attractive substitute for the visionary quality inherent in the prevailing Marxist ideology. Despite some positive first steps taken by the party in the direction of breaking out of its political isolation — the successful electoral pact with the Progressive Party, for example, in the *Reichstag* elections of 1912 and a degree of collaboration with the left-wing liberals and the Centre Party over questions of democracy and social policy — the revisionist approach was largely out of touch with the domestic situation in Germany. The constitution of the German Reich, the socio-political balance of power, and the intransigence of the ruling classes all stood in the way of the kind of purposeful, constructive co-operation envisaged by the revisionists and reformists.

The tone continued to be set by the broad spectrum of the centre of the party, which combined practical efforts in the direction of reform with adherence to a popular theoretical Marxism. This gradually became a mere group ideology that functioned as no more than a safety-valve for the aggressions arising out of the political and social situation. Although the party flatly refused to 'make revolutions' and in policy terms pursued an unambiguously reformist course, verbal radicalism continued to colour the image of Social Democracy with its revolutionary bombast. In fact, however, the party increasingly saw social revolution as an economic and political recasting process that would come about without any direct intervention on its part. The consequence of this interpretation of society was a dulling of the desire actively to shape events as one waited for the unpredictable great event to come. It was a question of being ready for that moment, of keeping the one firm bastion of the party's organisations intact, and of not jeopardising the power or the supposed power of those organisations through any rash manoeuvres.

When August Bebel died on 13 August 1913 he left behind him a party that was ill-equipped for the arduous tasks that lay ahead. As the hard core of the forces pushing for parliamentarisation, liberal democracy, and social justice, it had to defend itself against the attacks of all those who sought to block any change in the political and social structure of Wilhelmine Germany. The electoral successes of the SPD led at the same time to a hardening of the faction made up of 'Junkers and industrial tycoons', the Prusso-German army, and the racially nationalist Pan-Germanists. These forces found in imperialism a weapon — employed with notable success on the occasion of the 1907 general election — with which they were able to muster the bourgeois masses under the banner of a new ideology and lead them into the field against 'those unpatriotic fellows'.

# 5
# The First World War

## 1. Patriotic Duty and the Political Truce at Home

On 25 July 1914, with the stormclouds of war gathering ever more threateningly, the Executive Committee of the SPD raised a warning voice: 'There is danger ahead. World war looms! The ruling classes who muzzle and scorn and exploit you in peacetime now wish to use you — abuse you — as cannon-fodder. The ears of the powers-that-be must be made to ring with the cry: We don't want a war! Down with war! Long live the international brotherhood of peoples!'[1] Less than a week later the mood of the Socialist press was very different: 'When the fateful hour strikes, "those unpatriotic fellows" will answer the call of duty and not allow themselves to be outdone by the patriots in any way'.[2] And on 4 August the parliamentary party — Karl Liebknecht included — voted solidly in the *Reichstag* for the war loans requested by the government. Party Chairman Hugo Haase spoke for them all: 'We shall not forsake our own fatherland in its hour of danger'.[3]

How did it come about, this complete change of mood culminating in approval of the war loans? The question has always been a bitterly controversial one. Verdicts range from betrayal and references to original sin to the assertion that the stance adopted by Social Democracy was simply in line with a well-established tradition. Supporters of this view cite among other things the fact that Marx and Engels themselves had accepted the defensive war and August Bebel had declared that in the event of a Russian attack he would 'shoulder [his] gun'.[4] The Erfurt Programme, too, far from being pacifist, had called for 'training for universal fitness to fight' and 'a citizen army in place

---

1. Proclamation of the executive committee of the SPD, in *Vorwärts*, 25 July 1914.
2. *Vorwärts*, 31 July 1914.
3. *Stenographische Berichte des Deutschen Reichstags*, Vol. 306, pp. 8f.
4. Said in the *Reichstag* on 7 March 1904; *Stenographische Berichte . . .*, Vol. 198, p. 1588. As late as the summer of 1913, only weeks before his death, Bebel told the Budget Committee of the *Reichstag*: 'There is not a man in Germany who would wish to leave his country defenceless against attacks from abroad. This is true — particularly so — of Social Democracy as well.'

of the regular army'.[5] Opponents of this line of argument contended that on the contrary this was no defensive war but a case of imperialist genocide and the Social Democratic leadership had betrayed the resolutions of the International and the very principle of internationalism. The commitment made in the resolutions of the Socialist congresses in Stuttgart (1907), Copenhagen (1910), and Basel (1912) — 'to prevent the outbreak of war by employing what seem to them the most effective means and, if war is not to be avoided, to work for its swift termination'[6] — turned out to be flexible in the extreme. With no concrete measures agreed on, the whole question was left wide open.

The parties of the Second International were unanimous in their moral condemnation of war and did indeed seek ways of preventing the impending conflict from breaking out. In speeches in the *Reichstag* and at party conferences August Bebel repeatedly denounced the arms race and the warmongers. A well-founded fear that a nationalist and militarist faction in Germany was about to kindle the torch of war haunted him like a nightmare. It was what lay behind his talks in Zürich with Consul General Heinrich Angst, who passed Bebel's warnings on to the British government. In addresses to their congress in Basel cathedral in 1912, Europe's leading Socialists — August Bebel, Jean Jaurès, Victor Adler, Keir Hardie, Hermann Greulich, Edouard Vaillant — condemned war as the scourge of humanity. But their warning to governments that the rifle barrels might, if war came, be trained on them was exposed in August 1914 for what it was: a threat display designed to intimidate the warmongers but lacking any force when matters came to a head.

As long as it seemed to be a question of one of the usual Moroccan or Balkan crises, the massed battalions of the workers demonstrated solidly against war, as in July 1914. But when on 31 July the regional conflict finally turned into a major war, the Second International disintegrated. In Russia and Serbia, where the brutally suppressed and numerically feeble Socialists had plumped for violent revolution, war loans were opposed. In all other belligerent countries in which the labour movement enjoyed a broad and well-organised mass base and had adopted a parliamentary course as a democratic–socialist party of reform, most Socialists showed solidarity with their nation and backed the government. What the switch of mood among the masses on the outbreak of war indicates is the extent to which the working class in those countries felt itself to be a part of the nation and was integrated in the existing political order.

5. See Document 3, p. 240.
6. *Internationaler Sozialistischer Arbeiter- und Gewerkschaftskongress, Protokoll 1907*, pp. 41, 66, 162; see also Julius Braunthal, *Geschichte der Internationale*, Vol. 2

Susanne Miller has summed it up neatly: 'Whichever of the different justifications for the war policy adopted by the [German] party and trade-union leadership in August 1914 we choose to examine — alignment with the general mood of the people; defence against Russian tsarism, British imperialism, and French claims to Alsace–Lorraine; hope of an improvement of its own position as a result of domestic reforms; concern to safeguard Social Democratic and trade-union "achievements" and the material "assets" represented by their organisations — each of them individually and all of them together point to the fact that the German labour movement saw the German Empire as the ground of its being and as the operational base that it wished to preserve.'[7] This attitude was perhaps characterised most clearly by August Bebel when he told the 1907 party conference: 'If a time really comes when we have to defend the fatherland, then we shall do so because it is our fatherland; we shall defend it as the soil on which we live, as the country whose language we speak and whose customs we hold, and because we wish to make of this fatherland of ours a land of such perfection and beauty as shall be unmatched in all the world.'[8]

When war did break out, this avowal of the legitimacy of 'national defence' spread like wildfire among the masses who only days before had taken to the streets to demonstrate for peace. In the ranks of Social Democracy it was embraced even by those members of the parliamentary party who had argued against approving the war loans and only bowed to party discipline in the *Reichstag*. Karl Liebknecht himself did not uncompromisingly reject the principle of national defence at first. When at a meeting of the parliamentary party on 3 August 1914 fourteen deputies — including Chairman Hugo Haase — voted against approving the war loans, their real concern was with denouncing the global conflagration as an imperialist war of predation and defining their attitude toward the government and the bourgeois parties. Their resistance stiffened when in the so-called *Burgfrieden* the various political and economic pressure groups committed themselves to a domestic 'truce' for the duration of the war. Under the *Burgfrieden* the

---

(Hanover, 1961), pp. 325, 349ff., 370ff.

7. Susanne Miller, 'Die Sozialdemokratie in der Spannung zwischen Oppositionstradition und Regierungsverantwortung in den Anfängen der Weimarer Republik', in Hans Mommsen (ed.), *Sozialdemokratie*, p. 84. The same author provides a more detailed treatment in her book *Burgfrieden und Klassenkampf. Die deutsche Sozialdemokratie im Ersten Weltkrieg* (Düsseldorf, 1974).

8. *Protokoll über die Verhandlungen des Parteitages der Sozialdemokratischen Partei, abgehalten zu Essen a.d. Ruhr vom 15. bis 21. September 1907* (Berlin, 1907), p. 255. Bebel had addressed the *Reichstag* in very similar terms on 7 March 1904; *Stenographische Berichte . . .*, Vol. 198, p. 1588 (see also Vol. 199, p. 3263).

party majority saw itself as a kind of prop to Chancellor Bethmann Hollweg's government. It adopted an offensive posture only when it wished to denounce domestic grievances that particularly affected the working class or to attack war aims abroad and restoration attempts at home that seemed to go beyond the government's declared policy.

This siding with the government was made easier for the party not least by the political skill and tact of Bethmann Hollweg himself, who was careful not to lend open support to the activities of annexationist, arch-reactionary forces in the economy, the army, and the parties. Rather than negotiate specific, guaranteed domestic and foreign-policy concessions in return for its collaboration, the party majority placed its faith in a 'reorientation' in domestic affairs, chiefly in the shape of Prussian electoral reform. Right up until 1917 the Chancellor and the centre-left bourgeois parties repeatedly contrived to bind the Social Democrats to government policy by means of promises and superficial concessions.

## 2. The Split: Formation of the Independent SPD

Unlike the majority, the anti-war-loans group argued unequivocally in favour of retaining the party's traditionally oppositional role. There is every reason to believe that these differences need not have led to a split had the problem not cropped up again and again in all its poignancy with every fresh vote over war loans. Karl Liebknecht was the first to break ranks when on 2 December 1914 he voted openly in the *Reichstag* against the second War Loans Bill. He was joined on the occasion of the next bill by Otto Rühle, while other opposition deputies left the plenary chamber before voting began. By December 1915 as many as twenty deputies were voting against the loans, issuing a statement in which they accused the Chancellor of giving encouragement to the annexationists. The final break came in March 1916, when the majority of the parliamentary party voted for the emergency budget while a minority followed the party chairman, Hugo Haase, in rejecting it on the basis of a resolution of the Magdeburg party conference of 1910. Since this group had kept secret its intention of voting against the decision of the parliamentary party in the plenary *Reichstag* the majority saw their action not merely as a 'breach of party discipline' but as a 'breach of faith'. By 58 votes to 33 they expelled the twenty dissidents from the parliamentary party. These then formed a separate group, referring to themselves as the Social Democratic Fellowship (*Arbeitsgemeinschaft*).

The split in the parliamentary party did not at first mean a split in the party as a whole. It was not until the convocation of a *Reichskonferenz der Opposition* in January 1917, a move the central party council condemned as setting up 'a special organisation against the party', that the gap was seen to be unbridgeable. On 6–7 April 1917, in the *Volkshaus* in Gotha, the 'Independent [*Unabhängige*] Social Democratic Party of Germany' (USPD) was born.

The question whether this organisational split could have been avoided has yet to receive a clear answer. Its roots undoubtedly go back to the ideological, programmatical, and political differences that had characterised pre-war Social Democracy. The party had always stood by the principle that veteran campaigner Richard Fischer once reduced to the pithy formula: 'For as long as the party has existed we have had — and have not hidden — our differences of opinion. . . . But for as long as there has been a party its principle has been to preserve outward unity.'[9] Yet it was rigid operation of this very party tradition — now become a dogma — of 'outward unity', which put the 'breach of party discipline' virtually on a par with mutiny, that so exacerbated the differences. Whereas it had been possible before the war to absorb the tensions by means of a combination of more or less abstractly theoretical compromise resolutions and delaying tactics, the outbreak of the First World War placed Social Democracy in a position where further dodging was out of the question and immediate decisions had to be made.

The mere fact that, as war broke out, representatives of the radical left such as Konrad Haenisch and Paul Lensch fell in with the national mood while the 'revisionists' Eduard Bernstein and Kurt Eisner went over to the USPD indicates that the split was not between revolutionary Marxists on the one hand and revisionists and reformists on the other. On the contrary, the issues that divided people were the war loans, the political truce, and above all the stance to be adopted toward the government and the bourgeois parties. While the majority in the party embraced a policy of co-operation, the USPD pursued the line of blanket opposition. It saw itself as the true heir to the 'old-style' Social Democracy of Marx, Engels, Lassalle, and Bebel, an opposition party sharply divorced from all other social groupings. It wished to continue — uninhibited by the restraints of compromise — to fight against war and social abuses and in favour of peace, democracy, and Socialism.

As well as representatives of the centre left of the party — pro-pacifist revisionists such as Bernstein and Eisner — radical left-wingers too found a congenial field of operations in the USPD. While the

9. Said at a meeting of the parliamentary party on 20 December 1915; quoted in Erich Matthias and Eberhard Pikart (eds), *Die Reichstagsfraktion der deutschen Sozialdemokratie 1898 bis 1918* (Düsseldorf, 1966), Vol. 2, pp. 106ff., quotation p. 107.

so-callled 'Bremen Left' opted for independence as the 'International Communists of Germany', the 'Group International' that formed around Rosa Luxemburg and Karl Liebknecht on 1 January 1916 — known as the Spartacus Group from their 'Spartacus Letters' — initially associated itself with the USPD. Also associated with the breakaway party were the 'Revolutionary Shop Stewards', a group of skilled metalworkers active in Berlin who chiefly distinguished themselves in the organising of strike movements.

The strike of the spring of 1917, the navy rebellions of that summer, and the great strike of January 1918 showed just how much ground the Majority Social Democrats (MSPD) had lost among the workers. For many members of the starving, embittered, war-weary masses the USPD had become the party of hope. It is by no means clear why, as by-elections to the *Reichstag* showed, the breakaway group met with so little success at first. Sociological reasons alone do not account for this. The membership and following were heterogeneous. Factors of undoubted importance were that the MSPD continued to control the greater part of the party apparatus and the party press, that the USPD was harder hit by official censorship and other repressive measures, and finally that for many workers the MSPD, however irritating, was still *the* traditional Social Democratic Party, which one did not simply leave to join another one.

### 3. Majority Social Democracy and the Path to Governmental Responsibility

With the split into USPD and MSPD, Social Democracy forfeited its monopoly as *the* political representative of the German labour movement. Whereas the party had hitherto taken up the whole of the left of the political spectrum, the Majority Social Democrats now occupied only a segment. Moreover the appearance of a rival on its left wing had the effect of shifting the majority party towards the centre of the spectrum. Yet in spite of the efforts of the party's extreme right wing, which called for a radical reorientation, policy continued to be dictated by the broad centre, the chief representatives of which were Scheidemann and Ebert.

*Philipp Scheidemann* (b. 26 July 1865, d. 29 November 1939), a printer by trade, began his political career as an editor on various Social Democratic newspapers. Entering the *Reichstag* in 1903, he soon distinguished himself there as a brilliant speaker. Although he joined the executive committee of the party in 1911, parliament remained the principal forum of his activities, and after the death of

Bebel in 1913 this made him the best-known of the Social Democratic leaders. During the war the leadership of the parliamentary party — of which he had been elected a co-chairman in 1913 — in practice fell increasingly to him, Haase having begun to lose influence and importance even before his withdrawal. Scheidemann's basic political stance was of the middle-of-the-road kind typical of the party leadership. It was only during the war that, following the clashes with the minority, he and Ebert graduated towards the moderate right wing of the party. From 1917 to 1919 he was — with Ebert — co-chairman of the SPD.

*Friedrich Ebert* (b. 4 February 1871, d. 28 February 1925) joined the Social Democratic labour movement as a young saddler. After some bitter experiences on the road — unemployment, lockouts — he settled in Bremen in 1891 and there took an active part in agitation and labour organisation. By the age of twenty-three he held a number of key positions: as correspondent of Bremen's *Bürgerzeitung* or 'Citizens' Journal' and chairman of the local saddler's association, the Bremen trade-union cartel, and the Bremen SPD. From 1900 he held the post of labour secretary in Bremen. The 1905 party conference in Jena elected Ebert as full-time secretary of the executive committee; he also headed the 'Labour Youth' and was responsible for relations with the trade-union leadership. He entered the *Reichstag* in 1912 and in 1913 joined Haase at the head of the party, succeeding August Bebel. Ebert was another man who had no desire to shake the theoretical foundations laid down in the Erfurt Programme. His goal was the seizure of political power at the polls. Persistent work for reform, the preservation of party unity, and caution were the keynotes of his political approach.

Both Ebert and Scheidemann attached great importance to accounting for the policy of Social Democracy during the war as a logical extension of its traditional line. Although various annexationist tendencies showed through even within the party's own ranks when things were going well militarily, the rejection of any intention of conquest and the right of all peoples to self-determination remained — as proclaimed on 4 August 1914 — the basis of the 'negotiated peace' demanded by the SPD. The formula became personalised for friend and foe alike as the 'Scheidemann Peace'.

The Russian 'February Revolution' of 1917 gave an enormous boost to the disappointed hopes of the war-weary masses. An extensive wave of strikes in April 1917 gave expression to the workers' longing for peace and their protest against hunger, against attempts to prolong the war, and against the continued non-appearance of domestic reforms. The force of these events was reflected in a resolution of the MSPD leadership welcoming the 'victory of the Russian Revolution' with 'ardent sympathy' and expressing solidarity with the demand of the Petrograd Council of Workers and Soldiers for a peace 'without annexations and war indemnities on the basis of free development for all peoples'.[10]

With this the Majority Social Democrats in practice largely met the demands of the Independents. Undoubtedly the founding of the USPD itself helped to influence the decisions of the MSPD, which was inevitably afraid of losing its following to its left-wing rival. The big breakthrough was denied to the USPD, the pressure from the left was therefore contained, and the Majority Social Democrats remained free to put out feelers in the other direction. Instead of offering the Socialist groups a basis for unification, the slogan 'No annexations, no contributions!', coupled with the *Reichstag's* so-called 'Peace Resolution' of 19 July 1917, provided a joint platform for the MSPD, the Centre Party, and the Progressives. With a quick victory for German arms becoming a less and less realistic prospect, the left-wing liberals and the Centrists, among whom expansionist tendencies had long predominated, were turning increasingly towards a negotiated peace. Pressed by the tireless efforts of the Centre Party deputy Matthias Erzberger, the three parties gave themselves a forum for permanent contact in the 'Inter-Party Committee'. With this the traditional fronts in the *Reichstag* had undergone a shift. A new majority had emerged that set the pattern for the Weimar coalitions to come. To the left of it stood the USPD, which refused all co-operation from the outset; to its right, the conservative groups were for the first time forced into isolation.

This new party constellation was an important step in the progress of Social Democracy from being an almost exclusively oppositional party to being a potential party of government. Yet the question remains whether this new association did not unnecessarily restrict the party's scope with regard to the development and implementation of an independent policy. During the great strike of January 1918, when the cry for 'peace, freedom, and bread!' rang out more powerfully than ever before, the MSPD's bourgeois partners showed the party little loyalty, while its co-operation with them cost the MSPD a profound alienation of its own following. Even so, the Social Democrats felt at the end of September 1918 that they could no longer deny the call to join in forming a new government. It was at this point, with military defeat becoming manifest, that the parties of the subsequent Weimar coalition embarked on an attempt to ward off the impending collapse

10. *Protokoll über die Verhandlungen des Parteitages der Sozialdemokratischen Partei Deutschlands, abgehalten zu Würzburg vom 14. bis 20. Oktober 1917* (Berlin, 1917), p. 36.

with a government led by Prince Max of Baden and backed by the confidence of the majority in the *Reichstag*. No one in the parliamentary party raised any objection of principle; only tactical misgivings were expressed. With Philipp Scheidemann and Gustav Bauer — the second chairman of the General Commission, appointed after consultations with the trade unions — for the first time in German history Social Democrats joined a government as secretaries of state. Although the chief concern of this cabinet was to put a stop to the killing by means of a negotiated peace, it did at the same time realise another key aim of the SPD: the introduction of parliamentary government in Germany. Its democratic innovations were overshadowed, however, by the enormity of Germany's military collapse. The fact that for external purposes the responsibility for the armistice was assumed by the government and specifically by Erzberger in the forefront enabled the true initiators of that step to escape all responsibility in the public eye. It was the generals at the top of the army's supreme command, Hindenburg and Ludendorff, who insisted on the armistice, pushed the politicians into it, and in Hindenburg's case actually approved acceptance of the terms. The army leaders, together with the nationalists of every stripe, took advantage of this camouflaging of the true facts to discredit the forces of democracy with the promptly mobilised *Dolchstosslegende*, the 'stab-in-the-back legend', and to conceal the fact that it was they themselves who had brought the Empire to military defeat.

# 6

# From the Revolution to the Weimar Republic

## 1. The German Revolution of 1918–1919

When towards the end of October 1918 the German Admiralty tried behind the backs of the government and parliament to lead the fleet into one last battle, the sailors actually damped down the ships' boilers. With peace just around the corner, they saw no sense in giving their lives for their officers on a voyage that meant certain death. The entire 'November Revolution' was characterised by the same spontaneity. On 4 November a workers' and soldiers' council took over in Kiel, and in three days the rebels had almost the whole fleet under their control. As if fanned by a storm the spark of revolution spread from the ports right across the country. From Kiel to Munich, from Cologne to Breslau, and finally in Berlin itself soldiers and workers rose up against authority and against militarism, driven by their desire for 'peace, freedom, and bread' and buoyed up by the hope that now everything would be changed for the better.

Germany's monarchs could not vacate their thrones fast enough. Like crumbling masonry the governmental structures of the powers-that-be collapsed at the first push. In the workers' and soldiers' councils that mushroomed all over the country the mass movement created its revolutionary organs. Based on the Russian soviet, these had already made their appearance during the navy revolts of 1917 and more especially during the January 1918 strike. Yet despite these superficial reminiscences, November 1918 was not the large-scale, organised conspiracy that a tenacious legend backed up by a good deal of noisy chest-beating seeks to represent it as. Neither the Majority Social Democrats, nor the Independents, nor even the Revolutionary Shop Stewards and the Spartacists had 'engineered' this revolution. Its distinguishing feature was not systematic preparation or controlled leadership but a spontaneous rebellion of the war-weary masses. They chose the symbol of Socialism, the red flag, as their banner primarily because it stood for peace abroad and opposition to the ruling powers at home.

In the final analysis the Majority Social Democrats, like the leaders of the Independents, simply bowed to the pressure of circumstances. The long-awaited yet still-delayed prospect of peace and the revolutionary movement that was so much bound up with it together dictated the course of events. During the night of 7–8 November Kurt Eisner of the USPD, acting independently of the sailors, proclaimed a Socialist *Räterepublik* or 'republic of councils' in Munich. At the same time the MSPD in Berlin issued an ultimatum demanding the abdication of Emperor William II, though to no effect. But in the capital, too, the revolutionary wave was by now unstoppable. On the morning of 9 November the workers downed tools and left their factories. Forming huge processions, which were further swollen by soldiers and members of the war-weary populace, they marched on the government quarter and demonstrated in front of the *Reichstag*. Impressed by their mood, Prince Max of Baden took it upon himself to announce the Emperor's abdication and invite Friedrich Ebert, the chairman of the Majority Social Democrats, to become Chancellor. Ebert's idea of forgoing the abolition of the monarchy at first in order to avert the threat of chaos and civil war soon proved to be illusory. The monarchical system of government had fallen victim to the onslaught of the masses. In the early afternoon Philipp Scheidemann proclaimed a republic from the balcony of the *Reichstag* building, while from the balcony of Berlin castle Karl Liebknecht proclaimed a Socialist republic.

Yet it was not rivalry but co-operation between the different Socialist groups that — under the slogan 'Kein Bruderkampf' — set the tone during those heady days. This was the spirit of Ebert's offer to the Independents to form a joint government consisting of equal numbers of MSPD and USPD appointees. Ebert did not even oppose the suggestion that Karl Liebknecht be included; in fact he described it as 'welcome'. Liebknecht, however, turned down the invitation, as did Georg Ledebour, a representative of the radical wing of the USPD.

On 10 November the revolutionary government met for the first time in the Imperial Chancellery. This 'Council of People's Representatives' (*Rat der Volksbeauftragten*) comprised three MSPD nominees (Ebert, Scheidemann, and Otto Landsberg) and three USPD nominees (Haase, Wilhelm Dittmann, and Emil Barth, the latter representing the Revolutionary Shop Stewards). The Council owed its mandate to the revolution — a fact that was outwardly reflected in the confirmation of the revolutionary government by an assembly of Berlin's workers' and soldiers' councils convened at the Busch Circus. Of equal significance, however, was the fact that the prior 'Coalition Agreement' between the two parties stipulated that the serving (middle-class) secretaries of state should remain at their posts.[1]

Combining as it did most of the functions hitherto exercised by parliament, government, Emperor, and Federal Council, the Council of People's Representatives enjoyed very extensive powers. Equally extensive, however, were the problems with which it was confronted, notably the legacy of the lost war with its oppressive armistice terms and the continuation of the blockade by the former enemy powers. The German *Reich* threatened to founder in famine and chaos and break up. Here the revolutionary government did good work. The country's immediate plight was eased in that the worst consequences of the war were eradicated, food shortages relieved, the returning soldiers largely reintegrated, and important reforms introduced in the shape of a sheaf of socio-political provisions dealing with labour protection, health insurance, job creation, and unemployment relief. With Social Democrats in power, the abolition of censorship and discriminatory legislation went without saying, as did the safeguarding of freedom of expression and the freedom and security of the person. The introduction of universal, equal suffrage, the proportional system for all parliaments, and votes for women realised some of the party's main traditional objectives. The proclamation of the eight-hour day realised another; in the Weimar years the legal establishment of the eight-hour maximum working day was regarded by the working population as *the* great achievement of the revolution. With their deep-rooted sense of democracy the People's Representatives, led by Ebert and Haase, saw themselves as no more than a stopgap solution for the period of revolutionary upheaval. In promising a National Assembly the government committed itself immediately to a general election and a people's parliament as constituent organ of the new state. This course not only corresponded to what the MSPD wanted but also received the support of the USPD leadership and the majority of the workers' and soldiers' councils. Most members of these bodies, which were initially dominated by followers of Ebert and Scheidemann, also saw themselves as an interim solution born of revolution rather than as heralds of a 'councils system' or 'dictatorship of the proletariat'. The antithesis between 'national assembly' and 'councils system' that loomed so large in public discussion in no way reflected the real balance of political power. With its slogan 'All power to the councils' the Spartacus League had only a narrow base during this first phase of the revolution, as the elections to the General Congress of Workers' and Soldiers' Councils of Germany clearly showed. Among

1. See Gerhard A. Ritter and Susanne Miller (eds), *Die deutsche Revolution 1918–1919. Dokumente*, new edition (Hamburg, 1975), pp. 85f.

the 489 delegates who met in Berlin from 16 to 20 December as a kind of revolutionary parliament there were no more than ten 'United Revolutionaries'. The representatives of the councils decided by 344 votes to 98 to reject the Socialist republic proposed by Ernst Däumig on the basis of a pyramid of councils. The vast majority, made up of Majority Social Democrats, the right wing of the USPD, the soldiers' delegates, and the few middle-class democrats, plumped for a National Assembly elected by universal, equal suffrage. The election date set by the Congress — 19 January 1919 — was entirely in line with the wishes of the MSPD People's Representatives. The MSPD came out of that election with 37.9 per cent, the USPD with 7.6 per cent of the vote. Neither in the National Assembly election nor in the election held in Prussia a week later (MSPD 36.4 per cent, USPD 7.4 per cent) did the result produce a Socialist majority.

By then the coalition between the two Social Democratic parties had already broken up. During the night of 29–30 December 1918, after a dispute concerning the use of armed forces against insurgent sailors, the USPD People's Representatives quit their seats in the Cabinet and were replaced by two Majority Social Democrats, Rudolf Wissell and Gustav Noske. The euphoric mood of early November gave way to an atmosphere of confrontation within the Social Democratic labour movement.

One of the causes of the differences that had arisen lay in the assumption of governmental responsibility. This was true not only with regard to the positions of the various Socialist groups — MSPD, USPD, and the Spartacist/Communist alliance — toward one another but also of relations between leadership and following within those groups. In its utter contrast to the misery of the war, the day of 9 November had affected the revolutionary masses like the dawn of a new age. The working class, it seemed, was reunited and power in the land lay in the hands of its own representatives; all the long-cherished promises of Socialism ought now to come true. For decades people had been talking about the class struggle and the conquest of political power by the workers and imagined that the 'socialisation' of the means of production was the indispensable prerequisite of Socialism. Now, with revolutionary governments and revolutionary organs in charge both nationally and in the individual states, they expected the promises to be honoured.

Instead they were faced with the fact that in the civil service, in the army, and in the economy nothing much had changed. The offices of district administrator, the mayoralties, and the key positions in industry and the economy, in the army, and in the various authorities at national and state level continued, with the exception of a few 'inspectors' from the working class, to be occupied by the old representatives of the authoritarian state and the military caste, the landlords and the captains of industry. For example, six months after the outbreak of the revolution, of 470 Prussian district administrators only one was a Social Democrat. The troubles of Christmas 1918, when Berliners rushed to show solidarity with naval mutineers against the soldiers sent to crush them, gave clear expression to the first simmerings of discontent. Disturbances flared up in the Ruhr and in Upper Silesia, in Berlin, Bremen, and Brunswick, in Saxony and Thuringia. In addition to strike movements for higher wages and better food, other mass actions were aimed at socialising factories, at retaining workers' councils on a permanent basis, and even at overthrowing the capitalist system by force.

The democratic potential that lay in these mass movements remained largely unexploited. It was reflected in little more than formal legislative provisions such as the Socialisation Law of March 1919 and the 'Councils Paragraph' (165) of the Weimar Constitution — not, however, in any genuine permanent democratisation and restructuring of state and society.

Much has been written about the reasons for this. In the German Democratic Republic the Central Committee of the Socialist Unity Party defined the parameters of appraisal in its 'theses' regarding 'The November 1918 Revolution in Germany' as 'a bourgeois–democratic revolution that was to some extent implemented with proletarian means and methods'.[2] In addition to the initial absence of a 'Marxist–Leninist party of struggle', as far as Communist historiography is concerned the 'treachery' of the SPD leadership also played a decisive role. In the Federal Republic, on the other hand, historians long took the view that the choice in 1918–19 was simply between 'social revolution in alliance with the forces pushing for a dictatorship of the proletariat or a parliamentary republic in alliance with conservative elements such as the officer corps'.[3] Particularly along Social Democrats this idea of a concrete 'either/or' found many adherents. In Germany's hour of need, they said, the SPD had leapt into the breach and saved the country from Bolshevism and the dictatorship of the

2. 'Die Novemberrevolution 1918 in Deutschland. Thesen anlässlich des 40. Jahrestages', in *Zeitschrift für Geschichtswissenschaft*, 6 (1958), p. 21 (article pp. 1–27). Compare, in the same publication, Walter Ulbricht, 'Begründung der Thesen über die Novemberrevolution 1918'. The same basic line is followed in Georg Fülberth and Jürgen Harrer, *Die deutsche Sozialdemokratie 1890–1933* (Darmstadt and Neuwied, 1974), p. 127, and Jutta von Freyberg, Georg Fülberth, Jürgen Harrer, *et al.*, *Geschichte der deutschen Sozialdemokratie 1863–1975* (Cologne, 1975).
3. Karl Dietrich Erdmann, 'Die Geschichte der Weimarer Republik als Problem der Wissenschaft', in *Vierteljahrshefte für Zeitgeschichte*, 3 (1955), pp. 6f.

councils. It was pointed out by Willy Brandt, however, that allegations of a Bolshevist threat constituted 'an inadmissible simplification' and that the alternative had been represented more by the position of Rosa Luxemburg, that is to say 'a democratic-Socialist. . .not a terrorist–Communist' one.[4]

During the revolution Rosa Luxemburg occupied a place in the front rank of the Spartacus League. This was a somewhat heterogeneous group dominated by adherents of a Utopian-anarchist tendency who as early as 10 November persuaded Liebknecht not to join the Council of People's Representatives. Against the opposition of Rosa Luxemburg, Karl Liebknecht, and Paul Levi the vast majority at the founding conference of the Communist Party of Germany (KPD) held on 31 December 1918 and 1 January 1919 decided against participating in the National Assembly elections and chose the street as the principal platform for putting across its revolutionary slogans.

As with Rosa Luxemburg and Karl Liebknecht, fear of losing touch with the radical masses likewise determined much of the tactics of the USPD leadership under Haase and Dittmann. In the USPD the idea of concentrating on developing the 'achievements' of the revolution was bound up with that of parliamentary democracy and the National Assembly. As disillusionment spread among the working class, the left wing under Ernst Däumig and Richard Müller gained more and more influence until at the Congress of Workers' and Soldiers' Councils in December 1918 it defied Haase and secured the non-participation of the USPD in the Central Council. As a result this institution, which operated as a kind of control body over the central and Prussian governments, comprised only MSPD and soldier delegates. The position of the USPD People's Representatives was thus completely undermined. The party's left wing wanted to push it back into its customary oppositional role and sought refuge in a policy of confrontation with its Majority Social Democratic rival. On 28–9 December 1918 the USPD People's Representatives withdrew from the Cabinet.

The Majority Social Democrats in the persons of Ebert, Scheidemann, Landsberg, Rudolf Wissell, and Gustav Noske now alone constituted the government. Their guiding star, as it were, was a parliamentary democracy in which the adult population decided what was sensible in free elections and Social Democracy, with a mandate from the popular majority, could carry out social reforms in a climate of democratic orderliness. The arbitrary actions of individual councils and spontaneous mass demonstrations were something many Majority

4. Willy Brandt, '"Fünfzig Jahre danach", Rede auf der Feierstunde der SPD am 10.11.1968 in Godesberg', *Pressemitteilungen und Informationen der SPD*, 10 November 1968.

Social Democrats and trade-union leaders saw as betraying the deep-rooted democratic traditions of the labour movement, grossly violating the principle of the constitutional state, and creating 'Russian conditions' that rendered organised care of the population impossible, led to inequalities of income and supply, and threatened the entire structure of the economy. The People's Representatives, saddled with the responsibilities of government, thus increasingly found themselves coming into conflict with the workers' and soldiers' councils and increasingly fell back on such powers of the old system as gave them support. The civil service in particular was regarded by the Social Democratic government, including its USPD representatives, as indispensable for dealing with the serious problems of the transition period, and this enhanced its standing and influence.

Finally, the decision on the military issue went against an army imbued with the spirit of democracy and for the 'state within a state' of the *Reichswehr*. The old Imperial Supreme Command headed by Hindenburg and Groener retained a high degree of independence as controller of the armed forces. Attempts by the Berlin Executive Committee of the Workers' and Soldiers' Councils and by Ebert to build up a democratic *Volkswehr* or 'people's army' never got off the ground.

The 'Spartacus Week' uprising of January 1919, when armed insurgents threatened the virtually defenceless Council of People's Representatives, marked the decisive turning-point as regarded the future structure of the army. The street-fighting in Berlin not only confirmed the divisions within the labour movement; this violent threat to the new order from the left mobilised the counter-forces of the right and indirectly gave the military its longed-for chance to intervene. The government placed its faith not in the Majority Social Democratic volunteer units that proceeded to risk their lives in its defence but in the deployment by Noske of troops led by seasoned officers as well as the new Free Corps. Noske's chief concern was to make a show of military strength and set a lasting example. 'For Noske the use of force was not the *ultima ratio* but simply the means of restoring order at home.'[5] The character and political attitudes of the troops, among whom military discipline was paramount and democratic convictions not inquired about, were not of prime importance to him. These and similar bodies of men, who soon gave clear evidence of counter-revolutionary involvement, formed the nucleus of the military power deployed in the post-war years and the foundation of the *Reichswehr*.

---

5. Susanne Miller, *Die Bürde der Macht. Die deutsche Sozialdemokratie 1918–1920* (Düsseldorf, 1978), p. 270; for the context, see *ibid.*, pp. 225ff.

Machine-gun, cannon, and mortar set about stifling the aftershocks of the revolution.

The use of the army and the Free Corps against demonstrating and fighting workers, the total failure to recognise the looming dangers from the right, and the bestial murders of Rosa Luxemburg and Karl Liebknecht combined to mobilise the radical section of the working class against the government, while the latter's 'Noske policy' also incriminated it in the eyes of many of its own supporters. The January uprising marked a turning-point. That was the start of the self-amplifying oscillation between radicalisms of left and right, while at the same time the element represented by Social Democracy, which aimed at a democratic restructuring of society, was ground down and progressively lost. The republic founded on parliamentary democracy to which the Social Democratic People's Representatives aspired would have received the solid base people wanted for it only if democracy had not stopped short at the doors of the barracks, the factories, and the offices of the civil service but had made deep inroads into the power structures obtaining in the bureaucracy and the economy.

## 2. A New State on Old Foundations

In the National Assembly that was elected on 19 January 1919 the Majority Social Democrats won 165 seats while the Independents won only 22. Of the remaining deputies, 91 belonged to the Christian People's Party (i.e. the Centre Party), 75 to the German Democratic Party (DDP), 19 to the German People's Party (DVP), 44 to the German National People's Party (DNVP), and 7 to splinter groups. Most of the parties had new names, but only to some extent did these reflect new programmes. In the Centre Party, briefly appearing as the Christian People's Party, the workers' wing gained in influence and importance. The DDP essentially went on where the left-wing liberals had left off — though with an added social component. The DVP provided a home for the right wing of the former National Liberal Party under Stresemann, while the DNVP brought the old conservatives together with overtly German-nationalist circles. The outcome of the election, in leaving the Social Democratic parties in the minority, bolstered the confidence of the bourgeois parties.

A middle-class bloc government would have been possible numerically, but in practice such an arrangement was out of the question for both German Democrats and Centrists. When the USPD rejected the MSPD's offer to participate in a coalition government, the constellation of the 'Inter-Party Committee' was revived. In the Weimar theatre where the National Assembly met for security reasons, Friedrich Ebert was elected *Reichspräsident* on 11 February 1919 with a total of 277 out of 379 votes cast. Two days later the Assembly appointed Philipp Scheidemann Minister-President (the term *Reichskanzler* was reintroduced only when the Weimar Constitution came into effect on 14 August 1919). In the newly formed government the Majority Social Democrats filled six ministerial posts while six others were shared between the DDP and the Centre; the new Foreign Minister, Count Brockdorff-Rantzau, was officially a member of no party. Three MSPD conditions were accepted by the other two parties as the basis for the government's policy: 1. unreserved acceptance of the republican form of government; 2. in budgetary policy, severe subjection of wealth and property; 3. a far-reaching social policy to include socialisation of those industries that were ripe for it.

Of the multitude of problems facing the government and the National Assembly, arguing about the peace treaty and working out a new national constitution were the two most prominent. Not only parliamentary and government representatives of the MSPD but also USPD deputies laboured long and hard at drafting the constitution. Warnings voiced by the independents touched on several of the sore points that were to have such disastrous consequences for the development of the Weimar Republic. Their criticism of the emergence of a military system eluding any kind of democratic control highlighted a thorny problem to which the Majority Social Democrats paid too little heed and that Noske positively — and unpardonably — ignored. And with their warning against overestimating the powers of parliament in the face of virtually unchanged economic structures they actually identified the Achilles' heel of the new democracy.

However, the USPD's ability to get anything done remained limited. On top of the party's numerical weakness in parliament its growing internal dissensions proved a serious hindrance. In addition to those who advocated a parliamentary democracy, which they simply wished to see complemented by a parallel system of councils, there were the champions of a purely council-based system who, led by Ernst Däumig, eventually came to constitute the majority in the party. Their programme saw the workers' council in the political sphere and the works council in the economic sphere as *the* forms of organisation for the working population. The right to recall council representatives at any time was regarded as particularly democratic, yet in excluding whole sections of the population from being represented on the councils their models in fact thoroughly contravened the democratic principle of equality.

A different conception was represented by the motion successfully proposed by the MSPD group at the Second Congress of Councils in April 1919 calling for the establishment of a Chamber of Labour. According to this the councils were to operate not *'in place of* parliament but *alongside* parliament'.[6] The idea that economic democracy as well as political democracy must be institutionally anchored and the workers' councils be assigned specific functions had gained ground among Majority Social Democrats too since January 1919.

In the first weeks following the revolution the chief concern of political leaders — including even such men as Emil Barth and Kurt Eisner — was to get production going again. They put off making any fundamental inroads into the economic system of private capitalism, with which for all their socio-political involvement they were deeply unfamiliar. The trade unions themselves, in setting up a Central Alliance on equal terms with the employers, had decided to give their most urgent attention to relaunching the economy and combating hunger and unemployment. An agreement concluded with the employers' associations on 15 November 1918 gave them full freedom of combination, extended industrial agreements to all branches, and confirmed the eight-hour maximum working day. The People's Representatives gave these provisions the force of law.

Both the government and the trade unions shrank from making an immediate start on socialisation in the ruinous aftermath of the war. Two factors that had a further negative effect were the not unjustified fear that when it came to making reparation demands the Allies would start with socialised industries and secondly the complete absence, despite all the programmatic protestations, of any concrete plans for the introduction of public ownership. Reluctance to anticipate the National Assembly in a decision of such far-reaching importance, coupled with the bitter experiences of Soviet Russia, likewise dampened the resolution of the Socialists now occupying positions of governmental responsibility. Particularly a man like Karl Kautsky, for example, now a leading member of the USPD, saw the serious food and supply crises currently convulsing Lenin's Russia — still a predominantly agricultural country — as forbidding proof of where precipitate socialisation led to. The government's thesis was: no rash experiments; first increase production and get the economy working,

---

6. As expressed by Eberhard Kolb, 'Rätewirklichkeit und Räte-Ideologie in der deutschen Revolution von 1918/19', reprinted in Eberhard Kolb (ed.), *Vom Kaiserreich zur Weimarer Republik* (Cologne, 1972), p. 177. For the texts of the various motions, see *Zweiter Kongress der Arbeiter-, Bauern- und Soldatenräte Deutschlands vom 8. bis 14. April 1919 im Herrenhaus zu Berlin. Stenographisches Protokoll* (Berlin, 1919), pp. 267, 269f.

then introduce socialisation. But 'No increased production without socialisation!' was the antithesis that rang out ever louder from the shop floor.[7]

The soaring expectations of many workers and their new-found self-confidence, bolstered by the revolution, were frustrated by an undisturbed bureaucracy, a hostile army, material shortages, and the rigid 'I'm the boss here' attitude that long continued to prevail among entrepreneurs, particularly in mining and heavy industry. The revolution, they felt, had not brought about sufficient changes in their lives and at their place of work. As well as to socialisation they looked increasingly to the institution of the council as a means of remodelling managerial structures and replacing the old authoritarian order by a democratic managerial and economic system. Their dissatisfaction found expression in a plethora of strike movements and mass actions in the spring of 1919, the impact of which far exceeded anything that had occurred hitherto. The Government and the Weimar coalition parties — including the German Democrats and the Centrists — agreed that the crisis could not be overcome with prohibitions, penal sanctions, and armed force alone but that positive measures were called for. On 1 March 1919 the National Assembly — that is to say the votes of the Centre Party, the German Democratic Party, and the Social Democrats — passed a 'Socialisation Law'. This empowered the state to proceed 'by way of legislation and against adequate compensation. . .

1. to transfer to public management such economic enterprises as lend themselves to nationalisation, particularly those involved in the extraction of mineral resources and the exploitation of natural power;
2. in case of urgent necessity to administer in the public interest the production and distribution of economic goods.'[8]

The Socialisation Law provided the basis for a law regulating the coal industry passed on 23 March 1919 and others concerning the potash and electricity industries. They had very little practical effect.

Almost in parallel to the passage of the Socialisation Law the government adopted guidelines with regard to workers' councils. In addition to works, district, and national workers' councils these provided for economic councils in which employees and employers were to collaborate over matters of common economic interest — notably

---

7. See Hans Schieck, 'Die Behandlung der Sozialisierungsfrage in den Monaten nach dem Staatsumsturz', in Eberhard Kolb (ed.), *Vom Kaiserreich zur Weimarer Republik* (Cologne, 1972), p. 148.
8. *Reichs-Gesetzblatt 1919*, pp. 341f.

socialisation — and assist the political parliament. These guidelines found their way into the Weimar Constitution virtually unchanged as Article 165.

The preliminary work for this 'basic law' of the new republic had been done under the People's Representatives, a key contribution being made by the Secretary of State for the Interior, Hugo Preuss, a member of the DDP and a committed democrat. After prolonged discussion by expert commissions, the People's Representatives, representatives of the states, and the constitutional committee and plenum of the National Assembly, the constitution was finally adopted in Weimar on 31 July 1919. The Majority Social Democrats, the German Democrats, and the Centrists voted for it; the German National People's Party, the German People's Party, the Bavarian *Bauernbund* or 'League of Farmers', Dr Heim of the Bavarian People's Party, and the USPD voted against it. Signed by President Ebert on 11 August, the Weimar Constitution came into effect on 14 August 1919.

The new state was a parliamentary, democratic republic and the new supreme sovereign the people, that is to say the totality of men and women over twenty years of age. They elected the *Reichstag* as the central organ of power and the President as head of state, and they were able by means of petitions and referenda to give direct expression to their will. While the first section of the constitution dealt with the structure and functions of the central state, a second section concerned the basic rights and duties of the German people. This fell back on the catalogue of basic rights contained in the constitution adopted by the Frankfurt Parliament, sitting in St Paul's church in 1848; it guaranteed equality before the law, freedom of the person, freedom of opinion, assembly, and association, freedom of belief and conscience, and freedom of movement. This body of freedoms was extended by provisions granting equal rights of citizenship to men and women, laying down an eight-year minimum period of schooling, with teaching and teaching materials to be free of charge, and placing all citizens under an obligation to contribute towards public charges.

A third group of provisions was contained in Section 5 under the heading 'Economic Life'. The introductory Article 151 had laid down: 'The organisation of economic life shall be in accordance with the principles of justice, having as its object to guarantee every individual a life compatible with the dignity of man.'[9] This general postulate failed to conceal the compromise character of the section covering the

9. For the text of the Weimar Constitution, see Ernst Rudolf Huber (ed.), *Dokumente zur deutschen Verfassungsgeschichte*, Vol. 3 (Stuttgart, Berlin, Cologne, Mainz, 1966), pp. 129ff. The quotations in the following two paragraphs are from the same source.

economy. On the one hand it contained a profession of faith in freedom of trade and industry, in encouraging the self-employed middle class, and in guarantees of hereditary title and property while on the other hand it made room for specific Social Democratic demands.

On top of provisions regarding the protection of labour and guaranteed freedom of combination, the constitution committed the state to building up a comprehensive, democratically structured system of insurance for the 'maintenance of health and fitness for work, for the protection of motherhood, and to make provision against the economic consequences of old age, infirmity, and the vicissitudes of existence' and to providing for the keep of every citizen for whom no appropriate job opportunity could be created or shown to exist. In addition to these instruments of social policy, the guarantee of property was qualified by its social obligations, and it was laid down that any 'appreciation of land' that occurred 'with no outlay of labour or capital' should be made to redound to the common good. The state was further given the right to make compulsory purchases — against suitable compensation, of course — and to pass laws 'to transfer to public ownership such private economic enterprises as lend themselves to socialisation'.

Although both Social Democratic parliamentary parties championed the principle of compulsory purchase without compensation, they had been unable to incorporate it either in the Socialisation Law or in the constitution for want of a majority in parliament. Nevertheless, Article 156 did give them the possibility, on acquisition of the requisite number of seats, of introducing the socialisation of the means of production that they had advocated for so long. In addition to this instrument, Article 165 offered a quite different sort of approach to changing the structure of the economic system. The councils idea, so prominent in the revolutionary transitional period, found constitutional expression here, though in a much weakened and qualified form. Article 165 proclaimed as a basic principle: 'Workers and salaried employees are called to play an equal part, jointly with entrepreneurs, in determining wages and working conditions as well as the general economic development of the productive forces.' For the 'protection of their social and economic interests' workers and salaried employees were to have legally guaranteed works councils, district workers' councils, and a central national workers' council. At district and national levels employees' representatives were to meet together with 'the bodies representing the entrepreneurs and other interested sections of the population' in district economic councils and a national economic council and to collaborate in the 'performance of general economic functions and . . . in the execution of the Socialisation Law'. These directives plotted the outlines of an economic democracy. This part of the constitution, however, was never fully put into effect. The Works Councils Law of 4 February 1920 and the setting-up of a provisional National Economic Council in May of the same year were a very imperfect and incomplete implementation of it.

According to the letter of the constitution, Social Democracy had achieved objectives that went far beyond what it had dared to hope for before the war. Both its democratic heritage, which went back to the 1848 revolution, and its social policy programme were reflected in the Weimar document. Even the idea of socialisation found expression there, albeit in a very much watered-down form, and the principles of an economic democracy were now enshrined in law.

The adoption of the constitution was the occasion for rapturous celebration among Majority Social Democratic leaders in the party and in parliament. The SPD faction in the National Assembly even contended: 'The Constitution is made up as our Erfurt Programme demanded.'[10] No other constitution was 'more democratic, none gives the people greater rights'. The dominant feeling was that 'the German Republic is henceforth the most democratic democracy in the world',[11] and critical voices were drowned at first. Yet beneath all the euphoria there was an undertone of concern that the letter of the constitution and the reality were two different things. Despite Marx and Lassalle, the men who arrived at positions of political responsibility through the Revolution of 1918–19 paid too much attention to the external façade of democracy and did too little about altering the foundations. The old slogans about the class struggle and the socialisation of the economy had nourished expectations among the social strata providing the party's support, notably among the industrial work force, that Social Democracy ill succeeded in satisfying with its Weimar Constitution. 'The fervent appeal to its own supporters not just to stand there as onlookers and critics but to take an active part in furnishing the new house and filling it with life gave voice to the view that was to receive such bitter confirmation: a democracy can survive only on condition that enough democrats commit themselves to it.'[12]

10. The claim was made at the SPD conference in Kassel, 10–16 October 1920; see *Protokoll über die Verhandlungen des Parteitages der Sozialdemokratischen Partei Deutschlands, abgehalten in Kassel vom 10. bis 16. Oktober 1920* (Berlin, 1920), p. 89.
11. *Ibid.*, pp. 89ff., 93ff; see also *Stenographische Berichte der Verfassunggebenden Deutschen Nationalversammlung*, Vol. 329, pp. 2194f.
12. Heinrich Potthoff, 'Das Weimarer Verfassungswerk und die deutsche Linke', in *Archiv für Sozialgeschichte*, Vol. 12 (Bonn, 1972), p. 483.

### 3. 'Versailles' and its Aftermath

One of the heaviest burdens that the young democracy had to bear was the Treaty of Versailles. Social Democracy here found itself under pressure from two main directions: from its right-wing political opponents at home and from the allied governments of France, Britain, and Italy. The armistice terms that Marshal Foch dictated to the German negotiator, Matthias Erzberger, a leading member of the Centre Party, in the Forest of Compiègne struck not at the old powers in the land but at those who had espoused peace, understanding, and democracy. The severity of those terms lay not so much in the understandable obligation on Germany's part to surrender its war materials and withdraw from occupied territory. What hit the country's life nerve was handing over virtually a third of its locomotives, rolling-stock, and lorries, losing its merchant fleet, having the blockade continued and intensified, and being deprived of the left bank of the Rhine. Erzberger managed by dint of some tough negotiating to wrest a few concessions, which received the explicit approval of the army's supreme command. Nevertheless, the fears that had haunted not only him but also some Social Democrats, notably Scheidemann, all too soon came true.

The term *Dolchstoss* — literally 'dagger thrust' — entered the political vocabulary even before the November Revolution. After that event it rapidly gained currency as it was worked up into the claim that a carefully prepared revolution had attacked the fighting army from the rear and, as Hagen once did to Siegfried, treacherously knifed it in the back. The legend fell on fertile ground. For a long time war propaganda had been 'selling' far too rosy a view of the situation, repeatedly encouraging people's understandable tendency to indulge in wishful ьhinking. Consequently many Social Democrats, too, had a distorted picture of the military realities. Moreover defeat was not, as after the Second World War, directly experienced as an utter catastrophe and as a subjection to military occupation, for hostilities ended with the allegedly 'victorious' German armies still deep in 'enemy territory'. As a result, people were very ready to put the blame on others and to suspect some kind of betrayal. The scapegoats who had to bear that blame were all those who in one form or another had called for an end to the genocide. And it was the old ruling classes of the Empire and the military leaders — men like Hindenburg and Ludendorff who of course knew better — who most shamelessly propagated the *Dolchstosslegende* and used it as a weapon against the Social Democrats and the whole 'Erzberger/Scheidemann crew'.

By the time the peace terms — they were presented on 7 May 1919

— triggered off a wave of 'protests', the *Dolchstosslegende* already enjoyed wide currency. Up until then people had been reckoning with fairly mild peace terms. Particularly among Social Democrats the idea was prevalent that the new democracy was entitled to a just, impartial peace. They looked for a peace treaty based on the right of national self-determination, and they hoped for a league of nations enjoying equal rights and for the establishment of internationally binding social-policy guidelines. Their reaction to the terms of the Treaty of Versailles was that this was a dictated peace and an instrument of subjugation. 'Were this treaty actually to be signed,' said Scheidemann, justifying his rejection of the 'unacceptable' in the National Assembly on 12 May 1919, 'the corpse of Germany would not be the only one left lying on the battlefield of Versailles. Beside it would lie other corpses as noble: the right of national self-determination, the independence of free nations, and belief in all the fine ideals under the banner of which the Entente claimed to be fighting, foremost among them the belief in the loyal observance of treaties.'[13] In a blaze of indignation he dismissed all thought of signing as 'consenting to a pitiless dismemberment, assenting to enslavement and helotism,' and issued his celebrated challenge: 'What hand would not be doomed to wither that laid these chains upon itself and us?'

Scheidemann's speech echoed the feelings of many. It was not, however, conspicuous for its realism. At a time when most people's emotions were running away with them, the Independent Social Democrats were the only party in the National Assembly soberly to take up the only position possible in the circumstances. They too denounced the proffered peace terms as a 'dictate' of the worst kind; but, as they freely admitted, there was no way in which Germany could get around signing them. 'Non-signature will mean the retention of our prisoners-of-war, occupation of our mineral-deposit regions, aggravation of the blockade, unemployment, famine, thousands dead, a fearful catastrophe that will then in any case compel us to sign.'[14]

In time, as the ultimatum set by the Allies drew nearer, the Majority Social Democrats were themselves unable to ignore this argument any longer. While Scheidemann and the German Democratic Party continued to balk, Erzberger of the Centre Party and David of the MSPD led the pleading for acceptance as the lesser evil. They no longer saw any realistic alternative, as a report prepared by Groener and approved by Hindenburg also made clear: further military resistance was hopeless.

13. For the text of Scheidemann's speech, see *Stenographische Berichte der Verfassunggebenden Deutschen Nationalversammlung*, Vol. 327, pp. 1082ff.
14. A resolution of the USPD conference, quoted in Friedrich Stampfer, *Die vierzehn*

After Scheidemann had resigned in protest against the Versailles terms and the DDP had withdrawn from the government, a new coalition government made up of Majority Social Democrats and Centrists and led by the Social Democratic trade-unionist Gustav Bauer took the inevitable step. When after a fierce struggle the National Assembly had voted for acceptance by a simple majority, Hermann Müller (MSPD) and Johannes Bell (Centre) travelled to Versailles and there signed the treaty on 28 June 1919.

Knowing that the step was inevitable if Germany was not to be plunged into even greater misfortune, many people nevertheless soon put the knowledge out of their minds. As they came to see it, the signing of the Treaty of Versailles was yet another 'betrayal of Germany'. They found themselves constantly being reminded of the effects of so 'dishonourable' a contract. The partition of Upper Silesia in 1921, the continuing occupation of the Rhineland, the invasion of the Ruhr in 1923 by the French and Belgians, the controversy over the treaty's war-guilt paragraphs, and the perpetual struggle over reparations repeatedly confronted the German people with the consequences of a defeat it had not yet properly taken in. In the 'disgrace' of the Versailles *Diktat* many people saw the reason for their own, entirely personal plight and identified it with the nation's misfortune. The blame lay with the 'November gang', the 'traitors', and the entire 'system' introduced by them.

In this atmosphere there grew up among those opposed to the republic a mood of hatred and of uncontrolled agitation that not infrequently ended in murder. In a book entitled *Four Years of Political Murder* the statistician Professor Emil Gumbel took stock at the end of 1922: a government minister, Radbruch, confirmed officially that at least 376 political murders had been committed in Germany since 9 November 1918, nearly all of them by right-wing radicals, and that the vast majority of those crimes had gone unpunished.[15] Among the victims were Rosa Luxemburg and Karl Liebknecht, Leo Jogiches, Hugo Haase and Kurt Eisner, Gustav Landauer, Karl Gareis, Hans Paasche, Matthias Erzberger, and Walther Rathenau, to mention only the best-known. *Justitia* was usually quick to convict left-wingers, but when it came to dealing with criminals of the Right she was blind in more than the required sense.

Typical of the anti-democratic, anti-republican spirit of Weimar justice was its treatment of the President, Friedrich Ebert, who sought

---

*Jahre der ersten deutschen Republik*, third edition (Hamburg, 1953), pp. 117f.

15. Emil J. Gumbel, *Vier Jahre politischer Mord* (Berlin-Fichtenau, 1922; new edition Heidelberg, 1980), particularly pp. 5f., 78, 119f., 145.

in a number of actions to defend himself against the most outrageous slanders. One Weimar court went so far as to refer to the head of state in a judgement as a 'traitor to his country' (*Landesverräter*), simply because in January 1918 Ebert had joined a strike committee — with the declared intention of bringing the strike to an orderly conclusion. In a national campaign of incitement orchestrated around such catch-phrases as 'stab in the back', 'national betrayal', and 'November gang' and harping on the 'shame' of Versailles the democrats who had built up the new republic and on whose shoulders it rested were systematically reviled and attacked. Social Democracy, under simultaneous pressure from the left as well, was forced on to the defensive. Much of the diffidence and half-heartedness of its policy during the Weimar period must surely be put down to this. The party felt compelled to offer proof that it was not the party of revolutionary upheaval and treason but that it stood for the national interest and would guarantee law and order. This provided additional motivation for the tendency to prefer to go back into opposition and support the government indirectly instead of frankly assuming responsibility at the head of the government. The aim of this defensive strategy was to bring the bourgeois parties openly to accept a share of the responsibility for Versailles. Today the question imposes itself whether a different course might not have been possible, a more consistent course in the shape of a sober, purely pragmatic foreign policy coupled with an intensive campaign of education at home and effective co-operation between all democratic forces.

# 7

# The Weimar Democracy

## 1.  Labour Parties and Trade Unions in the Early Years of the Republic

In contrast to the pre-war period, when despite divergent tendencies and the organisational doubling of party and trade unions Social Democracy was a united force, the period following the 1918 revolution was characterised by a blend of co-operation and mutual opposition.[1] To start with, there were three parties laying claim to the tradition of the Socialist labour movement as the Weimar Republic got under way.

The Communist Party of Germany (KPD), initially no more than a splinter group, was dominated by adherents of a Utopian, revolutionary course of direct action. Rosa Luxemburg's conception had not survived the party's founding conference. Though many Communist historians refuse to admit as much, she decisively rejected Lenin's form of the dictatorship of the proletariat as a dictatorship of the party and of unfreedom. She saw the 'abolition of the principal democratic guarantees' such as freedom of the press and the right of association and assembly as a slap in the face for Socialism, and she challenged the Bolsheviks as follows: 'Freedom solely for the supporters of the government, solely for the members of one party — however numerous they may be — is no freedom. Freedom is always the freedom of the person who thinks otherwise. Not because of any fanatical belief in "justice" but because all the teaching, healing, cleansing qualities of

---

1. On the subject of Social Democracy in the Weimar Republic, see Friedrich Stampfer, *Die vierzehn Jahre der ersten deutschen Republik* (Hamburg, ³1953); Heinrich August Winkler, *Von der Revolution zur Stabilisierung. Arbeiter und Arbeiterbewegung in der Weimarer Republik 1918–1924* (Bonn, 1984) and *Der Schein der Normalität. Arbeiter und Arbeiterbewegung in der Weimarer Republik 1924–1930* (Bonn, 1985); and Richard N. Hunt, *German Social Democracy 1918–1933* (New Haven/London, 1964). For the early years, see also Susanne Miller, *Die Bürde der Macht. Die deutsche Sozialdemokratie 1918–1920* (Düsseldorf, 1978), and Alfred Kastning, *Die deutsche Sozialdemokratie zwischen Koalition und Opposition 1919–1923* (Paderborn, 1970). Good surveys of the overall development of the republic are provided by Karlheinz Dederke, *Reich und Republik. Deutschland 1917–1933* (Stuttgart, 1969), and Eberhard Kolb, *Die Weimarer Republik* (Munich and Vienna, 1984).

political freedom depend upon it and are ineffective when "freedom" becomes a privilege.'[2]

Following the murders of Rosa Luxemburg and Karl Liebknecht, the KPD got well and truly stuck in an impasse with its 'all-or-nothing' tactics. As the party was forced into illegality by official bans imposed for violent putsch-type activities, its ranks gradually became permeated by a process of reorientation that at the second party conference at 20–23 October 1919 led to a split. The far-left, anti-parliamentary wing broke away from the KPD, taking something like half the membership, and founded the Communist Labour Party of Germany (KAPD) in the spring of 1920. It continued to play a certain part in the bloody struggles of the ensuing years, but after that it became progressively less important. In the remainder of the KPD under the leadership of Paul Levi the principle of participation in parliamentary institutions had gained acceptance. In the general election of June 1920, the first one fought by the KPD, the party collected 2 per cent of the vote. The KPD did not become a mass party until the left wing of the USPD merged with the old KPD to form the 'United Communist Party of Germany' in November 1920.

Within the USPD it had become increasingly clear during the course of 1919 that the party harboured basically irreconcilable tendencies. The differences came out most markedly in attitudes towards parliamentarism. At the party conference in March 1919 two equally powerful wings opposed each other. One of them accepted the parliamentary system; for the other, parliament was at best an arena 'for the revolutionary rousing of the masses'.[3] The most desirable constitutional form in the eyes of the men and women who gathered round Ernst Däumig, Curt Geyer, and Klara Zetkin was the council system, and they were determined to fight for the dictatorship of the proletariat even without a majority in parliament. In the Munich *Räterepublik* and in a series of armed uprisings it was representatives of the radical wing of the USPD who chiefly distinguished themselves. The party was held together principally by its members' shared opposition to the ruling MSPD. With the Majority Socialists' return to opposition, that bond was removed.

In this difficult situation the USPD lost the man who had always tried to balance the different factions, namely its chairman Hugo Haase, who died on 7 November as a result of an assassination attempt by a mentally deranged person four weeks before. At the Leipzig party

2. See Document 5, p. 245.
3. Thus Däumig's motion, put forward by the left wing; see *Protokoll über die Verhandlungen des ausserordentlichen Parteitages* [der USPD] *vom 2. bis 6. März 1919 in Berlin* (Berlin, 1919), p. 250.

conference (30 November to 6 December 1919) the dominant left wing eventually pushed through a programme advocating the dictatorship of the proletariat in the form of rule by the councils. The conference majority then took the logical next step of breaking with the Social Democratic Second International and asking its executive committee to take steps to become affiliated to the Moscow-based Third International (the Comintern).

For all its internal differences and — in comparison with the MSPD — organisational weaknesses, the USPD was well on the way to becoming the protest party of the disillusioned masses. Large numbers of Majority Social Democrats abandoned their old party in the belief that the government it supported was doing too little for their material and social interests and for the goals of Socialism. In particular, its promises of socialisation had failed to materialise and the captains of industry were still at their desks, almost to a man and virtually unmolested. The use of troops against rebellious workers, the suppression of strike movements, constant supply crises, rapidly rising prices, and unemployment also played a part in leading workers uprooted by the war and young workers not moulded by the labour movement to join the ranks of the USPD.

USPD representatives occupied a dominant position in the shoemakers' union and in the textile-workers' union, for example. In the largest single trade union, the metal-workers' union, the USPD likewise secured control of the executive committee at the annual conference in October 1919 and appointed the experienced and capable former party secretary, Robert Dissmann, who had joined the USPD during the war, as the union's new chairman. In addition to the party's successes within the trade-union movement, its swelling membership and finally its performance in the general election of June 1920 showed that the USPD was successfully competing with the MSPD. While its share of the vote rose from 7.6 per cent in January 1919 to 18 per cent on this occasion, that of the MSPD dropped from 37.9 per cent to 21.6 per cent over the same period. If we add the KPD's 2 per cent to the 18 per cent secured by the USPD, outwardly two opposing camps of approximately equal strength now faced each other. If, however, we take attitudes to parliamentary democracy as our criterion, the dividing-line ran right through the middle of the USPD.

At its annual conference in Halle in October 1920 this conflict within the USPD led to a split. This was sparked off by the twenty-one conditions that Moscow had laid down for becoming affiliated to the Communist International. After furious discussion, principally between Rudolf Hilferding on the one hand and Gregor Sinoviev, chairman of the Comintern, on the other, the majority voted to become affiliated to the Third International and to merge with the KPD. The path of the newly founded United Communist Party was marked over the following years by tendency struggles, changes of course, and 'purges'. In the process the German Communists became increasingly dependent upon Moscow and were clearly seen to be operating as Moscow's tool.

Outvoted at the Halle party conference, the minority within the USPD, which included nearly three-quarters of the parliamentary party, at first attempted to keep the party going. In September 1922, however, this rump party, with the exception of an insignificant splinter-group, re-amalgamated with the MSPD to form the United Social Democratic Party of Germany.

Whereas for the USPD, up until the split, an oppositional role was taken for granted and any idea of participating in a coalition government was rejected out of hand, the development of the MSPD in the years following the revolution took place in the field of tension between governmental responsibility and opposition. The problems it faced in the period of the People's Representatives cropped up again repeatedly during the following period. Up until the summer of 1920 it was the leading government party. The Scheidemann Cabinet (MSPD, German Democratic Party, and Centre Party) was replaced after its resignation in June 1919 by a government comprising the MSPD and the Centre Party (under Chancellor Bauer), to which DDP ministers once again acceded in October of that year. Bauer's Cabinet resigned after the Kapp Putsch of March 1920 and was followed by the Hermann Müller government, which again rested on the 'Weimar Coalition'. In addition to the office of Chancellor, which fell to it as by far the strongest party, the MSPD filled two ministries right through these three cabinets, namely Economic Affairs and Labour. The Ministry of the Interior and the Ministry of Finance, on the other hand, remained in middle-class hands throughout. The other ministries were held now by one party, now by another. At the Foreign Ministry Hermann Müller (MSPD) replaced the previous incumbent, the professional diplomat Count von Brockdorff-Rantzau, in June 1919. On Müller's appointment as Chancellor, he was followed as Foreign Minister by his party colleague, Adolf Köster. At the Defence Ministry Gustav Noske, who had become an increasingly heavy liability for the party, had to step down after the Kapp Putsch. With that the Social Democrats relinquished control over this important department, which was now given to Otto Gessler of the DDP.

It had become clear soon after the revolution that the forces of the right were quickly recovering from their shock. The stronger the indications of the emergence of a new and combative anti-democratic faction became, the greater was the ferment that spread through the ranks of the Social Democratic Party membership. In the aftermath of the major strikes and disturbances of 1919, which the government met with a blend of toughness and conciliation, the council movement began to ebb. A powerful element of unrest among the working population persisted underground, as it were. Workers continued to feel that the state owed them, as the upholders of the 'revolution' and the new democracy, more than merely formal civic freedoms. Apart from the socialisation laws, which were virtually without practical effect, and some fine constitutional words about economic democracy and the eight-hour day, they could see nothing that had brought any real progress towards Socialism. After lengthy consultations and discussions taking up most of 1919, a labour-management law (the Works Councils Law) was finally passed on 4 February 1920. This gave workers legally guaranteed representation at their place of work as well as a right — opposed by the employers' organisations — of co-determination, for example in dismissals and appointments, in laying down working times and working arrangements, in regulations governing leave, and in the introduction of new methods of payment. But not only did the law provoke the anger of radical workers, who under the leadership of the USPD organised a protest demonstration outside the *Reichstag* on the occasion of the second reading, a demonstration that ended in violent clashes with the police. It also disappointed large sections of moderate labour opinion. They felt cheated of the fruits of the revolution and were unable to understand why the Social Democrats in the government had not done more for them. Irritation with the 'compromise government' that was not 'their' government but a coalition spilled over into a feeling of uneasiness with regard to the course adopted by the party's leaders. The result, as the chairman of the MSPD, Otto Wels, noted as early as the end of 1919, was 'a deep-seated agitation, an extraordinary dissatisfaction with the party and the party leadership'.[4]

Anyone looking only at absolute membership figures, which from a million in April 1914 had dropped to a nadir of 250,000 in April 1918 to return to the million mark in 1919 and rise to 1.18 million in the years 1920–22, will not at first be prepared to think in terms of a party crisis. However, if we compare this membership trend with the rapid growth of the USPD and above all with the meteoric rise of the trade unions, the only word to describe it is stagnation. The fact that the MSPD benefited so little from the trend towards organisations that

4. *Protokoll der Sitzung des Parteiausschusses, Berlin den 13. Dezember 1919* (Berlin, undated), p. 1.

was so symptomatic of this period constituted further proof of the serious erosion of its pulling-power.

It was a very different story with the Free Trade Unions, which at their congress in June–July 1919 gave themselves a firmer superstructure and took the name of General German Trade Union Congress (ADGB). The 'general commission' was replaced by a congress executive, and this was backed up by a congress committee, the organ of the association chairmen. The pre-war membership figure of 2.5 million (labour unions and the Socialist employees' associations allied to them), which the war then caused to sink to a low of less than 1 million at the end of 1916, was overhauled and left behind before the year 1918 was out. Membership continued to rise very quickly indeed; it stood at over 7.33 million by the end of 1919, and in June 1920 the congress reached its peak with a total of 8,144,981 members.[5]

While the soberly practical attitude that was so characteristic of the trade-union leadership continued to mould trade-union tactics, in contrast to the pre-war period this was now accompanied by fundamental theoretical discussions and a process of politicisation that ran right through the movement from bottom to top. There was a whole series of reasons for this: the mass influx of new and uninstructed members, the broad political spectrum covered by the membership from the radical, council-advocating wing of the USPD through critical Social Democrats to trade-unionists who concerned themselves solely with pay and conditions, the involvement of Majority Social Democracy in a government coalition with middle-class parties, the brutal use of soldiers against strike movements, and above all the existence of a plurality of Socialist parties. These factors led to the trade unions gradually abandoning their close ties with the MSPD and developing very considerable political weight in their own right. A quite new keynote was sounded when Carl Legien, the chairman of the general commission and a classic exponent of traditional trade-union policy, remonstrated with Scheidemann about Majority Social Democracy becoming an 'annexe' of this 'compromise government' and insisted that the party leadership ensure 'that we remain an independent party'.[6] No less instructive were the words of Theodor Leipart, Legien's successor-to-be, to the effect that he could understand why at the headquarters of the ADGB only the Independents' newspaper *Freiheit* was available and no longer *Vorwärts*, the official organ of the MSPD.[7]

5. For the background, see Heinrich Potthoff, *Gewerkschaften und Politik zwischen Revolution und Inflation* (Düsseldorf, 1979), particularly pp. 40ff.
6. *Protokoll der Parteikonferenz in Weimar am 22. und 23. März 1919* (Berlin, 1919), p. 19.

The feeling was spreading throughout the trade unions, right up to their supreme governing bodies, the congress committee and the congress executive, that the coalition government led by the Majority Social Democrats was not in a position to do anything effective for working-class interests. The trade unions must therefore step outside their traditional spheres of wage fluctuations and social policy and intervene in the economic and political spheres. This determination no longer to leave the political decision-making entirely to the parliamentary representatives of the working class but actively to take a hand in building a social democracy, operating as an independent political force, was put to the test on the occasion of the Kapp Putsch of March 1920.

## 2. The Kapp Putsch and its Aftermath

Confidence had been growing in right-wing nationalist circles in the years leading up to 1920 that the 'republican interlude' was nearing its end. Particularly within the Free Corps the nucleus of a new and combative anti-democratic nationalism took shape for which the constitutional government of the country was quite simply a 'scandal'. With the support of two such Free Corps, which had rejected a government attempt to dissolve them, a putsch was mounted against the democratic republic on 13 March 1920 by General Lüttwitz of the *Reichswehr*, the former East Prussian provincial administrator (*Generallandschaftsdirektor*) Wolfgang Kapp, Commander Ehrhardt of the Free Corps, and a number of other officers. Waving black-white-and-red flags and with swastikas on their helmets — a symbol of what lay in store for Germany — their troops occupied Berlin. The *Reichswehr*, whose job it should have been to protect the government, hesitated to intervene against the putschists. The army chief-of-staff, General Walther Reinhardt, remained loyal to the constitution, but he was the only one. General von Seeckt and his officers left the government in the lurch, now that it was a question, for the first time, of protecting it against the right and not as hitherto against the left.

President Ebert, Chancellor Bauer, and the ministers of the central government just managed to escape imprisonment by fleeing from Berlin. In this crisis — the worst to have hit the republic so far — it was the Free Trade Unions under Legien with their massive army of organised labour that came to the rescue. The General German Trade

---

7. See *Konferenz der Vertreter der Verbandsvorstände* [der Freien Gewerkschaften]. *Sitzung vom 25. April 1919* (Berlin, 1919), pp. 6, 26.

Union Congress (ADGB), together with the Alliance of Free Employees' Associations (AfA), summoned workers, salaried employees, and civil servants to stage a general strike against the putschists. The same watchword went out from the executive committee of the Majority Social Democratic Party and its representatives in the government. The Independent Social Democrats also added their voice to the call for a general strike. The German Civil Service Association (DBB), in which mainly the lower grades were organised, aligned itself with this defensive front, and the liberal trade unions (in the tradition of the Hirsch-Duncker *Gewerkvereine*) were likewise unable to remain aloof. Although the Christian German Trade Union Congress (DGB) officially condemned the general strike, in practice it too joined the campaign. Even the leadership of the KPD, which had at first refused to fight for the democratic republic on the orders of the Communist International in Moscow, was eventually compelled to participate. Determined action by organised labour — many civil servants in the ministries also refused to work for the illegal government — eventually forced Kapp and his accomplices to give up.

During the general strike Carl Legien, that straightforward, energetic trade-unionist, not only showed himself to be a brilliant organiser and co-ordinator but also became the central pivot between central government, the coalition parties, the USPD, and the mobilised working population. He was not satisfied with the surrender of those who had breached the constitution. The workers organised in the Free Trade Unions now expected a fundamental change of political direction. In a joint programme the ADGB, AfA, and DBB set nine conditions for bringing the first political general strike in German history to an end:

1. A decisive say 'in the reform of the central and state governments and in the reorganisation of economic and social legislation'.
2. The swift disarmament and punishment of all involved in the putsch.
3. The immediate resignation of Army Minister Noske (MSPD) and the Prussian ministers Wolfgang Heine (MSPD) and Rudolf Oeser (DDP).
4. The purging of the political and economic administration of all reactionary elements.
5. Rapid democratisation of the administrative process.
6. The immediate expansion of social legislation and of genuinely equal rights for workers, salaried employees, and civil servants.
7. The immediate socialisation of mining and power production.
8. The dispossession of landowners who sabotaged food supplies.

9. The dissolution of all counter-revolutionary formations and the takeover of the security service by organised labour.[8]

This attempt by the trade unions to put the Weimar democracy on a firmer footing by — belatedly — introducing some decisive reforms was destined to be unsuccessful. Although Otto Wels and the MSPD leadership made a strong commitment to it and leading representatives of the USPD likewise gave it their blessing, there was never any real chance of making up for what the November Revolution had failed to achieve. The trade unions, in alliance with other loyal forces, had rescued the democratic republic; that did not stabilise it. In fact their intervention turned out to be a two-edged sword. Campaigning under the banner of a struggle against the 'parallel government' that the trade unions were said to constitute and against the 'trade-union state', an anti-trade-union faction now evolved within the middle-class camp that proved more enduring in its effects than people's aversion to the putschists. The trade unions emerged from the Kapp Putsch as victors in appearance only. The real victor was in fact the army. The Cabinet that Hermann Müller (MSPD) assembled after a certain amount of wrangling was once again based on the old coalition. It did, after various ifs and buts, principally from the DDP, adopt the programme demanded by the trade unions, but only a small part of that programme was ever implemented. The Müller Cabinet's main domestic-policy problem was suppressing the rebellions that flared up in the wake of the general strike in Berlin, in central Germany, and above all in the Ruhr District, where after severe and often vicious clashes verging on civil war a 'Red Ruhr Army' came to control almost the entire industrial region for a time. With the backing of the government, State Commissioner Severing managed to negotiate a cease-fire and filter the moderate elements out of the Red Army to a very large extent. The resistance of the militant core was then smashed by the might of the *Reichswehr*. In the process the worker formations found themselves facing military units that had lent support to the putschists. The 'white terror' imposed by those units outdid the 'red terror' in brutality and intensity. Many workers, having by prolonging the strike and building up their own formations sought to defend the republic against a gross breach of the constitution and found instead that supporters of that breach were sent into action against themselves or their comrades on the orders of the Müller government, now became embittered beyond all measure. Under the terms of the state of

8. See *Korrespondenzblatt des Allgemeinen Deutschen Gewerkschaftsbundes*, Vol. 30, 27 March 1920, pp. 152f.

emergency, strikers loyal to the republic were often severely punished, chiefly by military courts, merely because they had come under suspicion or been denounced; no punishment by the republic of its enemies on the right followed.

The general election of June 1920 took place in the shadow of the Kapp Putsch and the worker rebellions that followed it. As we have seen, in comparison with the National Assembly election there was a landslide on this occasion between the two groups of parties representing the Socialist labour movement. Even adding to the MSPD's 21.6 per cent and the USPD's 18 per cent the 2 per cent of the vote captured by the KPD, we find that not only was there a shift to the left within the labour parties but that they suffered an overall loss of almost 4 per cent. The shifts among the middle-class parties were at least as serious. Of the MSPD's former coalition partners, the Centre Party lost 6.1 percentage points (with 13.6 per cent, against 19.7 per cent in January 1919), mainly because of the breakaway of the Bavarian People's Party, while the DDP slumped from 18.5 to 8.2 per cent. The biggest gains were recorded by the national–liberal DVP (from 4.4 to 13.9 per cent) and the far-right DNVP (from 10.3 to 15 per cent). Contrary to the expectations of Otto Wels, the chairman of the MSPD, the Kapp Putsch had not had the effect of damaging the right. Instead the civil-war conditions of the spring of 1920 had literally driven many voters into the arms of the 'system critics' on the right.

Hermann Müller did try to form another government under MSPD leadership, but the attempt failed. The new Cabinet headed by the Centrist Konstantin Fehrenbach included not a single Social Democrat. It was the first entirely middle-class government (DVP, DDP, and Centre) of the Weimar Republic. For the next eight years, until the formation of the second Müller Cabinet in 1928, the Centre Party rather than Social Democracy was the leading government party. In those eight years the SPD was no more than a junior partner in four short-lived Cabinets lasting a total of nine months.

## 3. Social Democracy from 1920 to 1928

The loss of governmental responsibility was registered by most Majority Social Democrats without either regret or concern. On the contrary, the predominant feeling was one of relief. Müller summed up the prevailing mood at the party conference in October 1920 when he said: 'None of us has any desire to rejoin the government'.[9] It was an

9. See *Protokoll über die Verhandlungen des Parteitages der Sozialdemokratischen*

attitude to which *Vorwärts* gave striking expression in 1925 when it wrote that the SPD had never been keen on participating in government and had only done so 'when the nation's uttermost need demanded this sacrifice of it'.[10] After the experiences of its one-and-a-half year involvement in government up until June 1920, a period in which its supporters had deserted it in shoals, it certainly had no wish to take up the burden of governmental responsibility except in an emergency.

Notwithstanding these reservations, the parliamentary party did feel compelled frequently to lend its support to governments in which it had no hand because otherwise they would have found no majority in parliament and fresh crises loomed. What the party expected from this tactics of 'toleration' was that the 'bourgeois' would themselves have to answer in the public eye for unavoidable measures dictated by internal and external necessity and that Social Democracy would thus get out of the firing-line of its opponents to right and left. This peculiar position between the two stools of government party and opposition was sharply criticised in 1928 by Julius Leber, who was to pay for his resistance to Hitler with his life in 1944: 'Either one must govern, or one must adopt a straightforwardly oppositional stance. To have neither the readiness to take responsibility for the one nor the courage for the other, in other words to prefer a policy of muddling through to one of making firm decisions, is the greatest mistake a political party can perpetrate.'[11]

Whenever unpopular decisions of great moment became unavoidable, the SPD leapt into the breach. Unlike many of its opponents on the right and on the left, it was not afraid to commit itself to what it saw as national political necessities. As a coalition partner it backed the attempt by the Joseph Wirth government (1921–2) to achieve a revision of the Treaty of Versailles by a 'policy of fulfilment'. Social Democracy had a great deal of sympathy with the left-wing Centrist Wirth, whereas towards his successor, the right-wing independent businessman Wilhelm Cuno, its predominant feeling was one of reserve. Even Cuno's Cabinet, however, in which the SPD had not a single representative, enjoyed the party's support in its attempt to answer the invasion of the Ruhr by French and Belgian troops in January 1923 with a policy of passive resistance. When that policy

---

*Partei Deutschlands, abgehalten in Kassel vom 10. bis 16. Oktober 1920* (Berlin, 1920), p. 270. A very similar view was expressed in 1924; see *Protokoll des Parteitages in Berlin 1924* (Berlin, 1924), pp. 83, 130.

10. *Vorwärts*, 6 December 1925.

11. Julius Leber (ed. his friends), *Ein Mann geht seinen Weg. Schriften, Reden und Briefe* (Berlin, 1952), p. 177.

sparked off an inflationary depreciation of the currency and the mark plummeted, the Social Democrats once again offered help in time of need. The Gustav Stresemann Cabinet, in which the SPD was a junior partner, took on the thankless task of calling a halt to the by now hopeless struggle for the Ruhr and subsequently restoring the currency.

1923 was one of the Weimar Republic's most critical years. The fight for the Ruhr, of which workers, salaried employees, and civil servants bore the brunt, saw thirteen Krupp workers killed by French troops on 31 March, and it became impossible to continue the struggle in the long run. The rocketing expenditure was financed by the expedient of printing banknotes. It was possible to peg the exchange rate against the dollar at around 20,000 marks until the middle of April; after that there was no holding it. In August the rate rose to 4.6 million, in October it was over 25 thousand million, and by 15 November, the day of the currency reform, it had reached 4.2 million million. Unimaginable hardship not only encouraged separatist movements in the Rhineland and in the Palatinate; on the right wing there was talk of a dictatorship and calls for a 'strong man' to restore control.[12] The Communists, particularly in Saxony and Thuringia, unmolested by governments they supported, prepared for an armed struggle. In Bavaria the Kahr government breached the constitution by rebelling against the central government. And in Munich, on 8 and 9 November 1923, Adolf Hitler felt his opportunity had come and with the backing of General Ludendorff launched a putsch attempt, which collapsed inside twenty-four hours.

With the vigorous support of Social Democracy, the republic survived this crisis under Stresemann's leadership. The measures resorted to by the government with the aid of an enabling act plunged the party into serious conflict. In Saxony and Thuringia, both of which had all-SPD governments with a strong leftward tendency, 'proletarian *Hundertschaften*' or groups of one hundred were raised to combat the threat of revolution from the right, and eventually Communists were taken into the Cabinets of both states. The SPD was now presented with the spectacle of the central government marching units of the *Reichswehr* into Saxony and Thuringia to compel the dissolution of the governments headed by Erich Zeigner and August Fröhlich while it took virtually no action against the Kahr government in Bavaria.

---

12. Thus, among others, Count Westarp, chairman of the DNVP group in the *Reichstag*, addressing Chancellor Stresemann. See also Karlheinz Dederke, *Reich und Republik*, op. cit., p. 70. Similar ideas were expressed by the leading industrialist Hugo Stinnes; see G. W. F. Hallgarten, *Hitler, Reichswehr und Industrie. Zur Geschichte der Jahre 1918–1933* (Frankfurt a. M., 1962), p. 66.

This double standard of being tough with the left and making concessions to the right was something for which the SPD did not wish to be co-responsible. Its withdrawal from the central government led to the fall of Gustav Stresemann. Ebert castigated what from the standpoint of the party was a comprehensible but in his eyes was a politically imprudent course of action with the words: 'The thing that has prompted you to bring down the Chancellor will be forgotten in six weeks, but the consequences of your stupidity will visit you for a further ten years.'[13]

This decision was influenced both by the pressure exerted by joint actions by Social Democratic and Communist workers and also by consideration for the party's left wing. In September 1922 the rump USPD had returned to the bosom of the mother party. The reunion brought an increase in membership, which in 1923 reached an all-time high of 1,261,072, but the party gained little from it in terms of external appeal. To the left of the SPD the KPD was now firmly entrenched. Its share of the vote rose from 2 per cent in 1920 through 12.6 per cent (May 1924), 9 per cent (December 1924), and 10.6 per cent (1928) to reach 13.1 per cent in 1930. The KPD's aggressive policy toward the republic and toward Social Democracy was one reason why the Social Democratic leadership often equated social–revolutionary tendencies among the working population with 'Communism'. This made any recovery of the allegiance of radicalised workers a quite hopeless undertaking.

Even in opposition the SPD never managed to make up for the serious setback it had suffered as a government party in the 1920 election. In May 1924 the reunited party collected 20.5 per cent of the vote. It achieved a notable success in December of the same year with 26 per cent, and in 1928 it came close to breaking through the 30 per cent barrier once again (with 29.8 per cent), but only two years later it dropped back to 24.5 per cent. The election results show clearly that the SPD was scarcely able to make good its losses to the KPD. Among workers, who according to the occupational census of 1925 accounted for 45.1 per cent of persons in full-time employment, it always won only a section of the vote, if by far the largest one. Catholic voters basically remained loyal to the Centre Party, while those with a Protestant allegiance, in so far as they were organised in Christian trade unions, tended to prefer the 'national' parties. Among agricultural workers, who politically and economically were still very much under the influence of the large landowners, the SPD likewise found it hard to make any headway.

13. Gustav Stresemann, *Vermächtnis*, Vol. 1 (Berlin, 1932), p. 245. See also Waldemar

Among other social strata such as office-workers and low-grade civil servants, pensioners and small farmers, and some craft-tradesmen and small retailers who were in a similar financial situation to the workers, the party managed to make only partial inroads even under the Weimar Republic. The proportion of working-class members did drop from around 90 per cent before the war to 73 per cent in 1926 and 60 per cent in 1930, while at the same time the proportions belonging to other groups rose: in 1930, 10 per cent of members were white-collar workers, 3 per cent civil servants, and 17 per cent housewives. But what we have to remember is that the working-class segment of the population was beginning to stagnate while the proportion of civil servants and white-collar workers was growing: by 1926 these made up a total of 16.5 per cent of persons in employment. The bottom section of the social pyramid now also included parts of the middle class that had got into economic difficulties as a result of inflation and had become proletarianised. Altogether, calculations based on social statistics show that in 1926 more than 50 per cent of the population belonged to the economic lower class.[14] A further 12 per cent belonging to the lower middle class were not much better off. These figures raise the question of why the SPD did not succeed in exploiting this voting potential to better effect and becoming *the* party of the under-privileged.

The burdens on the party that grew out of defeat, the revolution, and 'Versailles' constitute one reason. Another factor operating to the disadvantage of democratic Socialism was that in the distribution of social power in the Weimar Republic the balance soon tipped back towards the entrepreneurial side. Symptomatic of this was the fact that the eight-hour day was soon being challenged by employers. They argued that with it Germany would be incapable of bearing the burden laid upon it by the lost war and the reparation demands. The working population was well aware that it had its part to play in overcoming the burdensome consequences of the war, but it looked in vain for a corresponding readiness on the part of the entrepreneurial class. In a period of high inflation workers found their real income sinking steadily because prices were outstripping wages, while on the other side entrepreneurs and merchants sold their goods only against hard gold currency.

The loss of power suffered by trade-union organisations (dwindling membership figures and lack of funds) was paralleled by an enormous

---

Besson, *Friedrich Ebert, Verdienst und Grenze* (Göttingen, 1963), p. 89.

14. See Theodor Geiger, *Die soziale Schichtung des deutschen Volkes. Soziographischer Versuch auf statistischer Grundlage* (1932; reprinted Darmstadt, 1967), particularly p. 73.

growth in the power of property owners. The big industrialists in particular derived colossal returns from low manufacturing costs, high export profits, capitalised taxes, and debts that shrank to nothing overnight. The well-known industrial empire of Hugo Stinnes was by far the largest but by no means the only one. This first major process of concentration in industry was followed after the stabilisation of the mark by a second wave. Once reparations had been settled by the Dawes Plan of 1924, foreign capital poured into Germany, lured by high interest rates, and unleashed a powerful upswing. The loaned money provided the financial basis for the rapid process of rationalisation that now got under way. It was principally the big entrepreneurs who profited from this with their mass-production methods. Exemplary concentrations of economic power were the merger in the chemical industry in 1926 that led to the establishment of IG Farben, a complex comprising some nine-tenths of the chemical sector, and another in the same year that produced the United Steelworks, controlling some two-fifths of coal, iron, and steel production.

The working population itself profited from this economic boom. Workers' real wages, for example, rose by 37 per cent between 1924 and 1927. This figure begins to look a little less rosy, however, when we bear in mind that up until the inflation their actual earned income had fallen a long way behind the pre-war level. In only one year — 1929 — was the net real weekly wage of 1913 exceeded by a paltry 2 per cent. A further negative factor was that virtually throughout the Weimar period there existed a state of almost chronic unemployment. From something like 1 million unemployed in the middle of 1919, the figure did sink in the brief post-war boom to between 120,000 and 400,000 officially registered recipients of main relief. But in the winter of 1923–4 that figure rose rapidly to 1.25 million. Altogether around 4 million were wholly or largely out of work at that time. After a brief fall in the figures, by 1922 there were once again 2 million people dependent on unemployment benefit. Even in the period 1927–8 unemployment remained high, albeit with considerable seasonal fluctuations, at around 1.4 million averaged out over the year, before with the advent of the great economic crisis the figures went rocketing to unprecedented heights.

Immediately after the war the roots of this unemployment lay in the difficulties of readapting to a peacetime economy. After 1923 it was primarily demographic shifts and economic slumps but also the process of rationalisation, carried through without regard to its social consequences, that were responsible for the high figures. In addition to the increasing monotony of labour as a result of new production and operating methods (e.g. the assembly line), workers also found their jobs at risk. The working man or women dependent upon a wage was constantly threatened by economic insecurity. Increasing non-observance of the eight-hour day — in October 1926 53 per cent worked more than 48 hours — and the cessation of the government's social policy in 1923 highlighted the impotence of working-class organisations in comparison with what was known simply as 'the economy' and showed how the right-of-centre parties associated with the latter increasingly dictated events.

For a variety of reasons the scope for Social Democracy had narrowed sharply in the years following 1920. We are left with the question of how far the party's own theory and practice were responsible for its political weight and potential remaining so limited.

If we start by looking for evidence of a theoretical nature, we are struck by the fact that, except among fringe groups inside and outside the party, theoretical clashes were extremely rare occurrences. There were lively discussions within the party in 1921, when the MSPD gave itself a new programme at its Görlitz conference, but they revolved mainly around practical, concrete questions of the day. In its Görlitz programme the SPD presented itself as 'the party of the working people in town and country' and as being concerned with 'the formation of a joint force fighting for democracy and Socialism'. This 'people's party' label notwithstanding, the notion of the class struggle retained its programmatic importance. It was interpreted at Görlitz as a 'historical necessity' dictated by the capitalist economic order and further as a 'moral requirement'. The programme saw the 'transfer to public ownership of the major concentrated economic enterprises' and the 'progressive transformation of the entire capitalist economy into a Socialist economy' as being a 'necessary means . . . of leading mankind onward and upward to higher forms of economic and moral co-operation'. At the same time as making an unreserved commitment to the democratic republic, Social Democracy proclaimed its determination 'to make every effort to protect such freedom as has been achieved' and to repulse every assault on democracy 'as an attempt on the vital rights of the people'.[15]

Only a year after adopting the Görlitz programme, the party appointed a commission to prepare a fresh draft programme following the reunion with the USPD. This programme, in which Karl Kautsky, among others, once again had a hand, was adopted by the 1925 party conference in Heidelberg. Its introductory statement of principle drew extensively on the earlier Erfurt Programme. It was complemented by a number of passages — basically going back to Rudolf Hilferding —

15. See Document 8, pp. 253ff.

about the growing influence of finance capital on the state and the 'striving for imperialist aggrandisement' to which it gave rise. Long before other parties took up the cause of Europe German Social Democracy committed itself, in an official party programme, to 'the creation of European economic unity, which for economic reasons has now become urgent, and the formation of a United States of Europe'.[16]

The attempt to elaborate a specific agrarian programme, already undertaken in vain long before the war at the 1894 and 1895 party conferences, was resumed at the Kiel party conference in 1927. After some amendments a programme was passed unanimously promising support for rural settlement, land reform, and small farmers in general. This attempt to reach new classes of voter by means of a programme tailored to the needs of a particular social group made little impression on the reservations, accumulated over decades, with which small farmers regarded Social Democracy.

Of graver consequence for the party than the long absence of an agrarian programme was the fact that among the lower middle class and among salaried employees, small sections excluded, its political plans came up against a wall of mistrust. In its campaign to win over these social strata the SPD spoke critically of their 'erroneous awareness' and addressed them as proletarians or as proletarians in the making. The majority of them, however, had no wish to be class comrades with the workers. Some of them, being of proletarian origin themselves, were anxious to be rid of everything that reminded them of their former status. The other, larger group consisted in the main of members of the old middle class. As a result of changes in the structure of the economy and the consequences of inflation they were experiencing a social decline. Yet in spite of or precisely because of their depressed economic circumstances they retained an awareness of being something better. They tended to attribute the loss of their own security to the misfortune that had overtaken the nation. They were quick to blame that humiliation on the Social Democrats. Their ideal was not a classless society; instead they saw as the way out of their sorry plight a recognised place in the *Volksgemeinschaft* or national community and the rise of the *Reich* to new greatness and a new international standing.

Such emotionally charged visions of the future were held out to them by the right, by nationalist groups, and eventually by National Socialism, but not by the SPD. The Social Democrats also saw German recovery as an urgent necessity and set about promoting it by word and deed. But their policy was always very down to earth; it lacked

16. See Document 9, pp. 258ff.

sparkle and the power to inspire. Women owed the fact that they could vote to the government of the People's Representatives. But when they voted it was mainly the Catholic Centre Party and the German National People's Party that benefited; their contribution to the Socialist parties was below average. As far as young people were concerned, Social Democracy exerted comparatively little attraction. In 1930, for example, only 8 per cent of the membership were below 25 years of age. In the latter days of the Weimar Republic the Social Democratic parliamentary party had the highest average age of all the parties represented in the *Reichstag*. When someone was elected to the executive committee, he was virtually there for life. On only one occasion during the Weimar years was a member of the party's executive committee voted off — and he, significantly, was a representative of the left wing. Reliable, capable men without much in the way of personal radiance determined the image of the party. In painstaking, dogged, detailed work they led the campaign for social improvements and small reforms. The plebiscite about dispossession of the princes instigated by the KPD and the SPD in 1926 did admittedly managed to mobilise indifferent voters from well outside the ranks of the parties' own supporters. However, the whole thing went no further than a momentary demonstration and brought no lasting benefit or concrete success.

In thousands of municipalities and rural districts Social Democrats played an active part and evolved an exemplary modern local-government policy, although there were by no means as many 'red town halls' as is commonly supposed. They also exerted a good deal of influence in a number of states, and in 1929 they constituted a good third of all deputies in the *Landtage*. In Bavaria, that centre of 'law and order' where in the wake of the *Räterepublik* it was the forces of conservative reaction that called the tune, the party had declined almost to a splinter group (something over 10 per cent) by 1932, but in the state governments of Hamburg, Baden, Hesse, and Prussia, for example, it played a leading role. Apart from a few brief interruptions, in Prussia the SPD was in permanent command of the ship of state from 1919 onwards. After Paul Hirsch one of the most impressive political personalities of the Weimar Republic, Otto Braun, took over as Prussian Minister-President in 1920. With the aid of coalition governments made up of SPD, Centre Party, and DDP representatives (occasionally the DVP was involved as well), he sought to realise in Prussia the model of a 'republican *Volksstaat*'. Smooth-running, fairly administered democratic institutions and vigorous action by SPD ministers of the interior Carl Severing and Albert Grzesinski against subversive, anti-democratic activities pursued by right and left made

'Red Prussia' the favourite hate-object of the enemies of the republic.

Even in the 'Prussian bulwark' of the republic a distinctive weakness of the SPD in the Weimar period emerged with particular clarity. The Social Democrats regarded themselves, as the experienced campaigner Wilhelm Keil put it at the 1925 party conference, 'as the true upholders of the democratic republic', as 'champion of the poor, the workers, and the disinherited'. And indeed Social Democracy was *the* guardian of the constitution and of democracy. Yet its concept of democracy remained too narrowly restricted to the formal functioning of democratic institutions and to mere defence. Again and again the party's profession of faith in the democratic republic was justified in terms of its having secured therein a 'base' on the way 'to the Socialist republic'.[17] This typically defensive motivation was expressed as follows by the Minister-President of Hesse, Karl Ulrich, at the 1927 party conference in Kiel: 'We must tell the masses that we are determined to defend the democratic republic tooth and nail because we see it as a more promising context in which to fight for our socio-political demands and our Socialist goals than the monarchy.'[18] Yet the alternative to the Weimar Republic was not a monarchical restoration of the age of William II. The real threat was from the modern totalitarian state advocated by the forces of aggressive nationalism and by the Fascists, against which mere defence was quite inadequate. Hilferding's initiative to the effect that historically democracy 'had been' the task of the proletariat and that it still was lacking the power to inspire enthusiasm. From the fringes of the party, including the right and left wings, there came calls for the SPD not to confine itself to preserving democracy but actively to promote it and effectively to implement it in all spheres of political and social life.

Such a policy required a firm order of priorities and the consistent subordination of all other concerns and considerations to the *one* urgent objective. The man who had most decisively adopted such a position and possessed a corresponding degree of authority was taken from Social Democracy by an early death. On 28 February 1925 Friedrich Ebert succumbed to the consequences of protracted appendicitis. In the six years in which he had held office as head of state he had proved himself as a guardian of the republic and a committed, conscientious democrat. The struggle for a liberal socio-political system had taken precedence over everything else for him, and to it he had sacrificed his health and strength. However, with his rigidly anti-

17. Thus Paul Löbe, for example: see *Protokoll über die Verhandlungen des Parteitages der Sozialdemokratischen Partie Deutschlands, abgehalten in Kiel vom 22. bis 27. Mai 1927* (Berlin, 1927), p. 196.
18. *Ibid.*, p. 210.

leftist stance, his enormous faith in experts, and his failure to replace representatives of the forces of reaction by determined democrats, he must bear his share of the responsibility for the limited influence of Social Democracy. Ebert's place was taken by the legendary national hero, Field Marshal Hindenburg.

The first ballot for the election of the new President was held on 29 March 1925. In it the candidate nominated by the DNVP and the DVP, the Mayor of Duisburg, Karl Jarres, received 10.7 million votes, beating Otto Braun (SPD), who received 7.8 million, and Wilhelm Marx (Centre Party), who received 3.9 million. None of the candidates having secured the requisite overall majority, a second ballot took place on 26 April. The Centre Party, the DDP, and the SPD jointly nominated Marx, while the parties of the right this time put up Hindenburg. It was a close thing: Hindenburg won with 14,655,000 votes, with Marx close behind him (13,751,000 votes), while Ernst Thälmann, given a second nomination by the KPD, received 1,931,000 votes some of which would otherwise probably have gone to Marx. But a heavier share of the responsibility for the outcome falls to the Bavarian People's Party, a sort of forerunner of the present-day Christian Social Union, which asked its voters not to vote for Marx, the Centre Party man from the Rhineland and the candidate put up by its sister party, but for the aged field marshal. The highest office in the republic was thus placed in the hands of a man who transferred his military values to the political sphere and whose attitude towards parliamentary democracy was one of inner rejection.

## 4. The Second Hermann Müller Cabinet

In 1928 Social Democracy received a further opportunity to dictate policy from the government bench. A new parliament was elected on 20 May of that year. The SPD increased its share of the vote from 26 per cent (in the 1924 election) to 29.8 per cent and won 153 seats (previous total 131). Since the KPD also increased its share of the vote on this occasion from 9 to 10.6 per cent the gains cannot have come from the left but probably resulted from defections from the DDP, which had worn itself out in the bourgeois government coalition. After lengthy and difficult negotiations Hermann Müller formed a Cabinet that drew on the SPD, the Centre Party, the DDP, and the DVP. The involvement of the German People's Party was less than whole-hearted. Only the vigorous efforts of Gustav Stresemann had per-suaded it to join the 'Great Coalition' government.

Its internal tensions notwithstanding, the Cabinet managed to pursue a joint line in foreign affairs. The policy of rapprochement favoured by Stresemann, Foreign Minister since 1923, had already enjoyed the firm support of the SPD while the party was in opposition, whereas within the ranks of his own party Stresemann met with stubborn resistance. Following the signature of the 'Kellogg Pact' outlawing war on 27 August 1928, the government turned to the reparations problem. After some tough bargaining the so-called 'Young Plan' was adopted at a conference in The Hague on 21 August 1929. This brought Germany not only a reduction in the burden of reparations and a release from the supervision hitherto exercised by the Allies but also a speedy evacuation of the occupied territories. Allied troops were to leave German soil as early as 1930 — five years before the date laid down by the Treaty of Versailles.

This major foreign-policy success found no favour with the nationalists, however, any more than did Hermann Müller's plea at the League of Nations — of which Germany had been a member since 1926 — for the other states to disarm as well. So-called 'national' circles were less interested in general disarmament than in German rearmament. It was in this spirit that the previous bourgeois government had decided to build 'Cruiser A'. The SPD, which had fought the election with the slogan 'Kinderspeisung statt Panzerkreuzer' ('Food for the children rather than cruisers'), suddenly found itself confronted with the fact that the government it supported was prepared to put up funds for the ship. The party at large and the parliamentary party rebelled against their own comrades in the Cabinet. The SPD ministers bowed to the prevailing mood and to party discipline and voted against 'Cruiser A' in the *Reichstag*. Hardly had the party negotiated this hurdle before economic disaster struck, shaking the Weimar Republic to its foundations.

Even before the onset of the great world economic crisis with the crash on the New York stock exchange on 24 and 29 October 1929, the German economy was in recession with rising unemployment and worsening social tensions. The great labour struggle in the Rhine-Westphalia region in the late autumn of 1928, the so-called 'Ruhr Iron Dispute', threw a spotlight on the ruthless strategy of conflict with which entrepreneurs were seeking to take advantage of what for them were favourable times. In disregarding the arbitration order that Labour Minister Wissell declared to be binding the employers struck at the root of the existing wage-agreement and conciliation system. The protracted dispute over unemployment insurance that began in 1929 finally set the foundations of the Weimar social order rocking dangerously. The partly seasonal peak of 2.85 million unemployed in January 1929 did drop sharply in the summer, but in the following winter it climbed as high as 3.2 million. According to a compromise thrashed out in the Cabinet, the increasing outgoings of the state insurance agency were to be offset by raising employer and employee contributions from 3 to $3\frac{1}{2}$ per cent. The mounting deficit in unemployment insurance put the question back on the agenda in the spring of 1930. The industry- and employer-oriented DVP went along with the employers' associations in proposing to balance the books by reducing benefit payments to unemployed persons. The SPD, for whom what mattered was to protect the worker who had got into financial difficulties through no fault of his own, demanded an increase in contributions to $3\frac{3}{4}$ and subsequently to 4 per cent. A compromise proposal put forward by the Centre Party and accepted by the DVP failed to find a majority in the SPD parliamentary party. The Minister of Labour, Rudolf Wissell (SPD), and the trade unions saw unemployment insurance as the backstop behind the entire wage-rate system and as the cornerstone of social policy. It constituted the limit 'beyond which the patience with which the working population and its organisations put up with national–political considerations on the part of Social Democracy is exhausted'.[19] This inflexible stance was backed by the left wing of the party, which had already argued at the last party conference in favour of terminating the coalition. But for the party leadership too a government led by Social Democrats had made all the concessions it could. In the circumstances a majority within the parliamentary party rejected the compromise on 27 March 1930. The Centre Party and above all the German People's Party, which deliberately occasioned the break with the Social Democrats in order to implement its own ideas with regard to financial and social policy,[20] took the SPD's decision as a pretext for dismantling the coalition. The Müller Cabinet, the last government formed in accordance with the constitution, resigned the same day. The death struggle of the Weimar Republic had begun.

19. *Gewerkschaftszeitung*, No. 14, 4 April 1930, p. 209.
20. Thus, for example, internal remarks by the DVP chairman, Ernst Scholz; see Werner Conze and Hans Raupach (eds), *Die Staats- und Wirtschaftskrise des Deutschen Reichs 1929/33* (Stuttgart, 1967), p. 198, and Klaus Mammach, 'Der Sturz der grossen Koalition im März 1930', in *Zeitschrift für Geschichtswissenschaft*, XVI, 1968, No. 5, pp. 574, 579.

# 8

# The Destruction of Democracy in Germany

## 1. Elements of the Political and Social Crisis of the Early 1930s

The destruction of the Weimar Democracy and the seizure of political power by the National Socialists had many causes:[1] domestic and foreign, economic and social, rational and emotional, objective and subjective. Few if any of those in positions of political responsibility at the time can be completely exonerated from all guilt — and that includes the representatives of Social Democracy. Yet the extent and nature of their guilt, as of their failure, cover so vast a span that it is out of the question to look for a common denominator. That span reaches from active champions of the National Socialist regime on the one hand, through such men as Alfred Hugenberg of the German Nationalists, who deliberately encouraged Hitler as a public agitator, financial backers from industrial circles, and judges, scientists, and teachers who supported Hitler either directly or indirectly, all the way to the Communist Party, which directed its main thrust against Social Democracy in the belief that it, the KPD, would inherit the National Socialist vote. Anti-democratic tendencies in the middle class and in the so-called 'parties of the centre' prepared the soil in which National Socialism was able to grow.

If we look at the general election results for the period 1919 to 1933 we find that — with the exception of the National Assembly, which was a special case — the parties that championed the Weimar Republic never in fact managed to capture more than half of the vote. In the elections of 14 September 1930, 31 July 1932, 6 November 1932, and 5 March 1933 — the last of which, held after the National Socialists had seized power, was seriously interfered with — this democratic substance shrank even further. The SPD dropped from 29.8 per cent in

1. See especially Erich Matthias and Rudolf Morsey (eds.), *Das Ende der Parteien 1933* (Düsseldorf, 1960); and Karl Dietrich Bracher, *Die Auflösung der Weimarer Republik, Eine Studie zum Problem des Machtverfalls*, fourth edition (Villingen, 1964).

1928 to 24.5 per cent in 1930 and 21.6 and 20.4 per cent respectively in July and November 1932; in 1933, with Hitler already in power, it collected no more than 18.3 per cent of the vote. The German Democratic Party, which in 1930 began calling itself the German State Party (*Deutsche Staatspartei*), had almost completely disappeared by November 1932, when it captured a mere 1 per cent. The Centre Party, on the other hand, hung on to almost the whole of its Catholic vote in the four elections held between 1930 and 1933 (11.8, 12.5, 11.9, and 11.2 per cent, compared with 13.6 per cent in 1924 and 12.1 per cent in 1928). Politically, however, it had effected a change of course, with the new leadership elected at the 1928 conference in Cologne steering the party in a markedly conservative–nationalist direction. Its doing so echoed a development that its Bavarian sister party had already undergone much earlier. The German People's Party, which had joined the Hermann Müller government only after a tough struggle and which profited mainly from the respect accorded to Gustav Stresemann (until the latter's death in 1929), declined to the status of an insignificant splinter-group in the elections after 1930 (1.2 per cent in July and 1.9 per cent in November 1932).

To the right of the DVP was the DNVP or German National People's Party. The conservative, monarchist forces so strongly represented in it at first were pushed right into the background following the election of Alfred Hugenberg as chairman of the party in 1928. After the withdrawal of a moderate wing under Count Westarp in 1930 the party was recast as the 'Hugenberg Movement'. A structure based on the *Führer* principle, the activation of *Kampfstaffeln* or 'combat squadrons', and deliberate undermining of the democratic political order determined the direction of the party from this point on. Its election results had been describing a falling curve since 1924. In 1928 it still had 14.2 per cent of the vote, but after that the figure dropped sharply (7 per cent in 1930, 5.9 per cent in July 1932, 8.5 per cent in November 1932, and 8 per cent in 1933).

In Adolf Hitler's National Socialist movement, the DNVP faced a rival that outdid it both in unscrupulousness and in propaganda skills. Racist groups, among which National Socialism soon took the lead, first entered the Reichstag after the May 1924 election, in which they collected 6.5 per cent of the vote. In the years of economic and — comparatively speaking — political stabilisation, their share fell to 3 per cent in December 1924 and 2.6 per cent in 1928. But then it went rocketing up: 18.3 per cent in September 1930, 37.4 per cent in July 1932, and finally, after dropping to 33.1 per cent in November 1932, a massive 43.9 per cent in the atmosphere of intimidation and terror surrounding the election of 5 March 1933.

If we compare the curves of the National Socialists and the Communists we find certain parallels. After a decline in the period of stabilisation, the KPD's share of the vote rose to 13.1 per cent in 1930, 14.3 per cent in July 1932, and 16.9 per cent in November 1932. At the last election in March 1933 the KPD, which was the party worst affected by the National Socialists' terror tactics, dropped back to 12.3 per cent.

Both of these extremist groups, which radically challenged the existing political order and fought it with every means at their disposal, profited from the economic catastrophe that plunged the republic into unimaginable hardship and distress. By January 1930 there were already more than 3.2 million registered unemployed. After dropping to 2.7 million in July of that year the figure leapt to 4.887 million in January 1931 and 6.042 million and 6.014 million in January 1932 and January 1933 respectively. The highest level of unemployment was recorded in February 1932 with 6.128 million, though the actual figure was probably some 600,000 higher than that. Only about 12.7 million workers and salaried employees were still in employment, and several million of those were on short time. Averaged out over the year, 43.8 per cent of trade-union members were out of work in 1932 and a further 22.6 per cent were affected by short-time working.

After queuing for hours people who through no fault of their own found themselves plunged into destitution were finally paid their relief against a stamp on their dole cards. Up until June 1932 this was fixed at a level that was halfway adequate for subsistence. Then, however, the Cabinet of Franz von Papen, which ruled without parliament, backed only by the field marshal in the presidential chair, reduced the rate to a level below the minimum necessary for survival. For instance, a family of two adults and one child received 51 marks monthly, of which 32.50 marks went on rent, heating and light. That left 18.50 marks for food, which at current prices meant a per capita ration of half a loaf, a pound of potatoes, 100 grammes of cabbage, and 50 grammes of margarine. Three times a month the parents were able to purchase a cheap herring, and for the child they could even have an extra herring as well as half a litre of milk daily.

Comparatively speaking, such a family was much better off than many others. The reason for this was that unemployment relief, including a so-called 'crisis provision', was paid out for a maximum of one year. In February 1932 some 12.6 per cent of unemployed persons were receiving no relief whatever. A total of 29.9 per cent or 1.833 million people who were no longer receiving unemployment benefit or who like many poor, old, young, and formerly self-employed people had never joined the social-insurance scheme, were dependent on local public assistance. In many places this was not even sufficient to buy food, let alone pay for accommodation. Sleeping rough or at best in waiting-rooms or asylums for the homeless, people scraped along from one day to the next, waiting for a miracle that would put an end to poverty. They had long since given up any hopes they may have had in the government.

After the break-up of the 'Great Coalition' under Hermann Müller various elements in politics, the economy, and the army felt that the time had come for a 'Cabinet of the right' invested with special powers. By-passing parliament, this was to take things firmly in hand either through the medium of an Enabling Law or with the backing of the President. While a number of entrepreneurs, principally from the finished-goods sector of industry, had come to terms with a partnership system between capital and labour, others saw the 'trade-union state' as an obstacle to the full deployment of their economic power. Heavy industry in particular therefore gave its support mainly to associations and parties that promised to exercise control over the working population by means of an authoritarian form of government.

In mid-January 1930, with the Hermann Müller government still in power, Hindenburg was quite clear in his mind about the kind of Cabinet he wanted. It would be (a) anti-parliamentary, avoiding the need for the usual coalition negotiations, and (b) 'anti-Marxist', in order to exclude any Social Democratic influence. The Braun government in Prussia was likewise to be replaced by a Cabinet along these same lines.

In 30 March the field marshal and those who thought like him were able to regard their objective of a 'Hindenburg Cabinet' as achieved with the appointment of the Centre Party deputy Heinrich Brüning. The President empowered the new Chancellor to dissolve an unco-operative *Reichstag* and gave him a mandate, based on the constitution's sinister clause 48, to govern by emergency decree. As soon as the first major trial of strength occurred, when the *Reichstag* rejected Brüning's emergency decrees by a narrow majority, that body was simply dissolved — in clear contradiction to the spirit of the constitution.

Those who profited from the subsequent election, held on 14 September 1930 in the shadow of the economic crisis, Brüning's policy of strict economies, and a wave of nationalist disturbances, were the radical opponents of the democratic republic: the Communists to some extent, but to a far greater extent the National Socialists, who shot from 12 to 107 seats in the Reichstag. Brüning's government — 'above the parties' and backed by the President — fell when the field marshal withdrew his confidence in it on 29 May 1932 after some prompting from General Schleicher and under pressure from the large landowners of East Elbia.

The new Cabinet, under the ultra-conservative Papen, once a member of the Centre Party, pursued a course of open confrontation with parliament. This was government against the parties and no longer any pretended 'government above the parties'.[2] By abrogating the SA bans imposed by the Brüning Cabinet (see below), Papen let the terror of the 'Brown Army' loose on the streets once more. This time it was worse than ever. Dictatorship plans and the coup of 20 July 1932 that removed the Prussian government under Otto Braun (SPD) from office marked the political course of the 'Cabinet of barons'. On 1 December Papen was toppled, chiefly at the insistence of the army. For two months Hindenburg now, as he put it, let 'Mr [General] von Schleicher try his luck, in God's name'.[3] The general had no luck. On 30 January 1933 the ex-field marshal launched another government, this time under Adolf Hitler, with the words: 'And now, gentlemen, onward with God!'[4] They went onward all right — into the National Socialist dictatorship.

In the period of the Presidential Cabinets the National Socialists not only became the largest single party; they also became, for very large segments of the middle-class party spectrum, a potential party of government. The first to extend the hand of friendship to the Hitler movement was the chairman of the DNVP, Alfred Hugenberg. In a 'National Committee against the Young Plan' Hugenberg and Franz Seldte, the leader of a nationalist military organisation of former 'front-line soldiers' called *Stahlhelm* ('Steel Helmet'), joined together with Hitler to launch an unparalleled smear campaign against the republic and its representatives. A plebiscite initiated by the National Committee threatening those responsible for signing the Young Plan with imprisonment was not exactly a success, attracting only 13.8 per cent of votes cast.

The ones to profit from this co-operation were Hitler and his movement, which now started to impinge upon the awareness of broad sections of the population with all the instruments of demagogy. In the wake of the catastrophic economic crisis a mass influx of support began. Despite its name, the National Socialist German Workers' Party (NSDAP) never numbered more than a relatively small proportion of workers among its members and voters. Particularly Social

2. Karl Dietrich Bracher, *Deutschland zwischen Demokratie und Diktatur* (Bern/Munich, 1964), p. 45.

3. Franz Von Papen, *Der Wahrheit eine Gasse* (Munich, 1952), p. 240.

4. Quoted in Theodor Duesterberg, *Der Stahlhelm und Hitler* (Wolfenbüttel/Hanover, 1949), p. 41.

Democrats and those who were organised in Christian trade unions proved immune. The NSDAP drew first and foremost on the broad spectrum of 'the middle class and petty bourgeoisie', people who had been thrown off course by the war and by subsequent economic crises and who felt equally threatened by capitalism and Socialism alike. Small businesspeople, middle- and low-grade white-collar workers, schoolteachers, and students were particularly well represented in its ranks. As unemployment mounted, National Socialism increasingly cast its spell over the so-called 'unpoliticals' and in particular over large numbers of young people. When the latter left school or finished their training they looked in vain for work and in desperation turned to those who promised not only work and bread but power and greatness. People who were inwardly insecure and lacked firm social or religious ties felt particularly at home in the NSDAP. The 'Movement' compensated for their own inferiority complexes and provided an outlet for their aggressions. Jealousy and prejudice, anger and hatred, violence and destructiveness could all be vented to the full here, provided only that they were targeted at the enemy: the Jews, Bolshevism, Social Democracy, and the entire 'system'.

Instead of forming a united front against National Socialism, more and more parts of that 'system' became permeated with Fascism. Not surprisingly, National Socialism managed to gain a foothold in the army, that 'state within the state', where it was mainly the young officer corps who sympathised with the party's military-minded and aggressive ideas. But even among the army leadership there were signs of a certain interest in the NSDAP. With the knowledge of Chancellor Brüning, General von Schleicher approached Hitler and Röhm to examine the possibility of a 'strong national government of the right'.[5] The government took virtually no action at first against the party's vile terrorist excesses, Brüning wanting to win over the National Socialists for Hindenburg in the presidential election due in 1932.

Things turned out otherwise. Hitler — as well as Ernst Thälmann for the KPD and Theodor Duesterberg of the *Stahlhelm* — stood against Hindenburg on 13 March 1932. In the second ballot, held on 10 April 1932, the field marshal came out on top with 53 per cent of the votes cast (equivalent to 19.3 million), beating Hitler into second place (36.8 per cent or 13.4 million) and Thälmann into third (10.2 per cent or 3.7 million). In addition to the German People's Party and the Bavarian People's Party, which had already supported Hindenburg in 1925, a reversal of the fronts now brought the Centre Party, the

5. See the note made by Major General Curt Liebmann on 25 October 1930; reprinted in *Vierteljahrshefte für Zeitgeschichte*, 2 (1954), pp. 406ff.

German Democratic Party, and the SPD behind him too. But while the Centre Party extolled Hindenburg as the 'rock of national security' and as the 'saviour' and 'leader [*Führer*] of the German nation',[6] the SPD justified its decision with the watchword 'Against Hitler'. From this standpoint even the victory of Hindenburg was a victory for the republic.

Once again the National Socialist onslaught on the state had been halted. In April 1932 it even looked as if the government was about to rouse itself to vigorous defensive measures. At the insistence of the state governments, who felt they could no longer look on inactive while National Socialist bully-boys spread terror and murder in the streets, the party's military organisations — the *Sturmabteilung* (SA) and the *Schutzstaffel* (SS) — were banned. Following Brüning's resignation as Chancellor, the 'new boy', Franz von Papen, could not wait to dissolve the *Reichstag* and lift the ban on the SA and the SS. Papen was paying the price for the Nazis' toleration of him negotiated by General von Schleicher.

At the subsequent general election of 31 July the NSDAP secured 37.4 per cent of the vote and became easily the largest party. Much to his annoyance, however, Hitler still did not become Chancellor. Despite the brutal murder of a Polish Communist worker in his home in the Silesian village of Potempa (10 August 1932), when Hitler went out of his way to back the SA men responsible, the Centre Party did in fact conduct lengthy coalition negotiations with him and Göring, but in the end these came to nothing. Papen stayed, although the *Reichstag* expressed its lack of confidence in him by 512 votes to 42. Rather than resign he used the 'blank cheque' given him by the President to dissolve the *Reichstag*.

In the ensuing election (November 1932) the National Socialists dropped 4.3 percentage points, while the KPD for its part rose from 14.3 to 16.9 per cent. The Communist leaders saw this as confirming their expectation that NSDAP voters would eventually come over to them. In its political struggle the KPD threw all other political tendencies into a single pot labelled 'monopoly capitalism'. It did launch some attacks on 'National Fascism' (the NSDAP), but its main thrust was directed at 'Social Fascism' (the SPD). Even after the 1932 general elections, when Social Democracy managed to draw no more than something over 20 per cent of the vote, the Communists continued to attack the SPD as 'the social mainstay of the bourgeoisie'. From its analysis of the voting figures it concluded that 'the importance of the

6. See, for example, *Schulthess' Europäischer Geschichtskalender 1932*, p. 59; and *Das Zentrum* (news-sheet of the German Centre Party, Berlin), 3, 1932, pp. 89f.

SPD for the Fascist policy of finance capital' had in fact increased.[7] The deputy chairman of the KPD, Heinz Neumann, who wanted to direct the struggle more firmly against the Nazis under the slogan 'Hit the Fascists wherever you meet them!', was dismissed from office in the autumn of 1932 and his action condemned as 'sectarian'. The leading group around Ernst Thälmann held unswervingly to the tactical line dictated by Moscow. In August 1931, when the NSDAP and the DNVP in Prussia launched a petition for a referendum to have the SPD-led Braun government dismissed, the KPD gave them its backing, and when Berlin's transport workers took strike action at the beginning of November 1932 the party did not shrink from once again collaborating with the National Socialists. Fascists and Communists patrolled the streets side by side in an obvious manifestation of their common hostility to the republic and to Social Democracy in particular.

To left and right, as far as the eye could see, troops stood ready to deliver the death-blow to a democracy already hollowed out from within. Naked Fascism, Stalinist Communism, authoritarian power-hunger, and dreams of national supremacy threatened the republic from every side. Where there was not open hostility, the dominant elements were either a willingness to drift with the times or a mood of resignation. After the end of the Müller government and the transition to the presidential Cabinets of Brüning, Papen, and Schleicher 'Social Democracy stood out as the only consistent defender of the democratic constitution and the parliamentary system'.[8]

## 2. Social Democracy on the Defensive

After Brüning's appointment as Chancellor and the formation of his 'government above the parties', the Social Democratic parliamentary party at first pulled back into an oppositional posture along pre-war lines. In July 1930 there was an open confrontation when Brüning put his budget proposals into force as emergency decrees although the SPD had been prepared to vote for them on certain conditions. The parliamentary party rightly saw this as an attempt to by-pass the *Reichstag*. Its votes then went to revoke the emergency decrees,

7. See especially Siegfried Bahne, 'Die Kommunistische Partei Deutschlands', in Erich Matthias and Rudolf Morsey (eds), *Das Ende der Parteien 1933*, pp. 674ff.

8. Just one of many scholarly verdicts; see Hans Mommsen, 'Sozialdemokratie in der Defensive. Immobilismus der SPD und der Aufstieg des Nationalsozialismus', in Hans Mommsen (ed.), *Sozialdemokratie zwischen Klassenbewegung und Volkspartei* (Frankfurt a. M., 1974), p. 107.

whereupon the *Reichstag* was promptly dissolved by the Chancellor.

Huge gains by the anti-democratic parties in the general election of September 1930 threw the situation in the *Reichstag* into complete confusion. Of the 577 seats in the house, parties openly hostile to the state (NSDAP, DNVP, KPD) held over 225 or 39.1 per cent. Despite a general aversion to Brüning, whose election campaign had been conducted in terms of clear-cut opposition to the SPD, the party became imbued with the idea 'that in the current political situation there was no other course open to us but to support Brüning if we wished to prevent the National Socialists from snatching the leadership'.[9] The priorities at this time as far as the Social Democratic parliamentary party was concerned were the preservation of the democratic order, the safeguarding of the constitution, and the protection of a parliamentary system that was already badly holed. The policy of tolerating the Brüning Cabinet and its emergency decrees was regarded as the 'lesser evil'. At a purely theoretical level there was still the possibility of forming a parliamentary majority from the broad spectrum of parties lying between the KPD on the one hand and the DNVP and the NSDAP on the other. In practice, however, there was no question of the 72 deputies belonging to the splinter parties — most of them representing economic interest-groups — or of the 30 deputies belonging to the DVP ever collaborating with Social Democracy. Fearing that Brüning would otherwise seek NSDAP support or be replaced by a frankly right-wing Cabinet made up of all the country's reactionary and Fascist forces or by a dictatorship, Social Democracy got itself into a tighter and tighter corner. It had to accept unpopular emergency and economy measures that were passionately rejected by its supporters and allow laws to be passed that served the interests of the big landowners and no one else.

What other course could it possibly have adopted? Certainly not the one advocated by a handful of members, who believed that 'the right must be allowed to reach government in order that it may bring about its own collapse and that of the National Socialists along with it'.[10] Otto Braun's plea for a 'great coalition of men of good sense' and for linking central government closely with the Prussian state government was doomed to failure simply by Brüning's inability to change his mind about Social Democracy. But there was little readiness for such a solution even within the ranks of the SPD, given the competition represented by the Communists and pressure from the party's own left

9. As Wilhelm Keil admitted in late September 1930; quoted in Erich Matthias, 'Die Sozialdemokratische Partei Deutschlands', in Erich Matthias and Rudolf Morsey (eds), *Das Ende der Parteien 1933*, p. 106.

10. See Otto Braun, *Von Weimar zu Hitler* (New York, 1940), p. 308.

wing. At the 1931 party conference in Leipzig it became quite clear that the majority still placed its faith in a tactics of toleration. Even the young Wilhelm Hoegner, who warned his comrades against underestimating Fascism, ended by backing this course in decisive terms: 'Fascism is certainly not an enemy with whom we can comfortably cross swords. It is an enemy that seeks to go straight for our throat and is out to murder everything that is sacred to us: peace among nations, democratic equality, the working-class struggle for emancipation. We must therefore subordinate everything — even the tactics, indeed especially the tactics of the Social Democratic parliamentary party — to the requirements of this campaign against our most powerful enemy.'[11]

Similarly the SPD managed, despite internal opposition, to persuade itself to support Hindenburg in the 1932 presidential election. Its campaign statement of 27 February 1932 said: 'Hitler in place of Hindenburg means chaos and panic in Germany and throughout Europe, the utmost aggravation of the economic crisis and of unemployment, and the very greatest risk of bloody clashes both at home and abroad. Hitler in place of Hindenburg means: the victory of the reactionary section of the bourgeoisie over the progressive section of the middle class and over the working class, the destruction of all civic freedoms, the press, and political, trade-union, and cultural organisations, and increased exploitation and wage-slavery. Against Hitler! That is the slogan for 13 March.'[12]

In terms of that statement even the re-election of Hindenburg was a success that ought not to be under-rated. The replacement of Brüning by Papen and the outcome of the election of the Prussian state diet in April 1932, when the coalition parties supporting the Braun government lost their majority, together destroyed any nascent hopes that the crisis could be overcome. The onslaught of the anti-democratic forces was no longer to be repulsed by parliamentary and purely formal democratic means alone. Tendencies had long been in evidence, both within the SPD and alongside it, that called for the deployment of non-parliamentary weapons against 'reaction' and Fascism.

As on the occasion of the general-strike debate in the early years of the century, these calls for increased activity once again came mainly from the wings of the party — both left and right. In 1917 the Göttingen philosopher and mathematician Leonard Nelson had launched an organisation called the International Youth League. Ex-

11. *Sozialdemokratischer Parteitag in Leipzig 1931 vom 31. Mai bis 5. Juni 1931 im Volkshaus, Protokoll* (Berlin, 1931), p. 134.

12. Quoted in Walter Tormin (ed.), *Die Weimarer Republik* (Hanover, 1962), p. 214.

pelled from the *Sozialistische Arbeiterjugend* (SAJ; 'Socialist Labour Youth') and from the party in 1925, this body had founded the *Internationaler Sozialistischer Kampfbund* (ISK; 'International Socialist Fighting Alliance'). The ISK, whose theoretical course was a non-Marxist one taking its bearings from Kant, rejected the 'opportunism' of the SPD leadership and advocated a united front of the SPD and the KPD in the fight against right-wing radicalism.[13]

The same sort of aggressive activism in the defence of the democratic republic was shown by the *Sozialistische Arbeiterpartei Deutschlands* (SAPD: 'Socialist Labour Party of Germany'), founded in October 1931 under the chairmanship of three deputies, Max Seydewitz, Kurt Rosenfeld, and Heinrich Ströbel.[14] The poor electoral performance of this party, of which a Lübeck schoolboy named Willy Brandt became a member, may have been due primarily to the fact that traditional decision-patterns and organisational loyalties had more influence on the way people voted than criticism of and dissatisfaction with the party leadership.[15]

On the right wing of the party the so-called 'Hofgeismar Circle' of Young Socialists worked for a theoretical and practical reorientation of SPD policy. Their ideas aimed at a deliberately nationalist approach based on the concept of the *Volksgemeinschaft* or 'national community'. Other young reformists fought the immobilism of the party leadership. They called for a consistent, militant programme of action on behalf of democracy. The men who led them, for example Carlo Mierendorff, Julius Leber, Theodor Haubach, and Kurt Schumacher, risked their freedom and their lives under the National Socialist dictatorship in the struggle for a different Germany.

The emergence of new organisations such as the ISK and splinter groups such as the SAPD as well as the demand, particularly by the party's youth, for a more active course revealed a general unease at the rigidity and obsolescence of the party machine. Theodor Haubach noted that the criticism voiced by the *Young Socialist Press* and the *New Press for Socialism* was combated by the party's executive committee with considerable ruthlessness.[16] The anathema of disciplinary measures was directed both against right-wing and against left-wing opposition, the latter being too hastily equated with proximity to

13. On the subject of the ISK, see Werner Link, *Die Geschichte des Internationalen Jugend-Bundes (IJB) und des Internationalen Sozialistischen Kampfbundes (ISK)* (Meisenheim, 1964).
14. On the SAP, see Hanno Drechsler, *Die Sozialistische Arbeiterpartei Deutschlands (SAPD)* (Meisenheim, 1965).
15. See the essay by Hans Mommsen referred to in note 8 above.
16. See Hans Mommsen, as above. The publications in question were the *Jungsozialistische Blätter* and the *Neue Blätter für den Sozialismus*.

Communism. The fact that these critical wings occasionally found themselves in alliance against the centre of the party shows that the clashes had little to do with differences of opinion between pragmatic reformers and revolutionary Marxists. The dividing line tended to run between those who demanded action, whether from the right or from the left, and those who clung to the idea of historical inevitability and to the traditional tactics of Social Democracy. The political mentality of the latter was shaped by their experiences of imperial Germany; they thought in terms of power residing in organisation. Discipline and the unity of the movement were values that they were not prepared lightly to place at risk. Cautious manoeuvring, tolerating the lesser evil, and waiting for the next election constituted for them the yardstick of political action.

Not even the meteoric rise of the National Socialist vote on 14 September 1930 provoked any drastic change of policy, as Julius Leber bitterly criticised.[17] The grass-roots membership of the SPD reacted differently. Among them this alarm signal released a wave of militancy; here was no resignation but a stiffening of defensive resolve. Particularly the young refused to be content with the old familiar methods but insisted that the party take up a determined stance to defend democracy against the Nazi civil-war troops.

The 'league of republican front-line soldiers' known as the *Reichsbanner Schwarz-Rot-Gold* (named after the colours of the Weimar flag), which was founded by the SPD, the Centre Party, and the German Democratic Party in 1924, came to form the backbone of these endeavours.[18] Only six days after the September 1930 election the *Reichsbanner*, which in practice had increasingly evolved into a Social Democratic fighting force for the protection of the republic, decided to set up a combat-effective crack unit, the *Schufo* (short for *Schutzformationen* or 'protective formations'). The trade union movement began to set up similar units, known as *Hammerschaften*. Towards the end of 1931 the democratic combat units of the SPD, the trade unions, and the workers' athletic organisations amalgamated to form the 'Iron Front'. The effect of this initiative on the 'nameless masses of the old Bebel party', Julius Leber tells us, was like that of 'an old and half-forgotten charge signal on a battle-hardened body of men accustomed to victory'.[19] The Iron Front organised mass meetings to demonstrate the readiness of the Social Democratic membership to put

17. Julius Leber, *Ein Mann geht seinen Weg* (Berlin, 1952), p. 238.
18. On the *Reichsbanner*, see Karl Rohe, *Das Reichsbanner Schwarz Rot Gold. Ein Beitrag zur Geschichte und Struktur der politischen Kampfverbände zur Zeit der Weimarer Republik* (Düsseldorf, 1966).
19. Julius Leber, *Ein Mann geht seinen Weg*, p. 240.

up a fight. In addition to preparations for self-defence and the protection of party and trade-union premises, in certain places — Magdeburg was a good example — more comprehensive defensive measures were put in hand to deal with an eventual civil-war situation. The rousing effect of all this determination was reflected right up to the call issued by the parliamentary party for labour organisations to hold themselves in readiness to give the parliamentary battle for democracy and the safeguarding of social interests 'all appropriate means of support'.[20] In so far as anyone was contemplating actually using extra-parliamentary means they were thinking of the party and trade union organisations. The Iron Front, on the other hand, like the *Reichsbanner* in earlier years, continued to be regarded with a degree of mistrust that it never entirely overcame. This resulted not least from a certain element of competition but also from reservations regarding the character of an extra-parliamentary fighting organisation and regarding the individual use of violence in general.

This inner weakness due to cautious reserve was supplemented by another. Even the organisers of precautionary measures against an emergency took it for granted that they could count on the help of a functioning, democratic police force.

Their hopes rested particularly on the republican 'bulwark' of Prussia, where with Carl Severing as Minister of the Interior and Albert Grzesinski as chief constable of Berlin Social Democrats sat at the controls as far as the police were concerned. However, this 'stronghold' was wrested from them in the course of a single day. After the Prussian election of 24 April 1932, when the coalition parties lost their majority, the Cabinet remained in office — as was the case in other states too — purely as a caretaker government. A discouraged Otto Braun, who apart from this episode was distinguished among the politicians of the Weimar period for his energy and resolution, departed on sick leave on 6 June with the 'firm intention of never returning to office'.[21] After the election defeat, feeling no solid ground under his feet anymore, he suffered a personal collapse.

On 20 July 1932 Papen ventured the decisive blow. He lured the members of the Prussian Cabinet into the Chancellery and with the aid of the 'blank cheque' given him by Hindenburg announced the dismissals of Braun and Severing. The burden of responsibility at that moment lay chiefly on the shoulders of Carl Severing, the Minister of the Interior. Severing responded to this unconstitutional dismissal and

20. Quoted in *Der Kochel-Brief*, May/June 1955, p. 43. See also Erich Matthias, 'Die Sozialdemokratische Partei Deutschlands', in Erich Matthias and Rudolf Morsey (eds), *Das Ende der Parteien 1933*, p. 121.
21. Otto Braun, *Von Weimar zu Hitler*, p. 396.

the assumption of governmental authority by *Reichskommissar* von Papen, who had virtually no parliamentary backing, with the proud words that he would give way only to force.[22] All forewarnings notwithstanding, Papen's subsequent declaration of a state of emergency for Berlin and its environs and his placing of the Prussian police under the local army command passed off without a hitch. Following the arrest of the chief constable of Berlin and the police commander, Severing vacated his desk that same evening. The ruthless violence of Papen's approach was in stark contrast to the behaviour of the SPD.

The executive committee of the party had concerned itself with the threatened action against Prussia four days before, eventually allowing itself to be reassured by the reply from the Chancellery that nothing was planned 'for the present moment'. There had been warnings in plenty. Nevertheless, the news of the 'Prussian blow' hit the small number of men assembled on 20 July — Otto Wels of the executive committee, Franz Künstler of the Berlin party organisation, Theodor Leipart, chairman of the ADGB, and the head of the *Reichsbanner*, Karl Höltermann — with paralysing force. Otto Wels described the moment: 'The effect of the news was depressing. There was not a word of indignation, no visible sign of anger. I had the impression that we were all at a loss as to what was to be done.'[23] Those present at the meeting passed a negative verdict on the chances of a political general strike. It would face the opposition of the National Socialists and the Communists as well as the power of the state with the army at its head. A general strike, it was felt, would simply usher in an immediate military dictatorship and jeopardise the election due in eleven days' time. With Wels issuing the watchword 'Safeguard the general elec-. tion' the meeting broke up.

The key importance of that day for the end of democracy in Germany is undoubtedly one reason why the Social Democrats who occupied positions of decisive political responsibility at that time should afterwards have sought excuses. Probably each of them, in that exceptional situation, expected that one of the others would dare to take the crucial step. Yet neither Otto Wels and the executive committee nor Otto Braun and Carl Severing of the Prussian state government nor Leipart and the ADGB nor Karl Höltermann of the Iron Front was prepared to do so. The prospects for a political general strike were unquestionably poor in view of the vast numbers of unemployed. The effect of a

22. On this and what follows, see especially Hans J. L. Adolph, *Otto Wels und die Politik der deutschen Sozialdemokratie 1894–1939* (Berlin, 1971), pp. 240ff.
23. Handwritten notes by Otto Wels entitled 'Um den 20. Juli 1932. Einige Erinnerungen'; quoted in Hans J. L. Adolph, *Otto Wels und die Politik der deutschen Sozialdemokratie 1894–1939*, p. 243.

show of power by the Iron Front was likewise uncertain: it might easily spark off a civil war and lead to failure. Yet there is a wealth of evidence that in many places units of the Iron Front were waiting for the order to march — as workers in factories up and down the country were hoping for the signal to stage a general strike. They waited and hoped in vain: the trumpet-call summoning them to save the republic never came. No one in the leadership dared take the responsibility for being 'courageous at the comrades' expense', as Severing put it.[24] The apparent hopelessness of active resistance and their fear of possible bloodshed paralysed the resolution of trade unionists and party leaders alike. Moulded by a long humanitarian and democratic tradition, brought up to a politics of sober realism and the avoidance of experiment, and firmly anchored in the belief that their first task was to keep their own organisations as intact as possible, they took their case to the Constitutional Court and appealed in time-honoured fashion to the power of the ballot paper in the forthcoming election of 31 July 1932.

That election brought the National Socialists their biggest success — apart from what was no longer a free election in March 1933. Encouraged by the ease with which Papen carried out his coup in Prussia, the anti-democratic forces of the right relied more than ever on the surprise tactics and cold-blooded violence leading them to their objective. Joseph Goebbels' diary entry for 20 July 1932 typified their approach: 'Everything is going according to plan . . . We need only show the Reds our teeth and they'll knuckle under.' The next day he wrote: 'The Reds have missed their big moment. It will never come again.'[25] National Socialism saw for its part that the moment had come to launch the decisive assault on the republic.

Democracy's determination to assert itself, on the other hand, had received a mortal blow as a result of the absence of any vigorous defensive action on 20 July. Nothing — not even failure — could have had a more paralysing effect than that surrender without a struggle by the Social Democratic and trade union leadership. Yet there is one thing we must bear in mind if we wish to reach a just verdict here. The principles laid down in the Weimar constitution were in fact, in 1932, at home only within Social Democracy, the most reliable and the most consistent force for parliamentary democracy in Germany. Yet the party was strong only in comparison with the other democratic tendencies, which were barely clinging to life. With its share of the vote in 1932 lying only just above 20 per cent, Social Democracy was more than ever thrown back on its own resources. The last defenders

24. Carl Severing, *Mein Lebensweg*, Vol. 2 (Cologne, 1950), pp. 347ff.
25. Joseph Goebbels, *Vom Kaiserhof zur Reichskanzlei* (Munich, 1934), pp. 131ff.

of the constitution and of the democratic system in Germany saw no way out of the dilemma. They consoled themselves with the thought that the SPD 'has been through bad times before' and in the course of its development 'triumphed over many dangers. . . , overcome many enemies'.[26] Hard pressed from all sides, Social Democracy found itself fighting on two main fronts: with Socialist slogans against the social injustice of the capitalist system and with rational, democratic slogans against the irrational political agitation of Fascism. Its deep-rooted belief in the principles of good sense and humanity and of democracy and the rule of law actually prevented it from grasping the true essence of the National Socialist movement. For all the party's passionate condemnation of National Socialism, few in its ranks recognised the totalitarian character of German Fascism, which had no intention of abiding by the principles of law and freedom but rode rough-shod over them and made unscrupulous use of violence, terrorism, and murder against all who opposed it. The few months that were left to Social Democracy after the Prussian coup really gave it no further opportunity to mount a last-ditch defence against Hitler's bid for power. The *Machtübernahme* or 'seizure of power' on 30 January 1933 brought the darkness of dictatorship down over Germany.

26. Thus, for example, Rudolf Breitscheid in his address to the 1931 party conference in Leipzig entitled 'The overcoming of Fascism'; see *Sozialdemokratischer Parteitag in Leipzig 1931 vom 31. Mai bis 5. Juni 1931 im Volkshaus, Protokoll* (Berlin, 1931), pp. 119ff.

# 9
# In the Fight for a Better Germany

## 1. Against Totalitarian Co-ordination

On the afternoon and evening of 30 January 1933, as the streets reverberated to the sound of marching columns of SA troops, drunk with victory, many German cities saw spontaneous mass demonstrations against Hitler by the Socialist working population. Next day the federal committee of the ADGB, the central party council and the executive committee of the SPD, the members of the parliamentary party, and representatives of the Iron Front gathered for a meeting in Berlin. The outcome of that meeting appeared to have been an acceptance that the stage was finally set for action. Feverish preparations were made for mass action despite constant street checks by the SA acting as auxiliary police; all that people were waiting for was the promised signal for the central event. Many groups slept in their clothes for nights on end, expecting at every moment to get the green light for insurrection. But the reign of terror imposed by the National Socialists with all the power of the state began to have a visibly depressing effect on the will to resist. On 28 February, the day after the *Reichstag* fire, Hindenburg's decree 'For the protection of people and state' removed a number of important basic rights. The National Socialist tyranny was able to spread with less and less restraint. The Communist Party was banned; the Social Democratic press was muzzled during the election campaign and many party officials were maltreated or arrested. Despite all these difficulties, in the general election of 5 March 1933 the Social Democratic vote held up almost entirely. A total of 7.181 million voters — only 66,400 fewer than in November 1932 — had the courage even now to stand by their party. Some 4.8 million still voted for the KPD, but the party's 81 seats were simply taken away from it by arbitrary decree of the regime and many of its deputies and leading officials were arrested.

On 23 March 1933 Hitler received from a rump *Reichstag* sitting in the Kroll Opera House the crucial foundation on which to erect his totalitarian rule. In addition to the NSDAP and the DNVP, the German People's Party, the German Democratic Party, the Centre

120

Party, the Bavarian People's Party, and the various splinter groups also gave him their consent. Not a single member of those parties voted against the bill; not a single member abstained. Even a motion by the SPD group calling for the release of the arrested deputies was defeated, with the Centre Party voting against it. The parliamentary parties of the so-called 'middle-class centre' had urged the Social Democratic deputies beforehand either to stay away from the session or to abstain in the vote on the Enabling Law. The SPD stood firm, although some of its 120 deputies were already in prison and others had been forced to flee the country. Wilhelm Sollmann, a former Cabinet minister, lay in hospital after being badly beaten up. Julius Leber and Carl Severing were arrested en route to where the *Reichstag* was sitting.[1] The Social Democratic deputies made their way to their seats between lines of SA troops, and when they sat down they were immediately surrounded by armed SS men. Ninety-four members of the SPD parliamentary party were able to take part in that session of the *Reichstag*, and 94 voiced their courageous, unforgettable 'No' to Hitler's Enabling Law.

Otto Wels, the chairman of the party, spoke for them. No amount of warnings had been able to dissuade him from taking this dangerous task upon himself. For a brief moment there was dead silence in the auditorium — while the SA choirs droned on outside — as Otto Wels stepped up to the speaker's desk. Against the National Socialist ethos of violence and terror he set, on behalf of the SPD, the credo: 'Freedom and life may be taken from us, but not our honour.' Braving the death threats of the watching SS, Wels closed his speech with the following profession of faith: 'The Weimar constitution is no Socialist constitution. Yet we stand by the principles of the rule of law, equality of rights, and social justice that are laid down in it. In this historic hour we, the Social Democrats of Germany, solemnly pledge our faith in the principles of humanity and justice, of freedom and Socialism. No enabling law is going to give you the power to annihilate ideas that are eternal and indestructible. You yourselves profess Socialism. The Anti-Socialist Law did not destroy Social Democracy. Fresh persecutions can only give German Social Democracy fresh strength. We salute the persecuted and oppressed. We salute our friends throughout Germany. Their steadfastness and loyalty are worthy of admiration. Their courageous faith and their unbroken confidence are our guarantee of a brighter future.'[2]

That speech by Otto Wels is one of the great historical documents of

---

1. Severing managed to regain his freedom before the end of the session so was able to take part in the vote.
2. *Stenographische Berichte über die Verhandlungen des Deutschen Reichstages*, Vol. 457, pp. 33f.

freedom and humanity, of convictions courageously held, and of the determination to resist. Nevertheless, let us not forget that it still revealed a false estimate of Hitler's Fascism. The much-used comparison — reiterated here by Wels — of the NS regime with the Anti-Socialist Law shows that Social Democrats were scarcely capable of imagining the full horror of totalitarian rule. Many of them continued to hope that the present unconstitutional state of affairs was only temporary and that National Socialism would prove a short-lived episode. Hence the tendency, particularly in the trade unions but also within the party itself, to try everything possible to remain organisationally intact. By distancing itself from the SPD and declaring its neutrality vis-à-vis the state and the regime, the ADGB sought under Leipart's leadership to salvage trade-union independence. This policy of accommodation, which Siegfried Aufhäuser of the AfA had opposed with particular vehemence, was rejected by the party leadership. Nor did it do the trade unions any good. After many union offices had already been attacked in the weeks before 1 May, on 2 May 1933 SA and SS troops suddenly occupied all trade-union premises. Dozens of officials were arrested, maltreated, or — as in Duisburg — murdered.

In the wake of this blow the executive committee of the SPD expected a similarly sudden attack on the party. Otto Braun, Albert Grzesinski, Philipp Scheidemann, Wilhelm Dittmann, Artur Crispien, Rudolf Breitscheid, and Rudolf Hilferding had already had to emigrate; now the executive committee sent three of its members — Otto Wels, Siegmund Crummenerl, and Friedrich Stampfer — to Saarbrücken, which was still under French administration. Only days later Hans Vogel, Erich Ollenhauer, and Paul Hertz had to follow them. When on 17 May 1933 a rump group of the parliamentary party bowed to the death-threats of the NS Minister of the Interior, Wilhelm Frick, and, over-ruling the resistance of a minority, which included Kurt Schumacher, voted for a 'peace resolution' put forward by the Hitler government, they found themselves in conflict with the majority of the executive committee in exile. While many of those left behind in Germany clung like Paul Löbe to the belief that a legal oppositional stance could serve to moderate terrorism, the executive committee in exile, which now chose Prague as its headquarters (and adopted the acronym 'Sopade'), decided that the time had come for open resistance. The gulf that threatened to separate them was quickly bridged.

A certain amount of party property had already been confiscated on 10 May, but then on 22 June 1933 Interior Minister Frick banned the SPD on the grounds that it had not clearly dissociated itself from the 'treasonable' executive committee in exile. The end of any form of legal party work also removed the roots of the conflict between Prague and

Berlin. From now on there were only two possible locations for the fight against Hitler Fascism: underground or in exile.

## 2. Resistance among the Labour Movement

Resistance to Hitler among the German working class has so far aroused little public interest in the post-war Federal Republic, apart from a number of academic studies. A shortage of information and a one-sided concentration on the conspiracy of 20 July 1944 are not the only reasons for this state of affairs. Rather it reflects a specific self-image of the Federal Republic, which in so far as it relates to resistance movements at all does so exclusively to those proceeding from religious, conservative, and military milieux. Working-class resistance of a Socialist or Communist persuasion, to which the other German state — the one led by the Socialist Unity Party — has laid claim for its own purposes, has tended to be overlooked when the Federal Republic is reviewing its traditions.

Under the conditions of totalitarian rule it was not only active resistance that struck at the roots of the system but any kind of oppositional behaviour — from the political joke and listening to foreign radio stations right through to refusing to work and giving support to the victims of persecution. When between three and four thousand party colleagues attended the funeral of the former SPD deputy Clara Bohm-Schuch in May 1936 they not only showed great personal courage but bore demonstrative witness to an unbroken solidarity.[3]

Repressions and enticements notwithstanding, Social Democratic support proved exceptionally stable. How signally National Socialism failed to make any headway among the older organised working population was shown by the works councils elections of April 1933. The early results were so devastating for the so-called 'National Socialist Works Cells Organisation' that the elections were called off.[4] According to a summary of the partial results available, the Free Trade Unions alone received 73.4 per cent of the votes cast. Two years later the elections for the *Vertrauensräte* or consultative works councils held on 12–13 April 1935 turned out so negatively for the NS regime that the authorities resorted to falsifying the published figures. There

---

3. See Frank Moraw, *Die Parole der 'Einheit' und die Sozialdemokratie* (Bonn, 1973), p. 44.
4. On the subject of the works' councils elections, see Theodor Eschenburg, 'Streiflichter zur Geschichte der Wahlen im Dritten Reich, Dokumentation', in *Vierteljahrshefte für Zeitgeschichte*, 3 (1955), pp. 311ff.

was no question of a free and secret ballot. A combination of controls, chicanery, pressure, and manipulation was intended to compel workers to vote for the single list of the *Deutsche Arbeitsfront* (DAF; 'German Labour Front'), the NS monopoly organisation. Yet many still summoned up the courage to vote against the DAF — 68 per cent, for example, at the Schwarz metalworks in Eisenach, 75 per cent at Frankfurt's Municipal Tramcar Company, 50 per cent at the Berlin Allianz combine, 41 per cent at the Klöckner mining combine, 59 per cent at Hapag, the Hamburg shipping firm, 48 per cent at Ullstein Publishers, 51 per cent at the Demag engineering works in Duisburg, 54 per cent at Standard Oil, and 61 per cent at the Erzgebirge Coal-mining Company. The National Socialists never risked another works ballot after that.

The situation reports prepared by the Gestapo clearly reflect the anger of the working population and its widespread criticism of political and social conditions under the NS system. They expose the myth of a united, aggressively determined *Volksgemeinschaft* or 'national community' as a propaganda lie. Granted, such symptoms of discontent are not to be equated with resistance, but the basis for the latter was 'very much broader than outsiders are in a position to suppose and to assess. The organised members of Social Democracy maintained contact throughout the whole period even without their organisation.'[5]

Even before Hitler's seizure of power, various parts of the party machine had begun to prepare themselves for illegal operations in the event of an official ban. Some of the stimulus for this had come from Otto Wels himself. But the decisive push in the direction of forming Social Democratic resistance groups came from local initiatives. From May 1933 onwards groups operating underground rapidly expanded their activities.[6] Without the approval of the SPD rump executive left in Berlin, which clung desperately to legality, party workers in the more left-wing constituencies began to restructure the party for the

5. See Ludwig Bergsträsser, *Geschichte der politischen Parteien in Deutschland*, tenth edition (Munich, 1960), p. 297.
6. On this subject, see especially Richard Löwenthal and Patrik von zur Mühlen (eds), *Widerstand und Verweigerung in Deutschland 1933 bis 1945* (Bonn, 1982); Günter Weisenborn (ed.), *Der lautlose Aufstand. Bericht über die Widerstandsbewegung des deutschen Volkes 1933–1945*, second edition (Hamburg, 1954); Peter Grasmann, *Sozial-demokraten gegen Hitler 1933–1945* (Munich/Vienna, 1976); and Hans-Joachim Reichardt, 'Möglichkeiten und Grenzen des Widerstandes der Arbeiterbewegung', in Walter Schmitthenner and Hans Buchheim (eds), *Der deutsche Widerstand gegen Hitler* (Cologne/Berlin, 1966), pp. 169–213. Two local studies, for example, are Hans-Josef Steinberg, *Widerstand und Verfolgung in Essen 1933–1945* (Hanover, 1969); and Kurt Klotzbach, *Gegen den Nationalsozialismus. Widerstand und Verfolgung in Dortmund 1930–1945* (Hanover, 1969).

fight underground. Other groups, too — particularly from the *Sozia-listische Arbeiterjugend* (SAJ; 'Socialist Labour Youth'), from the *Reichsbanner* and the Iron Front, and from the Social Democratic student movement — sought to remain as closely knit as possible even under the conditions of National Socialist rule. Often only flimsily disguised, they nevertheless stood a rather better chance of pursuing oppositional activities in the early days than older and more prominent Social Democrats who were known to the authorities and to the Nazis. Such men were under suspicion from the outset. Franz Klühs, for example, the deputy editor of *Vorwärts*, soon fell victim to the Nazi state.

The full extent of Social Democratic resistance to the Hitler dicta-torship cannot be measured exactly. An interesting if very fragmentary glimpse is provided by the *White Book of German Opposition to the Hitler Dictatorship* published by the Sopade, as the SPD-in-exile called itself, in 1946.[7] In addition to the capital, Berlin, and the central-German belt of Thuringia and Saxony, where resistance cells were numerous, other important centres of resistance were the Rhine–Main–Neckar region, Stuttgart, Nuremberg, Cologne, and the Ruhr dis-trict. Hanover had a well-organised group calling itself the 'Socialist Front' and operating under the leadership of Werner Blumenberg. The group, which had prepared itself thoroughly for illegal operations even before the Nazi seizure of power, numbered some 3,000 staunch, active comrades. Careful though they were, a great many of these fell into the hands of the Gestapo in 1936, and in a show trial held in the following year more than 200 men and women were given lengthy prison sentences.[8] The 'Red Combat Patrol' — a group similar in structure and numerical strength that was active mainly in the Berlin region — was smashed as early as the end of 1933.

Special importance in the spectrum of resistance from the democra-tic Socialist camp attached to the splinter groups that in 1933 were critical of the party's executive committee or even stood outside the party altogether. With their greater militancy, their more realistic assessment of Fascism, and their organisational structure, which was often based on the cell principle, they were better equipped for the underground fight than were the SPD organisations. How successfully the ISK, for example, managed despite great sacrifices of freedom and life to make its presence felt and to survive was shown by the Gesta-po's situation report for 1937. This spoke of 'considerable activity' and

---

7. *Weissbuch der deutschen Opposition gegen die Hitlerdiktatur* (London, 1946; published by the executive committee of the SPD).
8. See Frank Moraw, *Die Parole der 'Einheit' und die Sozialdemokratie*, p. 37; and Günter Weisenborn (ed.), *Der lautlose Aufstand*, pp. 141, 179.

went on to say: 'A typical feature of ISK pamphlets is a symbol at the end representing a swastika hanging from a gallows.'[9]

In addition to the Socialist Labour Party of Germany,[10] which was based mainly in Saxony, a group that emerged more and more forcefully in these years was one that became known as 'New Beginning'. Originally a secret league of dissident young Communists and critical young Social Democrats, this group gained greater influence in the spring of 1933 when the Berlin-based SAJ switched to illegal operations — at first against the wish of the rump executive of the SPD. Co-operation between the relatively small league and the majority of the Berlin SAJ furnished the basis for an independently operating entity. Led initially by Walter Löwenheim (alias Miles) and later by Richard Löwenthal (alias Paul Sering), the group looked hard and successfully for effective methods of underground activity and for a close working relationship with the party-in-exile.[11] Among those active in this group was a young SAJ official named Fritz Erler. In 1938 he was arrested and in the following year sentenced to ten years' imprisonment. The apparatus of resistance organised on a decentralised basis by 'New Beginning' survived until 1944, when it finally fell victim to the regime. A great many of the leaders of individual groups were executed.

After 2 May 1933 most of the efforts of those opposing the NS regime in the ranks of the trade-union movement went initially towards keeping the structure of their shattered organisation in existence underground. As time went on, another objective gained greater and greater prominence: to bring to people's attention, both at home and abroad, the fact that there was another Germany besides that of the Nazi regime. Particularly active in this endeavour was the International Transport Workers' Federation, supported and encouraged by its general secretary, Edo Fimmen.

The banned Communist movement tried at first to offer resistance on the basis of its old organisational structure. The party's fight against Hitler, waged with exceptional vigour and daring, exacted a heavy toll of lives. The courage of many Communists and their loyalty to their convictions were no protection against a whole series of their resistance cells being infiltrated by informers and Gestapo agents. Mass

9. Quoted in Günter Weisenborn (ed.), *Der lautlose Aufstand*, p. 152.
10. On the SAPD, another source is Jörg Bremer, *Die Sozialistische Arbeiterpartei Deutschlands. Untergrund und Exil 1933–1945* (Frankfurt a. M./New York, 1978).
11. On the *Neu-Beginnen* group, see Kurt Kliem, 'Der sozialistische Widerstand gegen das Dritte Reich, dargestellt an der Gruppe "Neu-Beginnen"', unpublished thesis (Marburg, 1957); and Hans-Joachim Reichardt, 'Neu Beginnen, Ein Beitrag zur Geschichte des Widerstandes der Arbeiterbewegung gegen den Nationalsozialismus', in *Jahrbuch für die Geschichte Mittel-und Ostdeutschlands* (special edition), Vol. 12, 1963.

arrests, the KPD's accommodation to Moscow's 'popular-front strategy', and the abrupt U-turn of the Hitler–Stalin pact shattered the party's base so far as a mass offensive was concerned. Resistance was intensified once again after Hitler had attacked the Soviet Union, but this time it lacked the broad effect it had had before.

An obvious course for all resistance groups, if only for security reasons, was to fall back on previous political and trade-union amalgamations. In addition to the underground organisations of the Social Democratic Party there were others belonging to the Socialist trade unions, the Workers' Athletic League, the *Reichsbanner*, the SAPD, the ISK, 'New Beginning', the Christian trade unions and employers, and the KPD and the Communist trade-union opposition. The shared objective of the fight against Hitler and the danger to life and limb threatening every opponent of the NS regime gave rise to a feeling of solidarity. This helped to break down old prejudices and relativise political differences. Although supporters of democratic Socialism continued to have strong reservations with regard to the methods and objectives of the KPD, independently operating resistance organisations nevertheless achieved a degree of co-operation that transcended all former party boundaries. In the 'Saefkow Group', for example — one of the most widely distributed organisations, founded by a Communist Party official named Anton Saefkow — Social Democratic and Communist workers fought side by side with opponents of Hitler from middle-class circles.

Most resistance groups belonging to the labour movement were principally concerned with keeping democratic awareness alive through the medium of instruction and exposing the terrorism of the National Socialist regime. One way in which they did this was by secretly distributing handbills and leaflets or scattering them in street or factory at appropriate moments. Some of these pamphlets they produced themselves. In so far as such groups were in touch with the party-in-exile, the latter supplied them with material. Until that link was severed by the outbreak of war, huge quantities of brochures, usually disguised by misleading title pages and imprints, were smuggled into Germany and spread around the country. One of the most impressive and indeed shattering of these items was the report published by the SPD executive in Prague concerning the Oranienburg concentration camp. In it the former SPD deputy Gerhart Seger, one of the few who had managed to escape, gave early exposure to the horror of the concentration camps.[12]

---

12. Gerhart Seger, *Oranienburg. Erster authentischer Bericht eines aus dem Konzentrationslager Geflüchteten* ('Oranienburg. The first authentic report by a concentration-

A further crucial function of the resistance fighter was to provide assistance for the persecuted and for those threatened with prison, concentration camp, and execution. In 1944, for example, the 'People's Court' presided over by the bloodthirsty Roland Freisler declared in its judgment against the 'European Union' group, which had principally taken up the cause of foreign forced labourers: 'The shamelessness of the accused's attitude may also be seen in the fact that they gave systematic support to Jews living illegally and even foddered them. Worse than that, they actually provided them with false papers intended to deceive the police into thinking they were not Jews but Germans ... Another leaflet states in bombastic terms that the "European Union" campaigns in conjunction with the SPD, the SAPD, and the KPD but that it also does not spurn the representatives of bourgeois political tendencies. In even clearer terms than the manifesto the leaflets trot out all the lying human-rights principles of the Weimar constitution and even go so far as to point out that these people rely upon the enormous foreign-worker masses in Germany.'[13]

Lack of conspiratorial experience and organisational technique meant that resistance fighters were often swiftly tracked down by Hitler's police. The Gestapo had smashed most of the original Social Democratic resistance organisations by the mid-1930s. Thousands were arrested; others just managed to flee abroad at the last moment or go into hiding with the help of friends and colleagues. For the first year of the NS state alone the *Statistical Yearbook of the German Reich* recorded 20,565 convictions for political offences. These terrorist convictions were obtained mainly on the basis of decrees enacted 'for the protection of people and state', 'to combat political excesses', and 'to guard against treacherous attacks on the government of national edification'; or they were handed down for 'high treason' and on the basis of the 'law concerning firearms and ammunition'. In the early years the victims of this Nazi justice were chiefly supporters of the Socialist labour movement. They included officials of the KPD, members of Socialist splinter groups, leading Social Democrats such as the former president of the *Reichstag*, Paul Löbe, determined anti-Fascist fighters such as the young Kurt Schumacher, members of active resistance groups, and workers who told their workmates what they thought of the Hitler dictatorship. The devastating blows dealt by the

---

camp escapee'), with an introduction by Heinrich Mann (Karlsbad, 1934). See also the collection of documents published by the SPD executive-in-exile, *Konzentrationslager. Ein Appell an das Gewissen der Welt. Ein Buch der Greuel. Die Opfer klagen an* ('Concentration camps. An appeal to the conscience of the world. A book of horrors. The victims accuse'; Karlsbad, 1934).

13. Quoted in Günter Weisenborn (ed.), *Der lautlose Aufstand*, p. 169.

Gestapo virtually wiped out resistance in the labour movement as originally constituted. Subsequently, from about 1937, fresh initiatives were launched that drew on the experience already acquired. These were based for the most part on a system of three-, four-, or five-member cells so that even when individual groups were arrested the resistance work of the others could go on. 'A new generation of resistance fighters — young, experienced, and with no illusions — began to come into the groups. The result was "hard" groups that lasted, groups that covered their tracks so carefully that they remained intact for years on end, which was a colossal achievement when one considers how all-powerful the Gestapo machine was.'[14]

Altogether this resistance 'from below' demanded a high price. Thousands paid for their courageous stand on behalf of freedom, justice, and their fellow men with imprisonment, torture, and death. Straight figures do not begin to express the full extent of the sacrifice and suffering involved, the cost of the fight against oppression and tyranny and of support for the persecuted and threatened, or the courage of the individual man or woman who saved a Jew from certain death at the hands of the NS executioners. How many of us are aware that a Gestapo document of 10 April 1939 recorded precisely 302,562 political prisoners? Of the political prisoners of the NS tyranny it was the labour movement that provided by far the largest contingent. Tens of thousands were executed for oppositional activities, with Communists particularly numerous among them. According to a table drawn up by the Ministry of Justice, 11,881 death sentences were carried out between 1933 and 1944 in consequence of 'proper' court decisions. Military justice and special courts sent countless people to their deaths, especially in the last months of the war. The list of these victims does not of course include all those who died a 'natural death' in the concentration camps and in prison or were executed in connection with the conspiracy of 20 July 1944.[15] That 'rebellion of conscience' is well known today. We pay little or no attention to the 'silent rebellion' of the nameless host, the main burden of which was shouldered by the men and women of the labour movement.

The International Trade Union Congress did, however, remember those men and women in a speech made by its general secretary, Walter Schevenels, at the height of the Second World War. Addressing a rally organised by the 'Union of Germans Socialist Organisations in

14. Günter Weisenborn, in his *Der lautlose Aufstand*, p. 146.
15. See especially Bruno Gebhardt, *Handbuch der deutschen Geschichte*, ninth edition Vol. 4, Part 2 (Stuttgart, 1976), pp. 570, 572, 579. See also Günter Weisenborn (ed.), *Der lautlose Aufstand*, p. 149; and Peter Grasmann, *Sozialdemokraten gegen Hitler 1933–1945*, pp. 109f.

Great Britain' on 29 January 1943, he voiced his gratitude for the courageous efforts of the Socialist labour movement in Germany. May his words serve as a tribute to all who actively resisted National Socialism and fought for a Germany of freedom, democracy, social justice, and humanity. 'We too easily forget today that hundreds of German workers have lost their lives in these struggles and tens of thousands have placed their lives in jeopardy. It is true that the German labour movement has made mistakes and shown certain weaknesses, but it is not true to maintain that our German comrades have not fought . . . . I should like to add a word on behalf of our anti-Nazi fighters inside Germany. Before leaving Germany I had a meeting with our German colleagues. A week later most of the people who had taken part in that meeting were in custody. It was a meeting I shall never forget. In that overcrowded room the chairman shook me by the hand and said: "You are going back to the free world. Tell our friends that whatever mistakes we may have made in the past we were honest and sincere in what we were trying to do. Tell them that we shall remain true to our convictions and that they should not forget us." Today I can say that the majority of German workers have kept their word.'[16]

Exemplars of the unbroken will to resist shown by Social Democracy were such men as Kurt Schumacher, Julius Leber, Wilhelm Leuschner, Carlo Mierendorff, Theodor Haubach, Gustav Dahrendorf, and many others. Prison and concentration camp were powerless to dissuade them from continuing and renewing their resistance to an unjust regime. Even in the most murderous environment, fresh initiatives emerged. In February 1944, for example, Hermann Brill and Ernst Thape (both of the SPD) got together with Werner Hilpert (Centre Party, later CDU) and Walter Wolf (KPD) in Buchenwald concentration camp to form a popular-front committee and work out the terms of what was published after the liberation as the *Buchenwald Manifesto*.[17]

The young Kurt Schumacher earned the particular hatred of the Nazis for his militant opposition to National Socialism. On his arrest in July 1933 the *Stuttgarter Zeitung* crowed that 'one of the most bare-faced of Social Democracy's top agitators has been put behind bars'.[18] For this seriously disabled ex-serviceman it was the beginning

16. Quoted in Günter Weisenborn (ed.), *Der lautlose Aufstand*, pp. 181f.
17. Reprinted in *Buchenwald. Mahnung und Verpflichtung* (Frankfurt a. M., 1960), pp. 394ff.
18. *Stuttgarter Zeitung*, 12 July 1933. On Kurt Schumacher, see Lewis J. Edinger, *Kurt Schumacher, Persönlichkeit und politisches Verhalten* (Cologne/Opladen, 1967), pp. 80ff.; Willy Albrecht and Kurt Schumacher, *Ein Leben für den demokratischen Sozialismus* (Bonn, 1985), pp. 9ff.

of a ten-year trail of suffering through prison cells and concentration camps, ending in the notorious camp at Neuengamme, near Hamburg. Although tortured by his guards, Schumacher remained unbowed, and his courage and solidarity gained him a position of respect and authority among his fellow-prisoners. His execution was ordered as the Americans advanced, but he just managed to escape in time.

Wilhelm Leuschner, the deputy chairman of the now-dissolved ADGB, distinguished himself by building up a trade-union resistance organisation. Together with Jakob Kaiser of the Christian trade unions and Max Habermann of the *Deutschnationale Handlungsgehilfenverband* ('German National Commercial Assistants' Association') he created the concept of the unified trade unions of the future. With these they wished to tread together the 'right road for the German people, namely a healthy synthesis of Socialism and freedom'.[19] Leuschner's importance in the resistance movement is reflected in the fact that the 20 July 1944 movement planned to appoint him Vice-Chancellor. Like his friend Julius Leber, whom the same movement saw as Minister of the Interior, he had established early contact with the ex-mayor of Leipzig, Carl Goerdeler, and his circle. 'The decision of the trade unionists and Social Democrats involved on 20 July to work for the overthrow of the system through the generals was the right one. History's experience of totalitarian or authoritarian regimes since then has shown that successful subversion is impossible without the assistance of the military.'[20]

Colonel von Stauffenberg, the leading military brain behind the 20 July conspiracy, was a personal friend of Leber. An approach made to Communist groups that had been infiltrated by a Gestapo informer proved Leber's undoing on 4 July 1944. It was fear of the whole enterprise being discovered that drove von Stauffenberg to act quickly on 20 July. The revolt of the 'other Germany' failed. The bloody justice of Hitler's courts struck indiscriminately at those who were directly involved in the conspiracy, others who simply knew about it, and yet others who had had nothing to do with it. Savage methods of interrogation including brutal beatings were used against victims before they were handed over to the executioner. Julius Leber might have been speaking for them all — Leuschner, Haubach, Reichwein (Mierendorff had been killled in an air-raid), and many others — when he stated shortly before his execution in Plötzensee on 3 January 1945:

19. Quoted in Peter Hoffmann, *Widerstand–Staatsstreich–Attentat* (Munich, 1969), p. 229.

20. Hans Mommsen, 'Gewerkschaften zwischen Anpassung und Widerstand', in Heinz Oskar Vetter (ed.), *Vom Sozialistengesetz zur Mitbestimmung* (Cologne, 1975), pp. 297f.

'For a good and just cause, risking one's life is the proper price to pay.'[21] They gave their lives for the principles so impressively voiced in the *Reichstag* by Otto Wels on 23 March 1933, the Social Democratic principles of 'humanity and justice, of freedom and Socialism'.[22]

### 3. Ways, Means and Objectives of Democratic Socialism in Exile

For a long time the words 'exile' and 'emigration', when used in connection with the Hitler years, carried with them the unconscious reproach that a man or woman could not simply opt out of the common fate of the nation when threatened with personal danger. In fact even today such reservations, in which value judgements of the Third Reich are handed down from generation to generation, seem not to have been completely eradicated. Anyone arguing thus, whether maliciously or simply thoughtlessly, is either making light of the NS dictatorship or is himself caught up in its *Volksgemeinschaft* or 'national community' ideology. Not one of those who fled from Germany in the years after 1933 left without regret a country whose language he spoke and in which he had his roots. 'Nearly all emigrants, irrespective of whether they left the country because of their political vulnerability or because of their Jewish descent — and not infrequently both were involved — had in common the fact that they saw their livelihood, their freedom, and their life itself as being under threat from the dictatorship; and many among them only decided to flee after becoming personally acquainted with the terrorism, the concentration camps, and the prisons of the regime.'[23] For the Jewish refugees who managed to escape Hitler's clutches before the 'final solution' got under way in October 1941 there was no going back. And when Hitler began his lightning conquests tens of thousands who had thought themselves safe fell victim to the Nazi murderers after all.

The majority of those who emigrated were victims of racial persecution, Jewish citizens of a once free country who were now threatened

21. Julius Leber, *Ein Mann geht seinen Weg*, p. 295.
22. See note 2 above.
23. Erich Matthias, in Erich Matthias and Werner Link (eds), *Mit dem Gesicht nach Deutschland. Eine Dokumentation über die sozialdemokratische Emigration* (Düsseldorf, 1968), p. 8. Other recommended sources for the SPD emigration are Werner Röder, *Die deutschen sozialistischen Exilgruppen in Grossbritannien 1940–1945* (Hanover, 1968); Erich Matthias, *Sozialdemokratie und Nation. Ein Beitrag zur Ideengeschichte der sozialdemokratischen Emigration in der Prager Zeit des Parteivorstandes 1933–1938* (Stuttgart, 1952); Friedrich-Ebert-Stiftung (ed.), *Widerstand und Exil der deutschen Arbeiterbewegung 1933–1945* (Bonn, 1982); and Gerhard Hirschfeld (ed.), *Exile in Great Britain: Refugees from Hitler's Germany* (Leamington Spa, 1984).

with imprisonment and death in concentration camps and extermination camps. Approximately one emigrant in ten had to leave the National Socialist sphere of influence primarily for political reasons. This group included Social Democrats, middle-class democrats, Communists, pacifists, Christians, and other persuasions. It was mainly from their ranks that the hard core of active opponents of the Hitler regime was drawn. Exile, for them, was a political assignment, providing the base for their struggle against the National Socialist dictatorship and for a different, better Germany. The emigration to the Soviet Union apart, democratic Socialists formed the largest contingent among them.

The banning of the SPD on 22 June 1933 and the removal of its deputies from the *Reichstag* left the executive-in-exile as the mouthpiece of the party. This regarded itself as representing the party as a whole and set up its headquarters in Prague. Its members included the first chairman, Otto Wels, Hans Vogel as the second chairman, Siegmund Crummenerl as treasurer, Friedrich Stampfer, Paul Hertz, Erich Ollenhauer, and, from the autumn of 1933, Siegfried Aufhäuser, the chairman of the AfA. The executive-in-exile saw its chief task as being 'to tell the world the truth' and to do what it could to assist illegal operations back at home.[24] This included raising money and making it available, supplying informative material, which was often disguised as advertising brochures or cheap editions of the classics, providing assistance for the victims of the struggle, and attempting to open the eyes of the world to the true nature of the Hitler dictatorship. The executive committee threw a ring of frontier secretariats round Germany to maintain contact with its agents inside the country and to give all possible support to those fighting underground. In publishing Gerhart Seger's book about his experiences in Oranienburg concentration camp and its own collection of reports on the concentration camps of the 'Third Reich' the party-in-exile sought to rouse the conscience of the world. The same year — 1934 — saw the publication of the first of Erich Rinner's *Green Reports*,[25] in which information collected by the party's agents inside Germany was collated and passed on. Despite some understandable errors, these reports gave an unvarnished picture of the harsh realities of life under the NS regime. In the face of National Socialist violence and mendacity, Social Democracy placed its faith in the power of truth and information. 'Hitler means war' was the key watchword of their struggle against Hitler

---

24. *Neuer Vorwärts*, 18 June 1933.
25. *Grüne Berichte* — so-called because they were duplicated on green paper; their official designation was *Deutschlandberichte*. They have since been republished as *Die geheimen Deutschlandberichte der SPD 1934–1940*, 7 vols. (Frankfurt a. M., 1980).

Fascism before and after 1933. With words as their only weapons, the little group of emigrants tried to prevent the unleashing of the dogs of war. Friedrich Stampfer summed up their goal in a prophetic sentence in the party's exile newspaper, *Neuer Vorwärts*, which was published in Prague: 'If all Europe is not to become a rubble-heap burying the dismembered body of Germany we must not stand idly by as disaster approaches.'[26]

The appeal to the 'civilised world' to make a decisive stand against Hitler while there was yet time fell on deaf ears. On the contrary, for the European great powers the warnings of German Social Democracy constituted an embarrassing disturbance of their policy of appeasement towards the 'Third Reich'. As the British government admitted once war had broken out, reports were deliberately kept under lock and key in order not to cloud relations with Hitler's Germany. There was as little hope of their achieving this as there was prospect of a successful uprising taking place in Germany under the conditions of the National Socialist dictatorship. All the courage and all the dedication of active opponents of the NS regime, who before the outbreak of war came overwhelmingly from the Socialist camp, could not alter the fact that toppling Hitler's dictatorship by means of an isolated insurrection from below was a sheer impossibility.

The revolutionary elements that underlay this concept of the fight against Hitler found their most powerful expression in the 'Prague Manifesto' issued by the Sopade on 28 January 1934.[27] In this programmatic declaration by the party's executive committee Marxist theories regarding the nature of the Nazi counter-revolution, in which there was mention of 'mounting conflicts within capitalist society' and an 'objectively revolutionary situation', were interwoven with current political appeals to fight for freedom and the 'overthrow of tyranny'. 'The unity and freedom of the German nation can be saved only by the overthrow of German Fascism.' The appeal ended by acknowledging 'the great and imperishable ideas of humanity': 'We do not wish to live without freedom, and freedom we shall conquer — freedom without class rule, freedom extending to the total abolition of all exploitation and all dominion of man over man! . . . Through freedom to Socialism, through Socialism to freedom! Long live German revolutionary Social Democracy! Long live the International!'

This acknowledgement of the revolutionary character of Socialism arose automatically out of the circumstances of the fight against the NS dictatorship, which could not be other than revolutionary. The man-

26. *Neuer Vorwärts*, 8 April 1934.
27. See Document 10, pp. 265ff.

ifesto's rejection of compromise in the shape of 'reformism and legality' at the same time reflected an endeavour to bring the Socialist splinter groups operating on the fringes of the mother party back into the fold and unite them behind a common strategic objective.

In the exceptional situation in which the Socialists in exile found themselves it was inevitable that at first differences both old and new should have come to a head particularly virulently. Both the search for reasons for the victory of Fascism and the analysis of the mistakes made by democratic Socialism in the past gave occasion for lengthy and sometimes heated arguments. The tussle over the most effective ways of fighting National Socialism was likewise a protracted one. Furthermore, plans for a reorganisation of political and social life after the overthrow of the Hitler dictatorship were in need of clarification. Additional incendiary matter was supplied by the question of how far Communists ought to be incorporated in the united front of Socialists against Hitler Fascism. The KPD's united-front offer of November 1935, for example, sparked off some fierce controversy. Reactions ranged from unqualified rejection through partial co-operation towards the one common goal right up to hopes that the split in the Socialist labour movement might be healed at last.

A group calling itself the 'Revolutionary Socialists' and headed by Karl Böchel and Siegfried Aufhäuser, a former member of the USPD and the chairman of the AfA, called for a radical break with all reformist traditions and proclaimed the 'class struggle of the united German proletariat'.[28] In opposition to this so-called 'old left', which broke up again in 1937, the champions of a 'people's Socialism' led by Wilhelm Sollmann and Wenzel Jaksch advocated the abandonment of the theories of the class struggle and a move towards the 'patriotic Socialism of Lassalle'.[29]

In the case of the ISK it was primarily old and as yet unhealed wounds, ideological differences, and its participation in concentration attempts on the part of left-wing Socialist exile groups that stood in the way of a rapprochement at first. As late as 1939 the Sopade executive committee referred to membership of both organisations as being incompatible. During the war, however, under the leadership of Willi Eichler, who had had to flee from Germany in 1933, the ISK began to move closer to Social Democracy.

There were fierce and occasionally stormy clashes with the 'new left' concerning the 'New Beginning' group, to which Karl Frank, Richard

---

28. See 'Der Weg zum sozialistischen Deutschland / Plattform für die Einheitsfront'; published in *Zeitschrift für Sozialismus*, Nos. 12–13 (Karlsbad, 1934), pp. 375ff.

29. The words are Wilhelm Sollmann's, in *Zeitschrift für Sozialismus*, Nos. 24–25 (Karlsbad, 1935), p. 736.

Löwenthal (alias Paul Sering), Waldemar von Knoeringen, and Erwin Schoettle belonged, among others. What made the Sopade executive particularly bitter was that its own Paul Hertz and other colleagues had secretly worked for 'New Beginning' and that the group claimed parity of status in the International as representing a section of German Social Democracy.

The Socialist emigrant groups were scattered in many countries. Their headquarters was initially Czechoslovakia, which was like a second home to them. Eventually, however, the government of Czechoslovakia had to give in to Hitler's extortions, reinforced as these were by the interventions of the British Prime Minister, Neville Chamberlain, in his anxiety to achieve a settlement with the 'Third Reich'. The Sopade, like its Austrian counterpart, decided in 1938 to move to Paris. In the Czechoslovak republic it had, as Friedrich Stampfer wrote, 'breathed the air of freedom and found sympathetic friendship. All that was to change now. People began saying to one another, "This is where our exile really starts"'.[30]

Rudolf Breitscheid had already fled to France earlier and had written to tell the executive committee what awaited the Social Democrats in Paris: 'Never has an emigration had so many difficulties to combat as our own. We are regarded, at least in France, simply as troublesome foreigners whom people would like to get rid of as quickly as possible.'[31] With the German attack on France the emigrants, who had dedicated themselves whole-heartedly to the fight against Hitler Fascism, found themselves in an even worse position. The Daladier government, which had failed as far as containing the National Socialist expansionist urge was concerned, responded to a widespread mood of hostility toward 'enemy aliens' by indiscriminately herding German citizens into internment camps. As German troops carried their lightning campaign ever further into France, tens of thousands of Germans sitting in those camps had reason to fear for life and limb should the NS executioners get hold of them. Active politicians of all persuasions, non-political opponents of Nazism, and above all the huge numbers of Jews who had made their escape to France went through weeks of anxiety and appalling distress.

Not until the last minute were the camp gates thrown open. In headlong flight people sought safety from the Gestapo and the SS. The armistice agreement of 22 June 1940 committed the French government to handling over its German refugees. The only course left for most of them was to cross the frontier — illegally — into Spain, where

30. Erich Matthias and Werner Link (eds), *Mit dem Gesicht nach Deutschland*, p. 101.
31. *Ibid.*, p. 109.

General Franco had just established his dictatorship with the help of
Mussolini and Hitler at the end of a bloody civil war. The escape route
continued via Portugal to the United States, which is where most of
them went, or to Great Britain. But compared with the enormous
number of refugees who set out on that route, only a fraction succeeded in overcoming the obstacles and dangers encountered on the
way.

The chief contributions towards saving those refugees were made by
the United States, by the Socialist mayors of many French towns, by
the nameless strangers who risked their lives for others, and by a body
known as the 'German Labour Delegation' that operated in the USA.
This had been founded in New York on 10 March 1939 by a number of
Social Democratic emigrants including Albert Grzesinski, Rudolf
Katz, Gerhart Seger, Max Brauer, and Hedwig Wachenheim to serve
as an auxiliary organisation for the party's executive committee. With
strong support from the Jewish Labor Committee and encouragement
from the American Federation of Labor (the umbrella organisation of
the American trade unions) it organised an exemplary relief and rescue
operation. Hundreds owed it their freedom and their lives.

Not everyone got away. Others, too, shared the fate of the friends
Rudolf Breitscheid and Rudolf Hilferding, who were arrested by the
French authorities to be handed over to the Nazis. Hilferding died in a
Paris gaol, Breitscheid in Buchenwald concentration camp. A particularly tragic fate awaited the Frankfurt Social Democrat Johanna Kirch-
ner. After French resistance fighters had at first got her out of the
notorious Gurs internment camp she fell into the clutches of the Vichy
authorities and was handed over to the NS regime. Condemned by
*Blutrichter* ('blood-judge') Freisler, she died beneath the guillotine.

Those who managed to get away to Great Britain had escaped any
acute danger for the time being though hardships and difficulties
awaited them here too. The situation of these refugees, like that of the
emigrants who had sought refuge in Britain earlier on, usually on
account of their Jewish descent, looked somewhat bleak at first. A
series of private relief committees did take up their cause, making great
sacrifices on their behalf, but strict immigration regulations and a lack
of job opportunities drove many refugees to leave the country once
more and go overseas. Following the fall of France, thousands experienced the bitter fate of compulsory internment as 'enemy aliens'.
Nearly 8,000 persons were deported to Australia and Canada in July
1940, and almost twice that many were placed under strict police
surveillance.

Only after the shock of the first few months of the war had worn off
and spy hysteria had given way to more sober considerations did a

review of these internments get under way as a result of pressure from public opinion and the efforts of individual members of parliament. The British government had the grace to admit that it had made some serious mistakes. In consequence the representatives of the Sopade who had fled to Britain also regained some freedom of movement. The various Socialist emigrant groups received support from the Fabian Society, from individuals such as Victor Gollancz and James Middleton, and from the British Labour Party, with which the representatives of 'New Beginning' enjoyed particularly close contacts. At the same time the Labour Party launched various initiatives to bring the rival exile groups together.

With the furies of war now raging over Europe, many once fiercely disputed questions had lost some of their importance among democratic Socialists in exile. The idea of a popular insurrection in Germany and the hope of unreserved co-operation from the Social Democratic parties of the countries at war with Hitler repeatedly turned out to be illusory. No help could be expected from the Allied governments for opposition inside Germany. The 'Atlantic Charter' proclaimed by Roosevelt and Churchill on 14 August 1941 together with earlier statements by the Labour Party had fostered expectations of a negotiated peace following the fall of Hitler. Those expectations were bitterly disappointed. Where once the majority of the Labour Party had thought primarily in terms of solidarity with the German democrats, as the war dragged on a strongly national element gradually came to dominate their feelings. Britain's Conservative Prime Minister declared that the principles of the Atlantic Charter did not apply to Germany. The abortive rebellion of 20 July 1944 was in his eyes, as Churchill told parliament on 2 August 1944, no more than a power struggle among the 'highest-placed figures in the German Reich', who were seeking to kill one another off.

There was now virtually nowhere the German emigrant groups could look for support for the preservation of the territorial integrity of Germany after the overthrow of Hitler Fascism. Furthermore, with the signing of the Hitler–Stalin pact those tendencies within Social Democracy in exile that seemed prepared to co-operate with the Communists in the fight against National Socialism had lost much of their credibility and influence. With a new emphasis on 'Socialism without bureaucratic dictatorship' and 'with democratic freedoms' the London group of the Socialist Labour Party began to move rapidly closer to the Sopade.[32] Likewise in the 'New Beginning' group, fol-

32. Werner Röder, *Die deutschen sozialistischen Exilgruppen in Grossbritannien 1940–1945*, p. 44. On this and what follows, see *ibid.*, pp. 43ff.; and Jörg Bremer, *Die*

lowing the break with its founder Walter Löwenheim and under the influence of its leading theoretician, Richard Löwenthal, a move in the direction of the Social Democratic *Gesamtbewegung* (literally 'whole movement') became discernible. Once certain points of contention regarding organisation had been settled, no further questions of principle stood in the way of close co-operation with the SPD's executive-in-exile. The ISK, too, which under its leader-in-exile Willi Eichler was doing exemplary publicity work, showed itself willing to co-operate.

The *Auslandsvertretung Deutscher Gewerkschaften* (ADG; 'Foreign Agency of the German Trade Unions'), set up as an exile organisation in 1935 and headed by Heinrich Schliestedt until 1938 and by Fritz Tarnow thereafter, made some attempt to throw an organisational net over the emigrant groups in the different countries but did not get very far at first. There was broad agreement in principle over the concept of a future unified trade union. The argument was about whether this should take as its starting-point, as Tarnow proposed, the 'German Labour Front' broken up after Hitler's overthrow. It was in the 'National Group of German Trade Unionists in Great Britain', headed by Hans Gottfurcht and influenced by Walter Auerbach, that the idea of a total restructuring gained general acceptance. Under the umbrella of this emigrant trade unionists' organisation the different Socialist groups actually sat round a table together for the first time. To that extent it made its own contribution towards the founding of the 'Union of German Socialist Organisations in Great Britain'.

Force of circumstances helped considerably to overcome various reservations and differences, as did the fact that the people concerned knew one another and had endured the hardships of emigration together. Vogel and Ollenhauer of the Sopade, Knoeringen and Schoettle of 'New Beginning', and Eichler of the ISK were men who were capable of putting what they had in common above what divided them and who enjoyed relations of mutual personal trust.

Official negotiations for the foundation of a joint body comprising the Sopade (SPD), 'New Beginning', the ISK, the SAP, and the 'National Group of German Trade Unionists in Great Britain' opened on 25 February 1941. Agreement over the central questions was quickly achieved, and the 'Union' was launched upon the world less than four weeks later. It was headed by Hans Vogel (SPD) as chairman. In addition to him it was principally Ollenhauer, Fritz Heine (SPD), Schoettle ('New Beginning'), Eichler (ISK), and Hans Gottfurcht (trade unions) who determined the practical policy of the Union

---

*Sozialistische Arbeiterpartei Deutschlands*, pp. 252f., 259ff.

in the years that followed. In a unanimously approved state-ment issued on the day of the Union's foundation, 19 March 1941, the Socialists who had amalgamated to form that body proclaimed their determination to work 'with every means at their disposal' for the overthrow of the 'forces of totalitarianism' and to bring about a democratic peace that would give 'a new Germany the opportunity to make its contribution to the reconstruction of Europe as a free mem-ber of the European community of nations'. They further declared: 'The German Socialists in Great Britain are united in their conviction that the military defeat and overthrow of the Hitler regime, the final overcoming of German militarism, and the removal of the social foundations of the Hitler dictatorship constitute essential prerequisites for a lasting peace, for the reconstruction of Europe, and for a democratic and Socialist future for Germany.'[33]

Fruitful co-operation within the Union caused the old organis-ational demarcation lines to lose some of their importance. Similarly in discussions regarding the future course of democratic Socialism there were signs of a clarification of standpoints. There were still differences here and there, but on a series of crucial issues a joint line was increasingly beginning to emerge. Long-cherished hopes of toppling Hitler with an alliance of all free democratic forces inside and outside Germany had finally to be buried. Overthrowing the National Social-ist dictatorship now looked possible only by means of a military defeat. The Social Democratic emigration was thus faced with the dilemma that, while the joint struggle against Hitler Fascism bound it to the Allies, at the same time a gap was opening up between its own ideas with regard to a future peace settlement and the war-aims of the anti-Hitler coalition. After the Tehran conference between Stalin, Roosevelt, and Churchill in December 1943 it became clear that the war was going to end with a dismemberment of the German Reich.

Despite the increasing hopelessness of its endeavour, the Union directed a series of protests and memoranda against all partition and separation plans. It firmly opposed the theory of collective guilt and the growing 'Vansittartism' that blamed National Socialism on the German character and called for a blanket hostility to all things German.[34] In this struggle against the Allies' dismemberment and occupation plans the national factor began to gain prominence among the emigration as a unifying bond. More than ever the Social Demo-

33. Reprinted in *Zur Politik deutscher Sozialisten. Politische Kundgebungen und programmatische Richtlinien der Union deutscher sozialistischer Organisationen in Grossbritannien* (London, 1945), p. 26.
34. So-called after the Chief Diplomatic Adviser to the British government and former Under-Secretary of State for Foreign Affairs, Lord Robert Vansittart.

crats in exile felt themselves to be members of the German people, whose fate they must share once Hitler had been overthrown. As Germans among Germans they wanted to bear their share of the burden of the war's aftermath and, citing their moral claims as the earliest fighters against Fascism, to safeguard the interests of the nation vis-à-vis the victors.

This national preoccupation brought the Social Democrats in exile into conflict with the expansionist aspirations of the Soviet Union as evinced in the final stages of the war. After Hitler's attack on Russia, when the Soviet Union had become the bulwark of the Allied defence, paying for its stand with fearful sacrifices, few could overlook the decisive role played by Moscow in the fight against the NS dictatorship. The pro-Soviet feeling that was widespread in certain sectors of the Western Allied camp had little effect on the attitude of the Social Democrats towards the Communist system. Despite traditionally strong sympathies for the 'great Socialist experiment' of Lenin's soviet republic in the ranks of 'New Beginning' and the SAP, neither group could turn a blind eye to the excesses of the Stalinist system. The Hitler-Stalin pact showed how unscrupulous even Russian power politics could be. The Stalinist dictatorship with its 'purges' and show trials, which claimed as many victims among leading German Communists as did the NS regime, exposed the totalitarian nature of a system that claimed to be Socialist. The exile-KPD's almost unreserved loyalty to Stalin, its defence of annexations and expulsions by the victoriously advancing Soviet troops, and its revilement of Social Democracy as the 'agent of Hitlerism abroad'[35] wrecked all thought of a united front with the Communists even for the far left of the democratic Socialist spectrum.

'They did not belong to the unity of the Socialist movement',[36] the future outlines of which were emerging more and more clearly from discussions within the Union. The divisions in the ranks of the labour movement were to be overcome, and all organisations, groups, and tendencies taking their stand on free, democratic Socialism were to merge in a single Social Democratic Party. As early as 1943 it was possible to put forward a joint foreign-policy programme in which the Union committed itself to, among other things, a 'federation of European nations', disarmament, reparation, and an international security system. However, the permanence of any future peaceful coexistence between the nations depended, in its view, 'largely upon the German

---

35. Quoted in Werner Röder, *Die deutschen sozialistischen Exilgruppen in Grossbritannien 1940–1945*, p. 214. The insult gains colour in German from the use of the female form *Agentin* to agree with *die (f.) Sozialdemokratie* (Transl. note).
36. Willi Eichler, *Hundert Jahre Sozialdemokratie* (Bielefeld, 1963), p. 69.

people being given the opportunity to pursue its own initiative in shaping its internal political, social, and economic life'.[37]

How the democratic Socialists who made up the 'Union of Democratic Socialist Organisations in Great Britain' intended to turn Germany into a political embodiment of freedom, justice, and peace was laid down in their 'Programmatic Guidelines' of 1945. In statements about cultural policy, education, and the structure of justice and the administration and particularly in guidelines regarding economic policy and a 'German constitution' they traced the framework of a radical democratic republic that in its economic and political structure was intended to avoid the errors of Weimar. 'The goals of the Socialists with regard to the economy are: freedom from economic exploitation, equality of opportunity in terms of economic development, the guarantee of a livelihood for all compatible with the dignity of man, full employment for everyone fit to work, increased general prosperity, and the free development of the abilities of all.'[38] In the 'Preamble' to its 'Guidelines for a German Constitution' the Union[39] gave German Social Democracy the sum total of its experience to carry with it into the future. A fresh political and social order must be based on the following principles.:

Respect for and protection of the dignity of the human person are the inalienable foundations of the political and social life of the German republic.

In this spirit it aspires to:

a social order characterised by justice, humanity, and peace;

a political and social democracy founded on co-determination and co-responsibility on the part of every citizen;

the liberation of the economy from the fetters of private monopoly ownership and the planning of the economy;

protection against all economic exploitation; the guaranteed provision, for everyone, of a livelihood compatible with the dignity of man;

equality of opportunity in terms of economic and cultural development;

the promotion of the intellectual and cultural life of the nation and the education of its youth in the spirit of moral responsibility, democracy, and understanding among peoples;

37. Resolution adopted by the Union on 23 October 1943; reprinted in *Zur Politik deutscher Sozialisten*, pp. 16f.
38. 'Richtlinien für die Wirtschaftspolitik' ('Guidelines for an economic policy'), in *Zur Politik deutscher Sozialisten*, pp. 3f.
39. On 2 December 1945 the Union was officially superceded by an 'integrated party

the elimination of war as an instrument of politics;

international institutions to which individual national sovereignties shall be subordinate in the interests of securing peace and the prosperity of all peoples.[40]

organisation'.

40. 'Richtlinien für eine deutsche Staatsverfassung' ('Guidelines for a German constitution'), in *Zur Politik deutscher Sozialisten*, p. 5.

# 10
# Heritage and Mission

From the standpoint of today it may seem to many entirely natural that Social Democracy should have become the major party of democratic Socialism in post-war Germany. In 1945, following the collapse of the Nazi regime, it was far from that. To the left of Social Democracy the KPD — in contrast to the Weimar period, when it had grown to be the third-largest party — was reduced to those who followed the Leninist line. Not even for the millions of the starving and impoverished did it constitute a serious alternative in the western part of the country. In the eastern part, on the other hand, it was able with the aid of the Soviet occupier and enforced unification to become, as the SED, the official government party of a new, Communist-run state.

In Social Democracy the supporters of free Socialism had found *their* political home. Beyond the constricting bounds of Weimar it became the hope — and the party — of all who, whatever their theoretical footing, aspired to a democratic Socialist society living in freedom.

This was exemplified in 1945. Social Democrats who had come through twelve years of dictatorship under the Hitler regime linked arms with those who had suffered the bitter fate of emigration for all or part of that time. Their choice of Kurt Schumacher as chairman and Erich Ollenhauer as deputy chairman of the newly emergent party gave symbolic expression to their common preoccupation. Rising above old organisational and theoretical antagonisms, the banner of democratic Socialism drew together men and women of different origins and disparate points of departure. Social Democrats who had remained loyal to their party through storm and stress almost without question joined forces with Socialists who had long been in conflict with the old mother party and committed democrats who saw the SPD as the one guarantee of a better future. Their experiences of the National Socialist dictatorship and of Stalinist Communism, a recognition of the weaknesses of the Weimar Republic, and the need to stand together in the fight for a Socialist democracy threw a solid bridge over all that divided them.

For German Social Democracy, the year 1945 was not a break but a new beginning. Socialism had emerged in Europe as a protest movement against the cruel excesses of the early capitalist system, a party that campaigned against exploitation, oppression, and economic distress and advocated a solution of the social question through changing the structure of state and society. But whereas in western-European countries the liberal middle class became the crucial champion of parliamentary democracy, in Germany the chief burden of the struggle for democratic freedoms fell upon the shoulders of the Socialist labour movement. In this twofold task of fighting for social justice and wresting democratic freedoms German Social Democracy was largely thrown back on its own resources. In its battle for the removal of social evils it received some backing from the Christian Workers' wing of the Centre Party, while in the campaign for democracy it stood most chance of support from the left-wing liberals. Its opponents, of course, carried twice the weight. Banded against it were all the forces that wished to maintain or reaffirm their dominant position in the state and the economy. It had been the strongest — though still a feeble — opponent of National Socialism, to which it had put up the most consistent resistance.

It was precisely this experience of German Fascism and the perversion of Communism represented by Stalinism that made Socialists who were committed to freedom undertake a radical reappraisal of the forces that had driven and the principles that had guided that great movement of emancipation. Running like a red thread through the history of democratic Socialism is the fight against exploitation and oppression, be they directed against classes, races, creeds, or individuals.[1] The objective was and is to free people from poverty, fear, and economic and social insecurity, to achieve a just distribution of income and wealth, and to overcome inequality and injustice through the medium of an economic order harnessed to the interests of society as a whole. Democracy, for Social Democrats, is more than simply the principle that must shape the political order; it is the model for the structure of the totality of social life.

Democratisation in this sense means not just the provision of rights but the greater task of enabling man to avail himself of his freedom. In addition to the creation and extension of organisational and material preconditions, education and training occupy an important place. State and society have need of the critically-minded, mature citizen who through self-determination and respect for others takes an active part

---

1. Variously worded, these basic demands appeared in the party's Erfurt, Görlitz and Heidelberg programmes; see Documents 3, 8 and 9, pp. 240ff., 253ff., 258ff.

in moulding the life of the community. The preserving and safeguarding of peace abroad and the solution of conflicts by peaceful means are fundamental requirements for a better future and as such have been aimed at by Social Democracy since its inception. The great goal with which the labour movement was launched is still today, as it was more than one hundred years ago, an ever-fresh mission and commitment: a world of peace in freedom and justice, a social order in which the personality of each is able to develop freely in solidarity with others.

*Part Two*

## SUSANNE MILLER

# The SPD from 1945 to the Present

# 11
# Refounding the Party Organisation

On 10 April 1945 American troops occupied Hanover; on 19 April a meeting was held in the city at which Dr Kurt Schumacher and a number of other Social Democrats decided to reconstruct their party; on 6 May Schumacher delivered a programmatic speech at an assembly to refound Hanover's local branch of the SPD.[1] In two respects this chain of events was symptomatic. The reactivation of the party with the longest unbroken historical tradition started spontaneously almost as soon as the National Socialist tyranny collapsed and without waiting for the permission of the military governments regarding the formation of political parties, which was not forthcoming until several months later. And from the very beginning until his death on 20 August 1952 Kurt Schumacher was the dominant figure in German Social Democracy during the post-war years.

By early October 1945 the organisational framework of the SPD had been restored in much of the shattered German Reich — chiefly in the big cities; in small towns and in rural areas political life got under way again only hesitantly. So rapidly was the reconstruction process completed in many cases that, for example, a Social Democratic functionary returning to his home town in Hesse in July was told apologetically that he was too late: every position in the party machine was already filled. Members and functionaries were everywhere recruited principally from among Social Democrats who had remained true to their convictions for the past twelve years and were now reviving their party on the model of the Weimar period.[2] Undismayed by the heavy defeat suffered by the German labour movement in 1933, by the horrors of the Nazi tyranny and the war — which had been worse than anyone

1. Published in Kurt Schumacher, Erich Ollenhauer, Willy Brandt, *Der Auftrag des demokratischen Sozialismus* (Bonn, 1972), pp. 3ff.
2. See Albrecht Kaden, *Einheit oder Freiheit. Die Wiedergründung der SPD 1945–1946*, second edition (Berlin/Bonn, 1980), pp. 125f.; and Klaus Schütz, 'Die Sozialdemokratie im Nachkriegsdeutschland', in *Parteien in der Bundesrepublik. Studien zur Entwicklung der deutschen Parteien bis zur Bundestagswahl 1953* (Stuttgart/Düsseldorf, 1955), p. 158.

had ever experienced or even imagined before — and by the hardships that followed the collapse, a remarkably large proportion of the previous membership of the party had kept up an inner commitment to their ideal that often took the form of what was called *Organisationspatriotismus* — literally 'organisational patriotism'. On 30 September 1946, less than eighteen months after the unconditional surrender of the Reich, the SPD numbered 633,244 members in the three Western zones and Berlin, and it gained a further 70,000 before the end of the year — exceeding the membership figure for the same area at the end of 1931 by 18 per cent. The refounded SPD had also succeeded — largely thanks to the changes in the population structure brought about by war, flight, expulsion, and other factors — in extending its organisational network well beyond the level achieved in the Weimar period: by the end of 1946 the party had more than 8,000 local branches in the area covered by the Western zones — nearly 3,000 more than in the same area in 1931.[3]

Even before the SPD was able to hold its first post-war party conference, decisions had been taken that left no doubt as to how the question of choosing the leadership should be solved and what direction the party should take as a result. While Hans Vogel and Erich Ollenhauer, members of the SPD executive elected back at the end of April 1933 who had been living in London since March 1941, had offered to give up their seats to the party now operating legally in Germany once again,[4] leadership claims were advanced by a 'Central Committee of the SPD' formed in Berlin in mid-June 1945 under the chairmanship of Otto Grotewohl. Its first public statement of intent ended by declaring that it would 'wage the campaign for reorganisation on the basis of the organisational unity of the German working class'; the same statement had begun by welcoming 'most warmly' a proclamation issued by the central committee of the KPD on 11 June 1945.[5] Schumacher, in his speech of 6 May 1945 mentioned above, had gone very thoroughly into the problem of the 'unity of the working class'. He had cited as the crucial reason for his uncompromising rejection of a 'unity party' the Communists' dependence on Russia, and he had stressed that Social Democrats must refuse to become 'the autocratically manipulated instrument of some foreign imperial interest'. What divided Social Democrats from Communists was not 'a difference in degree of radicalism but a different way of looking at the political world, a different way of evaluating circumstances and ideas'.[6]

3. *Jahrbuch der SPD 1946*, pp. 18ff.
4. See Klaus Schütz, 'Die Sozialdemokratie im Nachkriegsdeutschland', *op. cit.*, p. 160.
5. See Albrecht Kaden, *Einheit oder Freiheit . . .*, *op. cit.*, pp. 26f.

When at this early stage Schumacher laid down guidelines on a central question concerning the organisation and policy of his party, it was not so much with the pressures soon to be exerted within the Soviet sphere of influence in mind as certain feelings and tendencies among some of his party comrades in the Western zones. As time went on, however, it emerged that these did not constitute a serious problem as far as building up an independent Social Democratic Party was concerned: joint campaigns with the Communists that had been launched in many cities in the Western zones after the war[7] were soon dropped without provoking any major conflicts within the party. The treatment of Social Democrats in the Soviet-occupied zone and the inevitability of their being forced into line had swiftly destroyed any lingering hopes of being able to work in partnership with Communists.

The real struggle centred on the party in Berlin, where it became increasingly clear that the 'Central Committee' was not going to be able to prevent the Communists from turning 'joint action' with them, which the committee had approved, into a full-scale merger of the two parties and in effect destroying the independence of the SPD by setting up a 'unity party'. This complex and dramatic struggle, in the course of which Schumacher and Grotewohl clashed head-on, was eventually decided by a ballot carried out at the instigation of the Berlin Social Democrats under the leadership of Franz Neumann in March 1946. While a majority came out in favour of loyal collaboration, over 82 per cent of Social Democrats in the three Western sectors of the city — in the Soviet sector the ballot had been banned by the Soviet military authorities — gave a negative reply to the question: 'Are you in favour of the immediate amalgamation of the two labour parties?'. On 7 April 1946 the Social Democratic Party of Greater Berlin was officially reconstituted. A fortnight later a 'unification conference' met in the 'Admirals' Palace' in the Eastern sector of Berlin and founded the *Sozialistische Einheitspartei Deutschlands* (SED; 'Socialist Unity Party of Germany'). With that the SPD ceased to exist in the Soviet-occupied zone.

The organisational framework of the SPD was thus already defined when on 9 May 1946 the delegates from the three Western zones and from Berlin assembled in Hanover for the first post-war party conference. Kurt Schumacher was unanimously elected first chairman of the

---

6. Kurt Schumacher *et al.*, *Der Auftrag des demokratischen Sozialismus*, *op. cit.*, p. 30.
7. On the subject of Bremen, see Peter Brandt, *Antifaschismus und Arbeiterbewegung* (Hamburg, 1976); on Hamburg, see Holger Christier, *Sozialdemokratie und Kommunismus. Die Politik der SPD und der KPD in Hamburg 1945–1949* (Hamburg, 1975); for a general account, see Lutz Niethammer *et al.* (eds), *Arbeiterinitiative 1945* (Wuppertal, 1976).

party. The conference also elected an executive committee, which consisted of five paid and twenty unpaid members and which appointed Erich Ollenhauer as Schumacher's deputy. The paid members of the executive — in addition to Schumacher and Ollenhauer these were Fritz Heine, Herbert Kriedemann, and Alfred Nau — formed the so-called 'Bureau', the staffing and powers of which were to play a major part in subsequent internal party disputes. The twenty-five member executive committee elected in Hanover consisted for the most part of men and women who had survived the years of the National Socialist tyranny in prisons or concentration camps or in exile abroad. They had all been members of the SPD since before 1933, though some of them had left the 'mother party' or been expelled from it during the Weimar period or the years of illegality and had been active in independent Socialist groups. From the time of its refoundation the SPD represented the 'unity party' of non-Communist Socialists.

## 1. The Programmatic Perspective

Since its adoption of the Erfurt Programme in 1891, German Social Democracy had been regarded within the Socialist International as being *the* Marxist party par excellence. The interpretation of that programme led to the biggest theoretical dispute — the revisionism debate — ever settled officially in the history of the SPD. It ended in 1903 when the party conference voted by an overwhelming majority in favour of Marxist orthodoxy. Twenty-two years later the SPD adopted a programme at Heidelberg that in terms of theory was an only slightly modified version of the Erfurt one. In terms of the realities of party business, however, it is to be noted that the theories underlying that programme were of at most indirect importance for practical political purposes and that neither the party leadership nor the broader membership seriously concerned themselves with them. During the Weimar years — in contrast to Social Democracy under the Empire — clashes over theory were in the main confined to groups on the periphery of the party. It goes without saying that, under the conditions of illegality that obtained in Germany under the Hitler regime, such discussions were very much inhibited. Among exiled party members, on the other hand, they became intense at times.[8] The Union of German Socialist Organisations in Great Britain, for example, an alliance of the SPD and three other groups formed in the spring of 1941, published after lengthy consultations its 'Programmatic

8. See especially Erich Matthias, *Sozialdemokratie und Nation*, op. cit.

Guidelines' for the future policy of German Socialists. These guidelines, whose authors included the future SPD executive members Erich Ollenhauer, Willi Eichler, and Erwin Schoettle, were not without importance as programmatic groundwork. They made no claim, however, to provide a completely rethought theoretical basis for Social Democratic policy. The rebirth of the party that for half a century had been proud of resting on the sure foundation of 'scientific Socialism' actually took place in a theoretical vacuum.

Yet despite — or it might have been because of — the relative lack of interest in ideological questions shown by the majority of the party's leaders, its functionaries, and its members, there soon emerged a 'party line' that encompassed the basic definitions of SPD policy, determined that policy for many years to come, and moulded the image of the party. By far the greatest contribution towards that process was made by Kurt Schumacher. This is therefore the place to say a few words about Schumacher the man.

He was born on 12 October 1895 at Kulm in West Prussia (now Chełmno in Poland), where he attended school. He volunteered as soon as war broke out, and two weeks after being sent into action he was badly wounded. He lost his right arm, was discharged, and subsequently devoted himself to his studies, which he completed by taking a doctorate in political science. He joined the SPD in 1918 and was elected a deputy to the Württemberg *Landtag* in 1924 and to the *Reichstag* in 1930. For ten years the National Socialists kept him in various concentration camps, almost torturing him to death; released in the summer of 1943, he was reimprisoned for several weeks following the events of 20 July 1944. From then until the end of the war he lived near Hanover. In that ancient stronghold of German Social Democracy he made his first contacts with party colleagues immediately after the collapse of the Hitler regime, leading the reorganisation of his party initially from the 'Schumacher Bureau' in Hanover, which after he had been joined by Ollenhauer and Heine in February 1946 (Hans Vogel had died in London in October 1945) became the 'Bureau of the Western Zones'.

However pointless it would be to try to construct a consistent political philosophy from Schumacher's thinking, nevertheless the elements of Socialist theory by which he was consistently influenced are unmistakable. Prominent among them were Lassalle's affirmation of the state and that thinker's characteristic emphasis on the indissoluble connection between the democratic freedom of a people within the state and that state's external independence. And when Schumacher called Marxism 'the method that, particularly as applied to analysis, we have to thank for more strength and more insights and more weapons than any other scientific and sociological method in the world',[9] he was doing more than simply paying his respects to the traditional doctrine of German Socialists, a doctrine to profess which was, for the space of twelve years, possible only at the risk of one's life. Schumacher's interpretation of social phenomena and their inter-relatedness, his general social criticism, and particularly his idea of the place of his party in the historical process were often couched in a conceptual language that was derived entirely from Marxist thought. But a more powerful influence on Schumacher's intellectual stance than any scientific system was his first-hand, personal *experience*: the First World War, the crisis-ridden Weimar years and the collapse of the Republic, the time of trial under the National Socialists, the Second World War, and the destruction of the Reich.

Schumacher's affirmation of state and nation and his fierce commitment to the Weimar Republic linked him to Social Democrats such as Carlo Mierendorff, Julius Leber, and Theodor Haubach. Though he was sharply critical of the immobilism and ineffectiveness of his party in the final Weimar years, the SPD nevertheless was and remained for him the representative of the 'other Germany', the moral and political antithesis of the Hitler state and those who supported it. That party's claim to leadership in the new Germany therefore seemed to him to be as imperative a moral and historical consequence as was the new Germany's claim to equality of national status and self-determination. Schumacher identified his own role totally with that of his party. And despite some criticism in its ranks directed at particular aspects of his policy and his personal style of leadership, no one challenged his unique position within the organisation. The positions of principle, too, that for almost a decade and a half were to be accepted as the foundation of Social Democratic policy were for the most part backed by the party's representatives with a remarkable degree of unanimity — if also, depending on the supporter's position in public life, with varying degrees of emphasis — or at least taken on board without contradiction. Where there were differences they concerned questions of political procedure, not of objective.

The harmony that the relaunched party enjoyed at the outset seems somewhat surprising in retrospect, given the fact that people had rallied to the SPD flag and risen at varying speeds to leading positions in the party whose political past and ideological patterning diverged from those that had characterised Weimar Social Democracy, indeed in

9. Speech at the SPD conference in May 1946; reprinted in Arno Scholz and Walther G. Oschilewski (eds), *Turmwächter der Demokratie. Ein Lebensbild von Kurt Schumacher*, Vol. 2 (Berlin, 1953), pp. 75–101.

some cases stood in direct contradiction to it, the best-known examples being Carlo Schmid, Adolf Arndt, Herbert Wehner, and Karl Schiller. There was also the fact that men such as Willy Brandt, Waldemar von Knoeringen, Erwin Schoettle, and Willi Eichler, who at the time of the Republic or during the years of exile had left the SPD because of differences of political opinion, now exercised important functions within the party organisation. This testified to a power of integration in the refounded party that was undoubtedly due to a great extent to the charismatic personality of Kurt Schumacher. It was Schumacher, too, who from the outset stressed the openness of the resurrected party in terms of ideology, inviting particularly those who subscribed to Socialism on Christian grounds to find their field of political activity within the SPD.

What, then, were the goals that Social Democrats pursued in the early post-war days? 'Sozialismus als Gegenwartsaufgabe' ('Socialism as a task for today') was the slogan, hammered home as the title of Social Democratic speeches and articles, that crystallised the emergent conviction that a country that lay in ruins could not and should not be reconstructed in accordance with the principles of a capitalist economy. These, it was felt, neither possessed the necessary efficacy, nor did they satisfy the demands of justice. At the first post-war conference of the SPD in Hanover Victor Agartz, who apart from Kurt Schumacher was the principal speaker, defined this position more precisely: 'Social Democracy rejects . . . as being unjust and inappropriate, particularly to the position of the German people today:

(a) liberalism in its original form . . .
(b) monopoly capitalism with imperialistic tendencies . . .
(c) the corporate state . . .
(d) centralised state capitalism in the form of a marketless economy . . .
(e) the neo-liberalism currently emerging . . .'.[10]

Conference's agreement was expressed in the elections for the executive committee: Agartz received the second-highest number of votes, only two fewer than Schumacher himself.[11]

'The planned economy and socialisation' — so Erik Nölting, as spokesman of the economic-policy committee, told the party executive in the following year — meant the 'implementation of the Socialist ideal in the economic sphere'; socialisation was not, however, to be

10. *Protokoll des SPD-Parteitags 1946*, pp. 65f.
11. *Ibid.*, p. 180.

equated with nationalisation.[12] 'A fresh framework on Socialist foundations' must be created for the German economy that should embrace 'the primary industries to be socialised and the state-controlled financial institutions'.[13] Addressing the party conference three years later, Hermann Veit once again catalogued the sectors of the economy that were to be socialised: the key industries of mining, iron, and steel, the power-producing industry, the large-scale chemical and building-materials industries, the big banks and insurance companies, and finally those monopoly industries with respect to which a transfer to common ownership was preferable to monopoly control.[14]

When Veit — who was then Minister of Economic Affairs in the state of Württemberg-Hohenzollern — made these demands it was already much too late for them to stand any chance of being even partially implemented. But in the initial phase of political reconstruction after the Second World War the idea of a radical structural alteration of the social system was very much in the air, so to speak. The concept of socialisation found expression not only in the Ahlen Programme adopted by the CDU in February 1947 but also in the constitutions of several states and — albeit in a watered-down form — in the Basic Law, the national constitution promulgated in May 1949. In the summer of 1948 a motion put forward by the SPD in the *Landtag* of North-Rhine-Westphalia requesting the permission of the British military government to transfer parts of the coal industry to common ownership was supported by something like a third of the CDU deputies. The intentions behind this socialisation project, which was frustrated by the opposition of the occupying power, were not simply economic and socio-political in character. Those who launched it were seeking to prevent an 'anti-democratic capitalist hegemony on the Ruhr' in future and to 'remove fears' that reconstruction on the Ruhr might come to constitute 'a threat to [European] security' — 'fears that are being advanced in justification of demands for an industrial dismantling programme'.[15] While 'the transfer of the means of production to common ownership' had been *the* classic demand of Social Democratic programmes from Gotha (1875) to Heidelberg (1925), in the years after 1945 it took on fresh aspects. Whereas Social Democrats had shrunk from taking any practical steps in this direction in the aftermath of the First World War on the grounds that one could not socialise a heap of rubble, after the collapse of 1945 they saw the

12. *Protokoll des SPD–Parteitags 1947*, pp. 158, 161.
13. Resolution of the 1947 party conference; *ibid.*, p. 228.
14. *Protokoll des SPD–Parteitags 1950*, p. 192.
15. Fritz Henssler, chairman of the Social Democratic parliamentary party in the North Rhine–Westphalia *Landtag*; *Protokoll des SPD–Parteitags 1948*, p. 54.

very ruin of the economy as their opportunity to erect a radicallly new system that would be egalitarian in its effects and ensure peace. In this they were making two assumptions: that all attempts to solve the problem of reconstruction by capitalist methods would swiftly and inevitably come to grief; and that the proletarised masses, having been through the ordeals of National Socialism, war, collapse, flight, and expulsion, would be filled with an anti-capitalist yearning that Social Democracy might and must satisfy by proceeding to take concrete action. Both assumptions were to prove erroneous.

In terms of foreign policy, which under Schumacher's influence attained a pre-eminent rank for the first time in the history of German Social Democracy, the reunification of Germany in freedom became the objective against which all considerations and all actions had to be gauged. At the heart of the reunification problem was of course the relation of the Soviet-occupied zone to the Western zones, but the policy of the SPD was in general directed at the restoration of Germany within its 1937 frontiers, which included the reincorporation of Saarland, the maintenance of Berlin's claim as the capital of the country, and non-recognition of the Oder-Neisse Line. The emphasis placed on these demands, particularly by Schumacher, has often been seen as expressing a new nationalism intended to eradicate the stigma of want of patriotism that had attached to Social Democracy under the Empire and the Weimar Republic. Such an interpretation overlooks how insistently the party supported the 'integrity of the Reich' in the First World War and how solidly the labour movement combated all separatist aspirations during the Revolution and the Weimar period. The 'unity of the Reich' as an aim may be traced back in the history of the SPD all the way to its foundation — certainly the party's policy after 1945 implied no break with tradition in this respect. It was given a topical emphasis by a further consideration springing from traditional Social Democratic values, namely that it must be the task of every German politician operating in freedom to work towards reunification in accordance with the right to national and democratic self-determination. Yet another factor was the conviction that a divided Germany would mean a permanent latent or manifest threat to peace in Europe and in the world. This fixation on reunification, while for the space of some fifteen years it lent an inner logic to the foreign policy of the SPD and its attitude to the defence question, at the same time gave it a rigidity that considerably reduced its chances of success.

The SPD's reunification policy must, of course, always be seen in conjunction with the fact that — as Hans-Peter Schwarz established through his penetrating analysis of the Social Democratic foreign policy of the early post-war period — Schumacher had 'from the outset pointed the SPD in a direction in which it could count on support only from the West. And since in 1945 and 1946 he was counting firmly on Social Democracy making the breakthrough to power, this meant nothing less than an early and — at least while he was leader — irrevocable option for a Western orientation for Germany.'[16] That option implied very much more than the expression, by a powerless object in the international interplay of forces, of a preference for one of the two power-blocs. It implied a commitment to the values and forms of the political system that had emerged from the Western tradition, though not — far from it — to the policies of the various Western powers. It was not only at the time that Schumacher's fundamental decision met with the full agreement of the party as a whole;[17] at no subsequent stage of the party's development was that decision ever questioned.

## 2. The Decision to Form the Opposition

When a question in an opinion poll run by the British military government in 1947 asked for the most-admired post-war politician, Kurt Schumacher was the only one people named. Around the same time a poll run by the American military government in its zone found that 40 per cent of those questioned had heard of Schumacher; Adenauer was not even mentioned.[18] However, the celebrity enjoyed by the party chairman was out of all proportion to the confidence shown in his party at the ballot-box, despite the fact that the SPD was seen by the public as 'the Schumacher party'. The earliest elections in the Western zones went very badly for the party. This emerges particularly clearly from a comparison of seats won. Let us look at a few figures, setting the results achieved by the SPD against those of its largest rival, the CDU:[19]

16. Hans-Peter Schwarz, *Vom Reich zur Bundesrepublik. Deutschland im Widerstreit der aussenpolitischen Konzeptionen in den Jahren der Besatzungsherrschaft 1945–1949* (Neuwied/Berlin, 1966), p. 500.

17. 'What we need most urgently,' Erich Ollenhauer wrote to the chairman of the Dutch Socialists on 6 April 1946, 'is the moral and political support of the West European labour movement and all truly democratic forces in the West. That support is the only possible counterpoise to pressure from the East. . . . We shall not yield and we shall pursue our course for as long as our strength lasts, because this is not about tactics and manoeuvring; what is at stake here is the existence or not of a free German labour movement and with it the survival chances of a new and viable German democracy'; quoted in Hans-Peter Schwarz, *Vom Reich zur Bundesrepublik, op. cit.*, p. 499.

18. See Lewis J. Edinger, *Kurt Schumacher, op. cit.*, p. 271.

19. Election results taken from Richard Schachtner, *Die deutschen Nachkriegswahlen* (1956), and the statistical yearbooks and monthly reports of the individual states. The figures for the French zone include the results from Saarland. 'CDU' covers the

*American zone*

| | | | | |
|---|---|---|---|---|
| Municipal elections (1946) | SPD | 17.3% | CDU | 35.2% |
| District elections (1946) | SPD | 27.2% | CDU | 62.6% |
| State and city parliamentary elections (1946–7) | SPD | 36.2% | CDU | 41.5% |

*British zone*

| | | | | |
|---|---|---|---|---|
| Municipal elections (1946) | SPD | 24.4% | CDU | 28.2% |
| District elections (1946) | SPD | 35.1% | CDU | 46.4% |
| State and city parliamentary elections (1946–7) | SPD | 49.0% | CDU | 27.4% |

*French zone*

| | | | | |
|---|---|---|---|---|
| Municipal elections (1946) | SPD | 11.9% | CDU | 45.9% |
| District elections (1946–7) | SPD | 23.9% | CDU | 61.0% |
| State parliamentary elections (1947) | SPD | 28.0% | CDU | 52.4% |

*Berlin*

| | | | | |
|---|---|---|---|---|
| City-council elections (1946) | SPD | 48.5% | CDU | 22.3% |
| Borough-council elections (1946) | SPD | 48.9% | CDU | 22.9% |

In only a few elections did the SPD manage to defeat the CDU, namely in the Hanseatic city-states (in the parliamentary elections of 13 October 1946 and in Bremen again on 12 October 1947), in all municipal, district, and state parliamentary (*Landtag*) elections in Hesse, Lower Saxony, and Schleswig-Holstein in 1946–7, and in the municipal elections in the Württemberg part of the state of Württemberg-Baden. Its most impressive results were achieved in Berlin.[20]

These election results in the three Western zones aroused disappointment among Social Democrats but did not spark off any general discussion. Admittedly, the outward opportunities for such a discussion were thoroughly unfavourable: communication between the zones was difficult, the French zone being virtually cut off from the others; there were no Social Democratic newspapers with a more-than-regional range; and above all the party's active functionaries, totally preoccupied in dealing with everyday cases of public and

Christian parties operating under different names in the various states. — The author wishes to thank Dr Rüdiger Wenzel for collating the figures.

20. See Willy Brandt and Richard Löwenthal, *Ernst Reuter, ein Leben für die Freiheit* (Munich, 1957), p. 357.

private distress, were scarcely in a position to embark on a thorough consideration of its future. Clearly, too, the party leadership failed to take the verdict of the electorate as indicating that many of the premisses on which the party's basic programmatic position had been erected might rest on false readings of the situation and need to be re-examined.

Indirectly the *Landtag* election results were of considerable importance in determining what was to be the position of the SPD for years to come. At the beginning of 1947 the British and Americans decided to unite their zones economically and by creating an Economic Council for the combined zones to grant the German people parliamentary representation at a higher level than hitherto. The members of the Economic Council, which was to sit in Frankfurt am Main, were delegated by the individual state parliaments and were required to elect the directors of five central economic administrations. Of the original 52 seats on the Economic Council (the number was later doubled, though the party quotas remained the same), which began its work in May 1947, 20 went to the SPD, 21 to the CDU, 4 to the FDP, 3 to the KPD, and the rest to smaller parties. The SPD claimed the right to fill the post of Director of the Administration for Economic Affairs with a Social Democrat. When its claim failed because the CDU, with FDP backing, insisted on giving the job to its own man, the SPD refused to participate in the Administration and decided to go into opposition — a decision that had been urged by Kurt Schumacher and that some leading Social Democrats (Fritz Henssler, for example, the chairman of the party in Westphalia) had sought to block. It was to be a 'constructive opposition', though, as the SPD stressed from the outset. In fact the Social Democratic members worked very hard on the Economic Council and were able, as their chairman noted with satisfaction after eighteen months of activity, to exert a considerable 'influence on the arrangement of matters of detail, which have unfortunately received no public recognition'.[21] Yet when in the wake of the currency reform of June 1948 living conditions in the Western sector gradually improved, the economic upswing was attributed to Ludwig Erhard and the parties backing him, while the SPD received the negative tag of 'the opposition'.

The SPD for its part had hoped that the oppositional role for which

---

21. Herbert Kriedemann, addressing the party conference in September 1948; see *Protokoll des SPD–Parteitags 1948*, p. 120. Deserving of mention in this context is the work done particularly by Anni Krahnstöver and Wilhelm Mellies (second chairman of the SPD, 1952–8) in connection with the 'equalisation of burdens' legislation (*Lastenausgleichsgesetz*) designed to compensate persons who had suffered materially as a result of the war.

it had plumped in the Economic Council would lead to a decisive increase in its vote and in its popularity. In the regional states created after 1945 coalition governments had been formed in which the SPD had usually received the economic-affairs portfolio, among others; external circumstances, particularly the dependence of those states on the military governments and the limited opportunities for getting the problems of reconstruction under control in the context of the state, were seen by Social Democrats as hampering their chances of success. Now they were counting on being able, in opposition, to open people's eyes to the fact that, as Schumacher said in his address to the 1948 party conference, so great was the 'ruthlessness of this class struggle from above . . . that over the last year there has been no important question on which agreement would have been possible without abandoning the interests of the working masses and betraying the struggle for Socialism as a job for today'.[22]

It was not only with regard to the effects of Erhard's economic policy that the SPD got it wrong. Even more crucially, it counted on the social injustices associated with that policy driving the 'working masses' into the Socialist camp, whereas it turned out that the majority was prepared to put up with them as long as its own standard of living — measured against the poverty of the immediate post-war years — was rising in relative terms. Furthermore, people's experience of the war economy and of the post-war economy had led to a widespread rejection of statism and to an identification of Socialist planning with rigid government control of the economy.

With hindsight it can be said that in later years the SPD would not have repeated its decision to go into opposition, faced with a situation comparable to that of the spring of 1947. It is worth noting, however, that that decision had given 'the young democracy a reliable opposition party that was above suspicion of radical intentions'.[23]. The political constellation in the Frankfurt Economic Council anticipated that which obtained in the parliaments and governments of the first seventeen years of the Federal Republic. The decision that made that constellation possible thus constitutes a turning-point in the history of post-war German Social Democracy. The roles were cast for a long time to come: a coalition of 'bourgeois' parties formed the federal government while Social Democracy provided the 'constructive opposition'.

22. *Protokoll des SPD–Parteitags 1948*, p. 32.
23. Ulrich Dübber, 'Die deutsche Sozialdemokratie nach 1945', in *Aus Politik und Zeitgeschichte*, a supplement to the weekly *Das Parlament*, B 21/62, 22 May 1963, p. 56.

### 3. The Establishment of the Basic Law

The attitude of the SPD towards the formation of the Federal Republic was the logical consequence of its decision for a Western orientation. Whereas Schumacher had rejected all initiatives towards reaching first economic but then also political agreements through conferences of the minister-presidents in the four zones — and had not shrunk, in the process, from clashing with leading Social Democrats whose loyalty to their party was beyond all doubt[24] — the attitude of the party leadership towards the London Resolutions of June 1948 was in the end essentially positive. The minister-presidents and the parties of the three Western zones decided to accept the principal task outlined in the resolutions, namely to work out a constitution for West Germany. The arguments of the elected — but not confirmed — Mayor of Berlin, Ernst Reuter, at the second meeting of the military governors with the West German minister-presidents on 20 July 1948 made a crucial contribution here. Reuter succeeded in convincing those present that 'the political and economic consolidation of the West is a fundamental prerequisite for our recovery too and for the return of the East to the motherland'.[25]

Granted, the contribution of the SPD to the work of the Parliamentary Council was governed by the party's view that the constitution to be established could only be of a provisional nature since for one thing 'rump Germany' possessed no sovereignty and for another the Russian zone of occupation as well as the territories beyond the Oder-Neisse Line were excluded from the discussion.[26] At the conferences of minister-presidents at Schloss Niederwald and on the Rittersturz (a hill near Koblenz), which met before the Parliamentary Council was summoned, the Social Democrats had made these points emphatically. Nevertheless it is a fact that the thoroughness of the Basic Law is due not least to the hard work put in by the Social Democrats. Yet even in retrospect Social Democratic members of the Parliamentary Council pointed out that their main concern was 'to avoid firm commitments'.[27]

In view of the numerical strength and the expertise of the Social Democratic group on the Parliamentary Council — of the 65 members

24. See especially Wilhelm Kaisen, *Meine Arbeit, mein Leben* (Munich, 1967), pp. 236ff., 267f.
25. See Willy Brandt and Richard Löwenthal, *Ernst Reuter*, p. 474.
26. See the report on the Parliamentary Council in *Jahrbuch der SPD 1948/1949*, pp. 12ff.
27. Letter from Fritz Eberhard to the author, 16 November 1972. See also Wilhard Grünewald, *Die Münchener Ministerpräsidentenkonferenz 1947. Anlass und Scheitern eines gesamtdeutschen Unternehmens* (Meisenheim am Glan, 1971).

of the latter, 27 belonged to the SPD, the same number as belonged to the CDU/CSU — and the pre-eminent position of its leading constitutional lawyer, Carlo Schmid, as chairman of the central committee, it may seem surprising that the Basic Law contains so few articles governing social questions. The chief reasons for this lie at two different levels. The SPD concerned itself with constitutional matters earlier than the other parties after 1945 and in fact adopted 'Guidelines for the Reconstruction of the German Republic', as drafted by its constitutional committee, at only its second party conference after the war.[28] But one looks in vain, both in those guidelines and in the detailed report made by the committee's chairman, Walter Menzel, for any remarks of substance regarding basic social rights and obligations[29] — a fact indicative on the one hand of programmatic uncertainty and on the other of a view of the party's objective 'according to which democracy was understood simply as the form of government of a Socialist-organised society'.[30] The fact that the Social Democrats 'confined themselves to the classic basic rights and deliberately avoided laying down so called social frameworks' was plausibly justified by Carlo Schmid on the grounds that they would otherwise have 'exceeded the scope of the task, which was simply to provide an interim solution'.[31] A more specifically Social Democratic motive was summed up twenty years later by an SPD member of the Parliamentary Council: social articles were 'not [to be created] without the Saxon comrades'.[32] In essence, what was behind the refusal to lay down social frameworks was Lassalle's theory that constitutional questions were power questions — in a reunited Germany Social Democracy, so it believed, would be in a position to mould the new constitution in accordance with its own economic and socio-political ideas.

While on the one hand the Social Democrats stressed the interim nature of the future Federal Republic, on the other hand they applied themselves energetically to ensuring that that provisional arrangement should be as effective as possible. This required them to form a

---

28. *Protokoll des SPD–Parteitags 1947*, pp. 225ff. For a detailed account, see Werner Sörgel, *Konsensus und Interessen. Eine Studie zur Entstehung des Grundgesetzes für die Bundesrepublik Deutschland* (Stuttgart, 1969), pp. 59ff.

29. *Protokoll des SPD-Parteitags 1947*, pp. 121ff.

30. Volker Otto, *Das Staatsverständnis des Parlamentarischen Rates. Ein Beitrag zur Entstehungsgeschichte des Grundgesetzes für die Bundesrepublik Deutschland* (Düsseldorf, 1971), p. 205.

31. Carlo Schmid, in his introduction to Werner Matz, *Grundgesetz für die Bundesrepublik Deutschland und Besatzungsstatut* (Stuttgart/Cologne, 1949), p. 7.

32. Volker Otto, *Das Staatsverständnis des Parlamentarischen Rates*, p. 86.

common front with the FDP against the federalism not only of the CDU/CSU and the German Party but also of the Americans and the French. This collaboration with the Liberals constituted a further reason — and a very cogent one — for the SPD to refrain from any precise definition of basic social rights. Under Schumacher's leadership the campaign against federalist solutions took a dramatic turn, culminating in the celebrated meeting in Hanover on 20 April 1949 to which the party chairman, scarcely recovered from his leg amputation, summoned the leaders of the party including the Social Democratic group on the Parliamentary Council and the Social Democratic minister-presidents.

The six-point resolution passed at that meeting took a stand against the intervention of the Western occupying powers, who were demanding a high degree of federalism in the structure of the Federal Republic, particularly as regarded its financial administration. It called for 'the necessary German freedom of decision' vis-à-vis the occupying powers, 'the preservation of German legal and economic unity', and a fiscal settlement 'that provides the federation with the ways and the means that it requires to fulfil its functions', and it announced that the SPD would reject a Basic Law that failed to satisfy one of its six demands.[33] Shortly afterwards an agreement was reached between the Parliamentary Council and the Allies that, while it did not entirely meet the Social Democrats' preconditions, nevertheless implied crucial concessions over the questions of legal and economic unity and federal powers in relation to finance. It was an unequivocal victory for Kurt Schumacher.[34]

Warned by the Weimar experience, the SPD endeavoured to make the constitution a factor for stability. This also explains the Social Democrats' insistence on the powerful position of the Federal Chancellor as anchored in the constitution. Their support for this was bound up with an optimistic assumption that it would fall to the SPD to nominate the first — and possibly the second, third, and so on — Chancellor of the Federal Republic. But something very different happened: the constitution allowed Adenauer to build up his 'Chancellor democracy' — a development that the Social Democratic authors of the Basic Law failed to foresee.

33. *Jahrbuch der SPD 1948/1949*, p. 139. Ernst Reuter, Wilhelm Kaisen, and the Minister-President of Schleswig-Holstein, Hermann Lüdemann, moved at the meeting that the concluding ultimatum be deleted, but their motion was rejected, eight of those present voting against it; see Willy Brandt and Richard Löwenthal, *Ernst Reuter*, p. 487.
34. Theo Pirker's view — in *Die SPD nach Hitler* (Munich, 1965), p. 100 — that this was a 'Pyrrhic' victory rests on his assumption that Schumacher wished to thwart the whole constitution-making process in order to prevent a deepening of the division of Germany as a result of the creation of a West German state. I regard that assumption as

# 12

# 'Constructive Opposition'

When the first *Bundestag* was elected on 14 August 1949 the SPD received 29.2 per cent of the vote, the CDU/CSU 31 per cent, the FDP 11.9 per cent, and the KPD 5.6 per cent, the rest being shared between smaller parties that without exception disappeared during the next few years. Given this result, Social Democratic participation in government was ruled out in advance, for the initiative in forming the Cabinet lay with the largest party in the *Bundestag*, the CDU/CSU, whose chairman Konrad Adenauer had neither occasion nor inclination to parley with his slightly weaker rival. There could be no doubt, judging from the experience of the Frankfurt Economic Council, that the FDP and other middle-class parties would opt for coalition with the party of Adenauer and Erhard. Thirteen years were to pass before there was any sign at all that the SPD's fixation on the role of opposition, as allocated to it by the verdict of the electorate, might relax. And not until a further four years had gone by did the party succeed in changing that role. Yet never before had German Social Democracy had in its midst a figure who laid claim to power for the party with such insistence and such self-assurance as Kurt Schumacher did, though at the same time there is no mistaking the contribution his policies made to the fact that power was denied it for so long.

A fortnight after the *Bundestag* election the executive committee of the SPD adopted the so-called 'Dürkheim Points' — sixteen political principles that were shortly afterwards approved by the parliamentary group and by the SPD minister-presidents as well. This document reflected the SPD's conception of its function and responsibility as a 'constructive opposition', as the statement by Erich Ollenhauer — who was now Schumacher's deputy not only in the party but also in the parliamentary group — underlined: 'Our opposition programme

---

false. Moreover, the view that Schumacher had been advised of the Allies' intention — formed as early as 8 April 1949 but kept secret — to give in whatever happened (see Volker Otto, *Das Staatsverständnis des Parlamentarischen Rates*, p. 118) is also regarded by close colleagues of Schumacher as wholly erroneous.

of today should be and will be our government programme of tomorrow.'[1] At Dürkheim the SPD proceeded, for the first time since 1945, to establish a comprehensive programme of its immediate tasks and objectives. Demands in the fields of economic and social policy formed the bulk of the Dürkheim resolutions. They planned to 'take away the power of the big proprietors and managers by socialising the primary and key industries' while 'securing the free development of small business and the rural middle class'.

In the first years of the Federal Republic the SPD directed its main criticisms of the government at the latter's passivity in the matter of job-creation — in the winter of 1950 there were nearly two million unemployed — and predicted a catastrophic aggravation of this problem. With the mounting success of Erhard's economic policy, however, the substance of the Social Democrats' criticisms changed: the effectiveness of the Erhard policy was called into question less and less, but they persisted in drawing attention to the social injustices and hardships to which that policy gave rise. It made the rich richer and the poor poorer, they claimed in a catchy formula. Nevertheless, the differences of principle between government and opposition over economic and social policy lessened as time went on. The programme of action adopted by the SPD at its Dortmund conference in September 1952 already showed an important change of emphasis as compared with the 'Dürkheim Points': where these had laid the main stress on planning and control of the economy and on the socialisation of primary and key industries, in Dortmund the SPD declared that in addition to planning it would promote 'genuine competition in all suitable branches of the economy' and 'small and medium-scale private ownership'. Two years later, at the party conference in Berlin, the programme of action was expanded and the relationship between planning and competition characterised in the slogan: 'Competition wherever possible, planning wherever necessary.'[2]

In the field of domestic policy in the broader sense the parliamentary practice of the SPD was wholly in accordance with its early decision to operate as a 'constructive opposition'. This found expression not only in the party's important contribution to the vast and intricate body of legislation created in the first legislative periods of the *Bundestag* — particular mention should be made of its role in housing legislation — but also in the fact that by far the greater part of all laws

1. *Protokoll des SPD Parteitags 1950*, p. 91. For the 'Dürkheim Points', see *Jahrbuch der SPD 1948/49* (Bonn, 1950), pp. 18ff.
2. The Dortmund/Berlin 'programme of action' is reprinted in Dieter Dowe and Kurt Klotzbach (eds), *Programmatische Dokumente der deutschen Sozialdemokratie* (Bonn, 1973), pp. 297ff.

went through the *Bundestag* with the votes of the Social Democrats behind them. Among the important pieces of social-policy legislation for which the SPD refused to vote because it had failed to get its way with its ideas about how they should be formulated were the Equalisation of Burdens Law and the Family Allowance Law (*Kindergeldgesetz*). In the sping of 1951 the law giving workers 'co-determination' in mining companies and in the iron and steel-producing industry was passed with the votes of both the CDU and the SPD, but the SPD stood alone with its proposals for the Works' Constitution Law (*Betriebsverfassungsgesetz*) and rejected the government's bill in a special vote by named cards that it had moved. The passage of the federal budget was regularly opposed by the Social Democratic parliamentary party — a traditional symbolic act of the parliamentary opposition.

However, the true confrontation — and it was a tough one — took place not in the sphere of domestic policy but in that of foreign, European, and defence policy.[3]

## 1. The Campaign for 'a New National Self-Awareness'

The most spectacular clash between the two dominant figures of the early years of the Federal Republic, Konrad Adenauer and Kurt Schumacher, occurred as early as 1949, two and a half months after the *Bundestag* first assembled. During the debate on the Petersberg Agreement, which granted limited sovereign rights to the federal government, Schumacher, heckling Adenauer, called him the 'Chancellor of the Allies' and was punished with exclusion from parliamentary proceedings for twenty days. Shortly before his death (on 20 August 1952) Schumacher summarised in the foreword to the draft of the Dortmund programme of action the basic ideas that had governed his policy since 1945. This impressive document, full of anger and pain, reads like a settling of accounts with Adenauer. 'Under no circumstances,' it says, must Germans be allowed to 'sink to the position of a subject people'; 'the policy of the German democracy must not be a function of the Western occupying powers'; the German people must be given 'a new national self-awareness . . . as far from the criminal wantonness of the

---

3. Attention has been drawn to the repercussions of differences regarding foreign policy questions on the chances of the CDU and the SPD reaching agreement over social and economic policy, as exemplified by the Works Council Law and the Equalisation of Burdens Law; see Klaus Schütz, 'Die Sozialdemokratie im Nachkriegsdeutschland', in *Parteien in der Bundesrepublik*, pp. 251ff.

past as from the present widespread tendency to see every Allied desire as a revelation of European thinking'. Even the reiterated statement that for the SPD 'German unity is no long-term objective but an immediate objective' had a polemical undertone.

It is only against the background of this view held by the SPD chairman, a view he championed ever more passionately the more sharply it contrasted with the objectives and the tactical flexibility of his victorious rival for power in the state, that the decisions of the SPD as arrived at by Schumacher and initially pursued by his successor, Erich Ollenhauer, can be understood. At issue were three sets of problems closely bound up with one another: the political and economic integration of the Federal Republic in Western Europe; its status within the Western bloc; and its military rearmament.

A difference of opinion among Social Democrats that to a far greater extent than occasional earlier clashes within the party took on a public dimension as well arose at the Hamburg party conference in May 1950 out of a debate about whether the Federal Republic should join the Strasbourg-based Council of Europe. Schumacher's arguments against joining had to do with the fact that the Saar region — not at that time a part of the Federal Republic — was likewise to be accepted as a member of the Council, which would have implied recognition of its national autonomy. More generally, however, he objected to the structure of the 'Europe of the Six' — symbolised by the Strasbourg body — as being 'conservative, clerical, capitalist, and cartellistic'.[4] A deeper motive was undoubtedly Schumacher's concern that the integration of the Federal Republic in Western European institutions, in which Socialists would be able to exert only limited influence, would erect ever greater obstacles to a reunification of Germany. Schumacher's objections to the Schuman Plan were of the same order. In addition they took on a certain nationalistic colour from the charge repeatedly advanced as the weightiest argument against the Federal Republic joining the European Coal and Steel Community, namely that the French partner would benefit at the Germans' expense.

Schumacher, who particularly over the Council of Europe received effective backing from Carlo Schmid, was given an overwhelming vote of confidence at Hamburg when the executive committee's resolution was adopted against only eleven dissenting votes. The dissenters, however, were no political lightweights, including as they did Ernst

4. 'Konservativ, klerikal, kapitalistisch, kartellistisch.' Schumacher repeatedly cited the 'four Ks' as characterising the 'Europe of the Six' or 'Kleinst-Europa' ('Minimal Europe'). The most concise summary of Schumacher's criticism of these plans is to be found in a speech of his that the SPD executive published as a pamphlet entitled *Deutschlands Forderung: gleiches Risiko, gleiches Opfer, gleiche Chancen!* ('Germany demands: the same risk, the same sacrifice, the same opportunities!'; Hanover, undated).

Reuter, Willy Brandt, Max Brauer, and Paul Löbe. The Mayor of Bremen, Wilhelm Kaisen, though not present at the party conference, also sided with the opposition and lost his seat on the executive at Hamburg.

A degree of confusion was sown among the rank and file when despite its rejection of German accession to the Council of Europe the party sent representatives to Strasbourg, where they were soon among the most highly respected members of the Council. In all the other European political and economic institutions, too, German Social Democrats played an important and in many instances even a leading role in the ensuing years. It was a role that, as far as the economic organisations were concerned, they owed to some extent to the fact that the German Trades Union Congress adopted a positive — if not uncritical — attitude towards the European Coal and Steel Community from the outset. In spite of its initial resistance to the 'Europe of the Six' the SPD made a great contribution towards developing, shaping, and extending it.[5]

The deepest rifts between government and opposition were provoked by the decision, initiated by the Federal Chancellor, to make a German contribution to the Western system of defence by rearming the Federal Republic. The resistance put up by the Social Democratic Party leadership towards the creation of the *Bundeswehr* and its incorporation in a European defence community was able to derive support from the widespread pacifist and anti-militarist attitude of the rank and file membership without identifying with that attitude in its political argumentation.

Like its rejection of German participation in the new European institutions, the Social Democratic Party's protest against the rearming of the Federal Republic was made mainly from the point of view of the priority of German reunification, although at first the party leadership placed other arguments in the foreground. A crucial role in Schumacher's complicated defence concept — which was characterised by his dictum that Germany must be defended on the Oder, not on the Elbe — was played by the demand that the Federal Republic must be an equal partner with the victorious powers in every respect before it could be expected to make a military contribution of its own. The SPD felt that Stalin's note of 10 March 1952 further justified its insistence that all possibilities of an agreement between the four occupying powers regarding a reunification of Germany must be explored exhaustively. The danger that a West German army operating within a

5. Impressive testimony to this from the standpoint of a leading French 'European' was provided by the letter from Jean Monnet to Herbert Wehner published in *Die Zeit* on 13 October 1972.

Western defence system might harden the fronts between the two blocs running right through Germany haunted the SPD. The government of the Federal Republic, however, was irrevocably committed to a Western 'policy of strength' and not prepared to talk to Stalin about a possible revision of that line.

In the first *Bundestag* the SPD was still in a position to prevent the constitutional changes required to raise armed forces from receiving the necessary two-thirds majority, but at the 1953 general election it lost that capability. Against the votes of the SPD the *Bundestag* decided in February 1954 to amend the Basic Law in such a way as to make it possible to introduce conscription. All the efforts of Social Democracy to block the creation of the *Bundeswehr* had come to nothing. Just how deeply the question of its attitude to the defence problem exercised the party from the grass roots to the leadership can be gauged from a resolution adopted by the 1954 party conference. This laid down five conditions that must be met if the SPD was to pronounce itself ready 'to participate in joint endeavours to safeguard peace and defend freedom by the use of military measures as well'. A party conference must establish whether this was the case. Those conditions were: that efforts to secure reunification be continued; that a European system of security be sought within the framework of the United Nations; that the treaties under which the Federal Republic entered into military commitments be made terminable; that all participants be granted equality of status; and that the armed forces be placed under democratic parliamentary control.[6]

After the SPD's negative attitude to the defence question had undergone increasing modification over the next four years under the influence of *faits accomplis* in the Federal Republic and political developments on the international stage — with the efforts of Fritz Erler to bring about such a change playing an important part here — the relevant resolution of the Stuttgart party conference in 1958 called for 'a numerically restricted but mobile and well-trained body of volunteers'.[7]

With respect to the whole body of defence legislation the Social Democratic parliamentary party likewise conducted itself as a 'constructive opposition', although vigorous voices were raised within its ranks in favour of non-participation in the committee stages. It rejected the 1955 Paris treaties and all the laws serving to recreate a German army — dismissing them as *Vertragsfolgegesetze* ('treaty-compliance laws'). On the other hand the laws concerning the basic

---

6. *Protokoll des SPD Parteitags 1954*, p. 341.
7. *Protokoll des SPD Parteitags 1958*, p. 488.

rights of soldiers and their social status were framed with the intensive co-operation of the SPD and passed with its votes.[8]

The SPD's committed opposition to rearmament took on a special quality not merely from the importance, complexity, and emotional resonance of the issue but equally from the fact that the campaign was also waged by the party in the extra-parliamentary arena.[9] After the signing of the Paris treaties, for example, it tried by collecting signatures for a 'German Manifesto' adopted at a rally in Frankfurt's famous Paulskirche on 29 January 1955 to launch a mass movement for which it counted on the support particularly of sections of the trade-union movement and the Protestant church. The result, however, fell short of the party's expectations. For its 'Campaign Against Nuclear Death' launched four years later with the object of demanding the creation of a nuclear-free zone in Europe the SPD elicited the co-operation of well-known writers, scientists, and theologians. It also managed to stage impressive mass demonstrations in some cities. But far from the movement bringing any direct political success, it neither helped to get the official opinion poll on nuclear arms that the SPD wanted nor did it influence the mood of the electorate in favour of the SPD, as was shown by the elections in North-Rhine-Westphalia in July 1958, when the CDU secured an overall majority. The abrupt termination of the anti-nuclear campaign was thus understandable in political terms, though it came as a disappointment particularly to those who had been drawn by it to make their first approach to Social Democracy.

A last, one might say desperate attempt to develop a concrete alternative to the government's policy with regard to the reunification of Germany as an 'immediate objective' was the SPD's 'Plan for Germany', which was drawn up very much under the influence of Herbert Wehner and presented in March 1959 by the executive committees of the SPD and its parliamentary group. This provided for a militarily 'thinned-out' zone in central Europe, discharged from NATO and the Warsaw Pact, and a gradual political and economic bringing-together of the two parts of Germany in preparation for elections covering the whole country. It was not only the fierce public attacks on the plan and the way in which it was ignored by both governments — in West and East Germany — that quickly sealed its fate. The fact that its publication coincided with the return of Fritz Erler and Carlo Schmid from a trip to Moscow, from which they brought back an impression

8. See Ulrich Dübber, 'Die deutsche Sozialdemokratie nach 1945', in *Aus Politik und Zeitgeschichte*, pp. 60ff.

9. See Hans Karl Rupp, *Ausserparlamentarische Opposition in der Ära Adenauer* (Cologne, 1970), especially pp. 47ff., 98ff., 127ff., 149ff., 173ff., 213ff., 250ff., 263ff.

of Soviet intransigence, may also have contributed to its being quietly buried.

The first decade of the Federal Republic thus ended for the SPD with the realisation that it was 'farther removed than at any time since the end of the war' from achieving its 'most essential national objective, namely to restore the unity of Germany in freedom'. On the domestic front, too, there had been 'no essential change in the antagonistic positions of Adenauer's one-party government and the Social Democratic opposition'. Yet when Erich Ollenhauer struck this balance of stagnation in July 1960,[10] signals had already been set within the party that allowed the stalled locomotive to continue along another track.

## 2. Party Reform and the Godesberg Programme

If we follow the development of the Social Democratic share of the vote in general elections from 1949 to 1972 we find it tracing a rising curve marked by an almost steady increase of between 3 and 4 per cent at each election. At first, however, there was a slight dip when in 1953 the SPD lost 0.4 per cent of the vote as compared with 1949 — despite the fact that in absolute terms it gained a million voters. The 1953 result sparked off a debate within the party of a breadth and vigour unparalleled in the post-war years, a debate that involved every level of the hierarchy from individual groups in the constituencies to key members of the national leadership. A great many critiques were drawn up at regional and local level and placed before the membership; a series of well-known Social Democrats spoke on the radio or wrote in the press about the consequences that the party must draw from its defeat at the polls.[11] Criticism was directed at the way in which the party was organised and also at its public image and the form taken by its propaganda. Surprisingly, the actual policy of the SPD since 1945 was virtually excluded from the debate. There was little call for this to be changed; rather it must be more effectively 'sold'.

If one wished to characterise the state of ferment that seized the party after 1953 with a greatly over-used phrase one might say it was a question of 'overcoming the past'. It was Carlo Schmid who referred

10. In his foreword to the party's 'Yearbook'; see *Jahrbuch der SPD 1958/59*, p. 7.
11. A brief account of the debate within the SPD in 1953 is given in Heinz-Joachim Mann, 'Das Godesberger Programm als Ergebnis innerparteilicher Willensbildung', in *Geist und Tat*, 24th year, No. 4 (1969). Unlike some other authors — Wolf-Dieter Narr, Theo Pirker, and Harold K. Schellenger, for example — Mann avoids the danger of mistaking the reality of the party as a result of sometimes unfounded categorisations of those involved in the debate.

to the need, ideologically speaking, to 'drop ballast', an expression that was immediately taken up and vigorously discussed both inside and outside the party. The 'ballast' included the old symbols and customs of the party — the red flag, calling people 'comrade', using the familiar form of address — but also, beyond these externals, the whole question of the influence of Marxism on the minds of Social Democrats.

To evaluate the discussion the executive committee of the party appointed two commissions: one to look at questions of organisation, the other to look at all the other matters. While the recommendations drafted by the commissions[12] and adopted by the executive committee and the central party council had no visible effect either within the party or on the outside world, a number of resolutions were passed by the executive committee in connection with the discussion that were important with regard to the further development of the party. Certain sections of the programme adopted in Dortmund in 1952 were expanded in 1954, and the whole thing was given a preamble that foreshadowed certain features of the Godesberg Programme — the ideological openness in the justification of Socialism, for example, and the SPD's awareness of itself as having evolved from a labour party into 'the party of the people'. Steps were also taken to increase educational work within the party and to found a theoretical journal. At the Berlin Party conference (1954), which is to be regarded as having in some ways wound up the debate of 1953 — the address by Willi Eichler summed up its key points and drew conclusions from them regarding the future work of the party — it was decided to appoint a commission to draw up a basic programme.

The leadership debate that had already played a certain part in the SPD after 1953 was intensified in the wake of a disappointing result in the 1957 general election, when although the SPD gained an additional 3 per cent of the vote the CDU/CSU secured an overall majority. It centered on the chairman of the party, Erich Ollenhauer, with whose lack of personality as the party's candidate as Chancellor the election defeat was associated. The impossibility of fielding personalities attractive to the mass electorate as the potential head of government and his Cabinet team was blamed on the 'party machine', in other words on the 'Bureau' of salaried members of the executive at party headquarters. The object of the reforms sought by influential figures and by the party organisations backing them was therefore to reduce the power of the 'machine' and to restructure and re-man the party leadership. This they managed to do at the party conference held in Stuttgart in May 1958, when although Erich Ollenhauer was re-elected

12. The recommendations were published in *Jahrbuch der SPD 1954/55*, pp. 320ff.

as chairman he was given two deputies, Waldemar von Knoeringen and Herbert Wehner, intended to express between them the breadth of the Social Democratic spectrum — Wehner being at that time regarded as the most prominent representative of the left wing while Knoeringen was an extremely popular politician particularly in Bavaria, a man in the tradition of his distinguished fellow-Bavarian Georg von Vollmar. The 'Bureau' was abolished as an institution, and two of its members — Hertha Gotthelf and Fritz Heine — failed to secure re-election to the executive committee. Changes to the party constitution made at Stuttgart henceforth placed the management of affairs in the hands of a *Präsidium* or standing committee elected by and from among the party's executive committee.

The Stuttgart conference also saw the first reading of the draft of a Basic Programme prepared by a commission sitting under the chairmanship of Willi Eichler. The fact that the draft was presented eight months after the SPD had suffered its third general-election defeat was closely bound up with the shock that the defeat aroused. The decision to draw up a Basic Programme to replace the programme of action adopted in Dortmund in 1952 and expanded two years later had been taken at the Berlin party conference of 1954. The thirty-four-member programme commission had not been appointed until March 1955, however, and its work and that of its various sub-committees had made only slow progress in the early years. It was Erich Ollenhauer's spontaneous reaction to the 1957 election defeat to herald the adoption of the Basic Programme as the most important consequence the party would draw from that bitter experience. And it was Ollenhauer again who urged the commission to present its findings as soon as possible. Ollenhauer's faith in the possibility of creating a basic programme at this stage and his belief that it would offer an important means of increasing the attractiveness and effectiveness of the party were by no means shared by the party leadership as a whole. Just such 'reformers' as Willy Brandt, Fritz Erler, Helmut Schmidt, and Herbert Wehner, for example, had misgivings about once again laying down the principles of democratic Socialism in a programme and so committing the party for some time to come. They would have preferred to see the party confine itself to programmes of action.

Before the Stuttgart conference the party as a whole had shown little or no interest in the preparation of the programme, and even after publication of the draft concern was only feeble at first. Subsequently, however, a debate got under way at all levels of the party organisation that revealed a degree of involvement that is without parallel in the history of Social Democratic programmes. At hundreds of meetings two men in particular, Eichler as chairman of the programme commission and Heinrich Deist as the author of the economic section of the draft programme, grappled with innumerable objections and suggested alterations. After a series of meetings of the commission — in the later stages involving the executive committee of the party as well — had tightened and revised the first draft and the section headed 'The Order of the State' had been rewritten by Adolf Arndt, an extraordinary party conference was summoned to discuss and adopt the document. A total of 340 delegates met in Bad Godesberg from 13–15 November 1959 to deal with 200 motions put down by local and regional branches relating to the second draft. In the final vote the draft, which even at Godesberg had undergone several amendments, was adopted almost unanimously; there were only sixteen votes against.

The most notable feature of the Godesberg Programme is its avoidance of any hard and fast ideological or theoretical commitment. It professes 'fundamental values' and puts forward 'basic demands' that are open to a variety of religious or philosophical justifications. This openness had the effect of removing barriers that had hitherto prevented German Social Democracy from gaining adherents, particularly among the religiously committed.[13] Furthermore, the 'special mission' of the churches and their 'autonomy' were explicitly affirmed.

The most controversial section of the programme — argued over even at the Godesberg conference — was that concerning economic policy. The importance of competition, already stressed in the Dortmund programme of action, was emphasised even more strongly in the Basic Programme. The term 'socialisation' was not used, though a paragraph was devoted to the function of 'public ownership', which was described as 'a legitimate form of public control' that was 'appropriate and necessary' wherever 'sound economic power relations cannot be guaranteed by other means'. An ambiguous concept not explained in concrete terms was introduced when in the context of remarks about 'Trade Unions in the Economy' reference was made to the co-determination that already existed in certain industries as marking 'the beginning of a new economic structure'.

Stronger on circumstantial detail than other sections of the Godesberg Programme is that devoted to 'National Defence', which starts by stating unreservedly that the SPD 'is in favour of national defence'. Nor is that statement qualified at all by the demands and objectives that follow it — 'an easing of international tensions', disarmament and the banning of 'the means of mass destruction', a ban on the produc-

13. Although there had been some relaxation in this regard since 1945, in North Rhine–Westphalia for example the SPD was still in the 1950s unable to secure a direct mandate in *Landtag* constituencies with electorates that were more than 40 per cent Roman Catholic.

tion and use of 'atomic or other means of mass destruction' in the Federal Republic, 'the inclusion of the whole of Germany in a European zone of reduced tensions', and so on.

For the rest the Godesberg Programme essentially sums up the principles that have guided the SPD since 1945: the belief in parliamentary democracy, the dissociation from Communism, the protection of individual liberty, the aspiration to social justice, solidarity with the weak, and the promotion of science and education. No attempt was made to define that controversial word 'Socialism'. The programme confines itself to a reference to the historical roots of democratic Socialism in Europe, namely 'Christian ethics, humanism, and classical philosophy'. Earlier conceptions, derived from Marxism, of a Socialist 'ultimate goal' are implicitly rejected by the statement that Socialism is 'a constant task — to fight for freedom and justice, to preserve them, and to live up to them'.

Undoubtedly the adoption of the Godesberg Programme did a great deal to reassure the party and clarify matters for the membership. Its greatest effect, however, was to transform the public image of the SPD, so creating the conditions in which it might achieve its goal of becoming a 'people's party' attractive to various classes of voters.

Further important decisions regarding both personnel and policy were of course necessary after Godesberg to get the party out of the rut of its 30 per cent share of the vote. But before we turn our attention to those decisions let us look at a crucial difference between the SPD after 1945 and the SPD in the Weimar and Wilhelmine periods to which it partly owed its eventual escape from that rut. In the old days Social Democracy had offered its members a total environment, as it were — 'Vaterhaus und Lebensinhalt' (literally 'parental home and life-substance'), as Otto Bauer pertinently expressed it — in the form of a whole range of associations: workers' gymnastic, sports, and hiking clubs, a Freethinkers' Union coupled with cremation facilities, workers' choral societies and orchestras, book clubs, people's theatre organisations, chess clubs, and so on. In so doing, however, it had at the same time cut them off from the rest of the population. After the Second World War either such associations were never resurrected or, where they survived as not unimportant sub-organisations, they had altered their character considerably. As a result the Social Democratic 'sub-culture' was largely dissolved. This led to a greater degree of integration of Social Democrats in the wider life of society, which in time increased the party's influence. The most obvious manifestation of this was the popularity that many of its representatives attained among the public in general at local and regional level, examples being Hinrich Wilhelm Kopf and Georg August Zinn, the Minister-

Presidents — known as *Landesväter* (literally 'fathers of the state') — of Lower Saxony and Hesse respectively, the city-state heads Max Brauer in Hamburg and Wilhelm Kaisen in Bremen, and the well-known figures of the Lord Mayors who in most cities from Kiel to Regensburg and from Cologne to Kassel belonged to the SPD. The Mayors of West Berlin, from Louise Schroeder onwards, were seen as incarnations of the city's desire for freedom and of its will to live. Ernst Reuter, of course, enjoyed an importance far beyond that of the head of a city government. In his relatively brief period of office — from 1947 until his death in 1953 — he became a statesman of European rank. The same is true of Willy Brandt, a later successor of Reuter as Governing Mayor of Berlin.

The reputation of Social Democratic politicians at state and local level of course rested primarily on their objective achievements. Many of them, however, acquired a special popularity on top of that as a result of their interest in traditional popular functions and festivities, through which they reached incomparably greater numbers than through political channels. These popular SPD politicians of the 1950s and 1960s were for the most part staunch Social Democrats from the Weimar period, when many of them — men such as Kaisen, Brauer, and of course Reuter, whose career and personality were altogether out of the ordinary — had already held responsible positions. To describe Kaisen and Brauer as representing a 'new type' of Social Democrat, as opposed to Ollenhauer and other 'functionaries' of the 'machine', as the American historian Harold K. Schellenger does, for example,[14] is to miss the fact that it is not a question of different 'types' but of people performing different functions. As far as the image of the SPD as a 'people's party' was concerned it was important to feature personalities who because of their position were independent of the party machine and whose achievements and demeanour made them known to and popular with large sections of the population. At state and local-government level the SPD possessed a greater reservoir of such politicians than the other parties. It is to the credit of Erich Ollenhauer and the men and women who had helped him to lay the foundations of the SPD after 1945 that the party was able to alter its image without in the process becoming a party of notabilities or a purely electoral organisation. It remained a party of the membership; indeed it succeeded in broadening its base considerably in the coming years.

---

14. See Harold K. Schellenger, *The SPD in the Bonn Republic. A Socialist Party Modernizes* (The Hague, 1968), pp. 131ff.

# 13
# The SPD's 'New Style'

'We have to realise that, given the present state of society, we are swimming not with the current but against it.' When Fritz Erler made that observation in 1950 before the supreme governing body of the party, the party conference,[1] the recognition he was voicing was by no means common knowledge among the membership. Yet the policy of German Social Democracy from the Second World War to the end of the 1950s cannot be more appositely portrayed than by Erler's image of a 'swimming against the current'. The Godesberg Programme broadened the party's scope for manoeuvre very considerably, but the real change in its policy was not dictated directly by the principles laid down at Godesberg but arose out of a fresh analysis of the situation and out of decisions taken as a result.

The clashes over the SPD's 'Plan for Germany' in the spring of 1959 had once again thrown the antagonism between government and opposition into sharp relief. Looked at in the light of wider developments, however, they have an anachronistic, unreal quality about them. Even at the time the SPD accepted the need to find a common starting-point with the government for dealing with the vital questions affecting the German people, one that should be based on a 'taking of stock' by government and opposition with regard to foreign and German policy. In view of the fact that at that time the integration of the Federal Republic in the organisations of Western Europe was a *fait accompli* while over the German question complete stagnation had set in, the Social Democrats' demand for a 'joint taking of stock' appears understandable and justified and the publication of their 'Plan for Germany' a self-inflicted sabotaging of their own efforts.

Having ground to a halt, the relationship between the government and the opposition suddenly lurched into motion — or so at least it seemed to the public — when following the failure of the Paris summit conference in May 1960 Herbert Wehner delivered what was regarded as a sensational speech in a foreign-policy debate in the *Bundestag* on 30 June 1960. Wehner stated explicitly that the 'Plan for Germany',

1. *Protokoll des SPD–Parteitages 1950*, p. 247.

together with the proposals put by the SPD to other, earlier conferences of foreign ministers, was a thing of the past. It was a question, he
said, of 'interpreting the signs of the times thus: not tearing ourselves
to pieces but working together in the context of the democratic whole,
albeit in businesslike mutual opposition over domestic policy'.[2] His
offer, in other words, went significantly further than the demand for a
'joint taking of stock'; it indicated a readiness to pursue a joint foreign
policy. The executive committee of the SPD, meeting the day after the
*Bundestag* debate, gave its unanimous acceptance to the course marked
out by Wehner's speech, and a few months later that course was
sanctioned by the party conference as well.

The SPD's 1961 general-election campaign was conducted entirely
in the 'new style'. The most striking feature of it were decisions
relating to personnel. At the end of November 1960 Willy Brandt was
presented to the Hanover conference as the party's candidate for the
chancellorship, together with his 'team' consisting of Max Brauer,
Heinrich Deist, Fritz Erler, Wenzel Jaksch, Alex Möller, Willi Richter,
Carlo Schmid, Fritz Steinhoff, Käte Strobel, and Georg August Zinn.
These had been selected by a seven-man commission of executive-
committee members from the point of view of their expert qualifica-
tions for government office but also in the light of their personal
popularity and electoral 'catchment area' (Jaksch, for example, was a
leading representative of the 'League of Expellees'; Richter was Chairman of the German Trades Union Congress).

The boldest decision, in traditional hierarchical terms, was the
nomination of Willy Brandt as the party's *Kanzlerkandidat*. Brandt
had only been elected to the executive committee in 1958 and was not
initially a member of its *Präsidium*; it was only after his nomination
for the chancellorship that he was invited to *Präsidium* meetings. His
'power-base' within the party lay in Berlin, where after a protracted
and — on his side — patiently and fairly fought struggle for power
with the Franz Neumann faction he had become chairman of the regional branch of the SPD in 1958. The reputation he enjoyed among a
vast public extending far beyond the frontiers of the Federal Republic
flowed from his activities as Governing Mayor of Berlin, a post he
had succeeded to on the death of Otto Suhr in 1957. Particularly in
the crises with which that city was afflicted he showed himself to be a
supremely level-headed politician — who also enjoyed in high degree
the confidence of the 'protecting power' in the shape of the United
States. Ernst Reuter's foreign-policy plan — which hinged on incorporating the non-Communist part of Germany in a strong Europe

2. *Stenographische Berichte*, Vol. 46, pp. 7058ff.

under American military leadership while at the same time pursuing cautious attempts to reach an understanding with the East — had been backed by Brandt and developed further by him after Reuter's death in 1953. The new course embarked on by the party leadership in the summer of 1960 was likewise in line with that plan.[3] Of the various aspects of Brandt's expertise and personality that recommended him as the party's candidate for the chancellorship, not the least important was the fact that at the age of forty-seven he was able in many respects to provide a positive contrast to the eighty-four-year-old Konrad Adenauer.

Even after Brandt's nomination Erich Ollenhauer remained chairman of the SPD and of its parliamentary group. Not until Ollenhauer's death on 14 December 1963 did Brandt take over the chairmanship of the party and Fritz Erler that of the *Bundestagsfraktion*. In the public eye, however, these two men together with Herbert Wehner were already regarded as the leading, most influential representatives of 'new-style' German Social Democracy.

At the Hanover party conference Brandt described the 'twin foundations of a new-style policy' as being 'solidarity and a sense of decency'.[4] The 'Appeal' adopted by the conference — as a prelude to the coming election campaign tailored entirely to Brandt's candidacy for the post of Chancellor — concentrated almost exclusively on domestic-policy demands while in the field of foreign policy it stressed the search 'for a broad basis' for insisting on the right to self-determination and reunification and preventing any separation of Berlin from the West.[5] However, the manifesto published in April 1961 made more concrete statements with regard to foreign policy too — for example in rejecting the 'two states' theory and in stressing the need to expand the European Economic Community, to improve relations with the East European nations, and to increase development aid.

At the general election of 17 September 1961 the SPD increased its vote by 4.4 per cent over 1957, achieving its best result yet at national level, but with a total of 36.2 per cent of the vote it remained the opposition party. Its suggestion that an all-party government be

---

3. The importance of Brandt's foreign-policy orientation as far as his nomination as *Kanzlerkandidat* was concerned is rightly recognised but is over-emphasised in Abraham Ashkenasi, *Reformpartei und Aussenpolitik. Die Aussenpolitik der SPD* (Berlin, Bonn, Cologne, and Opladen, 1968), p. 196: 'It was this unchanged foreign-policy stance that increased Brandt's attractiveness in the eyes of the Social Democratic king-makers and that rendered him indispensable to the SPD even after the two defeats of 1961 and 1965.'

4. *Protokoll des SPD–Parteitages 1960*, p. 674.

5. *Jahrbuch der SPD 1960–1961*, p. 420.

formed following the building of the Berlin wall met with no response. Talks took place between Herbert Wehner and the CDU/CSU deputies Paul Lücke and Karl-Theodor von Guttenberg towards the end of 1962 to explore the idea of a Great Coalition, but they were without result.

The activity of the SPD between the 1961 and 1965 general elections was so lacking in drama and spectacular climaxes as to remind one of Hegel's dictum that periods of good fortune form empty pages in history. The party quite clearly experienced a certain euphoria during that time. After years of disappointments it sensed for the first time the presence of 'Comrade Trend': things were beginning to go its way. It observed the end of the Adenauer era with hopes understandably high, its own leadership — Willy Brandt as *Kanzlerkandidat* and First Chairman after Ollenhauer's death, Herbert Wehner as Second Chairman and 'strong man' of the party, and Fritz Erler as a brilliant parliamentarian — clearly superior to the increasingly stale leadership of the government parties. Crises in the government camp helped to compromise the latter's standing, while the SPD's Godesberg Programme, its popular candidate for the chancellorship, and its 'course of unity' combined to present the party in a new and brighter light. The important thing now was to anchor this new image firmly in the public mind. It was a question, as an official SPD report put it, of persuading broad sections of the population that the party's 'new style' inaugurated in 1960–1 had not been a 'piece of electoral claptrap' but the 'outward and visible expression of an inner development towards becoming a people's party, one that has been proving its fitness to govern at many levels of German political life for decades'.[6]

The outcome of the 1965 general election, however, failed to live up to the party's expectations. With 39.3 per cent of the vote the SPD was still a long way behind the CDU/CSU, which secured 47.6 per cent. The disappointment of the Social Democrats at this success on the part of their political opponents was deepened by its having been achieved in spite of the fact that the Union parties had exposed some weak points, particularly in the replacement of Adenauer by Erhard, and cracks had begun to appear in the financial position of the Federal Republic.

6. *Ibid.*, p. 324. The programmatic recognition of church schools, albeit without abandoning the party's preference for non-denominational schooling, lay in the same direction; see the 'Guiding principles of the SPD with regard to educational policy' adopted in July 1962, in *Jahrbuch der SPD 1962–1963*, pp. 450ff.

## 1.  The SPD in the Great Coalition

The SPD got its chance of coming to power only when the old government coalition found itself in a situation of overt crisis that was generally seen as such. In the autumn of 1966 Chancellor Ludwig Erhard showed himself no longer equal to the domestic-policy difficulties then manifesting themselves in economic recession, mounting unemployment, and gains by the recently (in 1964) founded *National-demokratische Partei Deutschlands* (NPD; 'National Democratic Party of Germany') in *Landtag* and local elections. Moreover on the foreign-policy front there was a danger of the Federal Republic becoming isolated. Erhard was abruptly dropped by his party (CDU), while the FDP withdrew its four ministers from the government. The new *Kanzlerkandidat* elected by the CDU/CSU, Kurt Georg Kiesinger, tried at first to rebuild the coalition with the FDP. When the attempt failed, the negotiating commissions of the CDU/CSU and the SPD agreed on 26 November 1966 to recommend to their respective parties the formation of a joint government.

The forming of the Great Coalition in 1966 was the upshot of one of the most hotly disputed political decisions in the history of German Social Democracy.[7] An alternative would have been to form a government with the FDP, in which the SPD would have appointed the Chancellor and been by far the more powerful partner. However, the SPD could not bring itself to run the risk of governing with so small a majority in the *Bundestag*, a risk that would have been further increased by differences of opinion within the FDP. The other possibility — attempting to force a dissolution of parliament and fresh elections — also struck the SPD leadership as too risky since neither the CDU nor the FDP favoured such a course.[8] Nor did the SPD find it particularly tempting, if only because the *Landtag* elections in Hesse and Bavaria in November 1966 had brought only a tiny increase in its vote. Finally, to critics of the Great Coalition who maintained that the SPD should leave it to those who had made the mess to clear it up, Brandt replied: 'We are too big for that now.' The effort must be made 'to bring about the limited but nevertheless possible success for Germany, including the SPD, that, once it starts proving its worth in important areas, will win additional trust'.[9]

---

7. A good overall view is provided by the collection of documents published by the executive committee of the SPD, *Bestandsaufnahme 1966* (Bonn, 1966).
8. See Willy Brandt's speech to the central party council on 28 November 1966; reprinted in *Bestandsaufnahme 1966*, pp. 61f.
9. Willy Brandt, addressing the SPD central party council on 28 November 1966; *ibid.*

Subsequent developments proved the correctness of this assessment. The Great Coalition government under Chancellor Kiesinger, in which the SPD had nine ministers and eight secretaries of state, was successful 'in important areas', and the official kudos thus acquired was eventually to help the SPD to reach its objective.

The most decisive and immediately apparent results were achieved in the fields of economic and budgetary policy. The Minister of Economic Affairs, Karl Schiller (SPD), managed in collaboration with Finance Minister Franz-Josef Strauss (CSU) — whose membership of the coalition Cabinet had initially been the hardest pill for many Social Democrats to swallow — to bring unemployment down with amazing speed: by the autumn of 1968 it was below 1 per cent. Industrial production in 1968 rose by nearly 12 per cent. Much of the success of the economic and budgetary policy of the new government in Bonn was due to the fact that it had been able to win over both unions and entrepreneurs for a 'concerted campaign'. The co-operation of the trade unions and employers in general enabled the government to implement its plans for reviving the economy with relatively little friction.

Particular importance attached to the various measures taken by the state and federal governments working in tandem to remedy the crisis in the Ruhr coal industry. In the *Landtag* election in North-Rhine-Westphalia in July 1966 the SPD had become the strongest party, falling just short of an overall majority. Its breakthrough particularly in rural areas and small towns and its gains among the Roman Catholic population were unmistakable signs of the change in the political climate: the SPD now stood a chance of being elected even in former CDU strongholds. After fifteen months in office the CDU Minister-President of the state gave up in the face of growing difficulties and the Social Democrat Heinz Kühn formed a Cabinet in conjunction with the FDP.[10] The positive record of the 'Little Coalition' in the largest state of the federation and the personal influence of Minister-President Kühn were not without their effect on subsequent decisions of the FDP at national level.

After the initial misgivings felt by many members and supporters of the SPD over the link with the CDU had begun gradually to abate, they were re-aroused in the spring of 1968 by the passage of the Emergency Laws. No body of legislation had provoked so violent a public reaction nor released such a storm of protest in circles that

10. It is significant as regards the mood within the SPD that Kühn's original intention of collaborating with the CDU on the Bonn pattern was blocked by the resistance of the SPD deputies in the *Landtag*.

belonged to the SPD's traditional electorate since the clashes over the military rearmament of the Federal Republic. Even in the parliamentary party there was a minority that argued in the *Bundestag* for rejection of the Emergency Laws, exercised a not inconsiderable influence on the debate concerning them, and in the end voted against the legislation.

Afterwards, however, once the laws had been passed by a huge majority — of SPD votes too — the excitement quickly died down or at any rate ceased to play any further political role.

The activities of Foreign Minister Willy Brandt, on the other hand, met with an unreservedly positive response within the party from the outset. These were directed towards consolidating and extending the European Community, strengthening the Federal Republic's connections with its Western neighbours — here Brandt was concerned to restore a more cordial tone to relations with France, which had cooled somewhat under Foreign Minister Schröder — and complementing his predecessor's *Westpolitik* with a systematically developed *Ostpolitik*. Steps in this direction were the preparation of a non-aggression pact with the Soviet Union, the resumption of diplomatic relations with Yugoslavia (broken off in 1957), and finally a paving of the way for talks with the German Democratic Republic.[11]

However, in addition to the inestimable gains that the Great Coalition brought the SPD by providing it with its first opportunity at national level to persuade the public that the 'perpetual opposition party' was capable of governing, it also brought certain internal problems. During this period unrest among the section of the membership represented by the Association of Young Socialists (*Jusos*) became more apparent than ever before. Admittedly, the party leadership had already clashed so severely with the SPD-financed and protected *Sozialistischer Deutscher Studentenbund* (SDS; 'Socialist German Students' Association') back in the late 1950s that it had eventually, in 1960, made membership of the SDS incompatible with membership of the SPD and arranged for the *Sozialdemokratischer Hochschulbund* (SHB; 'Social Democratic Universities Association') to be founded. There had been rows and disagreements with the youth organisation known as 'The Falcons', too, but for twenty years the Young Socialists had never once given the party serious cause for concern — especially since at the time they did not constitute a power factor. Any attempt to go into the reasons why this changed under the Great Coalition and the extent to which the coincidence was accidental or causally deter-

11. An attempt by the SPD in the first half of 1966 to arrange an exchange of speakers with the SED at party level had met with failure.

mined would take us far beyond the scope of a brief party history and cannot be undertaken here. Let us merely note one circumstance that typified the party's internal affairs and was directly related to the efforts of the SPD leadership to get the party into shape to win elections, assume governmental responsibility, and show itself capable of running the country.

Once the Godesberg Programme had been adopted, discussion of questions of principle ceased abruptly; the new programme was cited but not interpreted. Moreover the party's new tendency to model itself on political success-stories sometimes so powerfully outweighed all other considerations that observers of the process described it ironically as the SPD's attempt to become the best CDU there had ever been. Younger party members reacted to it with scepticism, criticism, and opposition, an attitude for which they found no sympathy among the party 'establishment' and with which they often encountered what they saw as authoritarian rejection. Given this situation, the Young Socialists gradually learned to develop a strategy and tactics that put them into key positions within the organisation in many places and secured them important posts at local and state level. The fact that in this way the necessary change of generations in responsible positions was often accelerated, the pool of activists extended, and competition for seats intensified is one aspect of Young Socialist activity. The other, looked at in the long term, is even more significant: this was to counter the danger, which had set in after Godesberg, of the SPD stagnating intellectually. The *Jusos* relaunched a discussion that despite the immaturity of many of their political demands and their inflated emphasis on theories and 'models' stimulated a necessary re-examination of fundamental questions of Social Democratic policy.

## 2. The Brandt/Scheel Governments

It is unlikely that the architects of the Great Coalition ever regarded it as anything other than a necessary transition stage, a strictly interim solution. The prospect of a fresh constellation, more favourable to the SPD and promising greater permanence all round, emerged towards the end of the legislative period with the presidential election of March 1969. The parties of the government coalition each put up a candidate, the CDU/CSU backing Gerhard Schröder, then Minister of Defence, and the SPD backing Gustav Heinemann, the Minister of Justice in the Great Coalition Cabinet. The outcome of the election depended on how the two opposition parties, the FDP and the NPD, decided to vote. The latter declared against the SPD candidate from the start; the

FDP leadership had decided for him, but it was an open question right up until the day of the election whether the party's deputies would follow suit. In giving their united vote to Gustav Heinemann the Free Democrats not only tipped the balance in his favour but removed any Social Democratic doubts — generated by past experience — about the reliability of the FDP.

The late 1960s saw a change in the social climate of the Federal Republic. The movement known as the 'student revolt', which had begun in America and reached its European climax in Paris in May 1968, quickly spread to the universities of West Germany. The protest against existing conditions, while it received its most violent expression from the current generation of students, was shared by other milieux that had tended to be somewhat passive in their socio-political behaviour hitherto. Women voiced their dissatisfaction with their position in both private and public life and began with a fresh awareness and understanding of themselves to get organised in groups representing their interests. People at various levels of society began questioning established authorities and distributions of roles and challenging traditional patterns of thinking and modes of behaviour. Topics were tackled in public debate that had previously been the exclusive province of 'experts' or 'outsiders'. A growing number of citizens became convinced that there was a great deal that must be changed. Politically this mood of anti-conservatism precipitated in the form of support for the SPD.

On 28 September 1969, after an election campaign in which the SPD had received unprecedented backing from well-known personalities outside its ranks — actors, theatre directors, writers, scientists, journalists, sportsmen — the party won 42.7 per cent of the vote. Its most significant gains were among middle-class voters — and more among white-collar workers and civil servants than among the self-employed. Together with the FDP, which had received 5.8 per cent of the vote, it was able to form a Cabinet on a viable parliamentary base in the face of the massed opposition ranks of the CDU/CSU. The FDP received the ministries of Foreign Affairs, the Interior, and Agriculture. Foreign Minister Scheel also became Deputy Chancellor. The Education and Science portfolio was initially given to a non-party man, Professor Hans Leussink, which caused some astonishment among SPD members since educational reform was regarded as a specifically Social Democratic concern. When Leussink resigned three years later he was succeeded by the Social Democrat Klaus von Dohnanyi.

The policy of the Social–Liberal coalition was to be guided by the twin watchwords of 'continuity and renewal', Chancellor Brandt remarked in his governmental declaration of 28 October 1969.[12] Measuring the achievements of his government against those watchwords, we find that the first applied essentially to domestic policy and the second to foreign policy. Domestic legislation, particularly in the field of social policy, though extensive, did not in a single instance break fresh ground; rather it represented a logical continuation of the course pursued by the Great Coalition and to some extent by earlier governments as well. Some reforms were not passed because the period of office of the first Brandt/Scheel government ended after only three years. Others — for example relating to education and in particular the universities, to land law, and to the tax system — presented such enormous inherent difficulties that they fell short of their original purpose.

What on the other hand wholly bore the stamp of this first government of the Federal Republic under Social Democratic leadership was its foreign policy. Brandt himself always stressed that his *Ostpolitik* was merely the necessary complement to Adenauer's *Westpolitik*. Yet there is no mistaking the fact that through it fresh paths were trodden, ossified fronts received a new flexibility, and possibilities of an international *modus vivendi*, possibilities hitherto regarded as blocked, were now opened up. And a key factor in the response aroused by the policy was the way in which the treaties with Moscow, Warsaw, and East Germany not only did not damage relations between the Federal Republic and its Western allies and the European Community but actually furthered them. The granting of the Nobel Peace Prize to Willy Brandt in October 1971 strengthened large sections of the West German population in their belief that this government was coping with the country's political needs as they presented themselves a quarter of a century after the end of the war.

The vote over ratification of the *Ostverträge*, however, was taken by some deputies both of the SPD and of the FDP as an occasion for dissociating themselves from their respective parliamentary groups. The result was that the government parties lost their majority in the *Bundestag*. After a CDU/CSU motion of no confidence in the government had failed, all the parties reached agreement to the effect that fresh elections offered the only way out of the stalemate. The general election of 19 November 1972, brought forward in accordance with a complicated parliamentary procedure laid down by the Basic Law, saw the SPD, with 45.8 per cent of the vote, overtake the CDU/CSU for the first time (albeit by a mere 1.1 per cent) and the FDP achieve an unexpectedly high 8.4 per cent. Clearly the obvious problems of the Brandt/Scheel Cabinet, which manifested themselves particularly in

12. *Stenographische Berichte*, Vol. 71, p. 20.

ministerial resignations — most recently that of the once highly popular 'Superminister' of Economic and Financial Affairs, Karl Schiller — had not shaken the credibility of the government. In 1972 the SPD achieved its greatest election victory ever.

It had been an extremely hard-fought campaign, despite the fact that the objective differences at stake were smaller than had been the case in the 1950s, for example. However, political interest and degree of commitment among party sympathisers were now greater and capable of being roused more fiercely than in previous clashes by the political champions: Rainer Barzel and Franz-Josef Strauss on the one hand, Willy Brandt on the other. The negative aspect of this phenomenon — the danger of not only political but also moral defamation of the opposite number — ought not to blind us to its positive aspect: active participation in the political process by sections of the population that had hitherto been to a greater or lesser degree indifferent but that now professed loyalty to their favourite camp through the medium of 'electors' initiatives', street and house debates, canvassing, the wearing of badges, and other symbolic acts. This politicisation of the electorate benefited the SPD more than it did the CDU/CSU. The party made its largest gains, in comparison with earlier elections, among women, young voters, and working people in the lower income brackets. And with its record turnout at the polls the 1972 general election also scotched the belief that a high turnout would favour the SPD's opponents.

Not only the election victory of 19 November 1972, however, but also the internal development of the SPD revealed that the party's new conception of itself as expressed in the Godesberg Programme — 'from a party of the working class the Social Democratic Party has become a party of the people' — was in ever-increasing conformity with reality. Of new members joining the party in 1960, 55.7 per cent were manual workers, 21.2 per cent were white-collar workers and civil servants, 5 per cent were self-employed, 2.7 per cent belonged to the liberal and intellectual professions, 5 per cent were pensioners, and 9.3 per cent were housewives. The ensuing years produced some very remarkable changes in certain of these groups. The same breakdown of the 1969 new-membership figures shows manual workers accounting for only 39.6 per cent, white-collar workers and civil servants for 33.6 per cent, self-employed persons for 5.6 per cent, the liberal and intellectual professions for 7.8 per cent, pensioners for 5.6 per cent, and housewives for 9.6 per cent. The figures for 1972 show the shift towards the middle class continuing with only 27.6 per cent of new members manual workers but 34 per cent white-collar workers and civil servants; a further 15.9 per cent were students and schoolchildren (a group not previously isolated by the party statisticians), 9 per cent housewives, 3.7 per cent pensioners, and the remainder either self-employed, soldiers, or professional people.[13] Manual workers still constituted the largest group among new members of the SPD since some of those appearing as 'pensioners' or 'housewives' were undoubtedly retired manual workers or their wives, but the trend was unmistakably in the direction of pushing down the proportion of manual workers in the total membership.[14] A further feature of the development of the SPD was the diminishing average age of new members: whereas in 1960 55.3 per cent of those joining the party had been under forty years of age, in 1969 the figure was 67.2 per cent and in 1972 75.2 per cent (with 19.7 per cent under twenty-one). The trends visible here in the composition of the party in terms of profession and age-group would be much more pronounced still if one examined the make-up of the party's leadership and parliamentary representation at the various levels, but there are no comprehensive analyses available for this. In the spring of 1973 the membership of the SPD totalled nearly a million people, two-thirds of whom had joined the party within the last ten years.

German Social Democracy in the second half of the 1970s was thus a younger and a sociologically much changed party. Of the various questions that arose with regard to its further development, let us pick out just one, namely the relationship between party and government. The fate of the government led in 1928–30 by the Social Democratic Chancellor Hermann Müller had shown to what problems that relationship was exposed in Weimar. In Bonn it was not at first put to any real test, either during the Great Coalition or during the chancellorships of Brandt and his successor, Helmut Schmidt. One reason for this lay in the party's altered awareness of itself: tired of its opposition role, it had made a determined bid for power, and it now wanted to hang on to that power. But there were also personal factors. Herbert Wehner, the most influential man in the party organisation, had also been the prime mover behind the Great Coalition and as chairman of the parliamentary group during the Social–Liberal coalition was its staunch and indispensable supporter. The relatively smooth functioning of the Great Coalition in its early years, as regarded both the relations of the coalition partners to each other and those of the Cabinet to parliament, owed much to the efforts of Helmut Schmidt,

13. The figures are taken from SPD yearbooks and from documents made available to the author by the office of the SPD executive.
14. The proportion of manual workers in the population as a whole was going down too, but not as fast as in the SPD; between 1961 and 1970 it dropped by only 1.2 per cent.

who on the death of Fritz Erler in 1967 had taken over the chairmanship of the parliamentary group. Probably the most important factor
of all in ensuring a relationship of trust between party and government
was the fact that Willy Brandt remained — as Foreign Minister, as
Chancellor, and even after his resignation as head of government —
chairman of the Social Democratic Party. He led the party on a
somewhat loose rein at times, but in critical situations he contrived to
bring his immense authority and personal popularity to bear.

Although the loyalty of the SPD to the governments it manned was
not in question, it was significant that shortly after the election of 19
November 1972 Brandt emphasised strongly that the mandate from
the electorate implied a coalition of Social Democrats and Free Democrats.

Both he and Wehner issued stark warnings in the party's supreme
councils against any forming of factions within the party, whether on
the right or on the left wing. What prompted the party chairman and
his deputy to take that course was probably their fear that systematic
efforts might be made within the parliamentary group and the party
organisation to try to restrict the government's freedom of action and
decision, so undermining confidence in it.

The mere fact of the demand put forward by many local party
organisations that they be allowed to act in accordance with the
'imperative mandate' principle, by which an elected representative
must obey the dictates of the body that elected him or her, meant that
that fear could not simply be brushed aside. The growth of the party,
the shifts mentioned above in the social and age-rated make-up of the
membership, the increasing influence of young academics in the parliamentary group and in the organisational bodies of the SPD at all
levels, and above all the fact of the great election victory of 1972 and
the strong position of the SPD in the *Bundestag*, which removed the
earlier necessity for making concessions — all this made it more
difficult to avoid tensions between party and government. Besides, it
was inevitable that the party's programmatic ideas should go beyond
what was laid down by and could be directly implemented by the
coalition government.

This emerged clearly at the SPD's annual conference in Hanover in
April 1973. The leadership got its way in Hanover over almost all
policy questions. But its recommendations had already taken account
of the criticisms and suggestions put forward particularly by the
Young Socialists — though without any preparedness to make concessions as far as sticking to the Godesberg Programme and to the
foreign-policy course of the Social-Liberal coalition was concerned.
The executive committee elected in Hanover, which showed more

changes than were usual at such re-elections — something like a quarter of its members were classed as 'left-wing' — reflected the way the party was developing. The elections and resolutions of the Hanover party conference did not in fact lead to a polarisation within the party's own ranks. But what Hanover did very clearly show is that a 'people's party' of the size and breadth of the SPD naturally embraces a variety of tendencies — so had it at the time when it saw itself as a labour party — that seek to express themselves and to influence the decision-making process. To have ignored that fact — one that testifies to the democratic liveliness of an organisation and prevents it from becoming ossified — would have led to conflicts and crises. At the Hanover party conference Willy Brandt once again gave proof of his ability to unite his party by appreciating its members' problems and by inspiring confidence.

### 3. Contributions to the Social Democratic Programmic Debate after Godesberg

No party tried harder than the SPD to define its functions on the basis of what were to some extent freshly acquired insights into the international problems of the present and the future. Social Democrats who had for years, even for decades, been active in leading positions in the party organisation, in parliament, or in the government or been concerned academically with important political questions voiced their opinions in publications that won respect far beyond the confines of their own party.[15] Despite differences of approach, of style, and in some instances in the conclusions reached, the authors of such contributions were in agreement over three fundamentals: 1. the yardstick and the pointer of Social Democratic policy are and will always be the inseparably connected basic values of freedom, justice, and solidarity, as laid down in the Godesberg Programme; 2. the new challenges call not for any abandonment of reforms but on the contrary for their continuation, albeit with certain changes of emphasis; 3. Social Democratic policy can only and must only be implemented with the consent and co-operation of the citizens.

The differences in the way in which the problems were presented and in the order of priorities in proposals as to how they should be dealt with concerned the type of reforms: should these be cast in the traditional mould or should they reach out beyond it? A document

---

15. See, for example, the works listed in the bibliography by Willy Brandt, Helmut Schmidt, Erhard Eppler, Peter Glotz, Richard Löwenthal and Thomas Meyer.

drawn up by a team of politicians and academics working under Hans-Jochen Vogel, Heinz Ruhnau, and Hermann Buschfort called for the 'preservation of what has been achieved' as the 'immediate task'. Essentially what was meant was a defence against dangers that threatened what had been achieved, a defence operating on the firm foundation of the *status quo*.[16] On the other hand Erhard Eppler considered a 'structural policy' — that is to say, an alteration of existing power structures in the economy, in the bureaucracy, and in international relations — to be indispensable if values crucial to the life of man were to be preserved.[17] These differences of emphasis in statements about objectives had nothing to do with those confusing watchwords *Systemstabilisierung* or *Systemüberwindung*, which reflected the concern expressed in various quarters over whether to 'stabilise' or 'overcome' the system. They were related instead to the question of how much the policy of the SPD can and must be guided by long-term prospects. The answer to that question likewise governed the decision about the choice of means.

The SPD made its most important contribution towards solving this range of problems by continuing and bringing to a conclusion work on its 'Framework of Orientation '85'.[18] In accordance with a resolution of the Hanover party conference of the spring of 1973 the executive committee of the party appointed a commission consisting of eight members nominated by the executive committee and twenty-two by the districts; it was headed by Peter von Oertzen, Horst Ehmke, and (after the death of Klaus Dieter Arndt) Herbert Ehrenberg. The task of the commission was to produce an up-to-date, revised version of the 'Framework', taking account of the proposals that had already been made and of the debate about the first draft at the Hanover conference. In carrying out that task it received the help not only of a staff of academic assistants but also of the party's specialist committees. Hundreds of study groups at local and sub-district level and countless meetings of every sort of party body lent their efforts to the same theme, drafted proposals, and elaborated contributions of their own — some modest, some quite extensive. The draft presented to the Mannheim party conference for adoption in November 1975 was thus 'the outcome of a lengthy, comprehensive, and far-reaching discussion' — as witness the 1,007 motions brought before the conference.[19] That

16. Hans-Jochen Vogel, Heinz Ruhnau, Hermann Buschfort, *et al.*, *Godesberg und die Gegenwart* (Bonn, 1975), pp. 29ff.
17. Erhard Eppler, *Ende oder Wende?* (Stuttgart, Berlin, Cologne, Mainz, 1975), especially pp. 28–37, 72–9.
18. The 1973 party conference had only a first draft before it.
19. The first section of the 'Framework' is reprinted here as Document 15; see below, p. 290.

discussion was not confined to the SPD but embraced supporters as well as determined critics of the party — in fact the spectrum of those involved in it reached from the trade-union movement right through to the two major Christian churches.[20] It was an extremely valuable experience for the members of the commission and their colleagues to find an intensive working and learning process succeeding in co-ordinating different opinions and temperaments and achieving results through joint efforts.

At the Mannheim party conference (held from 11–15 November 1975) the 'Framework of Economic and Political Orientation of the Social Democratic Party of Germany for the years 1975–1985' was approved — after a small number of changes to the draft on the basis of conference motions — with only two votes against and two absten-tions. What this signified was summed up at the conference by Horst Ehmke: 'We have compiled a framework of orientation that while it contains no easy solutions nevertheless does what we wanted it to do: to the political work of the party and to politics in this country for the next ten years, which are certainly not going to be simple, it offers a sense of political direction. . . But what seems to me equally important is that is has proved possible, after long years of sometimes difficult but nevertheless necessary discussion, particularly with the younger generation and what is known as "the young left", to find our way back to a large measure of material agreement within the party. From that fact the party may draw fresh pride and fresh strength.'[21]

Willy Brandt, in a Foreword to the published version, described the 'Framework' as a 'linking piece between day-to-day politics and the Basic Programme'.[22] When Peter Glotz wrote of 'an indissolved re-sidue of perplexity' in a document that had 'picked up the thought impulses of the late 1960s but discarded the errors and illusions',[23] he put his finger on both the strengths and the limitations of such a 'linking piece'. In greater detail and at the same time more modestly than any other programmatic declaration in the history of Social Democracy it provides information about the aims and methods of the party. In the process those aims, as derived from the fundamental values of Socialism, and equally the practical political possibilities of

20. See the introductory address to the Mannheim party conference by von Oertzen, the chairman of the 'Framework' commission, in Peter von Oertzen, Horst Ehmke, Herbert Ehrenberg (eds), *Orientierungsrahmen '85, Text und Diskussion* (Bonn, 1976), pp. 79f. The book contains the most comprehensive bibliography to date on the subject of the 'Framework'; see *ibid.*, pp. 420ff.
    21. *Ibid.*, p. 297.
    22. *Ibid.*, p. 3; see also below, Document 15, p. 290.
    23. Peter Glotz, 'Der Mannheimer Parteitag der SPD 1975', in *Aus Politik und Zeitgeschichte*, supplement to the weekly *Das Parlament*, B 11/76, 13 March 1976, p. 3.

implementing them are underpinned by an analysis of the world in which we live. Much is admittedly left open, perhaps as a 'residue of perplexity' — the justification of the fundamental values, the clear alternative to the 'conventional concept of achievement', the principles of 'a just distribution', to name but a few of the subject-areas touched on in the 'Framework'. Its four main sections, however — 1. The aims of democratic Socialism; 2. Conditions and frame of reference; 3. The implementation of a policy of democratic Socialism as the task of the Social Democratic Party; 4. Fields of particular emphasis — did outline the crucial problems facing a modern, democratic party of reform. Of special and immediate importance for Social Democrats in office were the tasks identified as 'fields of particular emphasis': 'modernisation of our economy as the fundamental prerequisite for long-term security of employment', 'reform of vocational training', 'humanisation of the working world', 'reform of the health system', 'town planning and urban development', and 'equality for women'. In this section concrete demands were formulated, some of which were incorporated in the governmental programme for the forthcoming legislative period adopted by the SPD in June 1976.

More than a year before the adoption of the 'Framework', in October 1974 the executive committee of the SPD appointed a commission to give more precise and more concrete expression to the fundamental values of the Godesberg Programme — freedom, justice, and solidarity — in the light of the fresh problems that had arisen in the mean time.[24] Under the chairmanship of Erhard Eppler and his two deputies Richard Löwenthal and Heinz Rapp the *Grundwertekommission* produced discussion documents on the following subjects: 'Fundamental values in a world at risk' (1977), 'Fundamental values and basic rights' (1979), 'Concerning political culture in a democracy' (1980), and 'The labour movement and the change in social awareness and behaviour' (1982).[25] These publications drew attention to the opportunities and pitfalls that in a changing world faced a policy that must allow itself to be measured against the values of democratic Socialism. They furnished ideas and guidance for an absorbing as well as — within the SPD — self-critical discussion of those values, of their

24. The setting-up of the *Grundwertekommission* goes back to a suggestion made by Willi Eichler; this is contained in a memorandum of August 1971 that Eichler drew up at the request of Willy Brandt. See Willi Eichler, *Zur Einführung in den demokratischen Sozialismus* (Bonn, 1972), pp. 117ff.; and Klaus Lompe, Lothar Neumann (eds), *Willi Eichlers Beiträge zum demokratischen Sozialismus* (Berlin/Bonn, 1979), p. 187.

25. Erhard Eppler (ed.), *Grundwerte für ein neues Godesberger Programm* (Reinbek, 1984).

embodiment in the tradition of the labour movement, and above all of their consequences as regarded the present conduct of Social Democrats. In discussion meetings and published statements the commission also examined the programmes and positions of principle of other parties and social groups.

The 'Framework' and the work of the *Grundwertekommission* represented important contributions by the SPD towards clarifying its own programmatic positions. With them the party resumed the discussion of principles that had been broken off after the adoption of the Godesberg Programme. In giving its approval to the 'Framework' the party was not turning its back on Godesberg, as some unsympathetic journalists and politicians suggested, but continuing the Godesberg line of an undogmatic free Socialism based on fundamental values. The 'Framework' was not, however, able to provide 'political orientation' for the future, as expected. In the wake of the global economic crisis that set in in the second half of the 1970s Social Democracy was confronted with problems that placed a question mark against previous assumptions and that the authors of the document approved at Mannheim had not been able to take into detailed consideration. That was where the *Grundwertekommission* stepped into the breach. Its publications, while not laying the foundations for any broad discussion, nevertheless had some influence on the formation of opinion within the party as well as being heeded outside its ranks.

# 14

# The Social–Liberal Coalition in the Shadow of Global Economic Recession

Not many months after the Hanover party conference international relations received a blow that had far-reaching repercussions for the Federal Republic. The problems, which were of course discussed within the SPD as well, had in part been forseeable for some time. But their full significance could only be assessed when the immediate consequences became apparent in the autumn of 1973. The trigger was provided by the Middle East conflict, with the the the attack on Israel by Egypt and the Arab states — the so-called 'Yom Kippur War'. First the oil-producing countries of the Middle East imposed a supply boycott on the industrialised nations of the West; the lifting of the boycott was followed by substantial increases in the price of crude oil. The global economic recession that was aggravated by the ensuing energy crisis also affected the Federal Republic. Its gross national product, which in 1973 had risen by 4.9 per cent in real terms compared with the previous year, rose by only 0.4 per cent in 1974, and in 1975, at the height of the economic crisis, actually fell by 1.8 per cent. Not until 1976 did GNP go up again — this time by 5.3 per cent. The following years saw lower growth-rates for GNP: the figure stood at 2.8 per cent in 1977, 3.6 per cent in 1978, 4.5 per cent in 1979, and 2.5 per cent in 1980. The consequences of that recession were rising prices and increasing unemployment.[1]

Bitter past experience — the inflation of 1923, the unemployment of the 1930s, the collapse of the currency after the Second World War — helped to spread a mood of crisis that was less than justified in objective terms. In the international league the Federal Republic was still doing very well indeed: it had one of the lowest rates of increase for consumer prices of all industrialised countries and one of the lowest levels of unemployment. More than the symptoms present in

1. See below, Statistical information 12 (Basic economic and social data 1969–82) and 13 (Development of the labour market 1969–82), pp. 304, 305.

the country itself it was the overall development of the world economy that called for a thorough examination of the changed situation and of its consequences. The Godesberg Programme, the SPD's election platforms, and the reform plans contemplated by the Social–Liberal coalition governments since their accession to office all took for granted the possibility of a steady increase in material prosperity. That premise was now in question. A much-discussed study by the Club of Rome had already drawn attention to the 'limits to growth' back in 1972.[2] But the experiences of the autumn and winter of 1973–4, with Sunday driving banned and a series of wholly unfamiliar energy-saving measures in force, constituted a far more urgent challenge to rethink the aims and methods of political action than any impulses that could come from the — not undisputed — findings of academic research.

### 1.  Some Setbacks — and a Severe Test

The Mannheim party conference (11–15 November 1975), which was a manifestation of the discipline, solidarity, and intellectual liveliness of the SPD, occurred at a time when the party urgently needed a boost to its self-confidence. After the brilliant general-election victory of November 1972 it suffered a series of defeats in *Landtag* elections — most seriously in Hamburg and Bremen, where it lost about 10 per cent of the vote as compared with the previous *Landtag* elections. In local elections, too, the SPD turned in a poor performance. In big cities such as Frankfurt and Munich, where the party had been in the majority since the end of the Second World War, the office of Lord Mayor fell for the first time to a representative of the CDU or, in the latter case, the CSU. This retrograde trend could not be explained solely by the fact that the manifestations of economic and social crisis were blamed on the party of government — although they were actually a function of the international economic situation and were less in evidence in the Federal Republic than in many other countries. There were other factors as well. In traditional SPD strongholds such as Hesse, Lower Saxony, Hamburg, and Berlin signs of strain were beginning to show after decades in government. Some of the successors of the popular and universally respected Social Democratic 'princes' of certain states and cities failed to achieve the same sort of authority and were not up to preventing certain deplorable abuses in their administrations and in public institutions. Squabbling within the

2. Dennis Meadows, Donella Meadows, Erich Zahn, Peter Milling, *The Limits to Growth* (New York, 1972).

party, which took its most unsavoury forms in the Munich organisation, interfered with fruitful political activity and antagonised voters.
Anxiety was aroused in the SPD and in many circles concerned for the
future of freedom in the Federal Republic by the handling of the
so-called *Radikalenerlass*, an instrument designed to purge the civil
service of political extremists.[3] The mood of elation that followed the
election victory of November 1972 could not last; in fact it changed,
not always rationally, into disappointment at the government. Many
reform projects had in fact got stuck: in the fields of education and
science, for example, because of lack of funds; in justice because of the
verdict of the Constitutional Court on the amended Paragraph 218 of
the criminal code (concerning abortion); in co-determination in industry because of the attitude of the coalition partner, the FDP. In the
field of German policy vis-à-vis the GDR, too, notwithstanding
significant improvements — easier travel, the bringing together of
families, access to Berlin — the limits of what the federal government
could achieve were becoming apparent. On the one hand an increasingly polemical and aggressive CDU/CSU opposition accused the
Social–Liberal coalition of indulging in an irresponsible euphoria of
reformism; on the other the government came under criticism from
SPD members and electors for its lack of determination in combating
what was now an unmistakable trend towards Conservatism in the
Federal Republic.

In May 1974 Willy Brandt resigned as Chancellor after a member of
his staff, Günther Guillaume, had been exposed as an East German
spy. Helmut Schmidt, then Minister of Finance, succeeded Brandt as
Chancellor, while Brandt stayed on as chairman of the party. The
smoothness with which the changeover was effected and the sense of
personal responsibility that was manifest in Brandt's action obviated
the crisis of confidence that might easily have occurred not only
among the public but also within the SPD. The new Chancellor's
energy and expertise, particularly in the field of economic affairs, were
swiftly recognised both in the Federal Republic and abroad. Brandt's
position at the head of the party remained unchallenged. Nevertheless,
the broad resonance of the party that had mobilised significant sections
of young voters and floating voters and led to the election victory of
the autumn of 1972 proved impossible to restore, as became apparent
in the *Landtag* elections. In 1966 the SPD had been returned to Bonn
for the first time as the party of government in order to lead the

3. The 'anti-radical order' (official title: *Extremistenbeschluss*) was based on the
'Principles governing membership of civil servants in extremist organisations' adopted
by the Chancellor and the Minister-Presidents on 28 January 1972. A highly informative
account, with documents, is to be found in Peter Frisch, *Extremistenbeschluss*, second

Federal Republic out of an acute crisis. At the end of 1973 it had had to prove itself in 'crisis management' and had effectively done so. Early in 1976 Helmut Schmidt was able to summarise the comments of leading papers in the United States, France, and Britain as follows: 'They acknowledge that we have dealt better than other comparable industrialised countries with the problems of a dramatically changing world economy; that we are building a balanced and just society; that we are increasing — and that we recognise — the freedom and democratic participation of all citizens; and finally that we have become an asset as regards safeguarding peace in Europe.'[4] The general election of 3 October 1976 was the big test. The result: despite the SPD's recent losses at the polls, a majority — if a very slender one — remained loyal.

## 2. The Renewal of the Party's Mandate

The governments headed by Social Democratic chancellors successfully led the country through some difficult times. The Union parties had no constructive alternatives to offer. The opposition's often exaggerated attacks on the indubitable weaknesses of the SPD and the fact that it criticised and — whether in the *Bundesrat* (the Upper House representing the states) or by appealing to the Constitutional Court — blocked the government's measures, in many instances without offering any positive alternative, did not in themselves violate the rules of a working democracy. However, the CDU clearly abandoned the ground of a debate with political arguments when a prominent member of the party, Minister-President Hans Filbinger, fought the *Landtag* election campaign in Baden-Württemberg in the spring of 1976 with the slogan — already used by other Union politicians before him — 'Freedom or Socialism'. Although doubts were expressed even in the ranks of the Union parties as to whether so reckless a falsification of historical truth — the attribution to the SPD of objectives hostile to freedom — was permissible, the slogan was adopted by the CDU/CSU for the ensuing general-election campaign. This made a certain lack of objectivity the keynote of the campaign from the start. Real differences of opinion were obscured by the opposition or demagogically distorted in such a way that the electorate was only inadequately in-

edition (Leverkusen, 1976). See also Hans Koschnick (ed.), *Der Abschied vom Extremistenbeschluss* (Bonn, 1979).
4. Federal government statement on the state of the nation, delivered to the German *Bundestag* on 29 January 1976; see *Bulletin*, No. 13, 30 January 1976, p. 142.

formed about the questions actually in dispute between the parties and the parties' suggested solutions to them. The election was 'ultimately characterised by the fact' — as Werner Kaltefleiter, head of the Social Sciences Research Institute of the Konrad Adenauer Foundation, stated in his analysis of it, which incidentally does not go into the role of the Union parties' slogan — 'that in terms of public awareness of the problems it was a campaign virtually without thematic content'.[5]

'Weiterarbeiten am Modell Deutschland', appealed the programme of the government for 1976–80, the election platform of the SPD (roughly 'Let us continue working on our "Germany as a model"'). The document bore the powerful stamp of Chancellor Schmidt, centering as it did on a record of the achievements of the Social–Liberal governments, which was indeed impressive. They included, to mention only a few: a successful policy of peace and international understanding; a relatively high degree of economic stability; a close-woven welfare net with significant improvements such as flexible age limits, guaranteed superannuation schemes, old-age pensions for the self-employed, statutory health insurance for farmers, a new workers' protection law for young people, a reorganised family-allowance scheme, increased pensions for war victims, and rehabilitation measures and a preferential right to employment for the severely disabled; an extension of co-determination; a new matrimonial and family law; and the reform of Paragraph 218 of the Criminal Code (dealing with abortion). 'We know,' the campaign programme summarised the achievements of the past and the tasks that lay ahead, 'that millions of people would be happy if they could live under the material conditions of our republic and with the degree of personal freedom and social security that we take for granted. But we also know that there is still a great deal to be done in order to safeguard and develop our position.' Apt though this statement was, it is questionable whether the slogan with its allusion to 'Germany as a model' was well chosen. It definitely could not be said to have galvanised the party and the electorate. And many Social Democrats were made slightly uneasy by its tinge of arrogance.

In the general election of 3 October 1976 the SPD received 42.6 per cent, the FDP 7.9 per cent, and the CDU/CSU 48.6 per cent of the vote. In the last legislative period the SPD, as the largest parliamentary party, had filled the office of President of the *Bundestag* — with Annemarie Renger. This now passed to the CDU/CSU. In the *Bundestag* the SPD and FDP together had a majority of ten over the Union

5. Werner Kaltefleiter, 'Der Gewinner hat nicht gesiegt. Eine Analyse der Bundestagswahl 1976', in *Aus Politik und Zeitgeschichte*, supplement to the weekly *Das Parlament*, B 50/76, 11 December 1976, p. 31.

parties. Helmut Schmidt was re-elected Chancellor; Hans-Dietrich Genscher (FDP), Walter Scheel's successor at the Foreign Office after Scheel had been elected *Bundespräsident*, became Vice-Chancellor once again; and the Social–Liberal coalition in Bonn, in existence since 1969, was able to continue. Yet the SPD had every reason to be alarmed, because for the first time since 1953 it had failed to gain any votes at a general election; indeed it had even lost some. The reasons were many and various. It would be unrealistic to pretend that an understanding of them and appropriate efforts on the part of the party and the federal government would have been all that was needed to deal comprehensively, over the next few years, with the difficulties that stood between the SPD and greater success. On many of them — the development of the world economy, for example, or relations between the superpowers, or the age structure of the population with its adverse effect on pension funds — the government had little or no chance of having any effect. Yet the SPD's reaction to the general-election result showed that it was making a thorough examination of its own shortcomings and drawing the consequences.

Important groundwork was done by Holger Börner, general manager of the SPD (*Bundesgeschäftsführer*) from January 1972 to October 1976, and Hans Koschnick, deputy chairman of the party from November 1975 to December 1979. In an analysis of the 1976 general-election campaign they reached certain conclusions.[6] They found, for example, that the public image of Social Democrats was impaired by disagreements within the party, by shortcomings in the exercise of their public offices, and by a lack of adaptability to people's new habits. The list of achievements put forward by the SPD in the election campaign failed to make clear enough by what values the government allowed its policy to be guided;[7] it also failed to offer adequate prospects for the future. The SPD had not succeeded, as it had in 1972, in presenting topics and arguments that stimulated broad discussion and mobilised large sections of the electorate behind it. The danger from a CDU/CSU led by right-wing conservatives was not made clear

---

6. Holger Börner, Hans Koschnick, 'Bundestagswahlkampf 1976: Analyse und Folgerungen für die Arbeit der SPD'; printed as an appendix to *Protokoll der Tagung des SPD-Parteirats am 27./28. 1. 1977 in Bad Godesberg* (Bonn, 1977). The Bad Godesberg conference of the central party council was devoted to the question of the tasks facing the party.

7. An excellent treatment of this subject by Marie Schlei and Joachim Wagner, *Freiheit — Gerechtigkeit — Solidarität. Grundwerte und praktische Politik* (Bonn, 1976), appeared too late and was too lengthy a study to be adequately evaluated during the election campaign. The framework of values behind the government's social-policy reforms was also dealt with in Marie Schlei and Dorothea Brück, *Wege zur Selbstbestimmung. Sozialpolitik als Mittel der Emanzipation* (Cologne/Frankfurt a. M., 1976).

promptly enough or with sufficient vigour. In addition to these deficiencies with regard to content, there were also weaknesses in the way in which the campaign had been conducted that called for some reform of the party organisation. What this implied was hinted at by Egon Bahr, Börner's successor as *Bundesgeschäftsführer* of the SPD, when he told a meeting of the central party council: 'The organisation must therefore create links between people, between the people and the party and within the party itself. In modern German this is called "communication" [*Kommunikation*].'[8]

The government of the Social–Liberal coalition between 1976 and 1980 was characterised by a high degree of stability. This is especially remarkable since its period of office coincided with years of major upheavals and crises: global economic problems continued, with most of the industrialised countries particularly failing to prevent inflation and mass unemployment; terrorism in the Federal Republic reached sometimes alarming proportions; rising crude-oil prices aggravated the poverty of the developing countries; conflicts in the Middle East and the dictatorship of Islamic fanatics in Iran constituted a challenge to the United States, the principal partner in the Western alliance; the arms policy of the USSR and the Russian invasion of Afghanistan altered the military and political balance between the power blocs. Differences within the European Community constituted an additional burden for the Federal Republic, which had done its best to make the Community a workable institution and energetically advocated direct elections for a European Parliament.

The Social–Liberal coalition had succeeded in maintaining the standard of living of the people of its country, in avoiding serious social conflicts at home, and in convincingly upholding a policy of circumspection in the international sphere. This had earned the government and especially Chancellor Helmut Schmidt great respect both at home and abroad. The course of the governments headed by Schmidt was characterised by the steady pursuit of what had been begun and the successful parrying of threats to what had been achieved — not, however, by any bold departures in search of fresh horizons.

### 3. The SPD Faces Fresh Tasks

The trust that Helmut Schmidt had earned through his exercise of his office went far beyond the so-called *Kanzlerbonus*, the extra prestige accruing to the person of the Chancellor by virtue of his position.

8. *Protokoll der Tagung des SPD-Parteirats am 27./28. 1. 1977*, p. 57.

Naturally his party benefited from it, as the *Landtag* elections of the late 1970s showed, with the SPD doing better in most states than on the previous occasion. On the other hand the SPD had not, as an organisation, increased its power of attraction during Schmidt's chancellorship. This was apparent not only from the party's stagnating and at times even declining membership figures but also from other manifestations. In the 1976 and 1980 election campaigns far fewer people outside the SPD could be persuaded to give the party active support than had been the case in 1969 and especially in 1972. Even among the party membership there was in many instances a waning of activity, compared with previous campaigns. People who were prepared to make a social and political commitment, young people in particular, sought refuge in usually non-party 'citizens' initiatives' and in private organisations. The number of workers and active trade-unionists who took part in SPD-organised events had declined. The proportion of women among new members of the SPD had risen considerably but was still well below what might have been expected in view of the revolution in self-awareness that had begun to affect large numbers of young women in the late 1960s. In other words, the 'communication' called for by Egon Bahr had been but imperfectly achieved by the SPD. The party experienced no upswing in the second half of the 1970s comparable to that which it had enjoyed in the previous decade.

The fact that the SPD was now the party that for years had been playing the lead in a successful coalition government gave rise to a number of internal problems. Not a few members feared that the SPD was well on the way to becoming simply a 'Chancellor's party' or even degenerating into an appointments agency. Many had begun to adopt not merely a critical but at times even a distrustful attitude towards what they saw as the 'establishment'. Their personal commitment to the party had lessened.

Nevertheless, there was no shortage of new initiatives inspired and executed by the 'grass roots'. One thinks of the Social Democratic works, local, and ward newspapers that were published, financed, and distributed by party members. Also effective were the information stands set up week after week in many towns and cities, which as well as disseminating Social Democratic publications offered an opportunity of making personal contact with citizens, as did the party's local information and citizens' advice bureaux. Such activities showed that the SPD was still the party whose organisational life was most thoroughly grounded in the membership. Yet it had every reason continually to re-examine that organisational life and be open to fresh impulses in order to intensify what the 'Framework' had called 'the party's trust-winning work'.

Gaining new members, winning over supporters, and motivating larger sections of the membership and potential SPD voters — those were the main problems of the SPD as an organisation during the third term of office of the Social–Liberal coalition. On the other hand it had less trouble than it had had at many other times with tensions between different groups and tendencies within the party. There was one more fierce conflict with the Young Socialists in 1977 when Klaus-Uwe Benneter, a representative of the 'Stamokap' wing,[9] was elected their chairman. The chairman of the party was given grounds to intervene when Benneter began issuing press statements to the effect that the *Jusos* would not refuse to collaborate with the Communists, if it seemed to them to make political sense, and that as far as they were concerned membership of the SPD was 'no dogma' to which they clung 'at all events'. Since Benneter was not prepared to withdraw these statements, he was first removed from office by the executive committee of the party and then expelled from the SPD by due process. Benneter's standpoint was backed only by a section of the *Jusos* — he had been elected by a very small majority — and many regarded his trial of strength with the executive committee as at least tactically ill-advised. Consequently the whole affair was soon forgotten.[10] After the 'Benneter case' there were no further confrontations between the *Jusos* and the SPD executive at national level, although the *Jusos* remained fiercely critical of various aspects of current Social Democratic policy. In this they were by no means alone in the party.

Particular controversy both within the SPD and outside it was caused by the tightening up of the criminal law to combat terrorism, the treatment of Communists in the civil service (the so-called *Extremistenbeschluss*), security and defence policy, and the use of nuclear energy. The terrorist threat progressively receded in the Federal Republic after 1977, which meant that the measures introduced to combat it also lost some of their topicality. The states with Social Democratic governments considerably modified the *Extremistenbeschluss* in practice in accordance with the principles adopted by an extraordinary conference of the SPD in December 1978. Arms policy, however, and

9. 'Stamokap' is an acronym of 'Staatsmonopolistischer Kapitalismus', 'state monopoly capitalism'. See Hans Koschnick, Richard Löwenthal, Johano Strasser, *Zur Klärung des Verhältnisses zwischen Sozialdemokratie und Stamokap-Richtung* (Bonn, undated), p. 7: 'The nucleus of the Stamokap theory lies. . .in the dogmatic assertion that even economic planning and intervention by a democratic state necessarily and unilaterally serves the interests of monopoly capital.'

10. See Dieter Stephan, *Jungsozialisten: Stabilisierung nach langer Krise?* (Bonn, 1979), especially pp. 83–7.

questions regarding the use of nuclear energy remained problems of central importance. At the SPD's Berlin conference in December 1979 they were the most crucial and the most controversial subjects of debate. Helmut Schmidt made a vigorous and emphatic plea for the policy set out in great detail in the voluminous motions put forward by the executive committee. The debate on the security-policy motion became most inflamed over the question — which the majority of delegates answered in the affirmative — of whether the federal government, faced with the demand that the military balance between the blocs be maintained, should draw the consequence of agreeing to an increase in NATO's armaments (the so-called 'twin-track' resolution). In the debate on energy policy a minority opposed the proposition that the use of nuclear energy for peaceful purposes was indispensable. Both motions were eventually adopted, though with a substantial minority voting against them — even larger in the vote over energy policy than in that over security policy.

The weightiest argument of the opponents of nuclear energy concerned the incalculability of the risks — both for the present population and for future generations — associated with its use. The anti-nuclear ecology movement in the Federal Republic had started to form itself into organisations, the most determined of which was *Die Grünen* ('The Greens'), who were beginning to have some electoral success. First in Bremen (1979) and then in Baden-Württemberg (1980) they cleared the critical 5 per cent hurdle and entered the parliamentary arena. The Greens drew most if not all of their electoral support from potential SPD voters, which in the 1979 *Landtag* elections in Schleswig-Holstein, for example, tipped the balance towards the narrowest of victories for the CDU. Consequently the idea suggested itself that the SPD should espouse the Greens' cause, if only to prevent the new party from becoming a potentially dangerous balance-tipping factor. On the other hand renouncing the use of nuclear energy would have brought the SPD into conflict with a very important section of its supporters and voters, namely the trade unions, who were in favour of nuclear power stations. A rapprochement with the Greens would therefore hardly have been worthwhile for the SPD, even from the point of view of electoral tactics.

Undoubtedly considerations as to whether and in what way the 'Greens' and the 'Multi-Coloureds'[11] as well as the many citizens' initiatives launched by anti-nuclear and conservationist forces would develop further played at most a subordinate role in determining the

---

11. The 'Multi-Coloureds' (*Die Bunten*): a hodge-podge of splinter parties advocating alternative politics.

positions adopted by the SPD at the Berlin party conference. What was decisive in all the discussions there was the determination of the SPD to evolve its political plans as a party *jointly* with its representatives in the federal and state governments and to share the responsibility for their implementation. This had been an unmistakable feature of its attitude and conduct since it became a party of government in the Federal Republic, and it was particularly in evidence in connection with questions of such crucial importance as nuclear energy and defence policy. Equally apparent, however, were the repeated efforts of the SPD to influence the policy of the governments led by its representatives in such a way that it could be advocated and supported by the party. Inevitably this sometimes led to tensions between groups not only in the party at large but also between the parliamentary group on the one hand and the Social Democratic members of the government on the other. Such differences of opinion, which in one or two instances even found expression in votes in the *Bundestag*, may have furnished the opponents of the SPD with material for their propaganda, but they posed no threat to the Social–Liberal government.

In the ranks of the Socialist International the SPD occupied a preeminent position in the 1970s, for unlike most of the Social Democratic parties of Europe it enjoyed uninterrupted command of the reins of government during that period. In November 1976 Willy Brandt became President of the Socialist International — a tribute both to him personally and to his party. Following his election to that office he appealed to the International to launch offensives in three directions: towards a secure peace, towards new relations between North and South, and towards greater observance of human rights. Recognition of Brandt's endeavours on behalf of these objectives and encouragement to pursue them further were both implicit in his appointment, at the end of 1977, to the chair of the 'Independent Commission for International Development Questions' (the North-South Commission). The emergency programme presented by the commission in 1980[12] saw the most urgent tasks as being: to overcome world hunger; to reach comprehensive agreements in the field of energy policy; to step up the transfer of resources; to reform international organisations.[13]

The growing importance that the Federal Republic was acquiring in

12. See *Ensuring Survival. The Common Interests of the Industrialised and the Developing Countries*, Report of the North–South Commission (London, 1980).
13. According to a speech given by Willy Brandt in Santo Domingo on 26 March 1980; published in an SPD press release on 27 March 1980.

international politics as one of the wealthiest and most stable industrialised countries in the world also increased the sphere of responsibility of the SPD. Drawing a distinction between the national and
international tasks of a Social Democratic party, particularly when it
was in government, became more impossible than ever.

## 4. The General Election of 5 October 1980

An astonishing change came over the party-political scene in the
Federal Republic in 1979: the Union parties agreed to nominate
Franz-Josef Strauss, the Chairman of the CSU and Minister-President
of Bavaria, as their candidate for the office of Federal Chancellor.
Following the success of the Social–Liberal coalition in the 1976
general election, Strauss had abandoned all restraint in his criticisms of
the policies and personality of the Union parties' *Kanzlerkandidat* at
the time, CDU chairman Helmut Kohl. He had even considered
separating the Union parties and establishing his Bavarian-based CSU
on a national footing in order to be able to pursue a stiffer and — as he
thought — more effective opposition to the government. He subsequently dropped the idea of breaking up the joint CDU/CSU parliamentary group in favour of a fresh plan: he would become the
'strong man' of the Union parties himself. When after massive resistance within the CDU he eventually got his candidature for the
chancellorship accepted, he appeared to have achieved that objective.
The style of the 1980 general election campaign was thereby pro-
grammed in advance. It was not through objectivity and fairness that
Strauss meant to win over voters; he even very largely dispensed with
expounding alternatives to the government's policies. A demagogic
politician whose ruthlessness and intemperance were matters of common knowledge, he launched himself on a personal collision course
against the Social Democratic Chancellor and other SPD politicians. It
failed to bring him to his goal.

In the general election of 5 October 1980 the SPD gained 0.3 per
cent over its 1976 result while the FDP gained 2.7 per cent; the Union
parties lost 4.1 per cent. This gave the Social–Liberal coalition a
majority of 45 in the *Bundestag*, whereas in the previous legislative
period it had had a majority of only ten. The CDU/CSU continued to
constitute the largest parliamentary party.

Despite the improved parliamentary position of the coalition, the
SPD had no reason to regard the outcome of the 1980 general election
with satisfaction. After the party's huge success in the *Landtag* elections in North-Rhine-Westphalia in May 1980, when for the first time

in that state the SPD had won an overall majority and been able to form the government, a bigger increase in the SPD vote might have been expected. A further disappointment for the SPD lay in the fact that the massive advantage in terms of popular sympathy and trust that Schmidt possessed over his challenger Strauss, as all the opinion polls showed, failed to find concrete expression in votes for the Chancellor's party. It was also obvious that both the SPD and the FDP received votes on this occasion that were given to them purely in order to stop Strauss becoming Chancellor. The fact that the Greens secured only 1.4 per cent of the vote under these circumstances redounded mainly to the benefit of the SPD, while the FDP profited from the aversion that potential Union voters felt for the Union parties' *Kanzlerkandidat* and also received votes from people who actually supported the SPD but did not want to see the FDP fall at the 5 per cent hurdle.

The election of 5 October 1980 was a clear vote of confidence in the Social–Liberal coalition for its eleven years of government. The results showed that voters, particularly to the north of the River Main, did not want the 'change of direction' in national politics promised but never precisely defined by the Union parties. The election did not, however, bring the SPD the clear victory it had expected. Basically the party had held on to its vote without managing to extend it to new areas and new sections of the population.

# 15

# The Crisis and the End of the Social–Liberal Coalition

## 1. Dissatisfaction in the SPD over the Terms of the Coalition Agreement

The statements of both the SPD and the FDP in the 1980 general election campaign left no doubt about the intentions of both coalition partners to continue to govern in tandem. On 9 November 1980 the new *Bundestag* re-elected Helmut Schmidt as Chancellor. On the same day he appointed his third Cabinet, nearly all of whose thirteen SPD and four FDP ministers took up the same portfolios as they had held before. Continuity of co-operation appeared to be assured.

However, the decisions regarding the future policy of the Social–Liberal government — decisions reached only after some tough negotiating — put the coalition severely to the test from the outset. Those negotiations were dominated by the constraint, which neither the SPD nor the FDP had spelled out during the election campaign, of having to control the national debt by making cuts in expenditure and taking steps to plug the holes in the budget. It was clear from the start that compromises would have to be found over the questions of economic and budgetary policy that now occupied centre-stage; they were the object of deep-seated differences of opinion within the coalition. What was difficult to understand was that in the process it was the smaller partner that essentially got the better of the larger. The burden of the economy programme had to be borne primarily by those who traditionally voted for the SPD, as a widely-read news magazine summed up the results of the coalition negotiations.[1] The FDP influence in these agreements is particularly highlighted by three facts: no decisions were reached regarding measures to combat unemployment, the decision about safeguarding co-determination in the coal and steel industries was postponed, and the FDP Minister of Agriculture was able to block the projected revocation of certain privileges for agriculture. The

1. *Der Spiegel*, 10 November 1980, p. 20.

FDP insisted that the SPD must not attempt to push through laws with *ad hoc* majorities, for example by mobilising the working-class wing of the CDU against the Liberals.

The course agreed upon in the coalition negotiations for the future policy of the government was received with disappointment and concern, indeed in some instances with bitterness, by large sections of the SPD and the trade-union movement. But there was also, among Social Democrats, a thoroughly realistic recognition of the dilemma of their own situation. Even those — and they were numerous — who accused Helmut Schmidt of having made excessive concessions to the Liberals had no wish to break up the coalition and bring the era of Social Democratic government to an end. Moreover they were aware that the SPD owed its relatively good performances in the 1976 and 1980 general elections in large measure to Schmidt's personal magnetism and that for that reason alone his position within the party must not be allowed to be shaken. The possibility of once again being consigned to the opposition benches for years on end was a distasteful prospect for the SPD as a whole. On the other hand the party would not and could not forbear from criticising the policy of the government and above all urging the Chancellor not to let his concern for the future of the coalition persuade him to make concessions that his own comrades would find intolerable. Setting against the decisions and actions of the coalition ideas and demands that had crystallised out of the party's own discussions was not regarded by a large section of the Social Democratic membership as showing any disloyalty to their representatives in the government. They saw it as a legitimate and necessary endeavour to point the ruling Social Democrats in the right direction by means of criticism and counter-proposals and give them support against their coalition partner. 'We trade-unionists do not want a different government, we want a different policy,' wrote Leonard Mahlein, chairman of the print and paper industry's union in April 1982.[2] In so doing this champion of the left wing of organised labour was relaying not only the wish of his immediate colleagues but that of many Social Democrats, both of the left and of the right, as it had been expressed in various forms since the beginning of the third Schmidt Cabinet. However, the sub-group within the Social Democratic parliamentary group who called themselves *Kanalarbeiter* ('Navvies') — staunch supporters of the policies of Helmut Schmidt and his government — regarded this desire to 'square the circle' and the motives behind it as unjustified.

2. Quoted in Klaus Bohnsack, 'Die Koalitionskrise 1981/82 und der Regierungswechsel 1982', in *Zeitschrift für Parlamentsfragen*, 1/1983, p. 11.

In this third term opinions within the SPD differed more sharply than in either of the Social–Liberal coalition's two previous terms of office. Nevertheless, the dominant concern in the party was to preserve the Social–Liberal government. Even those members of the parliamentary group who opposed the 'Navvies' and were critical of the Chancellor refrained from taking any action in the *Bundestag* that might have jeopardised the coalition. When two left-wing deputies, Manfred Coppik and Karl-Heinz Hansen, resigned from the Social Democratic parliamentary group after years of disagreements with it they became isolated outsiders; their attempt to found a new party came to nothing.

## 2. Clashes within the SPD

While the government could count on the voting behaviour of the Social Democratic parliamentary group under the leadership of Herbert Wehner, conflicts outside the *Bundestag* were unavoidable. This became dramatically apparent on the occasion of a peace rally in Bonn on 10 October 1981 in which some 300,000 people participated, including many Social Democrats. Members of the SPD and FDP parliamentary groups also showed solidarity with the demonstrators. Helmut Schmidt saw this mass demonstration as a challenge to his own policy and was of the opinion — unlike Willy Brandt, the SPD chairman — that Social Democrats should be strongly advised not to take part. Even had such advice been given, however, it would probably not have led to the desired result as far as Schmidt was concerned. Certainly Erhard Eppler, who after the SPD's bad showing in the *Landtag* elections in Baden-Württemberg in March 1980 had resigned as chairman of the party in the state and in the *Landtag* but was still a member of the SPD *Präsidium* and chairman of the *Grundwertekommission*, would not have let it prevent him from addressing the peace demonstration as one of the main speakers.

It was not only the peace movement but also the ecology and alternative movements as well as various citizens' initiatives and protest campaigns, notably against the building of nuclear power stations and the expansion of Frankfurt airport, that attracted sections of the SPD and in particular the younger generation, formerly a reservoir of potential SPD voters. Opinions in the party were divided with regard to the validity of these movements and campaigns and the admissibility of Social Democrats taking part in them. There was controversy, too, over the question of whether sections of them might not be successfully won over to the SPD. Answering that question was important if only because the Greens were beginning to register successes in state and local elections.

On the subject of 'Social Democratic identity', Willy Brandt advocated openness towards new trends that 'aspire to nothing that is necessarily alien to the goals of democratic Socialism'.[3] Such trends, he said, 'make a stand against the uncontrolled triumphal march of a technology that is destroying nature and forms of living worth preserving. Some of them resist the growing anonymity with which people are treated, the inhumanity of large structures with their concomitant bureaucracies. Some are concerned with restoring coherence to life and experience. They are in search of new forms of community, new forms of the relationship between work and leisure, the bringing together of labour and culture.' Brandt concluded his sketch of the endeavours of 'restive youth', of those whom he called 'uncomfortable urgers', with two questions that he had already answered in the affirmative himself: 'Are these not also our own objectives? . . .Do they not precisely express something of the "Let us venture more democracy" principle that I adopted as my own motto in 1969 when we set about recasting the encrusted CDU state?'[4]

Willy Brandt encountered strong contradiction. The political scientist Professor Richard Löwenthal, vice-chairman of the SPD's *Grundwertekommission* and for many years a highly respected adviser of Social Democratic politicians, accused Brandt of making his answer 'rather too easy'.[5] Löwenthal referred to the fact that the SPD was on the one hand losing first-time voters to the Greens and on the other losing regular voters to the Union parties or causing them to become non-voters. Some groups, he pointed out, were not interested in the legal norms of parliamentary democracy and rejected an industrialised society based on the division of labour, and he warned the SPD against trying to integrate them in the party by making concessions to their attitudes and modes of behaviour. In the conflict between 'drop-outs' and 'the mass of the gainfully employed of all descriptions' the SPD must take up a clear position — against the 'drop-outs'. Otherwise it would 'only bring its own disintegration'.[6] This clash, which is often

3. Brandt's speech was given in Bonn on 21 October 1981 to a symposium organised by the executive committee of the SPD to commemorate the tenth anniversary of the death of Willi Eichler. It was followed by a frank, spontaneous discusssion between Social Democratic politicians, academics, and journalists, presided over by *Bundesgeschäftsführer* Peter Glotz. The proceedings are documented in *Die Neue Gesellschaft*, 28th year, 12 December 1981, pp. 1062ff.

4. *Ibid.*, pp. 1066f.

5. *Ibid.*, p. 1086. Löwenthal's contribution, 'Identität und Zukunft der SPD' ('Identity and future of the SPD'), occupies pp. 1085–9; it also appeared in the weekly, *Die Zeit*.

6. *Ibid.*, p. 1087.

interpreted as having been between Helmut Schmidt (whose position Löwenthal was seeking to strengthen) and Willy Brandt, received exceptional publicity when Löwenthal's argument, summarised in six propositions, was taken up by Annemarie Renger, the Vice-President of the German *Bundestag*, who asked prominent Social Democrats and trade-union leaders to put their names to it. Her action did nothing to resolve the differences of opinion within the party and had no effect on the state of the coalition.

### 3. Vice-Chancellor Genscher calls for a 'Change of Direction'

It was not the disputes in the SPD between 'right' and 'left' (whereby the meanings of those traditional terms needed to be substantially revised), disputes centering in the main around the issues of peace and conservation — and incidentally similar clashes were occurring within the FDP as well — that strained relations between the coalition partners in the summer and autumn of 1981 but the problems that were arising out of deteriorating economic developments. Finding joint solutions to those problems was becoming increasingly difficult for the government. The unemployed total had already passed the million mark and was still rising. High unemployment altered the balance of power between employers and employees, drove the trade unions on to the defensive, and gave rise to a feeling of resignation and disappointment among the traditional following of the SPD at the performance of their party and their government. At the same time rising unemployment rendered the problem of public funds and the financing of the welfare net acute. Sinking revenues as a result of the falling-off of social-security contributions and taxes contrasted with rapidly rising expenditure on the part of the insurers and the state. The financial problem was aggravated by the high-interest policy being pursued by all the industrialised countries of the West to combat creeping inflation. For the classical Keynesian counter-strategy the pre-conditions were poor: reserves had not been built up because for years politicians and economic experts had been in thrall to an uncritical belief in growth. There were misgivings about financing a job-creation programme by increasing net borrowing in view of high interest rates and the burden of public debt.

For the first time the Social–Liberal coalition was not able to mitigate distribution conflicts by allowing everyone to improve his own standard of living out of a growing national product. Any policy to overcome the financial and economic crisis must necessarily lay burdens on the population. It was over how those burdens should be distributed that the conflict broke out. Proposals put forward by the SPD to finance a job-creation programme by means of a supplementary tax on high incomes were rejected by the FDP, which placed its faith in the self-healing properties of the market. The FDP wanted to deal with the shortfall in public funds by reducing public expenditure, particularly in the welfare sector.

On 20 August 1981 the chairman of the FDP and Vice-Chancellor in the federal government, Hans-Dietrich Genscher, wrote a letter to the members of the party's leading councils and to its representatives in the national and state parliaments in which he said: 'Our country faces a major choice.' Discussions with the Social Democrats had shown that it was not a question, 'under different conditions', of waging 'a similarly fundamental conflict. . .as was fought in connection with the reconstruction that followed the Second World War'. The important thing was 'to break down a mentality of high expectation [*Anspruchsmentalität*]' that had come about 'because many laws positively encourage, not to say actually induce' it. Genscher's conclusion — much quoted subsequently — was: 'Eine Wende is notwendig' ('A change of direction is called for').[7]

Against the background of the policy of the coalition since October 1980, Genscher's remarks were hardly convincing. After all, even without a 'fundamental conflict' the FDP had managed, with Otto Count Lambsdorff as Minister of Economic Affairs, to get its way in the Cabinet over key questions. A critical observer with no noticeable sympathies regarding Social Democratic complaints about the economic and social policy of the coalition noted in retrospect: 'The business and industrial wing of the FDP governed, the labour wing of the SPD was listened to.'[8] A far more plausible motive for Genscher's appeal for a 'change of direction' than any 'fundamental' considerations of his was the outcome of the local elections in Hesse in March 1981 and the elections for the Berlin House of Deputies in May 1981. In both cases the CDU emerged as the strongest party, the SPD suffered heavy losses, and the FDP only just cleared the 5 per cent hurdle. National opinion polls also showed a steady decline in potential support for the SPD during those months. In this situation the FDP wished to display to the full the fact that it could choose its own coalition partner. Even during the foregoing years of the Social–Liberal coalition in Bonn the FDP had not committed itself to that

---

7. Wolfram Bickerich (ed.), *Die 13 Jahre. Bilanz der sozialliberalen Koalition* (a *Spiegel* book; Reinbek/Hamburg, November 1982), p. 241.
8. Wolfram Bickerich; *ibid.*, p. 47.

constellation. Its loyalty to the SPD ended at the point where its own chances of participating in government began to be at stake. In Rhineland-Palatinate, for example, it had stated as early as 1975 that it was prepared to form a coalition with the CDU if the latter failed to secure an overall majority. It had joined the CDU government in Saarland in March 1977. And in May 1979 it had given a sort of symbolic demonstration of how it was holding its options open when in the election for the office of President of the Federal Republic it voted neither for the Union parties' candidate, Karl Carstens, nor for the SPD candidate, Annemarie Renger. At local-government level, FDP support for the Union parties was not unusual. None of this, however, had jeopardised the Bonn coalition.

What crucially affected relations between the SPD and its partner in the federal government was the way things developed in Hesse. There the FDP had for twelve years formed part of an SPD-led state government. Before the *Landtag* elections due at the end of September 1982 it made a coalition declaration in favour of the CDU. There were no specifically Hessian reasons for this decision, the Minister-President of Hesse, Holger Börner (SPD), having defied fierce resistance from the left wing of his own party and especially from the Greens to steer a course to which the FDP could take no exception. It was not, however, clear whether after the *Landtag* elections the SPD would once again be forming the government in Wiesbaden. In June 1982 the Social Democrats had lost their overall majority in Hamburg, one of their traditional strongholds, while the CDU became the strongest group in the city parliament and the FDP, as had happened in 1978, fell victim to the 5 per cent clause. It naturally occurred to the FDP that it might profit from this trend towards the CDU. As far as Hesse was concerned the FDP had miscalculated: it failed to win a single seat in the September elections. For the Federal Republic, however, its coalition declaration in Hesse constituted a signal.

## 4. The Munich Conference of the SPD, 19–23 April 1982

In giving reasons for the break-up of the Social–Liberal coalition the FDP — as well as various commentators — made repeated reference to the resolutions adopted by the SPD conference in April 1982. The delegates who assembled in the Bavarian capital that spring were indeed concerned primarily to develop policy concepts steeped in

Social Democratic ideas, even if they were not going to be immediately implemented by the Social–Liberal government. As an SPD information sheet put it: 'This was not a party conference of the coalition but a party conference at which the Social Democrats redefined their position.'[9] This was explicitly accepted by the Chancellor, Helmut Schmidt, who declared at the Munich party conference: 'The party must think ahead towards practical solutions viable for the future. It must not wear itself down between the practice of government and the alternative movements. Not only may the party hurry on ahead of the government, the coalition government; it must.'[10] Immediately following the break-up of the Social–Liberal coalition Schmidt called upon the SPD to draw up a concise catalogue of its policy 'in continuity with our resolutions hitherto, of course including Munich'.[11]

The problem of unemployment and how to overcome it occupied a central place in the discussions at the Munich conference; it was also the subject that brought the differences between the coalition partners most clearly to light. Eventually, on the basis of a motion put forward by the executive committee and another tabled by conference delegates, a resolution was adopted by a large majority. A lengthy document, it bore the title 'Social Democratic perspectives for getting back to full employment — Work for all'. A fact widely noted by the public and much criticised by the Union parties, as by the FDP, was that it contained demands that had been rejected in Cabinet, mainly under pressure from Count Lambsdorff, the FDP Minister of Economic Affairs. These included: continued higher borrowing to prevent higher unemployment; a temporary supplementary tax on higher incomes and a labour-market levy for the residual financing of programmes to promote employment; the gradual removal of unjustified tax privileges; an increase in the surtax rate; and the introduction of an increment tax on land values. Agreement with the trade unions found expression in an emphasis on the need to extend opportunities for co-determination and to reorganise management structures in such a way as to ensure 'full parity of capital and labour in all important decision-making processes'. The demand for a shorter statutory working life likewise reflected the ideas of the trade-union movement.[12]

On defence policy the arguments that had arisen within the party

9. *Informationsdienst der SPD intern*, No. 7/82, 28 April 1982, p. 1.
10. *Ibid.*, p. 2.
11. Helmut Schmidt, addressing the central party council on 19 September 1982; SPD–Service 416/82, p. 5.
12. *Dokumente. SPD-Parteitag München 19.–23. April 82, Beschlüsse zur Wirtschafts- und Beschäftigungspolitik*, Part 1 (published by the Executive Committee of the SPD; Bonn, 1982), pp. 1–14.

and between the party and the government as a result of the resolution of the Berlin party conference of 1979[13] were avoided. The Munich conference resolved that the SPD should decide at a party conference in the autumn of 1983 what consequences it should draw from the state of negotiations between the USA and the Soviet Union at that time regarding the question of deploying new missile systems on German soil. The peace movements in the two Germanies and in the USA in particular received a sympathetic mention in the leading motion of the executive committee that was adopted by the party conference.[14]

The SPD, shaken by defeats in local and state elections, internal disputes, and compromising revelations regarding the behaviour of Social Democrats in the trade-union-owned housing association 'Neue Heimat' ('New Home'), drew fresh courage from the Munich party conference. In Munich the party had once again succeeded in 'thrashing things out', airing its disagreements openly and thereby proving its determination to act as one body. Never before at a party conference had examples of the activities of local branches and sub-districts been on display in such profusion and variety, testifying to the liveliness of the party and the wealth of ideas coming out of it. Helmut Schmidt, who was re-elected vice-chairman of the SPD — along with the Minister-President of North-Rhine-Westphalia, Johannes Rau (Schmidt receiving 365 out of 436 votes cast and Rau receiving 367 out of 432) — was once again assured of the fact that his party wished to continue the Social–Liberal coalition under his leadership.[15] Such an assurance was necessary because tensions were mounting within the coalition. That they were aggravated by the Munich conference of the SPD is one of the legends that were intended to justify the coalition switch by the FDP.

## 5. The Break-Up of the Social–Liberal Coalition

In the early summer of 1982 the basic figures for the 1983 budget were laboriously negotiated by the coalition partners. The result pleased no one, and the government found itself increasingly losing public confidence. It had been generally assumed since the 'change of direction' by the FDP in Hesse that the period of office of the Social–Liberal coalition would end prematurely; the question was simply how and

13. See above, p. 205.
14. *Dokumente. SPD-Parteitag München 19.–23. April 82, Beschlüsse zur Aussen-, Friedens- und Sicherheitspolitik* (published by the Executive Committee of the SPD; Bonn, 1982), pp. 3–7.
15. See below, Document 14, pp. 288–9.

when. Individual Social Democrats in prominent positions spoke out openly against remaining in the government. This was done most drastically by the Mayor of Saarbrücken, Oskar Lafontaine, a member of the executive committee. He saw the role of opposition as offering the SPD's only chance of regeneration, and he coupled his expression of this view with some extraordinarily offensive remarks about Helmut Schmidt.[16]

Yet the advocates of withdrawing from the government as soon as possible were not representative of the attitude of the members of the government and the parliamentary group, who were anxious to give no occasion for the reproach that the SPD had capitulated in the face of the difficulties of governmental responsibility and fled into opposition. Helmut Schmidt did occasionally, in conversation with party colleagues, make no secret of how hurt he was by criticism from within his own ranks, especially when it was as unqualified as Lafontaine's, and how badly he missed some reaction on the part of the party leadership.[17] But it never occurred to Schmidt to draw the consequence of quitting his post as head of the government.

As it happened, the *coup de grâce* was given to the Social–Liberal coalition by the FDP. Count Lambsdorff at the Ministry of Economic Affairs had drawn up a lengthy document that was handed to Schmidt on 9 September. Its outlines appeared that same morning in the weekly *Die Zeit*.[18] At a Cabinet meeting on 15 September 1982 Schmidt announced that Lambsdorff's plan was not in accordance with government policy and called upon Lambsdorff to clarify his position with regard to that policy before the *Bundestag* next day. Schmidt and the Social Democratic parliamentary group found Lambsdorff's comments in the *Bundestag* unsatisfactory.[19]

There was opposition to Lambsdorff's ideas within the FDP as well. However, the majority of its parliamentary group were not prepared to ditch their Minister of Economic Affairs in order to rescue — temporarily, at least — the coalition with the SPD. Genscher had

16. In a telephone conversation with a journalist named Jürgen Serke, Lafontaine said: 'Helmut Schmidt is still talking about sense of duty, calculability, feasibility, resolution. . . Those are secondary virtues. To put it bluntly, with those you can also run a concentration camp'; quoted in *Stern*, No. 29, 15 July 1982, pp. 55f. The remark also appeared in the mass-circulation tabloid *Bild* on 15 July 1982.
17. See the extracts from Schmidt's remarks to the Social Democratic parliamentary group on 26 October 1982 quoted in Helmut Herles, *Machtverlust oder das Ende der Ära Brandt* (Stuttgart, 1983), pp. 11f.
18. See Klaus Bölling, *Die letzten 30 Tage des Kanzlers Helmut Schmidt* (Reinbek/Hamburg, 1982), pp. 47f. On the subject of the dissemination of the Lambsdorff document in the press and its discussion in the highest councils of the FDP and the SPD, see Klaus Bohnsack, *op. cit.* (see above, note 2), pp. 19ff.
19. See Klaus Bohnsack, *op. cit.*, pp. 29f.

intended to hold the decision about a 'change of direction' in Bonn until after the *Landtag* elections in Hesse on 26 September. That plan was thwarted by Schmidt. The Lambsdorff memorandum — 'a catalogue of reactionary demands' that stood 'in blatant contradiction to the jointly formulated economic and budgetary policy of the coalition'[20] — so unambiguously justified a separation from a partner who would not dissociate himself from it that Schmidt hesitated no longer before setting the date of the divorce himself.

On 17 September 1982, in an impressive speech to the German *Bundestag*, Helmut Schmidt announced the end of the Social–Liberal coalition. He had given Genscher the text of the speech beforehand, and Genscher had promptly informed him of the resignations of the four FDP ministers. Schmidt stressed that the behaviour of the FDP had prompted him to suspend his efforts to work together with the party that had been his partner in the government hitherto. He proposed that the *Bundestag* be dissolved and fresh elections held as soon as possible. Consultations between himself, Willy Brandt, and Herbert Wehner had established, he said, that this was the best way 'of leading [us] out of the present domestic crisis'.[21]

Schmidt's proposal was not complied with. On 1 October 1982 the Union parties introduced a constructive vote of no-confidence against Chancellor Schmidt that resulted in a majority for Helmut Kohl (CDU). Four days later a new Cabinet formed from the Union parties and the FDP was appointed with Kohl as Chancellor.

A sizable minority in Genscher's parliamentary group had opposed the tactics whereby their leader had taken the FDP into a new coalition with the Union parties. However, the FDP deputies who took their opposition to its logical conclusion were few in number: Ingrid Matthäus-Maier, an acknowledged expert on finance, Günter Verheugen, formerly general secretary of the FDP, and Andreas von Schoeler, formerly parliamentary secretary of state at the Ministry of the Interior, joined the SPD — Frau Matthäus-Maier and Verheugen won SPD seats on 6 March 1983 — while Helga Schuchardt left the FDP without joining another party; shortly afterwards she joined the SPD government (*Senat*) of Hamburg in a non-party capacity as the head of its cultural department.

Helmut Schmidt had seen to it that he and his party made a dignified

20. Schmidt's words to the Social Democratic central party council on 19 September 1982; SPD–Service 416/82, pp. 1, 3.
21. For Schmidt's speech, see *Verhandlungen des Deutschen Bundestages. Stenographische Berichte*, Vol. 122, pp. 7072–7.

exit, and the party was grateful to him for it. He had freed it from a situation in which its self-assurance was being shattered. Many members experienced a sense of relief as a result. Yet there was scarcely a single Social Democrat, from the grass roots to the party leadership, who was not at the same time clear in his or her mind that the loss of governmental responsibility had ushered in a period of powerlessness that might last for years, a period in which the domestic-policy reforms and foreign-policy successes achieved by the Social–Liberal coalition would be placed in jeopardy.

## 6. The General Election of 6 March 1983

In his governmental declaration of 13 October 1982 Chancellor Helmut Kohl confirmed the intention of his government to call a general election for 6 March 1983. Although it had not yet been decided at that point which procedure would be used to bring about the dissolution of the *Bundestag*, the parties began to prepare themselves for an election to be held on that date. At the meeting of the Social Democratic central party council that took place two days after the collapse of the Social–Liberal coalition — the Schmidt Cabinet continued in office as a minority government until 1 October 1982 — Willy Brandt spoke in favour of a continuity of Social Democratic policy: 'Our party could not, in opposition, discover the world anew. It must take its stand on what had been done in government. Our decisions hitherto would all remain valid with the exception of those points that had been identified from the outset as concessions to the coalition partner.'[22] Helmut Schmidt underlined Brandt's statement.[23]

Yet Schmidt himself ended that continuity in personal terms. Despite being urged by his political associates to stand once again as the party's candidate for the chancellorship in the forthcoming general election, he declined to do so. He cited health grounds in the main but let it be known that political and personal differences with his party had helped to influence his decision.

The man who became the *Kanzlerkandidat* of the SPD was Hans-Jochen Vogel. The choice of Vogel was anything but a makeshift solution. Born in 1926, the son of a Bavarian professor and a brilliant jurist in his own right, he had joined the SPD in 1950 and ten years later been elected Mayor of Munich by a huge majority. The leftward

22. As recorded in the minutes of the central party council meeting held in Bonn on 19 September 1982 (unpublished), p. 2.
23. See above, p. 216 (note 11).

trend in the Munich SPD put him off further party work in Bavaria and he obeyed a summons from the government in Bonn to take over first the Ministry of Housing and then the Ministry of Justice. He won especial respect within the SPD for being prepared to give up his ministerial post in Bonn to help the crisis-ridden Berlin party out of the doldrums. In January 1981 he became Governing Mayor of Berlin. After losing that office to Richard von Weizsäcker (CDU) as a result of the elections for the city's House of Deputies in June of the same year, he stayed on in Berlin as chairman of the SPD group in the House. Even during this period, when for the first time in his political career he became acquainted with the difficulties and frustrations of life on the opposition benches, he remained a top figure in the national party as a member of the executive committee and of the *Präsidium* of the SPD. His experiences in Berlin — riots, squatters' movements, the whole alternative scene, and a deeply divided and politically dispirited SPD — had a formative influence on Vogel. From being a champion of the right wing of the party he became a man who was concerned to reconcile its differences. At the same time he set great store by preserving a style of his own.

Vogel had had a considerable hand in planning the 'Government Programme of the SPD 1983–1987' that was adopted by the Social Democrats' pre-election party conference in Dortmund on 21 January 1983.[24] It contained the key sentence: 'We take our stand in continuity with sixteen years of Social Democratic work in government.' Yet the implicit assurance that the decisions of Social Democracy were right even in retrospect was followed by some qualification: 'In a spirit of self-criticism we also, however, admit that we have not always shown the necessary courage and persistence in holding fast to the course of reform. In struggling over the right way to proceed we have made things difficult for ourselves. Many citizens failed to understand this, expecting more harmony and unanimity from us. — There is also the fact that throughout the world the causes and the extent of the economic crisis were for a long time not properly evaluated.' Just as characteristic of the programme as the ambivalence of these statements — on the one hand justification of the party's achievements and assurances that they would be continued, on the other an admission of its own weaknesses and mistakes — was the following observation: 'Many modern problems are so intricate that simple answers are often wrong. The process of democratic debate is a laborious one. Yet it is the best safeguard against disastrous errors, guaranteeing continuous

24. The basic features of the programme had been anticipated in Vogel's speech to the national conference of the SPD held in Kiel on 18–19 November 1982.

self-examination and providing for necessary corrections.'[25] Thought-ful considerations of this kind were capable of appealing to and winning over people who were aware of the problems and prepared to take part in a broad-based political dialogue. But in a programme that was supposed to convince the voting masses of the continued super-iority, in terms of competence to govern, of a party with sixteen years' experience of office, they were aimed rather above the average head.

The SPD's election programme and the campaign it fought were designed to examine the many and varied questions arising out of economic and social policy, the structure of society, legal problems, ecology, and the preservation of peace. The party failed, however, to get across to the broad mass of voters a convincing plan for beating unemployment and restoring economic prosperity. With around two and a half million unemployed, hundreds of thousands on short time, real wages declining, many large factories closing down, and growing deficits in local, state, and national budgets, these questions were naturally at the focus of interest for most citizens of the Federal Republic. The Union parties were able to derive extensive benefits here by reminding people of their own period in office, when an economic upswing, full employment, and a brimming national coffer had meant a rising standard of living for the whole population. The blame for changing that state of affairs they laid at the door of the SPD. Yet the opponents of the SPD offered no convincing solutions themselves of problems that had been created by a global economic recession coupled with developments in technology. Nevertheless, the majority of voters, including many former SPD voters, felt that the Union parties were in a better position than the Social Democrats to encour-age initiative and investment among entrepreneurs, both small and large, and so revive the economy.[26] Business associations and sections of the mass media did much to reinforce that feeling.

On 6 March 1983 the SPD suffered a heavy defeat. It received 38.2 per cent of the vote (compared with 42.9 per cent in 1980), the CDU/CSU 48.8 per cent, the FDP 7 per cent, and the Greens 5.6 per cent.

For the Social Democrats the result came as something of a surprise. They had done unexpectedly well in the *Landtag* elections in Hesse on 26 September 1982, when although the CDU remained the strongest party with 45.6 per cent the SPD secured 42.8 per cent and the Greens

25. *Das Regierungsprogramm der SPD 1983–1987* (Bonn, 1983), p. 7.
26. See Ursula Feist, Hubert Krieger, and Pavel Uttitz, 'Das Wahlverhalten der Arbeiter bei der Bundestagswahl 1983', in *Gewerkschaftliche Monatshefte*, 7/83, pp. 414ff.

8 per cent. It had been possible to interpret the fact that the FDP (3.1 per cent) disappeared from the *Landtag* and the CDU failed to achieve the majority it had hoped for as representing a verdict by the electorate against the rupture of the Social–Liberal coalition by the FDP. Hopes had been aroused within the SPD that further successes might follow. The same trend in voting behaviour had indeed reappeared in Hamburg on 19 December 1982. The elections to the Hamburg City Parliament on 6 June having failed to produce a majority capable of supporting a government, fresh elections had had to be held six months later with the result that the SPD recovered its overall majority (51.3 per cent, against 42.7 per cent in June) and the FDP (2.6 per cent, against 4.9 per cent in June) again failed to qualify for a single seat.

In the election campaigns in Hesse and Hamburg the active participation of Helmut Schmidt, whose treatment by the FDP had had the effect of solidarising voters, undoubedly constituted an important factor. And it is conceivable that with Schmidt as its *Kanzlerkandidat* the SPD might have improved its performance in March by a few percentage points. But that would not have altered the outcome of the 1983 general election to any decisive extent. His personal reputation notwithstanding, Schmidt would have been incapable of halting the migration of voters towards the parties from which they expected to see some better management of public funds and a boost to the economy as a result of entrepreneurial co-operation.

## 7. In Conclusion

As the main party of government the Social Democrats achieved the best result in their history in the 1972 general election. After that, however, the party suffered a series of reverses that it was only occasionally — as in the *Landtag* elections in North-Rhine-Westphalia in May 1980 — able to make good again. If we compare nine *Landtag* elections in the years 1974–5 with those that had taken place four years previously, in every case — except in Saarland — the SPD's share of the vote declined, most notably in Hamburg (by 10.4 per cent) and Berlin (by 7.7 per cent), while the Union parties registered gains, except in Schleswig-Holstein.[27] There was a similar trend in local-council elections in many big cities in which the SPD had had an overall majority for decades.

The party inevitably felt challenged to take a look at itself by the fact that Social Democrats at state and local level had failed to sustain the

27. See *Jahrbuch der SPD 1973–1975*, p. 241.

reputation that their party had formerly acquired for itself. This was not just due to adverse external circumstances but had other causes within the party itself: its internal squabbling, which in Munich, for example, completely undermined the position of the party in the city; the manning of official posts with party colleagues who were intellectually and personally not up to the job, whose actions were not subject to control, and whose failures were as far as possible hushed up afterwards; and miscalculations and poor leadership by Social Democrats in top positions in state governments and city halls, as evinced in the Hessische Landesbank affair in Hesse and the poisonous-waste scandal in Hamburg. Another miscalculation occurred in Lower Saxony in 1976 when the Minister-President of a Social–Liberal coalition, Alfred Kubel, a seasoned Social Democrat who had held various government offices since 1945, resigned by arrangement in the middle of a legislative period. This was a risk, and it turned out badly for the SPD: the men that the party had designated to succeed Kubel (first Helmut Kasimier, the Minister of Finance in Kubel's Cabinet, then Karl Ravens, who was Minister of Housing in the Bonn government) failed to secure a parliamentary majority; the CDU candidate, Ernst Albrecht, formed a new state government and won the next *Landtag* elections.

In addition to the weaknesses of the SPD in the personal sphere at state and local level came political measures that failed to win the support of large sections of the population. A key role was played here by educational policy, considered to be typified by certain Hessian guidelines for school instruction that attached less importance to the communication of knowledge than to the development of critical thinking. The overall concept came under attack from many quarters, not only from conservatively minded parents who were tired of the continual experimenting and longed for some order and stability. The policy of so-called 'territorial reform' (*Gebietsreform*) also came in for strong criticism, particularly in Lower Saxony and Hesse, states governed by Social–Liberal coalitions. The creation of larger administrative units, sometimes with new names, was seen as showing a lack of appreciation of deep-rooted traditions and of regard for local feelings and interests. The fiercest protest was provoked when two towns, Giessen and Wetzlar, were amalgamated as 'Lahn' — the name of the river on which they both lay; that decision was later revoked. 'Territorial reform' was not in fact specific to Social Democratic policy at state and local level; in Bavaria it was carried out by the CSU,[28] and in Hesse — where 'Lahn' lay — it was pressed most forcefully by the SPD's coalition partner, the FDP. Yet objections to the consequences of both educational and territorial reform were targeted primarily at the SPD. As the chief party of government in Bonn it was identified by the average citizen with all government measures at national and state level and was regarded as *the* party of reform. A further negative influence on the public's view of the SPD arose out of protest actions, for the most part by young people — demonstrations, not infrequently associated with acts of violence, sit-ins in university buildings, squatting in empty residential property — against which many people felt the Social Democratic authorities at state and local level did not proceed with sufficient vigour. The 'ungovernability' of Frankfurt, where Social Democratic mayors endeavoured to pacify the interminable disturbances that had begun with the 'APO'[29] generation of 1968 — two of these mayors, Willi Brundert and Walter Möller, wearing themselves out to the point where they died in office — was regarded almost as predestined. Yet after the SPD had lost its majority in Frankfurt and the CDU candidate, Walter Wallmann, had become mayor in 1977, the violence began to die down. The same thing happened in Berlin and in several university cities. This was probably because protesters realised that Conservatives would have fewer scruples than Social Democrats — with their concern for freedom — about responding to excesses with all the instruments of public authority, which had the effect of raising their threshold of inhibition. Possibly they also felt that there was no point in protesting against a Conservative authority, whereas Social Democrats were obliged to take account of such manifestations of grass-roots political feeling.

One of the basic conditions under which the SPD has to operate is that more is expected of it in government than is expected of the Conservatives. This is an understandable attitude with regard to a party whose goal it has always been to change society in the direction of greater freedom, greater justice, and greater humanity. In the sixteen years during which the SPD sat in government in Bonn it never lost sight of that goal. When in 1976 it drew up a record of the achievements of the Social–Liberal coalition — which had been preceded by three years of substantial participation by Social Democrats in the government of the Federal Republic — it did so with justifiable pride.[30] Yet it was already apparent then that problems had begun to

---

28. The report of the Bavarian SPD in the party's 1977–9 yearbook states: 'In countless motions the [Social Democratic] parliamentary group sought to push through the legitimate demands of many local authorities for the correction of nonsensical territorial reforms'; see *Jahrbuch der SPD 1977–1979*, p. 163.

29. 'APO' stands for *Ausserparlamentarische Opposition* ('Extra-parliamentary Opposition').

30. See above, p. 200.

arise for which the Social–Liberal government had no solutions to offer. Let us look at just a few of them.

The welfare net prevented people from being exposed to pauperisation — as became the fate of millions in the USA, the wealthiest industrialised nation in the world — and a large part of the population lived in what compared with other countries was a state of affluence. Yet the differences in income and standard of living between different groups in the Federal Republic remained glaring, so that social justice continued to constitute a distant ideal. Disadvantaged groups were able to accept this as long as they could count on constant economic growth and hope that in the course of time they might enjoy a share in it. But with declining growth-rates and rising unemployment the gap in the distribution of material goods once again began to widen.

People whose jobs and incomes were destroyed or threatened by economic developments — and they included not only employees but also self-employed craftsmen, small retailers and businessmen, members of the liberal professions, and small farmers — found their situation particularly burdensome in view of the fact that one group of people — and a fast growing group — was not exposed to the same risks: namely public employees and particularly civil servants. The privileges of this group were further extended under the Social–Liberal coalition. This gave rise to a great deal of ill-feeling among the population and fuelled mistrust of *die da oben* ('them up there'), who were seen as scratching one another's backs. The growing atmosphere of resentment that this produced influenced people's attitude to the state.

A further problem, placing an additional strain on the Social–Liberal coalition, was that of the foreign workers. The reckless way in which labour had been imported from all over the world since the mid-1950s to do jobs for which no Germans could be found — without either the employers or the state concerning themselves about the personal and material interests of the *Gastarbeiter* — was not something for which the SPD was answerable. In 1980 there were 4.5 million aliens living in the Federal Republic, around 2 million of them in work. In a time of rising unemployment this created additional difficulties. Mounting tensions, particularly between Germans and Turks — in other words people with totally different cultures — manifested themselves on housing estates, in schools, in the pubs, and to a lesser extent at work. These led to a widespread xenophobia that was most pronounced among manual workers because they came into most contact with foreigners, not only at work but in their daily lives generally, and also because they saw them as competitors on the labour market. Those in positions of political responsibility were worried about these tensions but had no clear policy with regard to the foreign population and could think of no remedies, apart from banning further recruitment of immigrant labour. The attempt to integrate the foreign population in German society met with rejection not only from the Germans but also — most notably — from the Turks. Repatriation was out of the question as far as the Social–Liberal government was concerned on legal and humanitarian grounds. None of this, of course, made the government any more popular.

Ecological problems had been addressed by the Social Democrats earlier than by other parties and movements. When in election campaigns in the 1960s the SPD called for the restoration of 'blue skies over the Ruhr' it was often ridiculed. In the 1970s, however, people suddenly woke up to the importance of ecology to quality of life, indeed to the survival of the human race. In the Federal Republic this new awareness joined forces with a sense of unease regarding the 'over-organised state' — and with a resurgent readiness to protest — to become a greater political force than in any other industrialised country in the West. Out of a stable three-party system that had lasted for decades — and at times had even seemed to be moving in the direction of a two-party system — there emerged, as it were from a standing start, a fourth, ecologically-oriented party, *Die Grünen*. Within a short space of time the Greens had seats on local councils and in over half the state parliaments; in March 1983 they entered the *Bundestag*.

The ecology question placed the SPD in a dilemma, not only in terms of current politics but in terms of its whole tradition. Technological progress had always been valued by Social Democracy; machine-breaking had been an alien concept in the German labour movement. The peaceful use of nuclear energy had long been seen by the SPD as a splendid opportunity for moving towards affluence and improved chances for all men to develop themselves to the full. Were the arguments sufficiently irrefutable to justify refusing to build nuclear power stations, as citizens' initiatives with Social Democratic backing and the Greens demanded in often dramatic ways? Even scientists differed in their opinions as to whether it was appropriate and advisable to rush ahead with the development of nuclear energy. It was therefore particularly difficult for politicians to make up their minds. That Social Democrats in positions of governmental responsibility did hesitantly and by no means unanimously decide on nuclear energy was seen by many as pandering to the Greens or even sympathising with 'drop-outs' from industrialised society.[31] In reality it showed an understandable and very responsible reluctance to take a step in what

31. See above, pp. 211ff.

might possibly be the wrong direction, involving unforeseeable consequences for future generations.

However, in the final years of the Social–Liberal coalition none of these publicly criticised failings of the SPD was as grave as the obvious inability of the government to get the better of the country's economic problems. The same difficulties were afflicting nearly all the other industrialised countries of the Western world — and under Conservative governments, for the most part — to a far worse degree than the Federal Republic. To make the SPD-led government responsible for those difficulties would therefore be absurd. One wonders, however, whether that government might not have been better able to counter the effects of the global economic recession if it had formed a proper estimate of their 'causes and extent', as the SPD's programme of government for 1983–7 put it.[32] It was short-sighted of the SPD — and soon back-fired on it — to make light of the problem of financing pensions in the 1976 election campaign and that of government indebtedness in the 1980 campaign. In each case, the government had to lay its cards on the table immediately after the election and expose itself to the charge that it had deceived the electorate.

For a long time the Federal Republic under the Social–Liberal coalition had coped better with its economic and social problems than most comparable countries. Presumably that was what made Helmut Schmidt in particular confident that it would continue to do so. It is astonishing that he above all, whose economic competence was an object of universal respect, did not recognise sooner that what the late 1970s were seeing was a deep-rooted, prolonged structural economic recession of global proportions and that it was inadmissible to offer voters the prospect of any speedy improvement in the economic situation. By the 1980 election campaign at the latest the electorate ought to have been familiarised with the fact the economy measures in various fields and cutbacks in social security would be unavoidable. Had people been prepared in this way, the government would have found it easier to take the decisions it knew to be necessary. There would still have been conflicts between the coalition partners, but a less fierce reaction from the groups hit by financial cuts would have left the SPD in a stronger position.

An important precondition for such a preparation for future hardships and for the management of the resultant conflicts would have been a closer relationship with the trade unions. The ties between the SPD and the unions, however, had grown rather slack. Their cooperation had been at its best in the early years of the Social–Liberal

---

32. See above, pp. 211f.

coalition; in these times of increasing difficulties it would have been particularly necessary. But in the year of the break-up of the Social–Liberal coalition the unions themselves were in deep trouble, weakened by high unemployment and compromised by the 'Neue Heimat' scandal. The disclosures about private enrichment on the part of directors of this trade-union-owned housing association as a result of shady deals and manipulations, the revelation of the high supplementary incomes of leading trade-unionists and the admittedly legal but for men in such positions hardly legitimate exploitation of potential tax advantages, and on top of all that reports about unfair treatment of 'Neue Heimat' tenants severely damaged the standing of the trade unions and indirectly of the SPD as well.

The Social Democrats were unable to carry out the intention announced in their 1976 election programme: '. . .there is still a great deal to be done in order to safeguard and develop our position.'[33] Their scope for action had been steadily restricted, in part by factors that might have been avoided or corrected but to a far greater extent by developments that it was scarcely in their power to influence. The most threatening of these in global terms was a deepening of the antagonism between the USA and the Soviet Union and a resultant increase in the level of armament in both military blocs. From the moment when the Republican Ronald Reagan was elected President of the United States in November 1980 there was evident in the Federal Republic, particularly in circles associated with the SPD, a deep distrust of the American government. The Reagan administration placed the enhancement of America's military potential at the centre of its policy, supported reactionary regimes in Central and South America and in other parts of the world, cut the welfare budget at home, allowed unemployment to rise, and pursued a high-interest policy that had an extremely adverse effect on economic developments in Europe. Conservatives in the Federal Republic were able to give their blessing to this policy and charged critics of it with 'anti-Americanism', which acted as an argument against the SPD. Helmut Schmidt had been one of the moving spirits behind the Twin-Track Resolution adopted by NATO during the presidency of Jimmy Carter[34] because he wanted to help make the USA and the Soviet Union sit down around a table and talk about the new nuclear missiles in Europe with the object of dispensing with them. For the Soviet Union this meant getting rid of the missiles it had already deployed. But the subsequent negotiations in Geneva held out little hope of that

33. See above, p. 200.
34. See above, p. 205.

object being achieved, which was partly due to the attitude adopted by the Americans. Feeling against NATO's Twin-Track Resolution grew within the SPD, yet the party did not go back on the decision taken by its 1979 conference in Berlin but meant to wait until 1983 before drawing the consequences from it. So the charge of disloyalty to Chancellor Schmidt cannot be brought against the SPD, even if the party was increasingly critical of his policy and of him personally.

This question of the party's relationship not only to Helmut Schmidt but also to other Social Democrats in government posts touches on a problem that had existed at least since the formation of the Great Coalition in Bonn in 1966 and had become gradually worse over the years: the mistrust of members and supporters of the SPD vis-à-vis 'them up there', the 'establishment'. Willy Brandt was more successful than Helmut Schmidt in countering that mistrust. While Schmidt's actions were shaped just as much as Brandt's by ethical considerations, Schmidt lacked his predecessor's ability to communicate to the public both within and outside his party the motives and objectives that guided his political decisions. There the image — nourished for years by the mass media — of Schmidt the successful pragmatist in fact operated against him. It blinded many to his real personality, which was that of a thoughtful, cultivated, and — in the true sense of the word — conscientious man.

★ ★ ★

The great achievement of the years of Social Democratic rule was the government's *Ostpolitik*, the policy of *détente* that can without hesitation be termed historic. This had been resolutely pursued by Foreign Minister Brandt with effective support from his chief negotiator, Secretary of State Egon Bahr, entered its crucial phase during Brandt's chancellorship with the Treaties of Moscow and Warsaw (1970), the Four-Power Agreement on Berlin (1971), and the Basic Treaty between the Federal Republic and the Democratic Republic (1972), and formed an integral part of the policy of the Social–Liberal coalition under Chancellor Schmidt. The position of the Federal Republic was strengthened by this normalisation of its relations with the Soviet Union and its allies coupled with a simultaneous commitment to the Western alliance and a deep involvement in the EEC. Its international standing as a major economic and political factor grew enormously in the 1970s. 'The once so apt definition of the West German economic giant who was at the same time a political dwarf disappeared from the international dictionary,' as Richard Löwenthal put it in a nutshell.[35] In concluding the *Ostverträge* the Federal Republic accepted, in the sight of the whole world, the consequences of the Second World War that Germany had unleashed. This enhanced the country's capacity to act on the international stage. Its efforts to reduce the tension between East and West made a major contribution towards preserving world peace. When that tension flared up again towards the end of 1979 with the Soviet invasion of Afghanistan, Helmut Schmidt made sure that the Federal Republic sided with America — for example, in boycotting the Olympic Games in Moscow — without bringing about any deterioration of its relations with the Eastern-bloc states. Schmidt was determined to do everything that lay within his power to prevent a return to the Cold War era, and he used his considerable international reputation to try to get the two superpowers to return to the conference table.

The Federal Republic managed to hang on to the advances secured by its *Ostpolitik*. The agreements with the Democratic Republic have given rise to a lively two-way traffic between the two German states, though this is associated with major restrictions in the East–West direction and in the other direction involves financial burdens as far as the visitor from the Federal Republic is concerned. At all events, the human contacts that were virtually severed by the closing of the frontier have been expanded and facilitated. As regards relations with the Soviet Union and the states within its sphere of influence, in addition to political and economic ties there are now also important cultural, scientific, and personal links. Although the *Ostpolitik* was highly controversial in its initial phase and details of the treaties came in for some sharp criticism, most people in the Federal Republic have come to recognise their fruits and many have actually enjoyed them. It is unlikely that this situation will change in the foreseeable future.

In the Federal Republic the provision of social security is a constitutional obligation. Since the adoption of the Basic Law in 1949 various social forces have collaborated, often with the Union parties acting jointly with the SPD, to pass laws and introduce measures to meet that obligation. Yet not until the advent of Social Democratic government in Bonn was the welfare net given the kind of close mesh that has been achieved in few other countries. Whether every individual measure adopted was appropriate and whether the giant centralised social-security institutions that the SPD helped to extend and bureaucratise have proved their worth or whether social policy should have made

35. Richard Löwenthal, 'Bilanz der deutschen Ostpolitik', in *Das Parlament*, No. 49, 11 December 1982, p. 12.

use of other methods are questions vigorously argued among Social Democrats themselves. In considering them they have stressed that what matters is on the one hand to dismantle such inequalities and abuses as may have arisen and on the other hand to give greater prominence once again to the idea of welfare being help towards self-help. The SPD has never disputed either the principle of the legal right to social-security benefits that must be provided by the community as a whole for the community as a whole or the view that those benefits are also intended to offset as far as possible the injustices that arise out of inequalities in the distribution of material goods and opportunities. Even under altered economic conditions the SPD will abide by the principles on which Social Democratic welfare policy has always been based and the measures it has prescribed. It will defend them against cuts — those already made and those that are anticipated — especially when such cuts are not of a purely quantitative nature but offend against fundamental notions of a modern welfare policy.

The formation of the Social–Liberal coalition was preceded, in the Federal Republic as in other Western countries, by a movement embracing many sections of society and insisting on shaking up ossified structures, saying goodbye to obsolete conventions, and seeking more humane forms of human coexistence. Students rebelled against the hierarchies of their universities, women developed a new self-awareness and a new group-awareness, kindergartens, schools, and families experimented with anti-authoritarian educational ideas. This wave of social renewal, which was characterised by a yearning for greater freedom, emancipation, and active participation in the organisation of social life, helped to carry the SPD through the elections and fostered its policy of reform.

Willy Brandt's challenge in his first governmental declaration — 'Mehr Demokratie wagen' (roughly 'Let us venture more democracy') — touched the hearts and minds particularly of those who had recently become SPD voters and supporters of the party. There was a lively interplay between the often prevailing mood of the time and the intention of the SPD to press for more democracy in public life, at work, in relations between the sexes and between the generations, and in cultural and educational institutions. Without the political climate engendered by that mood the SPD would probably not have reached the seat of government, and without the SPD in government the positive elements implicit in the 1968 movement would have atrophied. A policy of reform was welcomed by substantial sections of that movement; it therefore became possible to integrate it in the SPD.

But the reforming enthusiasm of the first years of the Social–Liberal government was not sustained. It was slowed down by diminishing public funds, by decisions of the Constitutional Court, by the attitude of the *Bundesrat*, the Upper House dominated by the Union parties, and by FDP obstructionism; it was also slowed down by the actions of Chancellor Schmidt and several of his ministers. What Schmidt attached more importance to than fostering that reforming enthusiasm — and in this he was supported particularly by his Minister of Justice, Hans-Jochen Vogel, and the FDP ministers of the interior Werner Maihofer and Gerhart Baum — was stressing the liberality of the state and society in terms of legislation and the administration of the law. Doubts about such liberality had already arisen under the chancellorship of Willy Brandt, when the *Radikalenerlass*[36] had been administered in a way that did not accord with the intentions of its initiators and had been fiercely criticised both at home and abroad. This was one of a number of examples during the Social Democrats' period of office where the results of a particular political measure in fact contradicted its original purpose.

The liberality of the Federal Republic was put to its severest test in the mid-1960s by a series of acts of violence committed by terrorists and involving variously hostage-taking, kidnapping, murder, and arson. Laws were tightened up, arousing misgivings not only in left-wing circles. Enhanced security measures, too, with barbed-wire entanglements, armoured cars, and armed police transforming the image of the government quarter in Bonn, gave rise to a feeling of unease. For many people unease turned to alarm when it became known that officers of the *Verfassungsschutz*, the Office for the Protection of the Constitution, had secretly broken into the home of the nuclear physicist Klaus Traube — who, as it turned out, was wrongly suspected of being in touch with terrorists — in order to install listening devices. The sensation caused by what the press called this *Lauschangriff* ('eaves-dropping assault') on Traube — the FDP Minister of the Interior, Maihofer, resigned from the government — was an indication of how sensitive the West German public had become with regard to encroachments by the authorities. This too was not a little to the credit of the Social–Liberal government, which had helped to promote the sensitisation process. Chancellor Schmidt reacted to the actions of the terrorists with firmness but without panicking. No state of emergency was declared; life in the Federal Republic went on as usual, even at the time when that was precisely what the terrorists were trying to prevent. The right to freedom was preserved — and turned out to be quite compatible with the obligation to protect the population against the terrorists.

36. See above, p. 198.

Sixteen years of Social Democratic government in Bonn reduced Adenauer's dictum of the 1950s — that an SPD victory would mean the ruin of Germany — to absurdity. From 1969 to 1982 the SPD, with Willy Brandt and Helmut Schmidt, filled the office of Federal Chancellor. Measured against what Brandt and the Social Democrats set out to accomplish in 1969, much was left undone. But the record of the Social–Liberal coalition is not a bad one. It launched some urgently necessary domestic reforms, and in the shadow of global recession the Social Democrats saw to it that the burden of economies did not fall unilaterally on the less well-off. With its *Ostpolitik* and the policy of *détente* the Social–Liberal government released itself from the burden of the Cold War and created the conditions in which the Federal Republic took its place in the international concert of powers, a place of growing economic and political importance. Much of all this was due to the personal stature of the two Social Democratic chancellors. With the SPD in office — and under its auspices — society underwent a change of character in the direction of greater openness, greater tolerance, and a determination to embrace more democratic co-determination and active, creative participation. *Ostpolitik*, *détente*, improvements in social security, and a more liberal society were fruits of the years of Social Democratic government that will continue to point the way in the future as well if the Federal Republic of Germany wishes to retain its standing in the world.

# Documents

# 1
# Programme of the Social Democratic Workers' Party, Eisenach 1869

I. The aim of the Social Democratic Workers' Party is the establishment of a free republic.

II. Every member of the Social Democratic Workers' Party undertakes to champion the following principles with all his might:

1. Present-day political and social conditions are in the highest degree unjust and are therefore to be combated most vigorously.

2. The struggle for the emancipation of the working classes is a struggle not for class privileges and prerogatives but for equal rights and obligations and for the abolition of all class rule.

3. The worker's economic dependence on the capitalist constitutes the basis of every form of servitude. The Social Democratic Workers' Party therefore aims to replace the present mode of production (wage system) by co-operative labour, giving every worker the full yield of his labour.

4. Political freedom is the essential prerequisite for the economic emancipation of the working classes. The social question is therefore inseparable from the political, the solution of the former being dependent on the latter and possible only in a democratic state.

5. In view of the fact that the political and economic emancipation of the working class is possible only if that class fights together and in concert, the Social Democratic Workers' Party has given itself a uniform organisation that will nevertheless allow each individual to bring his influence to bear for the common good.

6. In view of the fact that the emancipation of labour is neither a local nor a national task but a social one taking in all countries that have a modern social order, the Social Democratic Workers' Party considers itself, so far as the law on associations allows, to be a branch of the International Workingmen's Association, siding with the latter's endeavours.

III. The immediate demands of the political agitation of the Social Democratic Workers' Party are as follows:

1. The granting of universal, equal, direct, secret suffrage to all men of twenty years and over for the election of parliament, individual state diets, provincial and local representation, and all other representative bodies. The elected representatives are to be given adequate remuneration.

2. The introduction of direct legislation (that is, rights of proposal and rejection) by the people.

3. The abolition of all privileges of class, ownership, birth, and religion.
4. The establishment of a citizen army in place of the regular army.
5. The separation of church and state and the separation of education from the church.
6. Compulsory education in elementary schools and free instruction in all public educational institutions.
7. Independence for the courts, the introduction of assize and industrial courts, and the introduction of public, oral court proceedings and free justice.
8. The abolition of all press laws and laws of association and combination; the introduction of the standard working day; the restriction of female and the prohibition of child labour.
9. The abolition of all indirect taxes and the introduction of a single income and inheritance tax.
10. State backing for the co-operative movement and government loans for free producer co-operatives under democratic guarantees.

*Published in* Demokratisches Wochenblatt, *No. 33, 14 August 1869.*

# 2
# Programme of the Socialist Workers' Party of Germany, Gotha 1875

I. Labour is the source of all wealth and all culture, and since generally profitable labour is possible only through society, it is to society, that is to say to every member of it, that the total labour product belongs — given a general obligation to work — by the same right, to each according to his reasonable needs.

In present-day society the means of labour are a monopoly of the capitalist class; the resultant dependence of the working class is the cause of all forms of poverty and servitude.

The emancipation of labour requires the conversion of the means of labour into the common property of society and the co-operative organisation of all labour with the universally beneficial utilisation of and fair distribution of labour productivity. The emancipation of labour must be the work of the labouring class, as against which all other classes constitute a single reactionary mass.

II. Starting out from these principles, the Socialist Workers' Party of Germany aims to work by all legal means for a free state and a socialist society, to smash the iron law of wages by abolishing the system of wage labour, to end exploitation in whatever form, and to remove all social and political inequality.

The Socialist Workers' Party of Germany, while initially operating in a national context, is aware of the international character of the labour movement and determined to fulfil every obligation that the latter places upon workers in order to realise the fraternity of all mankind.

To pave the way for a solution of the social question the Socialist Workers' Party of Germany calls for the establishment of state-aided socialist producer co-operatives under the democratic control of working people. Producer co-operatives are to be created for industry and agriculture on such a scale as to give rise to the socialist organisation of all labour.

The Socialist Workers' Party calls for the following foundations of the state:

1. Universal, equal, direct suffrage with secret, compulsory voting by all citizens of twenty years and over in all elections and ballots at national and local level. Polling day must be a public holiday.
2. Direct legislation by the people. Decisions regarding war and peace by the people.
3. Universal fitness to fight. A citizen army in place of the regular army.
4. The repeal of all exceptive legislation, particularly the press laws and laws of association and combination, and of all laws restricting the free express-

ion of opinion and freedom of thought and research.
5. Jurisdiction by the people. Free justice.
6. Universal, equal public education by the state. Compulsory schooling for all. Free instruction at all public educational institutions. Religion to be declared a private matter.

The Socialist Workers' Party of Germany calls for the following within society as at present constituted:

1. The greatest possible extension of political rights and freedoms in line with the above demands.
2. A single progressive income tax for national and local government in place of all existing taxes, particularly indirect taxes, which are a burden on the people.
3. Unrestricted right of combination.
4. A standard working day to meet the requirements of society. The prohibition of Sunday working.
5. The prohibition of child labour and all such female labour as is harmful to health and detrimental to public morals.
6. Legislation to protect the lives and health of workers. Public-health inspection of workers' dwellings. Supervision of mines, factories, and workshop and home industry by officials elected by the workers. An effective law of liability.
7. The regulation of prison labour.
8. Full autonomy for all workers' provident funds.

> *From the minutes of the 'Unification Conference' in Gotha, 22–27 May 1875; see* Protokoll des Vereinigungs-Congresses der Sozialdemokraten Deutschlands, abgehalten zu Gotha vom 22. bis 27. Mai 1875 (*Leipzig, 1875*), *pp. 54f.*

# 3
# Programme of the Social Democratic Party of Germany, Erfurt 1891

The economic development of bourgeois society inevitably leads to the destruction of the small enterprise, the basis of which is private ownership by the worker of his means of production. It separates the worker from his means of production and turns him into an unpropertied proletarian, while the means of production become the monopoly of a relatively small number of capitalists and large landowners.

Hand in hand with this monopolisation of the means of production go the displacement of the fragmented small-business sector by gigantic big businesses, the evolution of the tool into the machine, and an enormous growth in the productivity of human labour. All the advantages of this change, however, are monopolised by the capitalists and large landowners. For the proletariat and the sinking middle orders — petty bourgeoisie, peasant farmers — it means a growing increase in the uncertainty of their livelihood and in poverty, pressure, enslavement, degradation, and exploitation.

The number of proletarians becomes ever greater, the army of surplus workers becomes ever more massive, the contrast between exploiters and exploited becomes ever sharper, and the class struggle between bourgeoisie and proletariat, which divides modern society into two hostile camps and is the common feature of all industrialised countries, becomes ever more vehement.

The gap between propertied and unpropertied is further widened by the crises inherent in the nature of the capitalist mode of production, which become more and more expensive and devastating, make the normal condition of society one of generalised insecurity, and prove that the forces of production have got beyond the control of present-day society and that private ownership of the means of production has become incompatible with their being utilised appropriately and developed to the full.

Private ownership of the means of production, once the means of protecting the producer's ownership of his products, has today become a means of expropriating peasant farmers, craft-tradesmen, and retailers and placing the non-workers — capitalists, large landowners — in possession of the product of the workers. Only the transformation of the capitalist private ownership of the means of production — land, mines, raw materials, tools, machinery, transport — into social ownership and the conversion of commodity production into socialist production, pursued by society for society's benefit, is capable of bringing it about that big business and the constantly increasing yield capacity of social labour cease to be a source of poverty and oppression for the hitherto exploited classes and become a source of supreme welfare and all-round, harmonious improvement. This social transformation means the emancipation not only of the proletariat but of the whole human race as suffering under present circumstances. It can only be achieved by the working class, however, because all other classes, despite conflicts of interest between them, take their stand on the private ownership of the means of production and have as their common goal the preservation of the foundations of present-day society.

The struggle of the working class against capitalist exploitation is of necessity a political struggle. The working class cannot wage its economic struggles and develop its economic organisation without political rights. It cannot effect the switch of the means of production to common ownership without first acquiring political power.

The task of the Social Democratic Party is to mould that struggle of the working class into a conscious, uniform process and direct it towards its immutable goal.

The interests of the working class in all countries with a capitalist mode of production are the same. With the growth of world trade and production for the world market the position of workers in one country is becoming increasingly dependent on the position of workers in all other countries. The emancipation of the working class is thus a task in which the workers of all civilised countries are equally involved. Recognising this, the Social Democratic Party of Germany feels and declares itself to be one with the class-conscious workers of all other countries.

The Social Democratic Party of Germany is thus fighting not for new class privileges and prerogatives but for the abolition of class rule and of classes themselves and for equal rights and equal obligations for all without distinction of sex and birth. Armed with these opinions it campaigns in present-day society not only against the exploitation and oppression of wageworkers but against every kind of exploitation and oppression, be it directed against a class, a party, a sex, or a race.

On the basis of these principles the Social Democratic Party of Germany demands firstly:

1. Universal, equal, direct suffrage with secret balloting for all German citizens of twenty and over without distinction of sex for all elections and votes. A proportional-representation system, and until that is introduced the statutory re-drawing of constituency boundaries after every census. Two-year legislative periods. Elections and votes to be held on a statutory public holiday. Remuneration of elected representatives. The abolition of any restriction of political rights except in the event of legal incapacitation.
2. Direct legislation by the people through the medium of rights of proposal and rejection. Self-determination and self-government of the people at national, state, provincial, and municipal level. The election of public authorities by the people, those authorities to be accountable and liable. An annual grant of supply.
3. Training for universal fitness to fight. A citizen army in place of the regular army. Decisions regarding war and peace to be made by parliament. All international disputes to be settled by arbitration.
4. The repeal of all laws restricting or suppressing the free expression of

opinion and the right of association and combination.

5. The repeal of all laws placing women at a disadvantage in terms of public and private law as compared with men.

6. Religion to be declared a private matter. The abolition of all expenditure out of public funds for ecclesiastical and religious purposes. Ecclesiastical and religious communities to be regarded as private associations that order their affairs in complete independence.

7. Secular schooling. Compulsory attendance at public elementary schools. Free education, teaching aids, and food in public elementary schools as well as in more advanced educational institutions for those pupils whose abilities are such that they are considered suitable for higher education.

8. Free justice and legal advice. Jurisdiction by judges elected by the people. Appeal in criminal cases. Compensation for those indicted, arrested, and convicted and subsequently proved innocent. The abolition of the death penalty.

9. Free medical attention including midwifery and medication. Free burial.

10. A graduated income and property tax to defray all public expenditure where this is to be covered by taxation. Compulsory self-assessment. Death duties, graduated according to size of inheritance and degree of kinship. The abolition of all indirect taxes, duties, and other politico-economic measures that sacrifice the interests of the people as a whole to the interests of a privileged minority.

To safeguard the working class the Social Democratic Party of Germany demands firstly:

1. Effective national and international legislation for the protection of labour on the following bases: a) the standard working day to be fixed at a maximum of eight hours; b) paid labour to be prohibited for children under fourteen; c) night work to be prohibited except in those branches of industry that require it by their very nature, whether for technical reasons or for reasons of public welfare; d) a continuous break of at least thirty-six hours in each week for every worker; e) the truck system to be prohibited.

2. The supervision of all industrial and commercial establishments and the study and regulation of labour relations in town and country by national and regional departments of labour and chambers of labour. Effective industrial hygiene.

3. The same legal status for agricultural workers and domestic staff as for industrial workers; the abolition of the special regulations for servants.

4. Guaranteed right of combination.

5. The assumption of all labour insurance by the state with workers playing a decisive part in the administration of it.

> *From the minutes of the SPD conference in Erfurt, 14–20 October 1891; see* Protokoll über die Verhandlungen des Parteitages der Sozialdemokratischen Partei Deutschlands, abgehalten zu Erfurt vom 14. bis 20. Oktober 1891 (*Berlin, 1891*), pp. 3ff.

# 4
# Eduard Bernstein: Letter to the Conference of the Social Democratic Party of Germany, Stuttgart 1898

It has been stated in certain quarters that the practical inference from my essays is a renunciation of the seizure of political power by the politically and economically organised proletariat.

This is a wholly arbitrary inference the correctness of which I strongly dispute.

I opposed the view that we are standing on the threshold of an imminent collapse of bourgeois society and that Social Democracy *ought to determine its tactics in the light of or make its tactics dependent upon the prospect of this kind of major social catastrophe being about to occur. I stand by this entirely.*

The adherents of this catastrophe theory rest their case essentially on the observations of the *Communist Manifesto*. They are in every respect wrong to do so.

The prognosis that the *Communist Manifesto* offered as to the development of modern society was correct in so far as it typified the general trends of that development. It was mistaken, however, in various specific inferences, chiefly in its estimate of the *time* that development would take. This last was unreservedly acknowledged by Friedrich Engels, co-author of the *Manifesto*, in his forward to *Class Struggles in France*. It is obvious, however, that since economic developments were taking very much longer than predicted they must also assume *forms* and lead to structures that were not predicted and could not have been predicted in the *Communist Manifesto*.

The aggravation of social relations has not occurred in the way in which the *Manifesto* portrayed it as occurring. It is not only futile but also the greatest folly for us to turn a blind eye to this fact. The number of the propertied has grown not smaller but larger. The enormous augmentation of social wealth is accompanied not by a shrinking number of capitalist magnates but by a growing number of capitalists of all degrees. The middle classes are changing in character but they are not disappearing from the social ladder . . . .

Politically we are seeing the privileged position of the capitalist bourgeoisie gradually giving way, in all advanced countries, to democratic institutions. Under the influence of these and under the impetus of a labour movement that is going from strength to strength, a social counter-action against the exploitative tendencies of capital has set in, a counter-action that, while as yet proceeding very timidly, feeling its way, is nevertheless there and is extending its influence to more and more areas of economic life. Factory legislation, the democratisation of local government and the extension of its field of operations, the freeing of trade unions and co-operatives from all legal impediments, and the taking of labour organisations into consideration in all works allocated by public authorities are typical features of this stage of development. That a person can still think, in Germany, of suppressing the trade unions marks not how advanced but how *backward* is his political development.

The more the political institutions of modern nations are democratised, however, the fewer the necessities and the opportunities for major political catastrophes. Anyone who clings to the catastrophe theory must seek as far as possible to oppose and obstruct this development, as indeed consistent advocates of that theory used formerly to do. But does the seizure of political power by the proletariat mean simply the seizure of that power as the result of a political catastrophe? Does it mean the exclusive appropriation and exploitation of the power of the state against the entire non-proletarian world? . . .

No one has questioned the need to fight for democracy for the working class. The argument is about the theory of collapse and the question of whether, given the present state of economic development in Germany and the degree of maturity of its urban and rural working class, Social Democracy can have any interest in a sudden catastrophe. I answered that question in the negative, and I continue to answer it in the negative because in my opinion a steady advance constitutes a greater guarantee of lasting success than the possibilities offered by a catastrophe.

And because it is my firm conviction that important epochs in the development of peoples cannot be missed out I set the very greatest store by the immediate tasks of Social Democracy: the struggle for the political rights of workers, the active political involvement of workers at municipal and rural-district level in the interests of their class, and the economic organisation of working men and women. It was in this sense that I once wrote that the movement is everything to me while what people *commonly* call the goal of Socialism is nothing, and in this sense I stand by that statement today . . .

The seizure of political power by the working class and the expropriation of the capitalists are not goals in themselves but simply means towards implementing particular objectives and endeavours. As such the demands of the Social Democratic programme are contested by no one. Regarding the circumstances of their implementation we can say nothing in advance; all we can do is campaign to bring them about. But the seizure of political power involves political rights, and the most important tactical question that German Social Democracy currently has to answer seems to me to be that of *the best way of extending the political and industrial rights* of German working people. Until a satisfactory answer is found to this question, stressing the others will ultimately be mere tub-thumping . . . .

*Reprinted in Eduard Bernstein*, Die Voraussetzungen des Sozialismus *(rororo Classics Vol. 14), pp. 10ff.*

# 5
# Rosa Luxemburg: from *The Russian Revolution,* a Critical Appraisal, Autumn 1918

... Granted, every democratic institution has its limitations and its short-comings, which it probably shares with all human institutions. But the remedy that Trotsky and Lenin have hit upon — the removal of democracy altogether — is worse than the evil it is intended to check, for it stops up the living spring from which alone all the inherent deficiencies of social institutions can be corrected, namely the active, uninhibited, vigorous political life of the broadest possible mass of the people ....

The very immensity of the tasks that the Bolsheviks approached with courage and determination called for the most intensive political education of the masses and accumulation of experience, something that is never possible without political freedom.

Freedom solely for the supporters of the government, solely for the members of one party — however numerous they may be — is no freedom. Freedom is always the freedom of the person who thinks otherwise. Not because of any fanatical belief in 'justice' but because all the teaching, healing, cleansing qualities of political freedom depend upon it and are ineffective when 'freedom' becomes a privilege.

The tacit assumption of the dictatorship theory in the Leninist–Trotskyist sense is that the Socialist revolution is something for which the party of revolution has a ready-made prescription in its pocket that merely needs to be energetically put into practice. This is unfortunately — or it may be fortunately — not the case. Far from being a body of prescribed instructions that simply need to be carried out, the practical realisation of Socialism as an economic, social, and legal system is something wholly shrouded in the mists of the future. What we have in our programme is simply a few major signposts that indicate the direction in which the requisite measures will have to be sought — and most of them are of a negative character ....

The practice of Socialism calls for a comprehensive mental change among the masses, who have been degraded by centuries of bourgeois domination. Social instincts in place of selfish ones, mass enterprise in place of lethargy, an idealism that will carry us through our afflictions, and so on and so forth. No one knows this better, says it more forcefully, or repeats it more persistently than Lenin. However, he is adopting entirely the wrong means: decrees, dictatorial powers for factory overseers, draconian penalties, and the rule of terror are all means that preclude this kind of rebirth. The only way to that rebirth is through the school of public life itself, unrestricted democracy of the broadest kind, and public opinion. The rule of terror in particular has a demoralising effect.

In the absence of all that, what is left in reality? Instead of representative bodies proceeding from general elections, Lenin and Trotsky have set up soviets as the only true representation of the working masses. But with the suppression of political life throughout the country, the life of the soviets too must increasingly flag. Without general elections, unrestricted freedom of the press and of association, and free public debate the life goes out of every public institution or rather it becomes a pseudo-life in which the only active element left is bureaucracy. No one is above this law. Public life gradually falls asleep, a couple of dozen party leaders of inexhaustible energy and boundless idealism run the government under the direction of perhaps one dozen really outstanding personalities, and a worker elite is summoned to assemblies from time to time in order to applaud their leaders' speeches and pass unanimously the resolutions placed before them, in other words basically management by a clique — a dictatorship, certainly, but not the dictatorship of the proletariat, rather the dictatorship of a handful of politicians, that is to say a dictatorship in the bourgeois sense, the sense of the rule of the Jacobins (the shifting of the congresses of soviets from three months to six months!). Worse, such conditions inevitably produce a degradation of public life, with assassination attempts, shooting of hostages, and so on . . . .

The fundamental mistake in the theory of Lenin and Trotsky is that, like Kautsky, they see dictatorship and democracy as opposites. 'Dictatorship *or* democracy?' is the question asked both by the Bolsheviks and by Kautsky. The latter naturally decides for democracy and specifically for *bourgeois* democracy since he in fact holds it up as the alternative to the Socialist revolution. Lenin and Trotsky, on the other hand, decide for dictatorship in opposition to democracy and hence for the dictatorship of a handful of people, that is to say dictatorship on the bourgeois model. These are two opposite poles, both equally remote from the true policy of Socialism. The proletariat can no longer, when it comes to power, follow Kautsky's advice and, pretexting the 'immaturity of the country', forgo the Socialist revolution and devote itself solely to democracy without betraying itself, the International, and the revolution. It should and indeed must immediately adopt Socialist measures in the most energetic, uncompromising, and relentless manner, that it to say exercise dictatorship but a *class* dictatorship, not that of a party or a clique, a class dictatorship, in other words one exercised in broad daylight, with the active and uninhibited participation of the broadest possible mass of the people, and in unrestricted democracy. 'As Marxists we have never been idolaters of formal democracy,' writes Trotsky. Certainly we have never been idolaters of formal democracy. Neither have we ever been idolaters of Socialism or of Marxism. Does it follow that, when we begin to find them uncomfortable, we can consign Socialism or Marxism to the lumber-room like the Cunow-Lensch-Parvus brigade? Trotsky and Lenin are the living negation of that question.

That we have never been idolaters of formal democracy means simply that we have always drawn a distinction between the social core and the political form of *bourgeois* democracy, we have always exposed the bitter kernel of social inequality and unfreedom inside the pleasant shell of formal equality and freedom — not in order to throw the latter away but in order to inspire the working class not to be content with that shell but to seize political power and fill it with fresh social content. It is the historical task of the proletariat, when it comes to power, to create a Socialist democracy in place of bourgeois democracy, not to do away with democracy altogether. Socialist democracy, however, does not begin only in the promised land, once the infrastructure of the Socialist economy has been created, as a ready-made Christmas present for the valiant people who have in the meantime loyally supported the handful of Socialist dictators. Socialist democracy begins at the same time as the dismantling of class rule and the erection of Socialism. It begins the moment the Socialist party seizes power. It is nothing else but the dictatorship of the proletariat.

Oh, yes: dictatorship! But that dictatorship consists in *the way democracy is used*, not in its *abolition*; it consists in vigorous and determined assaults on the duly acquired rights and economic conditions of bourgeois society without which the Socialist revolution cannot be implemented. But that dictatorship must be the work of the *class* and not of a small, leading minority in the name of the class, that is to say it must proceed step by step out of the active participation of the masses, be directly influenced by them, be subject to the control of the entire public, and be rooted in the growing political education of the mass of the people.

> *Rosa Luxemburg*, Die russische Revolution, *a posthumous publication edited and introduced by Paul Levi (Berlin, 1922), pp. 103, 109ff. A later edition was edited and introduced by Ossip K. Flechtheim (Frankfurt a. M., 1963).*

# 6
## The Programme of the People's Representatives, 12 November 1918

To the German people!

The government that has emerged from the revolution, the political leadership of which is purely Socialist, has set itself the task of implementing the Socialist programme. It issues the following proclamation with the force of law as of now:

1. The state of siege is lifted.

2. The rights of association and assembly are subject to no restrictions, not even for civil servants and employees of the state.

3. There will be no censorship. Theatre censorship is abolished.

4. Expression of opinion in speech and writing is free.

5. Freedom of religious practice is guaranteed. No one may be forced to perform a religious act.

6. An amnesty is granted for all political offences. Cases pending in respect of such offences will be quashed.

7. The law concerning auxiliary national service is abolished with the exception of the provisions relating to the settlement of disputes.

8. The regulations for servants are repealed, as are the laws discriminating against agricultural workers.

9. The provisions for the protection of labour abolished at the beginning of the war are hereby re-enacted.

Further statutory regulations relating to social policy will be published shortly. The eight-hour maximum working day will come into force by 1 January 1919 at the latest. The government will do everything to provide sufficient job opportunities. A regulation concerning unemployment benefit has been prepared. It spreads the financial burdens between central, state, and local authorities.

In the field of health insurance, the compulsory minimum will be raised above the present level of 2,500 marks.

The housing shortage will be combated by the provision of homes.

Steps will be taken to ensure adequate food supplies. The government will maintain regular production, secure property against interference by private persons, and protect the freedom and safety of the individual.

All elections to public bodies shall henceforth be conducted in accordance with equal, secret, direct, universal suffrage on the basis of the proportional electoral system, with all male and female persons of twenty years and over entitled to vote. The same suffrage shall apply in connection with the Constituent Assembly, regarding which further provisions will follow.

Berlin, 12 November 1918.

*Ebert, Haase, Scheidemann, Landsberg, Dittmann, Barth.*

Reichs-Gesetzblatt *('Imperial law gazette') 1918, pp. 1303f.; reprinted in Gerhard A. Ritter and Susanne Miller,* Die deutsche Revolution 1918–1919 *(Hamburg, 1975), pp. 103f.*

# 7
# Programmatic Declaration of the Independent Social Democratic Party of Germany, March 1919

In adherence to the guiding principles of the Erfurt Programme the party conference declares:

In November 1918 the revolutionary workers and soldiers of Germany seized power in the state. However, they have not consolidated their power, and they have not overcome capitalist class rule. The leaders of the right-wing Socialists have renewed their pact with the bourgeois classes and sacrificed the interests of the proletariat. They are pursuing a policy of confusion with the words 'democracy' and 'Socialism'.

In the capitalist social order, democratic legal forms are illusory. So long as political emancipation is not followed by economic emancipation and independence, there can be no true democracy. Socialisation as pursued by the right-wing Socialists is a delusion. They are content with a 'mixed' system of economic management that protects capitalist interests; they are even content with 'public control' of what in their own judgement are businesses ripe for immediate socialisation.

The class-conscious proletariat has come to realise that the struggle for its emancipation can only be fought by itself alone and not merely with the organisations available hitherto; a new proletarian fighting organisation is needed as well.

The proletarian revolution has created that fighting organisation in the *council system*. This unites the working masses in the factories in revolutionary action. It gives the proletariat the right of self-government at work, in local government, and in the state. It will realise the transformation of the capitalist economic order into the Socialist economic order.

The council system is developing out of the same economic conditions in all capitalist countries and becoming the vehicle of the proletarian world revolution.

The historical task of the USPD is to be the standard-bearer of the class-conscious proletariat in its revolutionary struggle for emancipation. The Independent Social Democratic Party takes its stand on the council system. It supports the councils in their efforts to wrest economic and political power. It aspires to the dictatorship of the proletariat, the representative of the great majority of the people, as the necessary precondition for the realisation of Socialism. Only Socialism will bring the abolition of all class rule, the abolition of all dictatorship, the advent of true democracy.

In order to achieve this goal the USPD will use every political and economic weapon available, *including parliaments*. It rejects aimless violence. Its goal is not the elimination of individuals but the abolition of the capitalist system.

The immediate demands of the USPD are for:

1. The incorporation of the council system in the constitution. Decisive participation by the councils in legislation, in national and local government, and at the workplace.

2. The complete dissolution of the old army. The immediate dissolution of the mercenary army formed by the volunteer corps. The disarming of the bourgeoisie. The formation of a People's Army from the ranks of the class-conscious working population. The People's Army to be self-governing and its leaders chosen by the men. The abolition of military jurisdiction.

3. The socialisation of capitalist enterprises to begin immediately. It is to be carried out at once in the fields of mining and energy production (coal, water, power, electricity), concentrated iron and steel production, and other highly developed industries as well as banking and insurance. Large landed estates and forests to be transferred to social ownership immediately. It is the task of society to bring the entire productive economy up to maximum efficiency by providing every kind of technical and economic assistance as well as by promoting the co-operative. In the cities, private ownership of land is to be transferred to communal ownership and adequate housing is to be provided by local authorities at their own expense.

4. The election of public authorities and judges by the people. The immediate appointment of a supreme court to call to account those guilty of the world war and of obstructing an earlier peace.

5. The whole of the increase in wealth created during the war to be taxed away. A part of all major fortunes to be made over to the state. For the rest, public expenditure is to be covered by graduated income, wealth, and inheritance taxes. The war loans are to be cancelled and compensation paid to the needy, to public-welfare associations and institutes, and to local authorities.

6. The extension of social legislation. Protection and assistance for mother and child. War widows and orphans and the wounded to be guaranteed a livelihood without financial worries. The homeless to be given the use of the surplus accommodation of the propertied. A thorough reorganisation of public health.

7. The separation of state and church and of church and school. Public comprehensive schools of a secular character to be organised in accordance with the principles of Socialist educational theory. Every child to have the right to an education suited to his abilities and the provision of the requisite means thereto.

8. The introduction of a monopoly under public law for advertisements and transferal to the associations of communities.

9. The establishment of friendly relations with all nations. The immediate initiation of diplomatic relations with the Russian Soviet Republic and with

Poland. The restoration of the Workers' International on the basis of the policy of revolutionary Socialism and in the spirit of the international conferences of Zimmerwald and Kienthal.

It is the belief of the USPD that the complete and permanent victory of the proletariat will be accelerated and assured by the kind of concentration of all proletarian forces towards which it strives. Active acceptance in word and deed of the principles and demands of this declaration is, however, the essential prerequisite for the unification of the working class.

> *From the minutes of the extraordinary conference of the USPD, 2–6 March 1919; see* Protokoll über die Ver-handlungen des ausserordentlichen Parteitages *[der USPD]*, vom 2. bis 6. März 1919 *(Berlin, 1919), pp. 3f.*

# 8
# Programme of the Social Democratic Party of Germany, Görlitz 1921

The Social Democratic Party of Germany is the *party of the working people* in town and country. It seeks to bring together all who do creative work with their bodies and with their minds and who are dependent upon the fruits of their own labour in the recognition of common perceptions, in the pursuit of common objectives, and in the formation of a joint force fighting for democracy and Socialism.

The *capitalist economy* has brought the greater part of the *means of production* so enormously developed by modern technology under the control of a relatively small number of large-scale proprietors. It has separated broad masses of the *working population* from the means of production and turned them into unpropertied proletarians. It has increased economic inequality and set against a small minority living in affluence large sections of the population languishing in poverty and destitution. In so doing it has made of the *class struggle* for the emancipation of the proletariat a historical necessity and a moral requirement.

The *world war* and the dictated peace that concluded it further aggravated this process. They accelerated the *concentration of firms* and of capital and widened the gulf between *capital* and *labour*, wealth and poverty. In industry, banking, commerce, and trade a new era of incorporations, mergers, cartellisations, and trust formations set in. While ruthless profit-seeking raised up a new bourgeoisie of war suppliers and speculators, others — small and medium-sized proprietors, tradesmen, manufacturers, hosts of intellectual workers, civil servants, office workers, artists, writers, teachers, and members of every kind of free profession — sank into proletarian living conditions. Inevitable consequences of this have been a *corrupting of public life* and a growing dependence of the bourgeois press upon all-powerful economic dictators who seek in this way to bring the *state* under their sway.

The development of high capitalism has further intensified the striving for control of the world economy by means of imperialist aggrandisement. In common with the unsatisfactory solution of the world's national and economic problems by the peace treaties now in force, it has given rise to the *danger of fresh bloody conflicts* that threaten to bring about the collapse of human civilisation.

At the same time the world war has *swept away decaying power systems*. Political upheavals have given the masses the *rights of democracy* that they need for their social betterment. An enormously strengthened *labour movement*, grown great as a result of the glorious and sacrificial work of generations, now opposes capitalism on an equal footing. There is now a greater determination than ever to overthrow the capitalist system by uniting the world proletariat and creating an international legal system, a true *league of equal nations*, for the purpose of protecting mankind from further war and destruction. It is the task of the Social Democratic Party to show this determination the way and to shape the necessary struggle of the working masses into a conscious, integrated campaign. The Social Democratic Party is itself determined to make every effort to protect such freedom as has been achieved. *It considers the democratic republic to be the form of government irrevocably given by historical development*, and it regards every assault upon it as an attempt on the vital rights of the people.

The Social Democratic Party cannot, however, confine itself to defending the republic against the attacks of its enemies. It is fighting for the supremacy of the people's will, organised in the free people's state, over the economy and for the *renewal of society in the spirit of Socialist solidarity*. It sees the transfer to public ownership of the major concentrated economic enterprises and beyond that the progressive transformation of the *entire* capitalist economy into *a Socialist economy operated for the common good* as the necessary means of freeing the working people from the fetters of the rule of capital, of increasing productive output, and of leading mankind onward and upward to higher forms of economic and moral co-operation.

The Social Democratic Party of Germany accordingly reiterates the profession set down in its Erfurt Programme. It is fighting not for new class privileges and prerogatives but for the *abolition of class rule* and of class itself and for equal rights and equal obligations for all without distinction of sex and origin. It is conducting this campaign in the knowledge that it will decide the fate of mankind in the national as well as the international community, in empire, state, and municipal or rural district, in trade unions and in co-operatives, at work and in the home.

In that campaign it makes the following demands:

*Economic policy*

Land, mineral deposits, and the natural sources of energy used in power production are to be removed from capitalist exploitation and transferred to the service of the people as a whole. Legal measures against the extensivisation or total non-utilisation of agricultural land or its squandering for private luxury use. National state control of the capitalist ownership of the means of production, principally of combines, cartels, and trusts. Progressive expansion of the companies owned by the state [*Reich*], the *Länder* and the public bodies, ensuring democratic administration and avoiding bureaucratisation. Promotion of non-profit-making co-operatives. The development of the system of economic councils into a system of representation of the social- and economic-policy interests of workers, salaried employees, and civil servants.

*Social policy*

Labour law to be standardised, the right of combination secured. Effective labour protection: the legal establishment of an eight-hour maximum working day, with a lower limit in businesses involving greater risks to life and health.

The greatest possible restriction on night work for men. The prohibition of night work for women and young people. A ban on work by women and young people in businesses particularly injurious to health and with machines with a particularly high accident rate. A total ban on the employment of children of school age. All firms and enterprises to be supervised. An uninterrupted weekly rest period of at least 42 hours. Annual paid leave. Support for all efforts to eliminate the evils of outwork and to do away with it where this is possible without causing serious economic loss to outworkers. The reorganisation of social insurance into a general public-welfare system. The promotion of international labour protection along these basic lines.

All women to have the right to paid employment.

The consolidation and extension of the civic and economic rights of civil servants.

A planned population policy adapted to the social requirements of the working class. Special relief for large families.

*Finances*

The consolidation and extension of income, wealth, and inheritance taxes and their adjustment to the alterations of value and to the efficiency of working [sic!] capital. The state [*das Reich*] to inherit in cases of more distant degrees of relationship; a statutory portion for the state, graduated according to the number of heirs. Effective prosecution of tax evasion and flight of capital. The considerate treatment of the labour force and the taxation of all wasteful over-consumption. Public-authority participation in the wealth of capitalist productive enterprises.

*Constitution and administration*

The safeguarding of the democratic republic. The consolidation of German unity. The development of the state into an organically structured unit; self-government for local authorities [*Gemeinden*] and the associations of local authorities (districts, regions, provinces [*Kreise, Bezirke, Provinzen*]) organised by law into higher self-governing bodies. Democratic popular representation to take precedence over professional organisations. The democratisation of all state institutions. Complete equality both constitutionally and actually for all citizens of twenty years and over without distinction of sex, birth, and religion.

*Local government*

The creation of a uniform system of local government for town and country together with a uniform body of local-authority representatives. Initiatives and plebiscites at local-authority level. All local-authority officials to be subordinate to the local representative body. The election of mayors for a limited period. The formation and encouragement of larger and more efficient local-government units. Central government's right of supervision to be restricted to the right of complaint against illegal administrative actions by the municipality; the right to confirm judgements to be removed from the supervising authorities for municipal organs. National legal decontrol of local-authority socialisation.

## Justice

The replacement of the prevailing private-law interpretation by a social interpretation of the law. The subordination of the law relating to property to that relating to the person and to the social community. Class justice to be combated; elected people's judges to play a decisive part in all branches of justice. Education for a general knowledge of the law; the language of the law to be of a colloquial nature. The judicial bench to be recruited from all classes; women to be involved in all judicial capacities. Training for the law to be reorganised in the spirit of Socialism. The entire judiciary to be transferred to national level. Appeal in criminal cases. The execution of punishment to be regulated at national level; criminal justice to be dispensed for protective and educative rather than retributive ends. The abolition of the death penalty.

## Cultural and educational policy

All citizens to have right of access to the nation's cultural wealth. The supreme right to educate to be vested in the people.

Religion is a private matter, a question of inner conviction, not a party matter and not a matter for the state; state and church to be separate.

Schooling to be organised along secular, comprehensive lines. Instruction, learning aids, and school meals to be free of charge.

Schools to be turned into largely self-governing living and working communities of young people. The two sexes to be educated together by both sexes. Lay people with outstanding pedagogic gifts to be employed as teachers, parents to share responsibility for the education of their children, and schools to be supervised by parent councils.

The younger generation to be educated in the family, at school, and in the free youth movement to become a conscious member of the national and international social community holding the ideals of the republic, of the performance of their social obligations, and of world peace.

Youth services (as an independent, public field of work with its own official organs), starting with the unborn child and ending with the onset of maturity.

Educational institutions for adult citizens as free associations for the development of a living folk culture.

## International relations and The International

The international union of the working class on a democratic basis as the best guarantee of peace.

A League of Nations that shall exclude no nation recognising its statutes and in which the parliaments of all countries shall be represented by delegates in accordance with the strength of the parties. That League of Nations to be developed into a genuine working alliance and legal and cultural community. All international disputes to be decided by an international court. Self-determination for all peoples in the context of an international law having equal validity for all. Protection under international law for all national minorities in accordance with the principle of full reciprocity. International disarmament guaranteed by the League of Nations; a reduction of the armed forces in all states to the level required by internal security and by the enforcement of international commitments by joint procedures on the part of the league of nations. All colonies and dependencies to be placed under League of Nations sovereignty. The implementation of the open-door principle for all areas of economic exchange. The democratisation and simplification of national diplomatic missions.

The revision of the Versailles peace treaty in the direction of economic alleviation and the recognition of rights of national existence.

> *From the minutes of the proceedings of the SPD conference in Görlitz, 18–24 September 1921; see* Protokoll über die Verhandlungen des Parteitages der Sozialdemokratischen Partei Deutschlands, abgehalten in Görlitz vom 18. bis. 24. September 1921 *(Berlin, 1921), pp. iiiff.*

# 9
# Programme of the Social Democratic Party of Germany, Heidelberg 1925

*Statement of principle*

Economic development has with inner inevitability led to a strengthening of capitalist big business, which is increasingly driving back and reducing the social importance of small business in industry, commerce, and trade. As industry develops with ever-increasing strength, the industrial population is growing steadily in relation to the agricultural population. Capital has separated the producer masses from the ownership of their means of production and turned the worker into an unpropertied proletarian. A large proportion of the land is in the hands of the big landowners, the natural allies of the big capitalists. As a result the economically crucial means of production have become the monopoly of a relatively small number of capitalists, giving the latter economic control over society.

At the same time the number and importance of salaried employees and intellectuals of all kinds are increasing as big business gains ground in the economy. These perform the functions of management, supervision, organisation, and distribution in the socialised labour process; they improve methods of production by carrying out scientific research. As their numbers grow they are increasingly losing all possibility of promotion to privileged positions and their interests are becoming increasingly concurrent with those of the rest of the working population.

With the development of technology and the monopolisation of the means of production, the productivity of human labour is increasing enormously. The big capitalists and the big landowners, however, seek to monopolise the fruits of the social labour process for themselves. Not only the proletarians but also the middle classes are being denied a full share in the material and cultural progress that the enhanced productive forces make possible.

Persistent tendencies within capitalism have the effect of depressing the standard of living of the working classes. Only by means of constant struggle is it possible for them to preserve themselves from increasing degradation and improve their situation. In addition their existence is highly insecure, with the constant threat of unemployment. This becomes particularly painful and embittering in the periods of crisis that follow every economic upswing and have their origin in the anarchy of the capitalist mode of production. The capitalist striving for monopoly leads to the concentration of branches of industry, the combining of successive stages of production, and the organisation of the economy in cartels and trusts. This process unites industrial capital, commercial capital, and banking capital in finance capital.

In this way individual capital groups become all-powerful controllers of the

258

economy, bringing not only wage-earners but the whole of society into economic dependence upon them.

As its influence increases, finance capital uses the power of the state to gain control of areas abroad as outlets, sources of raw materials, and locations for capital investment. This striving for imperialist aggrandisement continually threatens society with conflicts and the risk of war. However, as the pressure and as the dangers of high capitalism increase, so too does the resistance of the ever-growing working class, which is being educated and united by the mechanism of the capitalist production process itself as well as by the constant efforts of the trade unions and the Social Democratic Party. The proletarians are growing ever more numerous, the antagonism between exploiters and exploited ever more marked, and the class struggle between the capitalist rulers of the economy and those they rule ever more bitter. In fighting for its own emancipation, the working class represents the overall interests of society against the capitalist monopoly. An enormously strengthened labour movement, grown great as a result of the sacrificial work of generations, now opposes capitalism on an equal footing. There is now a greater determination than ever to overthrow the capitalist system by uniting the world proletariat and creating an international legal system, a true league of equal nations, for the purpose of protecting mankind from further wars and destruction.

The goal of the working class can be achieved only by changing the capitalist private ownership of the means of production into social ownership. The transformation of capitalist production into Socialist production for and by society will result in the development and augmentation of the forces of production becoming a source of the highest welfare and all-around perfection. Only then will society rise up from its subjection to blind economic power and from general disintegration to free self-government in harmonious solidarity.

The struggle of the working class against capitalist exploitation is not only an economic but inevitably also a political struggle. The working class cannot wage its economic struggle nor develop its economic organisation to the full without political rights. In the democratic republic it finds the form of government the preservation and development of which are an imperative necessity for its struggle for emancipation. It cannot bring about the socialisation of the means of production until it is in possession of political power.

The struggle for proletarian emancipation is one that involves the workers of all countries. The Social Democratic Party of Germany, conscious of the international solidarity of the proletariat, is determined to fulfil all the obligations that emerge therefrom. The permanent well-being of the nations can today be achieved only by their working together in solidarity.

The Social Democratic Party is fighting not for new class privileges and prerogatives but for the abolition of class rule and of classes themselves and for equal rights and equal obligations for all without distinction of sex and birth. Armed with these opinions, it campaigns not only against the exploitation and oppression of wage-workers but against every kind of exploitation and oppression, be it directed against a people, a class, a party, a sex, or a race.

It is the task of the Social Democratic Party to shape the working class's struggle for emancipation into a conscious, integrated campaign and to direct it towards its necessary goal. In constant contention and action in the political, economic, social, and cultural spheres, it strives to attain its ultimate objective.

## Programme of action

### *The constitution*

The democratic republic is the most favourable basis for the working-class struggle for emancipation and hence for the realisation of Socialism. The Social Democratic Party therefore defends the republic and supports its further development. It calls for the following:

The German *Reich* is to be transformed into a uniform republic on the basis of decentralised self-government. On an organically reorganised sub-structure of local and state authorities, a powerful central government is to be erected that shall possess the necessary powers, both legal and administrative, to provide uniform leadership and to hold the country together.

Direct central-government administration to be extended to justice; all courts to be administered at national level. Uniform principles for the security police to be laid down by legislation. A uniform national criminal police force to be created.

All monarchical and militaristic endeavours to be resisted and the German army to be transformed into a dependable organ of the republic.

Full implementation of constitutional equality for all citizens without distinction of sex, birth, religion, and economic standing.

### *The administration*

The objective of Social Democratic administrative policy is the replacement of the police-state executive inherited from the authoritarian state by an administrative organisation that gives administrative responsibility to the people on the basis of democratic self-government. The party therefore calls for:

The democratisation of the administration.

The standardisation at central-government level of the administration of the states.

The principles of administration to be laid down by central government. Their execution to be the responsibility of the self-governing bodies except in so far as concerns matters that because of their central character require direct administration by central government.

Scope is to be left for local and provincial peculiarities through the medium of skeleton legislation.

A central law governing the administration of the states to determine on an equal basis for all states the structure and competence of administrative areas and administrative organs.

A central local-authority code to create a uniform body of law governing local authorities and associations of local authorities (rural districts, municipalities, administrative districts [*Kreise*], provinces). The single-chamber system to be implemented for all self-governing bodies. Mayors to be elected for a fixed term. The self-governing bodies to attend to the affairs of their administrative area independently and on their own responsibility in the context of and referenda are to be introduced at local-authority level.

Legal control over administration, particularly the protection of the citizen against administrative actions encroaching on his legal sphere, is to be provided by administrative courts enjoying an independent position within the juridical hierarchy. The central administrative court to have the simultaneous function of a supreme administrative court in all state actions.

Central laws governing communalisation and compulsory purchase are to provide local authorities and associations of local authorities with the powers and the means of enforcing those powers necessary to implement and expand the communal social economy. The form of administration is to be such that on the one hand firms are freed from bureaucratic fetters on their management of their affairs but on the other hand the right of determination of public corporations is preserved without restriction.

A uniform code of service is to be created for all civil servants and salaried employees of public corporations, ordering their selection, appointment, promotion, and the representation and protection of their interests in accordance with democratic and social considerations.

## Justice

The Social Democratic Party opposes all class and partisan justice and advocates a legal and judicial order steeped in social consciousness and incorporating a crucial role for elected lay judges in all branches and at all levels of the law.

It particularly calls for;

In civil law, the subordination of rights of property to the rights of the social community, the facilitation of divorce, equality of status for men and women, and equality of status for legitimate and illegitimate children.

In criminal law, greater protection of the person and of social rights, the replacement of the principle of retribution by the principle of correction of the individual and the protection of society. The abolition of the death penalty.

In criminal procedure, the restoration of trial by jury and the extension of its area of competence, particularly to political trials and trials involving the press. Appeal to be allowed in all criminal cases, and all provisions prejudicial to the defence to be abolished.

In remand proceedings, protection of the prisoner against official encroachments; arrest, except in cases of apprehension *in flagrante delicto*, only on the grounds of a judicial order; oral hearing of appeals against arrest or remand. In the execution of punishment, central statutory regulation in the spirit of humanity and the corrective principle.

## Social policy

The protection of workers, salaried employees, and civil servants and the raising of the standard of living of the broad masses require:

The safeguarding of the right of combination and the right to strike. Women to have an equal right to paid employment. A ban on all paid employment for children of school age.

The statutory definition of an eight-hour maximum working day; that working day to be reduced for young people and in businesses involving greater risks to life and health. The restriction of night work. A continuous weekly rest period of at least 42 hours. Annual paid leave.

Attending to the execution of relief works to be left exclusively to the trade unions.

The abuses of outwork to be combated with the object of eliminating them altogether while providing a large measure of relief for those affected.

The supervision of all firms and business enterprises by the industrial inspectorate, which is to be expanded into a central-government institution involving workers and salaried employees as officials and as trustees.

The legal validity of tariff agreements to be ensured and assistance towards their conclusion to be provided by the arbitration authorities.

Independent labour courts having no connection with regular jurisdiction.

A uniform code of labour law.

The standardisation of social insurance until its eventual conversion into a general public-welfare system. The inclusion of those unfit for work and those out of work. Comprehensive, prophylactic, healing, and precautionary measures in the fields of public welfare, particularly education, health, and economic relief; the uniform regulation of welfare services under national law, with a guaranteed place for the working class in their implementation.

The encouragement of international treaties and legislation.

*Cultural and educational policy*

The Social Democratic Party aims to abolish the educational privileges of the propertied.

Education, training, and research are matters of public concern; their implementation is to be provided for by public funds and through public institutions. Instruction and teaching and learning aids to be free of charge; economic support to be provided for students.

The public institutions for education, schooling, training, and research are secular. Any influencing of these institutions under public law by the church or other religious or ideological communities is to be combated. State and church to be separate, school and church to be separate, schools, vocational-training colleges, and universities to be secular. No spending of public money for ecclesiastical and religious ends.

Education to be structured uniformly; the closest possible relations to be established at all levels between handicraft work and intellectual work.

The two sexes to be educated together by both sexes.

Uniform teacher-training at universities.

*Finances and taxes*

The Social Democratic Party of Germany demands thoroughgoing and comprehensive financial reform based on the principle of the taxation of sources and the distribution of charges in accordance with economic capacity.

In particular:

The further development of income, wealth, and inheritance taxes.

Uniform tax assessment with disclosure of tax lists. Effective prosecution of tax evasion, particularly by means of compulsory auditing.

A social subsistence minimum to be tax-free. Maximum relief for mass consumption. The abolition of turnover tax.

Public-authority participation in wealth and in the administration of capitalist business enterprises.

*Economic policy*

In its struggle against the capitalist system the Social Democratic Party of Germany calls for:

Land, mineral deposits, and natural energy resources used in the production of power to be removed from capitalist exploitation and transferred to the service of the community.

The development of the system of economic councils in order to implement a right of co-determination on the part of the working class in the organisation of the economy, with close co-operation with the trade unions being maintained.

National state control of capitalist combines, cartels, and trusts.

The promotion of increased production in industry and agriculture.

The promotion of housing affairs.

The dismantling of the protective-tariff system by means of long-term trade agreements to establish free exchange of goods and the economic integration of the nations.

The development of central [*Reich*], state [*Land*], and public-corporation owned businesses while avoiding bureaucratisation.

The promotion of non-profit-making co-operatives and public-utility enterprises.

The promotion of public-utility building; the regulations governing tenancy to come under public law; measures to combat housing profiteers.

*International policy*

As a member of the Socialist Workers' International the Social Democratic Party of Germany fights alongside the workers of all countries against the thrusts of imperialism and fascism and for the realisation of Socialism.

It opposes with all its strength every aggravation of antagonisms between peoples and every threat to peace.

It calls for the peaceful solution of international conflicts and their settlement before compulsory courts of arbitration.

It champions the right of national self-determination and the right of minorities to democratic, national self-government.

It is opposed to the exploitation of colonial peoples and the violent destruction of their economies and culture.

It calls for international disarmament.

It advocates the creation of European economic unity, which for economic reasons has now become urgent, and the formation of a United States of Europe as a step towards a solidarity of interests among the peoples of all continents.

It calls for the democratisation of the League of Nations and its development into an effective instrument of peace.

# Documents

*From the minutes of the proceedings of the SPD confer-*
*ence in Heidelberg in 1925; see* Sozialdemokratischer
Parteitag 1925 in Heidelberg: Protokoll mit dem Bericht
der Frauenkonferenz *(Berlin, 1925)*, pp. 5ff.

# 10
## The 'Prague Manifesto' of the Sopade — *The Struggle and the Goal of Revolutionary Socialism: the Policy of the Social Democratic Party of Germany,* January 1934

For a year the National Socialist dictatorship has lain heavy on Germany and on the world. The victory of the German counter-revolution has wrought an overwhelming change in the nature and functions of the German labour movement. The nation is delivered up to servitude and lawlessness in the Fascist totalitarian state. The task of the German labour movement lies in the revolutionary struggle to conquer servitude with the right to freedom, to overcome lawlessness with the ordered scheme of Socialism. . . .

In the struggle against the National Socialist dictatorship there is *no room for compromise*, no place for reformism and legality. The tactics of Social Democracy is determined solely by the goal of seizing power in the state, consolidating it, and asserting it for the purposes of realising the Socialist society. That tactics will make use of of *every* means serving to bring about the overthrow of the dictatorship.

A *revolutionary struggle* calls for *revolutionary organisation.* The old form — the old apparatus — is no more, and attempts to revive it are not appropriate to the new conditions in which we are fighting. New forms of organisation must emerge, with combatants prepared to make sacrifices. We are not free to choose those forms ourselves. It is still the enemy with his superior means and the brutality with which he uses them, it is still the condition of German society itself, which is under the most appalling pressure from economic, physical, and mental terrorism, that between them dictate the initiative. . . .

The reconquest of democratic rights has become necessary in order to restore the labour movement's viability as a mass movement and to wage the struggle for Socialist emancipation once again as a conscious movement on the part of the masses themselves. Every democratic right, however, is a threat to the continued existence of the dictatorship. The battle for democracy thus broadens out into the battle for the total overthrow of the National Socialist state.

That battle is simply a *revolutionary transition stage towards the conquest of overall political power.* The overthrow of tyranny, if not occasioned by external calamities, will occur only by virtue of violent conquest, only by virtue of victory in the revolutionary struggle. It will come about when the conditions of an objectively revolutionary situation are exploited by a resolute party of revolutionary Socialism, a party imbued with a radical fighting spirit and led by an experienced elite. It can arise only out of the action of the masses themselves. . . .

It its onerous, sacrificial, passionately committed striving for the overthrow of the dictatorship the labour movement is being filled *with a radical spirit of no-compromise*. The political upheaval of 1918 came at the end of a counter-revolutionary development brought about by the war and by much nationalist whipping-up of the popular masses. It was not by the organised, pre-planned, deliberate revolutionary struggle of the working class that the imperial regime was brought down but by defeat on the battlefield. As the only organised force still intact, Social Democracy assumed control of the state without resistance, a control it shared from the outset with the middle-class parties, with the old bureaucracy, indeed with the reorganised military machine. Taking over the old apparatus of government virtually unaltered was the grave historical error perpetrated by a German labour movement that had lost its way during the war.

*The new situation rules out any possibility of repetition.* The overthrow of the National Socialist enemy by the revolutionary masses will create a powerful revolutionary government supported by the revolutionary mass party of the working class, which controls it. The first and foremost task of that government will be to secure the power of the state for the victorious revolution, to root out any possibility of resistance, and to transform the machinery of government into an instrument of mass rule. . . .

It is not the task of Social Democracy to hope that the tyranny of National Socialism will be toppled by war. On the contrary, its task is *to prevent war*. For that reason it rejects all military concessions to Hitler's Germany. It warns the labour parties of all countries not to underestimate the danger of German nationalism. Equality of rights for the democracies, but no rearmament for a dictatorship lusting for war! Not a man and not a penny for this system — that is the watchword of Social Democracy, and that must be the motto of the Socialist Workers' International. The safeguarding of peace and the protection of the freedom of the nations call not for military concessions but for disarmament — and specifically for the disarming and disbandment of the SA and SS formations.

Should war, which the firmness and alert determination of the democracies under the influence of their labour parties are today still able to prevent, nevertheless break out the German Social Democrats will face the tyrant with *unaltered, implacable hostility*. The unity and freedom of the German nation can be saved only by the overthrow of German Fascism.

Social Democracy will resolutely oppose any attempt from outside Germany to exploit a military collapse of tyranny in Germany in order to dismember the country. It will refuse to recognise any peace that leads to Germany being torn apart and implies any restriction of its opportunities for free political and economic development. . . .

With the victory of the totalitarian state the question of how it is to be overcome is posed with brutal clarity. The answer is total revolution — moral, intellectual, political, and social!

In that struggle the Social Democratic Party will work towards one front comprising all strata of society opposed to Fascism. It will summon them all — peasant farmers, small tradesmen, businesspeople betrayed by the promises of the National Socialists, the intellectuals who under the present regime are suffering a once inconceivable degree of oppression and degradation — to fight alongside the working class.

We have pointed the way and shown the goal of the struggle. The differences within the labour movement are being eradicated by the enemy himself. The grounds for schism have been reduced to triviality. The struggle for the overthrow of the National Socialist dictatorship cannot be conducted by other than revolutionary means. Be he a Social Democrat, be he a Communist, or be he a supporter of one of the many splinter groups, the enemy of the dictatorship will become, as he fights — and through the very circumstances of his fighting — one and the same Socialist revolutionary. The *unification* of the working class *has become an obligation* imposed by history itself. . . .

The National Socialist powers-that-be brag of having destroyed the revolutionary Socialist labour movement and stamped out the idea of freedom. They are the victors, wreaking a cruel vengeance on the oppressed. But the greater their victory, the victory of the forces of capitalism, the graver will be their future defeat. The development of capitalism is producing its own gravediggers, and today's *triumph* is tomorrow's *demise.*

We are fighting Fascist barbarism on behalf of the great and imperishable ideas of humanity. We are the vehicle of the greatest historical development since the passing of medieval bondage; we are heirs to the imperishable traditions of the Renaissance and of Humanism, of the English and the French revolutions. We do not wish to live without freedom, and freedom we shall conquer — freedom without class rule, freedom extending to the total abolition of all exploitation and all dominion of man over man!

*The blood of the victims shall not have been shed in vain!*

*Workers of Germany, you have nothing to lose but the chains of your servitude, but you have the world of freedom and Socialism to win!*

*Workers of Germany, unite in the revolutionary struggle to destroy the National Socialist dictatorship!*

*Through freedom to Socialism, through Socialism to freedom!*

*Long live German revolutionary Social Democracy! Long live the International!*

*Prague, 28 January 1934*

The Executive Committee of the Social Democratic Party of Germany

*Published in* Neuer Vorwärts, *28 January 1934; reprinted in Dieter Dowe and Kurt Klotzbach (eds),* Programmatische Dokumente der deutschen Sozialdemokratie *(Berlin/Bonn, 1973), pp. 213ff.*

# 11
# Kurt Schumacher: 'What do the Social Democrats want? Not reconstruction but a fresh start!' Speech delivered in Kiel on 27 October 1945

[*heavily abridged*]

*A fresh start through Socialism*

The purpose of Social Democratic policy is to emancipate man economically in order to create for him the preconditions for political and moral freedom. Socialism cannot come as a gift but must find its democratic authentication in political volition. The mere establishment of a democracy that has not been fought for but imposed cannot bring Socialism unless the concerted political might of the working people of Germany aspires towards that goal.

All the intentions of reconstruction are attempts to revive capitalism. But people's belief in the authority of the old ruling classes has been shaken. It can no longer provide the basis for any constitution of society. 'The ruling ideas are the ideas of the ruling class,' said Marx.

But what is the ruling class today? A battered, shattered host that has gone into bankruptcy both at home and abroad. Undoubtedly many individuals are still in possession of their material foundations, and equally undoubtedly they have no intention of giving them up in order that the nation as a whole may survive. Using all the resources of tactical cunning, social interconnections, economic organisations, and now of the bourgeois parties as well, they would like to start again where — for the most part voluntarily and with criminal short-sightedness — they left off in 1932–3. But the political and social situation of Weimar cannot be reproduced. . . .

The crucial point on the agenda today is the abolition of capitalist exploitation and the transfer of the means of production from the control of the big proprietors to social ownership, the management of the economy as a whole in accordance not with the interests of private profit but with the principles of economically necessary planning. The muddle of the capitalist private-enterprise economy, the agents of which know no concern greater than that of making more money tomorrow than they made today, cannot be tolerated. Planning and control are not Socialism; they are only the prerequisites for it. The crucial step is to be seen in drastic socialisation.

Germany is too poor to be able to afford the luxury of planless production of goods or extra profits for monopoly capitalism. The social product even of a fully relaunched German economy will at best suffice to feed the working population and provide social assistance for the needy.

Socialism is no longer the concern of the working class in the old, narrow sense of the term. It is the programme for workers, peasant farmers, craft-tradesmen, small businessmen, and the intellectual professions! They are all in a position of irreconcilable antagonism to the real exploiter class. It has resulted in national and economic catastrophe that the so-called middle classes, ensnared by the propaganda of reactionaries, militarists, and Nazis, allowed themselves to be used as political cannon-fodder against democracy and Socialism. . . .

The fact that many of the means of production are today demolished and large numbers of capitalist economic leaders have been removed from the production process proves nothing as regards the abolition of capitalism as a system. That system is everywhere seeking to re-establish itself, and the true object of the policies of the bourgeois parties is to revive it and to win over chiefly middle-class mass support for such ends by means of ideological deception tactics.

The entrepreneurial nimbus is fading. The management of enterprises has long since passed into the hands of paid personnel who could just as well be appointed and remunerated by the representatives of the people. Even prior to 1933 Germany was probably, of all the countries in the world, economically and technically the one most suited to socialisation. German capitalism contrived to avoid that consequence by successfully unleashing a storm of political propaganda against the proponents of the ideas of Socialism and democracy. In the years of plenty the Germans did not wish to be Socialists; they will now, in poverty, have to be Socialists. Anyone with any judgement and sense of responsibility must recognise that the German people is no longer wealthy enough to pay for entrepreneurial profits, capital profits, and ground-rents. The destruction and diminution of the economic substance currently available renders a capitalist profit economy impossible and necessitates a public-utility economy planned and run in accordance with criteria relating to the common economic interest.

The nationalisation of *big industry* and *high finance* and the resettlement of *large land holdings* are an absolute necessity in economic terms. Particularly mining, heavy industry, the power-producing industry, transport, a very large part of manufacturing industry, insurance, and banking are not only ripe for socialisation; they must be socialised if the German economy is to function adequately.

Big property is seeking with the aid of all the political and economic tendencies and institutions whose ear it has to avoid Socialist consequences being drawn from the present situation. Its satellites continue, as before, to maintain that Social Democracy wishes to expropriate and socialise all owner-ship. As before, their diversionary propaganda smoke-screen lumps together the consumer ownership and labour ownership of small and medium-scale property with the capitalist profit and exploitation ownership of the upper bourgeoisie. As before, however, ownership in terms of small and medium-scale property is under no threat from Social Democracy.

The deprivatisation of the means of production and their transfer from big property to communal ownership do not only constitute an economic prob-lem; they also raise a crucial political question. Monopoly capital helped Hitler to power and on his orders prepared and waged the great war of predation against Europe. As long as it is possible in Germany for great wealth to accumulate in irresponsible private hands, democracy is not assured. The enormous economic power of the combines must be brought under public control; otherwise it will turn its political power against the new state. The peculiar predisposition of German class psychology and the compelling realities of German history will forever induce big property to convert its money into political power, which it will then use against democracy and peace. Democracy will be assured only in a Socialist Germany. Unlike in the countries of the older democracy of the West, in this country capitalism and democracy cannot coexist. . . .

### Europe and Germany

. . .The German problem cannot be settled from the German standpoint and in accordance with German views alone. There is no German question that is not at the same time potentially a European question. It is true as regards international politics too that one cannot build a new world from old materials and that, when circumstances have undergone a world-revolutionary upheaval, altered methods are called for as well.

Yet the Social Democratic Party regards itself, precisely because of its emphatically international character, as representing the nation as a whole. It is probably the only party in Germany that can escape the charge that it rallied to the principles of right and reason only in the hour of defeat. It lays claim, without any nationalist hysteria and without the arrogance that has typified Germans in recent years, to national recognition for the German people. The Social Democratic Party does not feel incriminated, nor is it incriminated, and it wishes to play its part in procuring for the German people the respect and sympathy that will be due to this nation too, once it has overcome the ghastly aberrations and brutalities in its history. The Social Democratic Party will devote all its efforts to preserving Germany as a national and economic entity in the context of the European balance of power and of the necessity for Europe. . . .

Social Democracy cannot conceive of a new Germany as an isolated, nationalistic Germany. It cannot think of Germany as anything but a constituent part of Europe. However, it wants to see that Germany not as an outcast but as an equal partner. Social Democracy, a party that because of the international nature of its policy has been rejected by the blind, nationalistically infected sections of its own people, is able to advance this claim openly and with calm assurance.

Not only politically is Europe a system of equilibrium; all its parts are also economically dependent on one another, and ultimately it constitutes a unit socially as well. The forces of Europe will increasingly direct themselves towards these goals as time goes on. So far as a German contribution to this is possible, the Social Democratic Party wishes to make it. It knows that the harnessing of all German forces is necessary for this. But it also knows that without the help of the United Nations it will be impossible to build Germany anew. That help must not stop at material aid. Political aid is a most urgent necessity. However appallingly and importunately our present poverty is knocking at the gates, the future is more important! Never mind about the older and middle-aged generations in Germany. They have taken much upon themselves already and will have to take more in order to make life possible for the generations coming after them. It is the young that matter!

Youth needs the help of the United Nations. We must be able to say to young people that democracy is not the political condition of a Germany lying beaten on the floor, Socialism is not the economy of poverty and hopelessness. If the world can give our young people the feeling that these are great ideas that will make life worth living once more and give it content and stability, then the decision for democracy will have been made in Germany!

There is no point in avoiding the issue. For everyone in Germany who taps deeper springs of knowledge and feeling than simply concern for his own pocket there are two questions that are indissolubly linked. One has to do with the possibility of *social justice*. The other is how his own nation can regain *equality of status* among the nations of the world.

The Social Democratic Party pursues this course unreservedly, drawing its strength from the knowledge that its ideals today are the ideals of the whole nation and of all forward-looking forces throughout the world!

*Reprinted in Arno Scholz and Walther G. Oschilewski (eds),* Turmwächter der Demokratie. Ein Lebensbild von Kurt Schumacher, *Vol. 2 (Berlin, 1953), pp. 36–50.*

# 12
# Kurt Schumacher: Dissociation from the Communists, January 1946

*[Extracts from a commentary on a resolution of the SPD of the British zone of occupation at a conference in Hanover, 3–4 January 1946]*

If what we see in the East were really Socialism, European humanity would have sentenced Socialism to death. Moreover the fundamental general view emerges that the destruction of the bourgeoisie or parts of that class does not give rise to the condition of Socialism.

We cannot be and have no wish to be anti-Russian, but neither do we wish to give preference to the national and imperial policy of Russia over that of any other country. We are prepared on principle, in considering these matters, to disregard certain events in the eastern zone. After all, we cannot be anti-Russian on principle because a permanent fellowship of peace among the nations is impossible if so large a country is excluded. A leading member of the Communist central committee said recently that we ought not to conduct an anti-Soviet smear campaign but that what we need are 'close' normal relations with Soviet Russia. The wishes of Social Democracy vis-à-vis Russia could not be better expressed. 'Normal relations' — that is the condition we desire, but at the moment relations are abnormal because in the eastern zone the occupying power is doing something that the other occupying powers notably do not do. In the East it is interfering in the internal thinking and significance of the political parties. We have seen this in the dismissal of the CDU leadership. We have seen it in the compulsory forming of blocs, and we are now seeing it at its most painful and most sweeping in the attitude of the occupying power aimed at giving the Social Democratic membership a Communist leadership. . . .

For German Social Democrats Socialism is a means to the economic emancipation of the human person. Socialism in Germany wants the human person — a person of a kind that individualism and liberalism were unable to create, a person on a socially secure foundation. German Social Democracy cannot conceive of a Socialism of authoritarian control and loss of individuality. Even if all differences of principle, tactics, and historical background were settled — and in reality not a single one is settled — this question alone would be decisive.

Union — as distinct from conquest — is only possible between autonomous elements. Want of autonomy among Germany's Communists has gone so far that they have become Russian patriots and deep down Germany and Socialism have become secondary concerns to them. . . .

We want to be patriots of no other country; we want to be as good Germans as we are international Socialists. When the Communists now suddenly say that they too want a new unity party to be autonomous, we know despite all assurances to the contrary that beneficiaries can never be autonomous.

Social Democracy has no intention of sacrificing itself to the foreign-policy interests of a victorious power. . . .

> *Reprinted in Arno Scholz and Walther G. Oschilewski (eds), Turmwächter der Demokratie. Ein Lebensbild von Kurt Schumacher, Vol. 2 (Berlin, 1953), pp. 61–8.*

# 13
# Basic Programme of the Social Democratic Party of Germany
## Adopted by an Extraordinary Conference of the Social Democratic Party held at Bad Godesberg from 13–15 November 1959

This is the *contradiction* of our time:

Man has unleashed the power of the atom and now fears the consequences of his own creation;

Man has developed the productive forces to a point hitherto unknown, and amassed tremendous wealth, but has failed to give everyone a fair share of the common achievement;

Man has conquered the earth and brought continents closer together but power blocs armed to the teeth separate peoples more than ever before, and totalitarian systems threaten his freedom.

This is why man, warned by wars of destruction and barbarism in the recent past, is afraid of his own future, because at any moment, somewhere in the world, human failing may throw the human race into the chaos of self-destruction.

Yet this is also the *hope* of our time:

Man can make his life easier in the atomic age, free himself from anxiety and distress and create prosperity for all if he uses his ever growing power over the forces of nature solely for peaceful ends;

Man can secure world peace if he establishes the rule of international law, reduces mistrust between peoples and stops the arms race;

For the first time in history it will then be possible for everyone to develop his personality in a securely-founded democracy and to broaden his cultural outlook free from want and fear.

*All men* are called upon to solve this contradiction. In our hands lies the decision as to whether man advances towards a happier future or towards self-destruction.

Only a new and better order of society can open man's way to freedom.

Democratic Socialism strives to achieve this new and better order.

### Fundamental Values of Socialism

Socialists aim to establish a society in which every individual can develop his personality and as a responsible member of the community, take part in the political, economic and cultural life of mankind.

Freedom and justice are interdependent, since the dignity of man rests on his

274

claim to individual responsibility just as much as on his acknowledgement of the right of others to develop their personality and, as equal partners, help shape society.

Freedom, justice and solidarity, which are everyone's obligation towards his neighbours and spring from our common humanity, are the fundamental values of Socialism.

Democratic Socialism, which in Europe is rooted in Christian ethics, humanism and classical philosophy, does not proclaim ultimate truths — not because of any lack of understanding for or indifference to philosophical or religious truths, but out of respect for the individual's choice in these matters of conscience in which neither the state nor any political party should be allowed to interfere.

The Social Democratic Party is the party of freedom of thought. It is a community of men holding different beliefs and ideas. Their agreement is based on the moral principles and political aims they have in common. The Social Democratic Party strives for a way of life in accordance with these principles. Socialism is a constant task — to fight for freedom and justice, to preserve them and to live up to them.

### Basic Demands for a Society Worthy of Man

From the acceptance of Democratic Socialism follow certain basic demands which must be fulfilled in a society worthy of man.

All peoples must submit to the rule of international law backed by adequate executive power. War must be ruled out as a means of policy.

All peoples must have equal opportunities to share in the world's wealth. Developing countries have a claim to the help of other peoples.

We are fighting for democracy. Democracy must become the universal form of state organisation and way of life because it is founded on respect for the dignity of man and his individual responsibility.

We resist every dictatorship, every form of totalitarian or authoritarian rule because they violate human dignity, destroy man's freedom and the rule of law. Socialism can be realised only through democracy and democracy can only be fulfilled through Socialism.

Communists have no right to invoke Socialist traditions. In fact, they have falsified Socialist ideas. Socialists are struggling for the realisation of freedom and justice while Communists exploit the conflicts in society to establish the dictatorship of their party.

In the democratic state, every form of power must be subject to public control. The interest of the individual must be subordinated to the interest of the community. Democracy, social security and individual freedom are endangered by an economic and social system in which striving for profit and power are the distinguishing features. Democratic Socialism therefore aspires after a new economic and social order.

All privileged access to educational institutions must be abolished. Talent and achievement should be the sole criteria of advancement.

Freedom and justice cannot be guaranteed by institutions alone. Technology and organisation are exerting a growing influence on all areas of life. This creates new dependencies which threaten freedom. Only diversity in economic, social and cultural life can stimulate the creative powers of the individual without which man's mind is paralysed.

Freedom and democracy are only thinkable in an industrial society if a constantly growing number of people develop a social consciousness and are ready to help shoulder responsibility. A decisive means to this end is political education in its widest sense. It is an essential objective of all educational efforts in our time.

## The Order of the State

The Social Democratic Party of Germany lives and works in the whole of Germany. It stands by the Basic Law of the German Federal Republic. In accordance with the Basic Law it strives for German unity in freedom.

The division of Germany is a threat to peace. To end this division is a vital interest of the German people.

Not until Germany is reunited, will the whole people be able freely to determine the content and form of the state and society.

Man's life, his dignity and his conscience take precedence over the state. Every citizen must respect the convictions of his fellow men. It is the duty of the state to protect freedom of faith and freedom of conscience.

The state should create the conditions in which the individual may freely develop his personality, responsible to himself but conscious of his obligations to society. Established fundamental rights do not only protect the freedom of the individual in relation to the state; they should also be regarded as social rights which constitute the basis of the state.

The social function of the state is to provide social security for its citizens to enable everyone to be responsible for shaping his own life freely and to further the development of a free society.

The state becomes a truly civilised state [*Kulturstaat*] through the fusion of the democratic idea with the ideas of social security and the rule of law. It depends for its content on the forces prevalent in society, and its task is to serve the creative spirit of man.

The Social Democratic Party affirms its adherence to democracy. In a democracy the power of the state is derived from the people and the government is always responsible to Parliament whose confidence it must possess. In a democracy the rights of the minority as well as the rights of the majority must be respected; government and opposition have different tasks of equal importance; both share in the responsibility for the state.

The Social Democratic Party aims to win the support of the majority of the people by competing under equal conditions with other democratic parties in order to build a society and a state that accord with the essential demands of democratic Socialism.

Legislature, executive and judiciary should operate separately and it is the duty of each to serve the public interest. The existence of three levels of authority — Federal, State, and Local — ensures the distribution of power, strengthens freedom and through co-determination and co-responsibility gives the citizen manifold access to democratic institutions. Free local communities are vital to a living democracy. The Social Democratic Party therefore supports the principles of local self-government which must be extended and given adequate financial support.

Associations in which people of different groups and sections of the population unite for common ends are necessary institutions of modern society. They must be democratically organised. The more powerful they are, the greater is the responsibility they carry, but the greater also is the danger of their abusing their power. Parliaments, administration and courts must not be allowed to come under the one-side influence of vested interests.

Press, radio, television and cinema fulfill public tasks. They must be independent and free to gather information wherever they wish, to comment on it and to distribute it, and to form and express their own opinions. Radio and television should remain under the control of public corporations, and be directed by free and democratic boards. They must be safeguarded against pressure from interest groups.

Judges must have outer and inner independence if they are to serve justice in the name of the people. Lay judges should play an equally important part in jurisdiction. Only independent judges can pass judgment on criminal offences. Neither wealth nor poverty should have an influence on people's access to courts or on jurisdiction. Legislation must keep pace with the development of society if justice is to be done and if the people's sense of justice is not to be violated.

## National Defence

The Social Democratic Party affirms the need to defend the free democratic society. It is in favour of national defence.

National defence must be adapted to the political and geographical position of Germany and therefore stay within the limits imposed by the necessity of creating the conditions for an easing of international tensions, for effectively controlled disarmament and for the reunification of Germany. Protection of the civilian population is an essential part of a country's defence.

The Social Democratic Party demands that the means of mass destruction be banned by international law in the whole world.

The Federal Republic of Germany must neither produce nor use atomic or other means of mass destruction.

The Social Democratic Party is striving for the inclusion of the whole of Germany in a European zone of reduced tensions and of a controlled limitation of arms, a zone to be cleared of foreign troops in the process of German reunification in freedom and in which atomic weapons and other means of mass destruction are neither produced nor stored nor used.

The armed forces must be under the political direction of the government and under the control of Parliament. A relationship of trust should exist between soldiers and the democratic forces in the country. The soldier must retain his civic rights and duties.

The armed forces must only be used for national defence.

The Social Democratic Party pledges itself to protect every citizen who for reasons of conscience refuses to do military service or operate means of mass destruction.

The Social Democratic Party stands for general and controlled disarmament and an international authority equipped with the means of coercion to safeguard the rule of international law. These would supersede national defence forces.

## The Economy

The goal of Social Democratic economic policy is the constant growth of prosperity and a just share for all in the national product, a life in freedom without undignified dependence and without exploitation.

### Constant Economic Expansion

The Second Industrial Revolution makes possible a rise in the general standard of living greater than ever before and the elimination of poverty and misery still suffered by large numbers of people.

Economic policy must secure full employment whilst maintaining a stable currency, increase productivity and raise general prosperity.

To enable all people to take part in the country's growing prosperity there must be planning to adjust the economy to the constant structural changes in order to achieve a balanced economic development.

Such a policy demands national accounting and a national budget. The national budget must be approved by Parliament. It is binding on government policy, provides an important basis for the policies of the autonomous central bank, and establishes guiding lines for the economy which keeps its right to make independent decisions.

The modern state exerts a constant influence on the economy through its policies on taxation, finance, currency and credits, customs, trade, social services, prices and public contracts as well as agriculture and housing. More than a third of the national income passes through the hands of the government. The question is therefore not whether measures of economic planning and control serve a purpose, but rather who should apply these measures and for whose benefit. The state cannot shirk its responsibility for the course the economy takes. It is responsible for securing a forward-looking policy with regard to business cycles and should restrict itself to influencing the economy mainly by indirect means.

Free choice of consumer goods and services, free choice of working place, freedom for employers to exercise their initiative as well as free competition are essential conditions of a Social Democratic economic policy. The autonomy of trade unions and employers' associations in collective bargaining is an important feature of a free society. Totalitarian control of the economy destroys freedom. The Social Democratic Party therefore favours a free market wherever free competition really exists. Where a market is dominated by individuals or groups, however, all manner of steps must be taken to protect freedom in the economic sphere. As much competition as possible — as much planning as necessary.

### Ownership and Power

A significant feature of the modern economy is the constantly increasing tendency toward concentration. Large-scale enterprises exert a decisive influence not only on the development of the economy and the standard of living but also on the structure of the economy and of society.

Those who control large industrial concerns, huge financial resources and tens of thousands of employees do not merely perform an economic function but wield decisive power over men; wage and salary earners are kept in a position of dependence, and not only in purely economic and material matters.

Wherever large-scale enterprises predominate, free competition is eliminated. Those who have less power have fewer opportunities for development, and remain more or less fettered. The consumer occupies the most vulnerable position of all in the economy.

Increased power through cartels and associations gives the leaders of big business an influence on politics and the state which is irreconcilable with democratic principles. They usurp the authority of the state. Economic power becomes political power.

This development is a challenge to all who consider freedom, justice, human dignity and social security the foundations of human society.

The key task of an economic policy concerned with freedom is therefore to contain the power of big business. State and society must not be allowed to become the prey of powerful sectional groups.

Private ownership of the means of production can claim protection by society as long as it does not hinder the establishment of social justice.

Efficient small and medium sized enterprises are to be strengthened to enable them to prevail in competition with large-scale enterprises.

Competition by public enterprise is an important means of preventing private enterprise from dominating the market. Public enterprise should safeguard the interests of the community as a whole. It becomes a necessity where, for natural or technical reasons, economic functions vital to the community cannot be carried out in a rational way except by excluding competition.

Enterprises which are built up on a voluntary collective basis and whose purpose it is to satisfy demand rather than earn private profits help to regulate prices and serve the interests of the consumer. They perform a valuable function in a democratic society and should be supported.

Large-scale publicity should give the people an insight into the power structure of the economy and into business practices in order that public opinion may be mobilised against abuses of power.

Effective public control must prevent the abuse of economic power. The most important means to this end are investment control and control over the forces dominating the market.

Public ownership is a legitimate form of public control which no modern state can do without. It serves to protect freedom against domination by large economic concerns. In these concerns power is held today by managers who are themselves the servants of anonymous forces. Private ownership of the means of production is therefore no longer identical with the control of power. Economic power, rather than ownership, is the central problem today. Where sound economic power relations cannot be guaranteed by other means, public ownership is appropriate and necessary.

Every concentration of economic power, even in the hands of the state, harbours dangers. This is why the principles of self-government and decentralisation must be applied to the public sector. The interests of wage and salary earners as well as the public interest and the interests of the consumer must be represented on the management boards of public enterprises. Not centralised bureaucracy but responsible co-operation between all concerned serves the interests of the community best.

## Distribution of Income and Wealth

The competition economy does not guarantee by itself just distribution of income and wealth. This can only be achieved through measures of economic policy.

Income and wealth are distributed unjustly. This is not only the result of mass destruction of property through crises, war and inflation but is largely due to an economic and fiscal policy which has favoured large incomes and the accumulation of capital in the hands of a few, and which has made it difficult for those without capital to acquire it.

The Social Democratic Party aims to create conditions in which everybody is able to save part of his rising income and acquire property. This presupposes a constant increase in production and a fair distribution of the national income.

Wage and salary policies are adequate and necessary means of distributing incomes and wealth more justly.

Appropriate measures must ensure that an adequate part of the steadily growing capital of big business is widely distributed or made to serve public purposes. It is a deplorable symptom of our times that privileged groups in society indulge in luxury while important public tasks, especially in the fields of science, research and education, are neglected in a way unworthy of a civilised nation.

## Agriculture

The principles of Social Democratic economic policy apply also to agriculture. The structure of agriculture, however, and its dependence on uncontrollable forces of nature call for special measures.

The farmer is entitled to own his land. Efficient family holdings should be protected by modern laws on land tenure and leases.

Support of the existing system of co-operatives is the best way of increasing the efficiency of small and medium sized holdings whilst maintaining their independence.

Agriculture must adjust itself to the changing economic structure in order to make its proper contribution to economic development and to assure an adequate standard of living to the people working in it. These changes are determined not only by technical and scientific progress, but also by the changes in the location of the market within the framework of European co-operation and by the fact that the German economy is increasingly linked with that of the rest of the world.

The modernisation of agriculture and its efficiency are a public responsibility.

The interests of the farming population are best served by the integration of agriculture into an economy with high productivity and an ever more widely distributed mass purchasing power. Price and market policies necessary to protect agricultural incomes should take into account the interests of the consumers and of the economy as a whole.

The cultural, economic, and social condition of the entire farming population must be improved. The lag in social legislation must be overcome.

## Trade Unions in the Economy

All wage and salary earners and civil servants have the right to free association in trade unions. They would be helplessly exposed to those in positions of command in enterprises and concerns unless they were able to confront the latter with the united force of their free and democratically organised trade unions and freely to agree on working conditions.

Trade unions fight to secure wage and salary earners a fair share of the country's wealth and the right to a voice in decisions affecting economic and social life.

They fight for greater freedom and act as representatives of all working people. This makes them an important element in the constant process of democratisation. It is the unions' great task to enable every employee to shoulder responsibility and to see to it than he can make use of his abilities.

Wage and salary earners whose contribution to production is decisive have so far been deprived of an effective say in economic life. Democracy, however, demands that workers should be given a voice and that co-determination be extended to all branches of the economy. From being a servant the worker must become a citizen of the economy.

Co-determination in the iron and steel industry and in coal mining marks the beginning of a new economic structure. The next step should be the establishment of a democratic organisational structure in all large enterprises. Co-determination by employees in the independent administrative bodies set up in the economy must be secured.

## Social Responsibility

Social policy must create the essential conditions which allow the individual to unfold himself freely in society and which determine his life according to his own responsibility. Social conditions that lead to individual and social hardship cannot be accepted as inevitable and unchangeable. The system of social security must correspond to the dignity of responsible individuals.

Every citizen has the right to a minimum state pension in case of old age or inability to earn a living, or at the death of the family's provider. This pension is supplemented by other personally acquired pension claims. In this way the individual standard of living will be sustained. Social allowances of all kinds, including pensions for war-disabled and their dependents, must be regularly adjusted to the rise in earned incomes.

Technology and modern civilisation expose people to many dangers to their health. They threaten not only the living generation but future generations as well. The individual is unable to protect himself against these hazards. The Social Democratic Party therefore demands comprehensive health protection. Health policy must be perfected, and the conditions and ways of living must be shaped in a way conducive to making life in sound health possible. Public health protection, especially protection at work and effective methods of preventing damage to health in individuals, must be developed. A sense of personal responsibility in respect of one's health must be aroused and the doctor of one's choice must be given full facilities for the preservation of health and prevention of illness. The professional freedom of decision of doctors must be ensured. The provision of adequately equipped hospitals is a public task.

Since all people should have an equal chance to live, all must have access to the treatment made available through modern technical research when they are in need of it, regardless of their financial position. Such medical treatment must be supplemented by adequate economic assistance in the case of illness.

Working hours should be progressively shortened without prejudice to income levels and in step with the development of the economy. In order to cope with particularly difficult situations in life and in special cases of need, the general social allowances must be supplemented by individual care and social aid. Social aid should be given in co-operation with independent voluntary welfare organisations and institutions for mutual aid and self-help. The independence of free welfare organisations must be protected.

All labour and social legislation should be ordered and compiled in a surveyable code on labour legislation and a code on social legislation.

Everyone has a right to a decent place in which to live. It is the home of the family. It must therefore continue to receive social protection and must not be the mere object of private gain.

The housing shortage must speedily be eliminated through effective building programmes. Public housing must be encouraged and social considerations must be taken into account when determining rents. Speculation in real estate should be prohibited and excessive gains from the sale of real estate taxed away.

### Woman—Family—Youth

Equality of rights for women should be realised in the legal, economic and social spheres. Women must be given equal opportunities in education and occupational training, in the choice and practice of professions and in earnings. The special psychological and biological characteristics of women should not be disregarded because they have equal rights. The work of the housewife should be recognised as an occupation. The housewife and mother is in need of social assistance. Mothers of children of pre-school age and school-age should not be compelled by economic need to seek gainful employment.

State and society must protect, support and strengthen the family. By supporting the material security of the family, society recognises its moral value. Effective help should be given to the family by generous tax allowances for parents, and by maternity benefits and family allowances.

Young people must be enabled to manage their own lives and grow up ready to assume their responsibilities towards society. It is therefore the task of state and society to strengthen the eductional function of the family, to supplement it where it does not suffice, and, if need be, to provide an alternative. A system of grants and scholarships must ensure that special abilities and aptitudes of young people are fully developed in their vocational and professional training.

The protection of the young workers must be adjusted to present-day social conditions and educational experience. If the young people are entrusted at an early stage with a share in the work and responsibilities of adults, they will become well-informed and determined democrats. Progressive youth legislation should guarantee the young people's right to education and development of their personality. In all areas of life which concern education or the encouragement and protection of youth, the welfare of youth must have priority over all other considerations.

## Cultural Life

The creative powers of the individual must be given a chance to unfold freely in a full and diverse cultural life. The state should encourage and support all forces willing to make a contribution to cultural progress. The state must protect the citizen against all attempts by power groups or sectional interests at making the people's spiritual and cultural life subservient to their own purposes.

### Religion and Church

Only mutual tolerance which respects the dignity of all men regardless of differences in belief and conviction, offers a sound basis for political and human co-operation in society.

Socialism is no substitute for religion. The Social Democratic Party respects churches and religious societies. It affirms their public and legal status, their special mission and their autonomy.

It is always ready to co-operate with the churches on the basis of a free partnership. It welcomes the fact that men are moved by their religious faith to acknowledge their social obligation and their responsibilities towards society.

Freedom of thought, of religion and of conscience, and freedom to preach the gospel must be protected. Any abuse of this freedom for partisan or anti-democratic ends cannot be tolerated.

### Education

Education must give an opportunity to all freely to develop their abilities and capacities. It must strengthen the will to resist the conformist tendencies of our time. Knowledge and the acquisition of traditional cultural values, and a thorough understanding of the formative forces in society, are essential to the development of independent thinking and free judgment.

School and university should bring up youth in a spirit of mutual respect. Youth should be taught to appreciate the values of freedom, independence and social responsibility as well as the ideals of democracy and international understanding. The aim should be to encourage tolerance, mutual understanding and solidarity in our society in which so many philosophical viewpoints and sytems of value exist side by side. The curricula of schools should therefore pay proper attention to education for citizenship.

The arts and crafts should have an important place in education. It is the task of state and society to enable everyone to become familiar with the arts and artistic work through schools and adult educational institutions.

Sport and physical training deserve the support of state and society. They help to keep the people in good health and are important elements in the formation of a spirit of solidarity.

Parents should have a voice in the education of their children at school and forms of self-government by pupils should be developed everywhere. School systems and curricula must give full scope of the development of talent and ability at all stages. Every gifted pupil should have access to advanced education and training. Attendance at all state supported schools and universities should be free. Books and other study material should be available to students free of charge.

The period of compulsory school attendance should be increased to ten years. Trade and technical schools should not only provide occupational training but also general education.

New paths to university education must be opened. Since not all talented young people can reach university via the usual elementary and higher school training, other opportunities to do so must be made available via vocational work, occupational schools and special educational institutions.

All teachers should be trained at universities. A good school system demands educators able to judge independently the problems of their time.

### Science

Scientific research and teaching must be unfettered. The results of scientific research must be made known to the public. Adequate public means must be spent on research and teaching.

The state must see to it that the results of scientific research are not misused to the detriment of mankind.

An independent council of scientists should be formed which would regard itself responsible for making proposals for urgent research projects and for undertaking some itself. Research and teaching should be furthered in every field of science without exception.

Generous grants should secure for all students the full benefits of academic education. All students should be taught the basic elements of political and social science.

Mastering the political, human, and social problems of the developing industrial society and maintaining human freedom in it call for a perfection and intensification of the science of man and society. Efforts in this field must be made to correspond to those exerted to develop natural science and technology.

The freedom and independence of universities must remain untouched. But the university must not remain isolated from other spheres of life and should therefore work together with other institutions of a democratic society, especially in adult education.

A modern system of adult education should provide opportunities for everyone to acquire knowledge, power of judgement and other abilities after the completion of formal education. Responsible participation in the democratic state depends on these qualities.

## *The Arts*

The freedom of artistic work must be guaranteed. State and municipality should make public means available to support the creative elements in the community. No regimentation, especially no censorship, must restrict free artistic creation.

## The International Community

The greatest and most urgent task is to preserve peace and protect freedom.

Democratic Socialism has always stood for international co-operation and solidarity. At a time when all interests and relationships are internationally linked, no nation can any longer solve its political, economic, social and cultural problems by itself. The Social Democratic Party is guided by the realisation that the cultural, economic, legal and military tasks of German politics must be solved in close co-operation with other peoples.

Normal diplomatic and trade relations with all nations are indispensable in spite of differences in system of government and social structure.

International courts of justice and treaties, the acknowledgement of the right to national self-determination and of the equality of all nations, the inviolability of sovereign territory and non-interference in the affairs of other peoples — all these are necessary to secure peace which must be guaranteed by a world authority.

The United Nations Organisation must become the universal body which it was meant to be. Its principles must be universally binding. The right of national minorities must be recognised in accordance with the human rights proclaimed by the Charter of the United Nations. The Social Democratic Party of Germany proclaims the right of all people to a homeland, a national tradition, a language and culture.

Regional security systems within the United Nations framework should be established as a step towards general disarmament and the easing of international tension. The reunified Germany should become a member of a European security system with full rights and obligations. Economic developments make co-operation between the states of Europe necessary. The Social Democratic Party recognises the need for such co-operation which, in the first place, should serve economic and social progress. Regionally limited supra-national association must not be allowed to result in "closed-door-policies" with regard to the rest of the world. The prerequisites of peaceful co-existence are co-operation between equal partners and a system of world trade open to all nations.

Democratic state must express their solidarity especially with the developing countries. Half of the world's population still lives in extreme poverty and ignorance. So long as the wealth of the world is not redistributed and the productivity of developing countries raised considerably, democratic development is in jeopardy and peace continues to be threatened. All peoples are obliged to fight starvation, misery and disease by a common effort. Their economic, social and cultural development must be inspired by the ideas of democratic Socialism if they are not to become the victims of new forms of oppression.

# Documents

## Our Way

The Socialist movement has an historic task. It began as a spontaneous moral protest of wage earners against the capitalist system. The tremendous development of the productive forces with the help of science and technology brought wealth and power to a small group of people, but only destitution and misery to the workers. To abolish the privileges of the ruling classes and to secure freedom, justice and prosperity for all was and remains the essence of the Socialist aim.

The working class had to rely on its own resources in its struggle. It acquired self-confidence by becoming conscious of its own position and by its determination to change this position by united action and the experience of success in its struggle.

Despite heavy setbacks and some errors the Labour movement succeded in the nineteenth and twentieth centuries in winning recognition for many of its demands. The proletarian who was once without protection and rights, who had to work sixteen hours a day for a starvation wage, achieved the eight-hour day, protection at work, insurance against unemployment, sickness, disability and destitution in old age. He achieved the prohibition of child labour and night work for women, the legal protection of youth and mothers, and holidays with pay. He successfully fought for the right to assemble and to form trade unions, the right to collective bargaining and to strike. He is about to obtain the right to co-determination. Once a mere object of exploitation, the worker now occupies the position of a citizen in the state with equal rights and obligations.

In several countries of Europe the foundations of a new society have been laid under Social Democratic governments. Social security and the democratisation of the economy are being realised to an increasing extent.

These sucesses represent milestones on the march forward of the Labour movement which has demanded so many sacrifices. The emancipation of the workers helped to enlarge the freedom of all men. From a party of the working class the Social Democratic Party has become a party of the people. It is determined to put the forces unleashed by the industrial revolution and the advance of technology in all spheres of life to the service of freedom and justice for all. The social forces which built the capitalist world cannot tackle this task. Their historical record is one of impressive technical and economic advance, but also of destructive wars, mass unemployment, inflation which robbed people of their savings, and economic insecurity. The old forces are unable to oppose the brutal Communist challenge with a better programme for a new society, in which individual and political freedom is enhanced, and economic security and social justice guaranteed. This is why they cannot satisfy the claims for assistance and solidarity from the young states which are about to throw off the yoke of colonial exploitation, to shape their destinies in freedom and to insist on participation in the world's wealth. These states are resisting the lure of Communism which is trying to draw them into its sphere of influence.

Communists are radical suppressors of freedom and violators of human rights and of the self-determination of individuals and peoples. The people in the countries under Communist domination are increasingly opposing the Communist regime. Even in those countries changes are taking place. Even there, the longing for freedom is growing which no system can wholly suppress in the long run. But the Communist rulers are fighting for their own survival. They are building up military and economic power for which their peoples have to pay the price and which represents an increasing threat to freedom.

Only the prospect of a society based on the fundamental values of democratic Socialism can offer the world new hope, a society resting on respect for human dignity, on freedom from want and fear, from war and oppression, which is built in co-operation with all men of good will.

This message is addressed to all men and women in this country as well as in other parts of the world.

In Germany Socialists are united in the Social Democratic Party which welcomes to its ranks all who accept the fundamental values and demands of Democratic Socialism.

# 14
# The 'Munich Declaration' of the SPD, 19 April 1982

At the conclusion of the Munich party conference SPD Chairman Willy Brandt delivered the following 'Munich Declaration':

In a period of global recession that could become a global depression, in a period of continuing instability in relations between the superpowers, in a period of structural change affecting the economies of the industrialised societies, in a period of changing awareness and changing values in our society, when Neo-Conservatives and young 'alternatives' share a common temptation to seek simple solutions to complex problems; in this situation we make 10 statements:

1. The Social Democratic Party of Germany is the political force that is capable of protecting our people from the curse of over-simple solutions. Those who brand the ability to compromise as opportunism bring misfortune upon mankind. Social Democrats deal in concrete terms; they acknowledge the legacy of the European Enlightenment, and they will oppose every false step into irrationalism.

2. The Social Democrats, at the conclusion of their Munich party conference, confirm their claim to the political leadership of the Federal Republic of Germany. They proclaim their faith in Chancellor Helmut Schmidt. They are determined continually to reforge the social alliance between employees, the progressive middle class, the younger generation, and intellectual Germany.

The coalition with the Free Democrats has our positive assent. In difficult times it has a fresh chance of proving its worth.

3. Our people must not be allowed to come under the control of those who are today trying to sell it the drastic remedies of Neo-Conservatism. In other countries these have plunged large sections of the working class into renewed poverty. We continue to advocate active state intervention in the economic process in order to help prevent unemployment, instances of social collapse, and unacceptable ecological burdens. We wish to encourage a spirit of enterprise at all levels of working life and to impede profit-making without performance. The SPD is and will always be a party of labour. It backs job-creation, energy-saving, and reduced working hours. We abide by our course with regard to co-determination and the formation of assets in employee ownership. The party conference has made important proposals here.

4. We realise that lower growth places the financing of the systems of social security fought for by the labour movement in jeopardy. We will not tolerate the burden of the major risks that life holds being thrown back on the

individual citizen. We are prepared to consolidate our systems of social security under conditions that preserve the principle of equity.

5. We Social Democrats are aware that progress becomes pointless in a destroyed environment.

We therefore see the conservation of nature as a communal responsibility; there are also jobs here for the future. For the tasks that are currently most urgent — a ten-year 'Clean Lakes and Rivers in the Federal Republic' programme and a concerted plan to combat the threat to our forests from acid rain — a proper financial programme will need to be worked out.

6. A special challenge to our good sense and to our humanity is posed by the question of how we behave towards the foreign fellow-citizens who have been summoned to our country. The SPD is determined to combat with all its strength the hatred of foreigners now arising under the influence of unemployment. We call upon the trade unions, the churches, and all social groups and parties to launch a major initiative against xenophobia. At the same time we realise that the Federal Republic of Germany is not capable of integrating an unlimited number of foreign fellow-citizens. We shall therefore exert ourselves to the utmost in order humanely to ensure that the number of foreign fellow-citizens does not grow any further.

7. Without peace, all is in vain. Social Democrats are therefore resolutely opposed to every threat to peace. We campaign for disarmament in East and West.

Successful pursuit of *détente* is an urgent necessity. Only such a policy is capable of creating the kind of trust without which arms limitation will be impossible. We accept the Western alliance as well as a policy of security partnership with the Eastern-bloc countries.

8. The guarantee of peace and the right to freedom are prerequisites for the physical and moral survival of the human race. We stand by the weak, oppressed, and exploited peoples of the Third World. We proclaim our solidarity with the forces of freedom, wherever they are oppressed — from Poland to Turkey and from Afghanistan to El Salvador.

9. In the local community the citizen has direct experience of democracy. The Social Democrats are determined to oppose any undermining of the financial position of local authorities, to make our towns and villages better places to live in, and to launch a new offensive in local-government policy.

10. The Munich Party Conference of 1982 has demonstrated the Social Democrats' capacity to act. We are and shall always be a community of like-minded people that is able to open its ranks in discussion and close them in action. We have no illusions:

The 1980s will require all our strength. German Social Democracy gives notice of its intention to shape the future of our country.

Informationsdienst der SPD intern, *No. 7/82, 28 April 1982, pp. 8f.*

# 15
# The Aims of Democratic Socialism
## Foreword from the *Framework of Economic and Political Orientation of the Social Democratic Party of Germany for the years 1975–1985*

What is the "Orientation Frame 85" about, which so intensively occupied many in the SPD — and many outside it as well — before it was adopted on November 14th, 1975, by the Mannheim party conference? Well, those involved with it know and it won't harm others to take note that here the strongest political party in the Federal Republic of Gemany has made the attempt to create the linking piece between day-to-day politics and the Basic Programme and thus to define the tasks extending into the coming decade. The resolution in Mannheim in a way concluded a debate of almost 10 years. The preceding lively discussions led to a new conciseness of Social Democratic policy.

The discussion about mid- and long-term political planning began when, after almost 20 years in opposition, the SPD at the end of 1966 for the first time assumed co-responsibility in the federal government. The social Democrats took seriously the obligation to a forward-looking, responsible policy. In 1968 the "Perspectives — Social Democratic policy in the transition to the 1970s" was presented and in the spring of 1970 the Saarbruecken party conference appointed a commission which was charged to work out "a long-term socio-political programme on the basis of the Godesberg Basic Programme" which had to be "concretised" and "quantified". The commission, under the leadership of Helmut Schmidt, Hans Apel and Jochen Steffen presented the first draft of a "Framework of Orientation to 1985" in 1972. After lively discussion, the party conference in Hannover in the spring of 1973 charged a new commission with revising and supplementing it. We learned a lot in this discussion; including that our intention to quantify a long-term political programme could not be realised in the originally intended way if we were going to be responsible in our statements.

The Hannover "Resolution on the Framework of Orientation to 1985" thus charged the second commission with new tasks and recommended separation into a basic "General Part" and a "Special Part" of detailed statements which should be updated as required.

The second "Orientation Frame 85" commission under the chairmanship of Peter von Oertzen, with Horst Ehmke and (after the death of Klaus Dieter Arndt) Herber Ehrenberg presented its draft to the party Executive Committee on January 14th, 1975. It led, as I have already remarked, to lively and in the main fruitful discussion within and outside the SPD.

The commission appointed to process motions regarding the Orientation Framework worked out a new revised version of the General Part for the Mannheim party conference, taking into account 1,007 motions from party branches as well as the proposals of special commissions and working groups. After making further changes and additions the party conference then adopted this version. (The Special Part and the motions connected with it were referred for further deliberation to the special commissions of the Executive Committee.)

The Orientation Framework is no substitute for the Godesberg Basic Programme. It not only confirms the fundamental positions of Godesberg, it supplements them in important fields and formulates solutions for problems we are likely to face in the period running up to 1985.

The 1985 Orientation Framework has worked out, for example, that the economy and the society of the Federal Republic of Germany will only cope with the tasks of the coming years if reform policies continue. It makes clear the the SPD not only successfully tackles difficult economic problems but, in contrast to other parties in our country, makes the attempt to show answers to questions which face the Federal Republic in a time of worldwide economic transformation. Prerequisites for the success of our economic policy and for the securing of jobs are longer-term political perspectives and a structural policy in tune with them.

The Union parties have so far not been in a position clearly to present their goals for a longer period of time. Nor are they able to say with what concrete instruments and in what priorities they would achieve such aims. Because of internal contradictions neither are they able to arrive at anything near the outlining of socio-political tasks as given in the 1985 Orientation Framework.

The SPD cannot afford to forego clarification of the contents and long-term orientation of its policies. This is why it is stating more precisely for a 10-year period the content of its political concept and explains how it wants to achieve its aims. I consider one of the great advantages of the now adopted Orientation Framework to be that with it the attempt is made to outline the tasks of Social Democratic policy as precisely as possible under the conditions now prevailing while in regard to instruments of economic policy, various possibilities are realistically and flexibly kept open. The Mannheim party conference followed my advice that we should not over-extend ourselves in formulating our economic policy instruments.

I wish to extend my heartfelt thanks to all those who worked to compile this important document of German Social Democratic policy. This goes for the members of the commission and their expert staff. It goes for those who worked for changes and additions even though they were naturally not able to assert all their wishes. And it goes not least for those who, out of their specific, non-party responsibility in society provided valuable stimuli.

The job now is to disseminate the Orientation Framework in our own party and among the interested public. The citizens should know with what the Social Democratic Party intends to contribute to solve the problems ahead of us. They should see what aims we pursue, how we assess the premise from which to proceed, what means we regard as suitable and in what democratic ways we intend to implement our policies.

The discussion before and in Mannheim has confirmed that the German

Social Democrats are able not only to debate courageously and freely but also to take realistic, forward-looking decisions and jointly to act on them.

**Willy Brandt**

*English translation published by the Research Institute of the Friedrich Ebert Foundation, Bonn, 1976.*

# Statistical Information

**1.** Voting strength and Reichstag representation of the SPD, 1871–1912 (%)

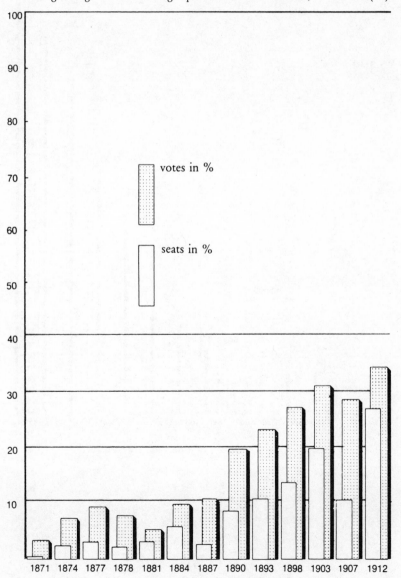

**2.** Reichstag election results, 1871–1912 (000s)

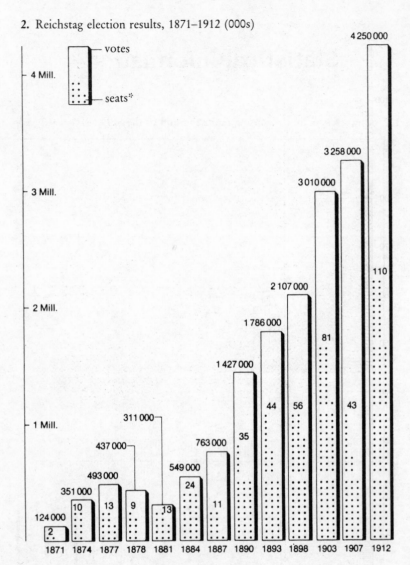

* out of a total of 397 representatives; 1871 only 382 representatives

**3.** Reichstag election results, 1919–1933

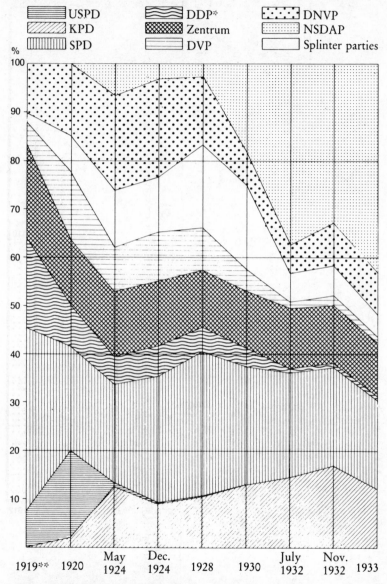

* From 1930 'Deutsche Staatspartei'
** 1919 elections for the National Assembly

**4.** Reichstag election results, 1919–1933 (%)*

| Party | Jan. 1919 (Nat. Ass.) | June 1920 | May 1924 | Dec. 1924 | May 1928 | Sept. 1930 | July 1932 | Nov. 1932 | March 1933 |
|---|---|---|---|---|---|---|---|---|---|
| NSDAP | — | — | 6.5 | 3.0 | 2.6 | 18.3 | 37.4 | 33.1 | 43.9 |
| DNVP | 10.3 | 15.1 | 19.5 | 20.5 | 14.2 | 7.0 | 5.9 | 8.5 | 8.0 |
| Splinter** | 1.6 | 7.4 | 11.8 | 11.2 | 17.0 | 17.8 | 5.9 | 5.9 | 4.3 |
| DVP | 4.4 | 13.9 | 9.2 | 10.1 | 8.7 | 4.5 | 1.2 | 1.9 | 1.1 |
| Zentrum*** | 19.7 | 13.6 | 13.4 | 13.6 | 12.1 | 11.8 | 12.5 | 11.9 | 11.2 |
| DDP | 18.5 | 8.3 | 5.7 | 6.3 | 4.9 | 3.8 | 1.0 | 1.0 | 0.9 |
| SPD | 37.9 | 21.6 | 20.5 | 26.0 | 29.8 | 24.5 | 21.6 | 20.4 | 18.3 |
| USDP | — | 18.0 | 0.8 | 0.3 | 0.1 | — | — | — | — |
| KPD | — | 2.0 | 12.6 | 9.0 | 10.6 | 13.1 | 14.3 | 16.9 | 12.3 |

* *Source: Statistik des Deutschen Reiches*
** Refers to all parties which did not receive more than 5% of the votes at any of these elections.
*** 1919 incl. the Bayerische Volkspartei (BVP)

**5.** Strength of parties in the *Bundestag*, 1949–1983

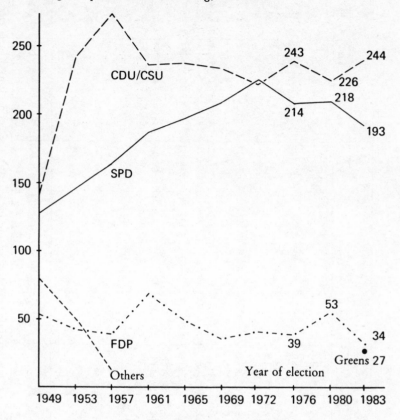

## 6. SPD results in the *Bundestag* elections, 1949–1983

| | | Bundestagswahl[1] | | | | | | | | | |
|---|---|---|---|---|---|---|---|---|---|---|---|
| | | 14.8.1949 | 6.9.1953 | 15.9.1957 | 17.9.1961 | 19.9.1965 | 28.9.1969 | 19.11.1972 | 3.10.1976 | 5.10.1980 | 6.3.1983 |
| Baden-Württemberg | abs. | 655 506 | 825 704 | 1 009 019 | 1 342 885 | 1 470 040 | 1 675 702 | 2 069 169 | 1 980 976 | 2 031 035 | 1 777 511 |
| | %[2] | 23,9 | 23,0 | 25,8 | 32,1 | 33,0 | 36,5 | 38,9 | 36,6 | 37,2 | 31,1 |
| Bayern | abs. | 1 075 416 | 1 184 262 | 1 394 811 | 1 652 642 | 1 869 467 | 1 983 020 | 2 483 136 | 2 201 692 | 2 220 681 | 2 014 399 |
| | %[2] | 22,7 | 23,3 | 26,4 | 30,1 | 33,1 | 34,6 | 37,8 | 32,8 | 32,7 | 28,9 |
| Bremen | abs. | 104 509 | 138 846 | 184 003 | 212 734 | 215 487 | 232 779 | 284 028 | 255 544 | 238 913 | 222 935 |
| | %[2] | 34,4 | 39,0 | 46,2 | 49,7 | 48,5 | 52,0 | 58,1 | 54,0 | 52,5 | 48,7 |
| Hamburg | abs. | 358 873 | 403 410 | 528 645 | 560 038 | 572 859 | 637 051 | 673 517 | 614 284 | 572 012 | 521 509 |
| | %[2] | 39,6 | 38,1 | 45,8 | 46,9 | 48,3 | 54,6 | 54,4 | 52,6 | 51,7 | 47,4 |
| Hessen | abs. | 684 042 | 862 701 | 1 037 166 | 1 233 312 | 1 366 010 | 1 492 916 | 1 697 322 | 1 626 365 | 1 655 039 | 1 513 449 |
| | %[2] | 32,1 | 33,7 | 38,0 | 42,8 | 45,7 | 48,2 | 48,5 | 45,7 | 46,4 | 41,6 |
| Niedersachsen | abs. | 1 125 295 | 1 136 522 | 1 255 204 | 1 526 824 | 1 614 540 | 1 797 376 | 2 235 911 | 2 129 502 | 2 231 784 | 2 015 731 |
| | %[2] | 33,4 | 30,1 | 32,8 | 38,7 | 39,8 | 43,8 | 48,1 | 45,7 | 46,9 | 41,3 |
| Nordrhein-Westfalen | abs. | 2 109 172 | 2 553 014 | 2 965 616 | 3 549 359 | 4 149 910 | 4 534 471 | 5 509 886 | 5 153 959 | 5 107 264 | 4 782 220 |
| | %[2] | 31,4 | 31,9 | 33,5 | 37,3 | 42,6 | 46,8 | 50,4 | 46,9 | 46,8 | 42,8 |
| Rheinland-Pfalz | abs. | 408 905 | 482 686 | 578 203 | 659 830 | 754 175 | 825 379 | 1 067 953 | 1 013 574 | 1 049 145 | 959 714 |
| | %[2] | 28,6 | 27,2 | 30,4 | 33,5 | 36,7 | 40,1 | 44,9 | 41,7 | 42,8 | 38,4 |
| Saarland[3] | abs. | — | — | 138 309 | 194 003 | 250 797 | 253 485 | 349 801 | 344 187 | 361 342 | 329 436 |
| | %[2] | — | — | 25,1 | 33,5 | 39,8 | 39,9 | 47,9 | 46,1 | 48,3 | 43,8 |
| Schleswig-Holstein | abs. | 413 257 | 357 798 | 404 595 | 495 728 | 549 901 | 633 537 | 804 446 | 779 599 | 794 881 | 728 903 |
| | %[2] | 29,6 | 26,5 | 30,8 | 36,4 | 38,8 | 43,5 | 48,6 | 46,4 | 46,7 | 41,7 |
| Bundesrepublik Deutschland (without Berlin) | abs. | 6 934 975 | 7 944 943 | 9 495 571 | 11 427 355 | 12 813 186 | 14 065 716 | 17 175 169 | 16 099 019 | 16 262 096 | 14 865 807 |
| | %[2] | 29,2 | 28,8 | 31,8 | 36,2 | 39,3 | 42,7 | 45,8 | 42,6 | 42,9 | 38,2 |

1. From 1953, number and % of valid votes (from 1953, of valid second votes); 2. % of second votes; 3. The Saar participated in the elections for the first time in 1957, after region's re-integration into the FRG.

7. Average per capita income in Germany, 1871–1979 (in DM, based on present-day purchasing power)

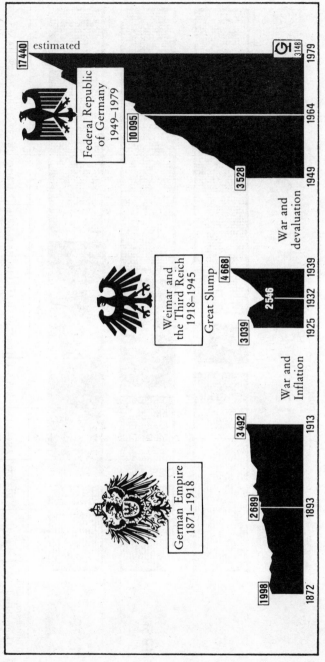

Globus

8. Occupational distribution of the labour force (%)

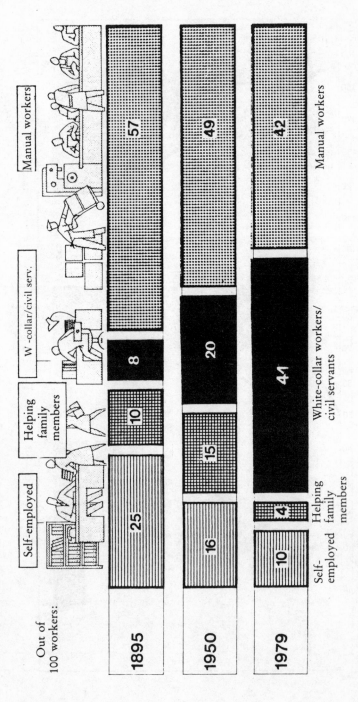

Out of 100 workers:

Self-employed | Helping family members | W.-collar/civil serv. | Manual workers

1895 — 25 — 10 — 8 — 57

1950 — 16 — 15 — 20 — 49

1979 — 10 — 4 — 41 — 42

Self-employed | Helping family members | White-collar workers/ civil servants | Manual workers

Source: Statistisches Bundesamt

Die Zeit/Globus

**9.** Nominal weekly wages in industry and cost of living index, 1871–1932
    Index 1913 = 100

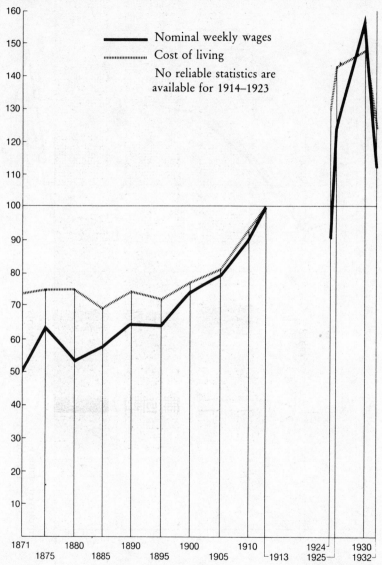

10. Real weekly wages in industry, 1871–1932
    Index 1913 = 100

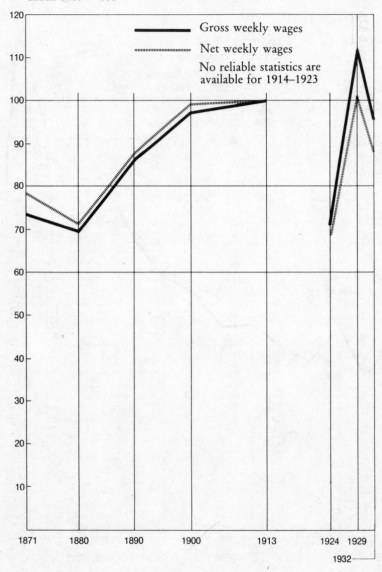

11. Unemployment, 1919–1933 (000s)*

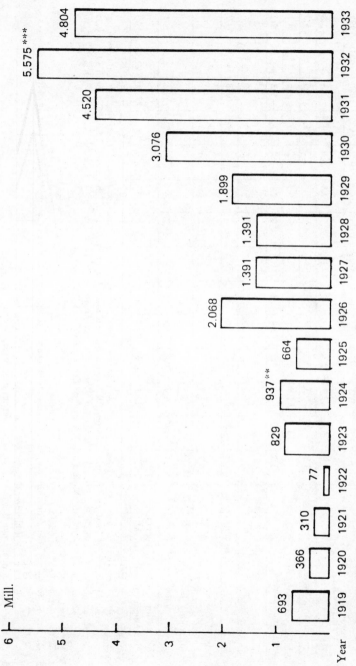

| Year | 1919 | 1920 | 1921 | 1922 | 1923 | 1924 | 1925 | 1926 | 1927 | 1928 | 1929 | 1930 | 1931 | 1932 | 1933 |
|------|------|------|------|------|------|------|------|------|------|------|------|------|------|------|------|
| | 693 | 366 | 310 | 77 | 829 | 937** | 664 | 2.068 | 1.391 | 1.391 | 1.899 | 3.076 | 4.520 | 5.575*** | 4.804 |

\* See Bry, *Wages in Germany*, pp. 325–9 — respective annual averages

\** From 1924 the statistics were changed: up to 1923 only those unemployed who received unemployment benefit were included; from 1924, all registered unemployed. The relevant figures — old system — were: 1924 — 841,000; 1925 — 384,000.

\*** Maximum level in February 1932 — 6,128,429.

**12.** Basic economic and social data, 1969–1982

| | 1969 | 1970 | 1971 | 1972 | 1973 | 1974 | 1975 | 1976 | 1977 | 1978 | 1979 | 1980 | 1981 | 1982 |
|---|---|---|---|---|---|---|---|---|---|---|---|---|---|---|
| Annual growth rate (%) | 7,9 | 5,9 | 3,3 | 3,6 | 4,9 | 0,4 | −1,8 | 5,3 | 2,8 | 3,6 | 4,5 | 2,5 | −0,3 | −1,0 |
| Annual price increase (%) | 1,9 | 3,4 | 5,3 | 5,5 | 6,9 | 7,0 | 6,0 | 4,5 | 3,7 | 2,7 | 4,1 | 5,5 | 5,9 | 5,3 |
| Annual variations of wages and salaries (%)[1] gross[2] | 9,2 | 14,7 | 11,8 | 9,0 | 12,0 | 11,4 | 7,2 | 7,0 | 6,9 | 5,2 | 5,5 | 6,5 | 5,0 | 4,1 |
| net[3] | 5,3 | 8,9 | 4,4 | 3,5 | 1,4 | 2,9 | 1,1[4] | 0,0 | 2,1 | 3,7 | 1,9 | −0,3 | −1,3 | −2,2 |
| Index-linked increase (%) Pensions | 8,3 | 6,35 | 5,5 | 9,5 | 11,35 | 11,2 | 11,1 | 11,0 | 9,9 | 0,0 | 4,5 | 4,0 | 4,0 | 5,76 |
| Net overall level[5] | 57,9 | 56,9 | 54,6 | 57,3 | 56,6 | 57,4 | 59,5 | 63,3 | 66,2 | 65,2 | 64,4 | 63,8 | 63,4 | 64,9 |
| Annual variations of income from self-employment and of capital (%) gross | 6,0 | 9,5 | 6,4 | 7,6 | 7,5 | 0,1 | 5,4 | 12,8 | 6,0 | 9,1 | 8,3 | 0,4 | −0,9 | 6,7 |
| net | 4,3 | 14,7 | 5,9 | 7,9 | 3,2 | 0,3 | 8,2 | 11,2 | 1,4 | 12,6 | 10,6 | 2,1 | 0,7 | 8,1 |
| Net lending rate of the Federal Government (in milliard DM) | 0,001 | 1,11 | 1,44 | 3,98 | 2,68 | 9,48 | 29,93 | 25,78 | 21,82 | 26,09 | 25,66 | 27,11 | 37,60 | 37,00 |

*Sources:* *Statistisches Taschenbuch 1982. Arbeits- und Sozialstatistik. (Eine Information des Bundesministers für Arbeit und Sozialordnung),* Tables 1.10, 1.13, 1.15; *Gesellschaftliche Daten 1982. Reihe Berichte und Dokumentationen,* Table 116; OECD. *Economic Outlook 32,* December 1982, Table R10; *Aktuelle Beiträge zur Wirtschafts- und Finanzpolitik* (BPA), no. 65/1981, Tables 2, 3: 14/1983, Tab 2, 3; for 1982, information from the Ministry of Labour and Social Security, 9 August 1983.

1. Per employed worker.
2. Without employers' national insurance contributions.
3. Based on 1976 prices, after deduction of tax and national insurance and correlated with the cost of living index of a family of four with average employee income.
4. To be increased by 4% if childrens' allowance is included.
5. As a % of the annual wage based on insurance contributions over 40 years.

**13.** Development of the labour market, 1969–1982

| Year | Unemployed (000s) | Rate of unemployment[*] | Workers on short time (000s) |
|------|-------------------|-------------------------|------------------------------|
| 1969 | 179 | 0,8 | 1 |
| 1970 | 149 | 0,7 | 10 |
| | | | |
| 1971 | 185 | 0,8 | 86 |
| 1972 | 246 | 1,1 | 76 |
| 1973 | 273 | 1,2 | 44 |
| 1974 | 582 | 2,6 | 292 |
| 1975 | 1047 | 4,8 | 773 |
| | | | |
| 1976 | 1060 | 4,7 | 277 |
| 1977 | 1030 | 4,6 | 231 |
| 1978 | 993 | 4,4 | 191 |
| 1979 | 876 | 3,8 | 88 |
| 1980 | 889 | 3,9 | 137 |
| | | | |
| 1981 | 1272 | 5,5 | 207 |
| 1982 | 1833 | 7,5 | 606 |

*Sources: Arbeits- und Sozialstatistik. Der Bundesminister für Arbeit und Sozialordnung. Hauptergebnisse, 1982, p. 60; for 1982, information from the Ministry of Labour and Social Security, 9 August 1983.*
[*]% of dependently employed persons.

# Chronology

**1848**

February      Karl Marx and Friedrich Engels' *Communist Manifesto* is published in London.

March      Revolutions in France, Germany, Austria, Hungary.

April      Workers' associations are formed in many cities.

28 August –
3 September      A German workers' congress meets in Berlin. The 'Brotherhood of Workers' is founded under the leadership of Stephan Born.

**1854**

July      Under a law on associations passed by the Bundestag all workers' associations are dissolved.

**1861**

The ban on associations is lifted in Saxony.

**1863**

1 March      Ferdinand Lassalle responds to the Leipzig committee with an 'Open Reply' in which he advocates founding an independent political party for the working class.

23 May      The *Allgemeine Deutsche Arbeiterverein* (ADAV: General German Workers' Association) is founded in Leipzig. Lassalle is elected president for five years. The ADAV demands as its primary objective 'the introduction of universal, equal, direct suffrage'.

**1864**

31 August      Lassalle dies after a duel.

28 Sept.      Founding of the International Workingmen's Association (IWA: First International) in London.

**1865**

December      The *Allgemeine Deutsche Zigarrenarbeiterverein* (General German Cigar-Workers' Association) founded in Leipzig.

**1866**

May　　　　Formation of the *Deutscher Buchdruckerverband* (German Book-Printers' Union).

19 August　Bebel and W. Liebknecht, in association with middle-class Democrats, found the *Sächsische Volkspartei* (Saxon People's Party).

**1867**

Karl Marx publishes the first volume of *Das Kapital.*

12 February　Bebel, W. Liebknecht and Schraps are elected to the North German *Reichstag.*

**1868**

5 September　At the conference of the Union of German Workers' Associations a majority decides to subscribe to the programme of the IWA. Support is given to the formation of trade unions.

**1869**

7–8 August　Founding of the *Sozialdemokratische Arbeiterpartei* (SDAP: Social Democratic Workers' Party) in Eisenach. The SDAP expressly states that it is the German branch of the IWA.

**1871**

March　　　Revolt of the Paris Commune.

**1875**

22–27 May　The Lassalleans and the Eisenachers unite at the Gotha party conference to form the *Sozialistische Arbeiterpartei Deutschlands* (Socialist Workers' Party of Germany). Adoption of the Gotha Programme, so fiercely criticised by Marx.

**1876**

1 October　The first issue of *Vorwärts* (*Forward*), the central organ of the Socialist Workers' Party, published in Leipzig.

**1878**

30 July      Despite massive obstruction the Socialist Workers' Party receives 437,158 votes and wins 9 seats in the *Reichstag* at the general election.

19 October      Bismarck's 'Law against the criminal endeavours of Social Democracy', proposed originally in May, is passed by the Reichstag by 221 votes to 149.

**1880**

20–23 Aug.      Congress of the Socialist Workers' Party in Wyden, Switzerland.

**1883**

14 March      Karl Marx dies in London.

**1889**

July      An international workingmen's congress appoints 1 May as the day for the campaign for the eight-hour day.

**1890**

25 January      The *Reichstag* refuses to renew the Socialist Law.

20 February      At the general election the SPD becomes numerically the largest party, receiving 1,427,000 votes.

November/ December      Formation of the *Generalkommission der Gewerkschaften Deutschlands* (General Commission of the Trade Unions of Germany).

**1891**

16–23 Aug.      Congress of the Second International.

14–20 Oct.      Erfurt party conference. Adoption of the Erfurt Programme.

**1895**

5 August      Friedrich Engels dies in London.

**1899**

January      Bernstein publishes his book, *The Requirements of Socialism and the Tasks of Social Democracy*.

9–14 Oct.      Clashes over revisionism at the Hanover party conference.

## 1903

13–20 Sept.  Revisionism is condemned at the Dresden party conference.

## 1905

22–27 May  General-strike debate at the fifth congress of trade unions in Cologne. The congress refuses to give its backing to the political general strike.

17–23 Sept.  At the party conference of the SPD in Jena the general strike receives approval only as a defensive measure.

## 1906

23–29 Sept.  The general strike debate continues at the Mannheim party conference. The Mannheim Agreement grants the trade unions a large measure of independence.

## 1912

12 January  At the general election the SPD receives 34.8 per cent of the vote (4.25 million).

## 1913

13 August  August Bebel dies in Switzerland.

## 1914

3 August  The SPD group in the *Reichstag* decides by 78 votes to 14 to approve the war loans requested.

4 August  The SPD group votes unanimously in the *Reichstag* in favour of the War Loans Bill. Chairman Haase declares: 'We shall not forsake our own fatherland in its hour of danger'.

2 December  Karl Liebknecht votes alone against the second War Loans Bill.

## 1916

January  The International Group forms around Rosa Luxemburg and Karl Liebknecht; publication of the 'Spartacus Letters'.

24 March  The SPD group in the Reichstag splits. Formation of the Social Democratic Fellowship.

## 1917

7 January  Convocation of the *Reichskonferenz der Opposition*,

|   | condemned by the central party council. |
|---|---|
| 6–8 April | The *Unabhängige Sozialdemokratische Partei Deutschlands* (USPD: Independent Social Democratic Party of Germany) is founded in Gotha. |

## 1918

| January | Strike movement, mainly in the armaments industry. |
|---|---|
| 4 October | Social Democrats participate in the government of Prince Max of Baden. |
| 4 November | A workers' and soldiers' council assumes political and military power in Kiel. |
| 7–8 Nov. | The revolutionary uprising of workers, sailors and soldiers spreads throughout Germany. Independently of the sailors' movement a republic is proclaimed in Munich. |
| 9 November | Prince Max of Baden hands the reins of government to Ebert. Scheidemann proclaims the republic. |
| 10 Nov. | The revolutionary government of the *Rat der Volsbeauftragten* (Council of People's Representatives) brings together MSPD (Ebert, Scheidemann, Landsberg) and USPD (Haase, Dittmann, Barth). Executive council of the Berlin workers' and soldiers' councils. Ebert accepts the supreme army command's offer of co-operation. |
| 12 Nov. | The Council of People's Representatives announces its intention of 'implementing the Socialist programme'. |
| 15 Nov. | Trade unions and employers' associations conclude an agreement meeting most trade-union demands and setting up a *Zentralarbeitsgemeinschaft*. |
| 16–20 Dec. | National conference of workers' and soldiers' councils. The councils decide on elections for a National Assembly and call for immediate socialisation measures. |
| 29 December | The USPD members quit the Council of People's Representatives. |
| 30 December | The *Kommunistische Partei Deutschlands* (KPD: Communist Party of Germany) is founded. |

## 1919

| 4–13 January | Clashes between revolutionary workers and soldiers and troops ordered in by the Ebert government. |
|---|---|
| 15 January | Rosa Luxemburg and Karl Liebknecht are murdered. |
| 19 January | At the National Assembly elections the SPD receives 37.9 per cent and the USPD 7.6 per cent of the vote. |

11 February    Ebert elected *Reichspräsident*.

13 February    Scheidemann forms the first Weimar coalition government of SPD, DDP and Centre Party.

7 April    Proclamation of the *Räterepublik* in Bavaria.

10–15 June    Party conference of the SPD in Weimar.

20 June    Following the resignation of Scheidemann, Gustav Bauer (SPD) forms a new coalition government with the Centre Party. This is subsequently rejoined by the DDP.

### 1920

18 January    The Works Councils Law is passed.

13–17 March    The Kapp Putsch. A general strike called by the trade unions and the SPD forces Kapp to retreat.

27 March    Following the resignation of the Bauer Cabinet Hermann Müller forms another government with the Centre Party and the DDP.

6 June    At the general election the SPD's share of the vote drops (from 37.9 to 21.6 per cent) whereas the USPD scores a big success (up from 7.6 to 18 per cent).

12–17 Oct.    At an extraordinary party conference of the USPD in Halle a majority accepts the twenty-one conditions for admission to the Communist International. The vote provokes a split in the USPD.

4–7 Dec.    The left wing of the USPD joins the KPD to form the United Communist Party of Germany.

### 1921

18–24 Sept.    The Görlitz party conference of the SPD adopts a new party programme.

### 1922

24 Sept.    Re-amalgamation of the rump USPD with the MSPD to form the United Social Democratic Party of Germany.

### 1923

Trade unions and Social Democracy support passive resistance to the occupation of the Ruhr.

### 1924

15 January    The *Allgemeiner Deutscher Gewerkschaftsbund* (ADGB: General German Trade Union Congress) withdraws from

the *Zentralarbeitsgemeinschaft* formed with the employers' associations on 15 November 1918.

### 1925

28 February   Death of Friedrich Ebert.

13–18 Sept.   The party conference of the SPD in Heidelberg adopts a new programme.

### 1928

20 May   General election. SPD share of the vote up to 29.8 per cent.

28 June   Hermann Müller forms a Great Coalition government with the SPD, DDP, Centre Party, DVP and the Bavarian People's Party.

### 1930

27 March   A projected reorganisation of unemployment insurance leads to the break-up of the Great Coalition.

14 Sept.   In view of the general election success of the NSDAP the SPD decides to tolerate the Brüning government.

### 1931

22 Dec.   Founding of the Iron Front to ward off the Fascist threat; it comprises SPD, ADGB, *Reichsbanner* and workers' sports clubs.

### 1932

13 March   The SPD backs the election of Hindenburg as *Reichspräsident*.

20 July   The Otto Braun government in Prussia is deposed with the aid of Article 48.

### 1933

January   Hitler becomes *Reichskanzler*.

23 March   The SPD group in the *Reichstag* votes against the Enabling Law

2 May   Occupation of the premises of the Free Trade Unions.

22 June   The SPD is banned. A huge wave of arrests begins.

### 1934

28 January   The Sopade (SPD in exile) issues its Prague Manifesto: *The Struggle and the Goal of Revolutionary Socialism*.

**1941**

19 March      Founding of the Union of German Socialist Organisations in Great Britain.

**1945**

19 April      At a meeting between Kurt Schumacher and other Social Democrats in Hanover it is decided to refound the SPD.

15 June      The SPD in Berlin issues a call for a 'united proletarian fighting organisation of the working class'. The Berlin central committee of the SPD under the chairmanship of Otto Grotewohl lays claim to the leadership of the German party.

19 June      Representatives of the central committee of the KPD and the central committee of the SPD in Berlin decide to set up a 'joint action committee'.

September      The Schumacher Bureau in Hanover reconstitutes itself as the Bureau of the Western Zones.

5–6 October      A conference of Social Democratic functionaries from the Western zones is held in Wennigsen, near Hanover.

20–21 Dec.      A conference in Berlin bringing together thirty SPD and thirty KPD functionaries rejects the Communist demand for joint electoral lists.

**1946**

30 March      In a ballot of SPD members in the three Western sectors of Berlin 82 per cent vote against immediate amalgamation with the KPD.

9–11 May      Party conference of the SPD in Hanover. Schumacher is elected chairman, Ollenhauer first deputy chairman, and Willi Knothe (Frankfurt a. M.) second deputy chairman.

**1947**

May      The SPD group in the Economic Council for the United Economic Zones (Frankfurt a. M.) decides to go into opposition.

**1948**

1 September      The Parliamentary Council is set up. Konrad Adenauer is elected chairman; Carlo Schmid is elected chairman of the SPD group within it.

11–14 Sept.      The party conference of the SPD in Düsseldorf calls for a statute of occupation as the legal basis for relations between the occupying powers and the Germans.

10–11 Dec.   The SPD executive finds that the question of a German army constitution does not lie within the sphere of German jurisdiction.

**1949**

8 May   The Parliamentary Council passes the Basic Law, with the SPD voting in favour.

14 August   Election of the first *Bundestag*.

31 August   The SPD group in the *Bundestag* elects Schumacher as its first chairman, Ollenhauer as its second chairman and Carlo Schmid as its third chairman.

13 October   The *Deutscher Gewerkschaftsbund* (DGB: German Trade Union Congress) is set up under chairmanship of Hans Böckler.

**1950**

21–25 May   The party conference of the SPD in Hamburg endorses the decision of the executive to resist any remilitarisation of Germany and is critical of both the Council of Europe and the Schuman Plan.

**1951**

21 May   Promulgation of the Co-determination Law for the coal and steel industries, passed with the votes of CDU/CSU and SPD.

30 June–3 July   The Socialist International is refounded in Frankfurt a. M. It adopts a declaration of principal: 'Goals and tasks of democratic Socialism'.

**1952**

19 July   Against the votes of the SPD the *Bundestag* passes the Labour Management Law.

20 August   Death of Kurt Schumacher.

24–28 Sept.   The party conference of the SPD in Dortmund adopts a programme of action. Erich Ollenhauer is elected chairman and Wilhelm Mellies deputy chairman.

**1953**

17 June   Protest movement by the workers of East Berlin and the German Democratic Republic.

6 September   General election. The heavy defeat suffered by the SPD

provokes extensive discussion within the party.

**1954**

20–24 July   The party conference of the SPD in Berlin decides to set up a commission headed by Willi Eichler to work out a basic programme.

**1955**

29 January   On the initiative of the SPD a meeting in the Paulskirche, Frankfurt a. M., adopts a German Manifesto calling for a four-power agreement concerning the reunification of Germany and warning against re-armament in both Germanies.

**1956**

10–14 July   The party conference of the SPD in Munich tackles some of the problems of the Second Industrial Revolution.

**1957**

May   The *Gesamtdeutsche Volkspartei* (All-German People's Party) decides to dissolve itself and issues a recommendation to its members to join the SPD. Its chairmen Gustav Heinemann and Helene Wessel become SPD candidates for the forthcoming general election.

14 Sept.   General election.

**1958**

23 March   The Campaign Against Nuclear Death opens with a meeting in the Paulskirche, Frankfurt a. M.

18–23 May   The party conference of the SPD in Stuttgart decides to alter the party's constitution, setting up a presidium elected by and from among the executive committee. Ollenhauer remains chairman; Waldemar von Knoeringen and Herbert Wehner are elected deputy chairmen; Willy Brandt becomes a member of the executive committee.

**1959**

13–15 Nov.   An extraordinary party conference of the SPD in Bad Godesberg adopts the Basic Programme.

**1960**

30 June       In a speech in the *Bundestag* Herbert Wehner advocates a joint foreign policy for government and opposition on the basis of existing treaty obligations.

21–25 Nov.       The party conference of the SPD nominates Willy Brandt as the party's *Kanzlerkandidat*.

**1961**

August       The building of the Berlin Wall.

17 Sept.       General election.

**1962**

26–30 May       SPD party conference in Cologne. Willy Brandt elected to join Wehner as deputy chairman.

**1963**

14 Dec.       Death of Erich Ollenhauer

**1964**

15–16 Feb.       An extraordinary party conference in Bad Godesberg elects Willy Brandt chairman and Fritz Erler and Herbert Wehner deputy chairmen of the SPD.

3 March       Fritz Erler is elected chairman of the SPD group in the *Bundestag*.

**1965**

19 Sept.       General election.

**1966**

10 July       *Landtag* election in North-Rhine–Westphalia. With 49.5 per cent of the vote the SPD for the first time outstrips the CDU in the largest state of the confederation.

2 November       Herbert Wehner lays eight points before the *Bundestag* as the basis for SPD participation in government.

1 December       The new central government of the Great Coalition is sworn in. Willy Brandt becomes Foreign Minister and deputy to Chancellor Kurt-Georg Kiesinger (CDU).

8 December       Heinz Kühn becomes Minister President of North-Rhine–Westphalia and forms a coalition government with the FDP.

**1967**

22 February   Death of Fritz Erler.
14 March      Helmut Schmidt becomes chairman of the SPD group in the *Bundestag*.

**1968**

31 May        The office of *Bundesgeschäftsführer* of the SPD is created.

**1969**

5 March       Dr Gustav Heinemann (SPD) is elected President by the *Bundesversammlung* with the votes of the FDP.
28 Sept.      General election.
October       Formation of the Social–Liberal coalition government under Chancellor Willy Brandt, with Walter Scheel (FDP) as Foreign Minister and Vice-Chancellor. Herbert Wehner becomes chairman of the SPD group in the Bundestag.

**1970**

29 June       The SPD executive expresses disapproval of the action of a Young Socialist delegation received by Chairman Walter Ulbricht (SED) of the German Democratic Republic.
14 Sept.      The SPD executive welcomes the treaty with the Soviet union concluded on 12 August 1970.
14 Nov.       Executive, party council and control commission of the SPD declare themselves opposed to any joint action with Communists.

**1971**

20 October    Willy Brandt is awarded the Nobel Peace Prize.
18–20 Nov.    An extraordinary party conference of the SPD in Bonn–Bad Godesberg discusses the following subjects: tax reform, the mass media, abortion and reform of the party organisation.

**1972**

June          The draft of a 'Framework of Economic and Political Orientation for the years 1973–1985' ('Long-term Programme') is sent out to the party for comment and criticism.

19 Nov.        General election. Formation of the second Brandt–Scheel government.

**1973**

10–14 April    The party conference of the SPD in Hanover passes resolutions in connection with the Framework of Orientation relating to land law and employee profit-sharing.

**1974**

7 May          Willy Brandt resigns as Chancellor and is succeeded by Helmut Schmidt.

15 May         Walter Scheel (FDP) is elected President, Gustav Heine-mann having declined to stand again.

**1975**

11–15 Nov.     The party conference of the SPD in Mannheim adopts the Framework of Orientation '85 almost unanimously.

**1976**

18 March       The Co-Determination Law, binding on all firms with more than 2,000 employees, is passed by the *Bundestag*.

3 October      General election. The Social–Liberal government with Helmut Schmidt as Chancellor continues in office.

25 Nov.        Willy Brandt becomes president of the Socialist International.

**1977**

28 Sept.       Willy Brandt becomes chairman of the Independent Commission for International Developmental Questions (North–South Commission).

**1978**

9–10 Dec.      An extraordinary party conference of the SPD in Cologne adopts a programme and lists of candidates for the European elections.

**1979**

7–10 June      In the first direct elections to the European Parliament the SPD wins 35 seats (1 in Berlin) out of the 81 seats assigned to the German Federal Republic (3 to Berlin). The European Parliament has a total of 410 seats.

3–9 Dec.     At the party conference of the SPD in Berlin a majority votes for the security and energy policy of the Social–Liberal government.

**1980**

11 May     In the *Landtag* election in North-Rhine–Westphalia the SPD wins an absolute majority for the first time in this state and forms the government on its own.

5 October     The general election results in a broadening of the parliamentary base of the Social–Liberal coalition. Helmut Schmidt remains Chancellor and Hans-Dietrich Genscher his deputy.

**1981**

10 October     Some 30,000 people take part in a peace demonstration in Bonn.

11–13 Dec.     Chancellor Helmut Schmidt holds talks with Erich Honecker, General-Secretary of the SED and Chairman of the Council of State in the German Democratic Republic.

**1982**

February     Chancellor Schmidt asks for a vote of confidence in the *Bundestag* and receives all the votes of the SPD and the FDP.

17 June     The FDP in Hesse makes a coalition declaration in favour of the CDU.

20 August     Foreign Minister Hans-Dietrich Genscher, chairman of the FDP, calls for a 'change of direction'.

17 Sept.     Chancellor Schmidt declares the Social–Liberal coalition terminated.

1 October     The *Bundestag* elects Helmut Kohl (CDU) Chancellor by means of a constructive vote of no-confidence.

18–19 Nov.     At an SPD conference in Kiel the party's *Kanzlerkandidat*, Hans-Jochen Vogel, delivers a programmatic speech.

**1983**

6 March     General election. The SPD is defeated.

# Bibliography

## I. General Works

Braunthal, J.: *History of the International*; London 1967
Bry, G.: *Wages in Germany*; Princeton 1960
Dahrendorf, R.: *Society and Democracy in Germany*; Garden City 1967
Desai, A. V.: *Real Wages in Germany 1871–1913*; Oxford 1968
Geary, D.: *European Labour Protest 1848–1939*; London 1981
Grebing, H.: *History of the German Labour Movement*; Leamington Spa 1985
Hohorst, G., et al.: *Sozialgeschichtliches Arbeitsbuch*; vols. 1/2/3 Munich 1975/78/81
Huber, A. (ed.): *Frauen in der Politik: die Sozialdemokratinnen*; Stuttgart, Herford 1984
Joll, J.: *The Second International*; London 1955
Kuczynski, J.: *Die Geschichte der Lage der Arbeiter unter dem Kapitalismus*; 21 vols., Berlin 1961ff.
Lehnert, D.: *Sozialdemokratie zwischen Protestbewegung und Regierungspartei, 1848–1983*; Frankfurt 1983
Meyer, T., S. Miller, J. Rohlfés (eds.): *Lern- und Arbeitsbuch. Geschichte der deutschen Arbeiterbewegung*; 3 vols., Bonn 1984
———, K.-H. Klär, S. Miller, K. Novy, H. Timmermann (eds.): *Lexikon des Sozialismus*; Cologne 1986
Mommsen, H. (ed.): *Sozialdemokratie zwischen Klassenbewegung und Volkspartei*; Frankfurt 1974
Tormin, W.: *Geschichte der deutschen Parteien seit 1848*; Stuttgart 1967

## II. Pre-1945

Angress, W.: *The Stillborn Revolution*; Princeton 1963
Balser, F.: *Sozial-Demokratie, 1848/49–1863*; 2 vols., Stuttgart 1962
Berlau, A. J.: *The German Social Democratic Party, 1914–1921*; New York 1970
Breitman, R.: *German Socialism and Weimar Democracy*; Chapel Hill, N.C. 1981
———: 'German Social Democracy and General Schleicher'; *Central European History* (1976), 352–78
Burdick, C. B., and Lutz, R. H.: *The Political Institutions of the German Revolution*, New York 1966
Calkins, K. R.: 'The Election of Hugo Haase to the Co-Chairmanship of the

320

# Bibliography

Pre-War German Social Democratic Party'; *International Review of Social History* (1968), 174–88

Carsten, F. L.: *Revolution in Central Europe*; London/Berkeley 1972

Chalmers, D. A.: *The Social Democratic Party of Germany*; New Haven 1964

Comfort, R. A.: *Revolutionary Hamburg*; Stanford 1966

Conze, W.: 'From "Pöbel" to "Proletariat". The Social-Historical Preconditions of Socialism in Germany'; in Iggers, G. (ed.), *The Social History of Politics*; Leamington Spa and New York 1986

Cooper, R.: *Failure of a Revolution;* Cambridge 1955

Crew, D.: *A Town in the Ruhr*; New York 1979

Dominick III, R. H.: *Wilhelm Liebknecht and the Founding of the German Social Democratic Party*; Chapel Hill 1982

Dowe, D.: 'The Workers' Choral Movement before the First World War'; *Journal of Contemporary History* (1978), 269–76

Edinger, L. J.: *German Exile Politics*; Berkeley 1956

Evans, R. J. (ed.): *The German Working Class 1888–1933*; London 1982

Feldman, G. D.: *Army, Industry and Labor in Germany, 1914–1918*; Princeton 1966

Fowkes, B.: *Communism in Germany under the Weimar Republic*; London 1984

Fromm, E.: *The Working Class in Weimar Germany*; Leamington Spa and Cambridge, Mass. 1984

Gates, R. A.: 'German Socialism and the Crisis of 1929–1933'; *Central European History* (1974) 332–59

Gay, P.: *The Dilemma of Democratic Socialism*; New York 1952

*Die Geheimen Deutschlandberichte der SPD, 1934–1940*; 7 vols., Frankfurt 1980

Groh, D.: *Negative Integration und revolutionärer Attentismus*; Frankfurt 1973

Guttsman, W. L.: *The German Social Democratic Party, 1875–1933*; London 1981

Hall, A.: *Scandal, Sensation and Social Democracy*; Cambridge 1977

Heckart, B.: *From Bassermann to Bebel*; New Haven 1974

Hunt, R. N.: *German Social Democracy 1918–1933*; Chicago 1964

Kaelble, H.: *Industrialisation and Social Inequality*; Leamington Spa and New York 1986

Kautsky, K.: *Social Revolution*; Chicago 1902

Kehr, E.: *Battleship Building and Party Politics in Germany, 1898–1901*; Chicago 1973

Kocka, J.: *Facing Total War. German Society 1914–1918*; Leamington Spa and Cambridge, Mass. 1984

Kolb, E.: *Die Weimarer Republik 1918–1933*; Munich 1984

Langewiesche, Dieter, and Schönhoven, Klaus (eds.): *Arbeiter in Deutschland. Studien zur Lebensweise der Arbeiterschaft im Zeitalter der Industrialisierung*; Königstein/Ts. 1980

Lidtke, V.: *The Outlawed Party*; Princeton 1966

Löwenthal, Richard and von zur Mühlen, Patrik (eds.): *Widerstand und Verweigerung in Deutschland 1933 bis 1945*; Berlin/Bonn 1982

Lutz, R. H.: *The Causes of the Collapse in 1918*; New York 1969

# Bibliography

Maehl, W. H.: *August Bebel. Shadow Emperor of the German Workers*; Philadelphia 1980

Maier, C.: *Recasting Bourgeois Europe, Stabilization in France, Germany and Italy in the Decade after World War I*; Princeton 1975

Matthias, Erich: 'Kautsky und der Kautskyanismus. Die Funtion der Ideologie in der deutschen Sozialdemokratie vor dem ersten Weltkrieg'; *Marxismus-Studien*, 2, Tübingen 1957

——, and Morsey, Rudolf (eds.): *Das Ende der Parteien 1933*; Düsseldorf/Königsstein/Ts. 1979

Mehring, Franz: *Geschichte der deutschen Sozialdemokratie*, 4 vols.; Stuttgart 1921 (new ed., 2 vols., Berlin (GDR) 1960).

Miller, Susanne: *Die Bürde der Macht. Die deutsche Sozialdemokratie 1918–1920*; Düsseldorf 1978

——: *Burgfrieden und Klassenkampf. Die deutsche Sozialdemokratie im Ersten Weltkrieg*; Düsseldorf 1974

——: *Das Problem der Freiheit im Sozialismus. Freiheit, Staat und Revolution in der Programmatik der Sozialdemokratie von Lassalle bis zum Revisionismusstreit*; Berlin/Bonn 1977

Mishark, J. W.: *The Road to Revolution*; Detroit 1967

*Mit dem Gesicht nach Deutschland. Eine Dokumentation über die sozialdemokratische Emigration*, ed. Erich Matthias and Werner Link; Düsseldorf 1968

Mitchell, A.: *Revolution in Bavaria*; Princeton 1966

Mommsen, Hans (ed.): *Arbeiterbewegung und industrieller Wandel. Studien zu gewerkschaftlichen Organisationsproblemen im Reich und an der Ruhr*; Wuppertal 1980

Morgan, D. W.: *The Socialist Left and the German Revolution*; New York 1975

Morgan, R.: *The German Social Democrats and the First International, 1864–1872*; Cambridge 1965

Moses, J.: *German Trade Unionism from Bismarck to Hitler*; 2 vols., London 1981

Nettl, P.: *Rosa Luxemburg*, 2 vols.; Oxford 1966

——: 'The German Social Democratic Party as a Political Model'; *Past and Present* (1965) 75–95

Nichols, Anthony, and Matthias, Erich: *German Democracy and the Triumph of Hitler. Essays in Recent German History*; London 1971

Pore, R.: *A Conflict of Interest: Women in German Social Democracy, 1919–1933*; Westport, Conn./London 1981

Potthoff, H[einrich]: 'Das Weimarer Verfassungswerk und die deutsche Linke', *Archiv für Sozialgeschichte*, vol. 12 (1972) pp. 433–483

——: *Gewerkschaften und Politik zwischen Revolution und Inflation*; Düsseldorf 1979

Quataert, J. H.: *Reluctant Feminists in German Social Democracy*; Princeton 1979

——: 'Feminist Tactics in German Social Democracy'; *Internationale Wissenschaftliche Korrespondenz* (1977) 48–65

Ritter, G. A.: 'Workers' Culture in Imperial Germany'; *Journal of Contemporary History* (1978) 165–89

_____: *Die Arbeiterbewegung im Wilhelminischen Reich. Die Sozialdemo-kratrische Partei und die Freien Gewerkschaften 1890–1900*; Berlin 1963
_____: *Staat, Arbeiterschaft und Arbeiterbewegung in Deutschland. Vom Vormärz bis zum Ende der Weimarer Republik*; Berlin/Bonn 1980
_____, and Miller, Susanne: *Die deutsche Revolution 1918–1919, Dokumente*; Hamburg 1975 (rev. ed.)
Röder, Werner: *Die deutschen sozialistischen Exilgruppen in Grossbritannien. Ein Beitrag zur Geschichte des Widerstandes gegen den Nationalsozialismus*; Bonn-Bad Godesberg 1973
Rosenberg, A.: *History of the German Republic*; London 1936
Rosenhaft, E.: *Beating the Fascists*; Cambridge 1983
Roth, G.: *The Social Democrats of Imperial Germany*; Totowa, N.J. 1963
Russell, B.: *German Social Democracy*; London 1896 (1965)
Ryder, A. J.: *The German Revolution of 1918*; Cambridge 1967
Scheidemann, P.: *Memoirs of a Social Democrat*; London 1929
Schorske, C. E.: *German Social Democracy, 1905–1917*; New York 1955
Sheehan, J. J.: *German Liberalism in the 19th Century*; Chicago 1978
Snell, J. L.: *The Democratic Movement in Germany, 1789–1914*; Chapel Hill, N.C. 1976
Steenson, G. P.: *Karl Kautsky, 1854–1938. Marxism in the classical Years*; Pittsburgh 1978
_____: *Not One Man. Not One Penny. German Social Democracy, 1863–1914*; Pittsburgh 1981
Steinberg, Hans-Josef: *Sozialismus und deutsche Sozialdemokratie. Zur Ideologie der Partei vor dem 1. Weltkrieg*; Berlin/Bonn 1979
Thonessen, W.: *The Emancipation of Women: The Rise and Decline of the Women's Movement in German Social Democracy, 1863–1933*; London 1973
Varain, Heinz Josef: *Freie Gewerkschaften, Sozialdemokratie und Staat. Die Politik der Generalkommission unter der Führung Carl Legiens (1890–1920)*; Düsseldorf 1956
Veblen, Th.: *Imperial Germany and the Industrial Revolution*; New York 1915 (1966)
Wachenheim, Hedwig: *Die deutsche Arbeiterbewegung 1844–1914*; Cologne/Opladen 1967
Weber, H. (ed.): *Der Deutsche Kommunismus*; Cologne 1963
_____: *Kommunismus in Deutschland 1918–1945*; Darmstadt 1983
Winkler, H. A.: *Der Schein der Normalität. Arbeiter und Arbeiterbewegung in der Weimarer Republik 1924–1930*; Berlin/Bonn 1985
_____: *Von der Revolution zur Stabilisierung. Arbeiter und Arbeiterbewegung in der Weimarer Republik 1918–1924*; Berlin/Bonn 1984

## III. Post-1945

Albrecht, W. (ed): *Kurt Schumacher. Reden—Schriften—Korrespondenzen 1945–1952*; Berlin/Bonn 1985
Ashkenasi, Abraham: *Reformpartei und Aussenpolitik. Die Aussenpolitik der SPD*; Berlin 1968

# Bibliography

Benz, W. (ed.): *Die Bundesrepublik Deutschland.Geschichte in drei Bänden;* Frankfurt 1983

Bölling, Klaus: *Die letzten Tage des Kanzlers Helmut Schmidt. Ein Tagebuch,* Spiegelbuch, Reinbek/Hamburg 1982

Brandt, W.: *Links und frei. Mein Weg 1930–1950;* Hamburg 1982
_____: *People and Politics, 1969–1975;* Boston 1978

Brandt, W.: *In Exile;* London 1971

Braunthal, G.: *Socialist Labor and Politics in West Germany;* New York 1978

Carr, J.: *Helmut Schmidt;* London 1985

Childs, D.: *From Schumacher to Brandt;* Oxford 1966

Conradt, D. P.: *The West German System. An Ecological Analysis of Social Structure and Voting Behavior 1961–1969;* Beverly Hills 1972

Cullingford, E. C. M.: *Trade Unions in West Germany;* London 1973

Edinger, L. J.: *Kurt Schumacher;* Stanford 1965

Eichler, W.: *Zur Einführung in den demokratischen Sozialismus;* Bonn-Bad Godesberg ²1973

Eppler, E. (ed.): *Grundwerte für ein neues Godesberger Programm. Die Texte der Grundwerte-Kommission der SPD;* Reinbek/Hamburg 1984
_____: *Wege aus der Gefahr;* Reinbek/Hamburg 1981

Glotz, Peter: *Der Weg der Sozialdemokratie. Der historische Auftrag des Reformismus;* Vienna etc. 1975

Graf, W. D.; *The German Left since 1945;* Cambridge 1976

Kaden, Albrecht: *Einheit oder Freiheit. Die Wiedergründung der SPD 1945/46;* Berlin/Bonn ²1980

Klotzbach, Kurt: *Der Weg zür Staatspartei. Programmatik, praktische Politik und Organisation der deutschen Sozialdemokratie 1945 bis 1965;* Berlin/ Bonn 1982

Lafontaine, O.: *Der andere Fortschritt. Verantwortung statt Verweigerung;* Hamburg 1985

Löwenthal, Richard (Paul Sering): *Jenseits des Kapitalismus. Ein Beitrag zur sozialistischen Neuorientierung. Mit einer ausführlichen Einführung: Nach 30 Jahren;* Bonn 1978

Meyer, T. (ed.): *Demokratischer Sozialismus. Geistige Grundlagen und Wege in die Zukunft;* Munich/Vienna 1980

Moraw, F.: *Die Parole der 'Einheit' und die Sozialdemokratie. Zur Parteiorganisation und gesellschaftspolitischen Orientierung der SPD in der Periode der Illegalität und der ersten Phase der Nachkriegszeit 1933–1948;* Bonn 1973

Narr, Wolf-Dieter: *CDU–SPD. Programm und Praxis seit 1945;* Stuttgart etc. 1966

Oertzen, Peter von/Ehmke, Horst/Ehrenberg, Herbert (eds.): *Orientierungsrahmen '85. Text und Diskussion.* ed. Heiner Lindner; Bonn 1979

Pirker, Theo: *Die SPD nach Hitler. Die Geschichte der Sozialdemokratischen Partei Deutschlands 1945-1954;* Munich 1965

Prittie, T.: *Willy Brandt. Portrait of a Statesman;* London 1974

Schellenger jr., Harold Kurt: *The SPD in the Bonn Republic: A Socialist Party Modernizes;* The Hague 1968

Schmidt, Helmut: *Freiheit verantworten;* Düsseldorf/Vienna 1983

Schwan, Alexander/Schwan, Gesine: *Sozialdemokratie und Marxismus. Zum Spannungsverhältnis von Godesberger Programm und marxistischer Theorie;*

Hamburg 1974

Weber, H.: *Geschichte der DDR*; Munich 1985

Wehner, Herbert: *Wandel und Bewährung. Ausgewählte Reden und Schriften 1930–1967*, ed. Hans-Werner Graf Finckenstein and Gerhard Jahn. With an introduction by Günter Gaus; Berlin/Hanover 1968

# Index

# Index